# Seam Framework

## Second Edition

# Seam Framework

## Experience the Evolution of Java™ EE

## Second Edition

Michael Juntao Yuan
Jacob Orshalick
Thomas Heute

PRENTICE
HALL

Upper Saddle River, NJ • Boston • Indianapolis • San Francisco
New York • Toronto • Montreal • London • Munich • Paris • Madrid
Capetown • Sydney • Tokyo • Singapore • Mexico City

Many of the designations used by manufacturers and sellers to distinguish their products are claimed as trademarks. Where those designations appear in this book, and the publisher was aware of a trademark claim, the designations have been printed with initial capital letters or in all capitals.

The authors and publisher have taken care in the preparation of this book, but make no expressed or implied warranty of any kind and assume no responsibility for errors or omissions. No liability is assumed for incidental or consequential damages in connection with or arising out of the use of the information or programs contained herein.

The publisher offers excellent discounts on this book when ordered in quantity for bulk purchases or special sales, which may include electronic versions and/or custom covers and content particular to your business, training goals, marketing focus, and branding interests. For more information, please contact:

U.S. Corporate and Government Sales
(800) 382-3419
corpsales@pearsontechgroup.com

For sales outside the United States please contact:

International Sales
international@pearsoned.com

Visit us on the Web: informit.com/ph

*Library of Congress Cataloging-in-Publication Data*

Yuan, Michael Juntao.
  Seam framework : experience the evolution of Java EE / Michael Juntao Yuan,
Jacob Orshalick, Thomas Heute.—2nd ed.
      p.   cm.
  Includes index.
  ISBN 978-0-13-712939-3 (pbk. : alk. paper)
 1. JBoss. 2. Web servers—Management. 3. Java (Computer program language)
I. Orshalick, Jacob. II. Heute, Thomas. III. Title.
  TK5105.8885.J42Y832 2009
  005.2'762—dc22

                                                              2008047478

ISBN-13: 978-0-13-712939-3
ISBN-10:    0-13-712939-4

Text printed in the United States on recycled paper at R.R. Donnelley in Crawfordsville, Indiana.
First printing, February 2009

*Michael dedicates the book to Ju.*

*Jacob dedicates the book to Jennifer and Talia.*

*Thomas dedicates the book to Isabelle.*

# Contents

# About This Book

Six months after its initial release, JBoss Seam has already become one of the hottest frameworks in enterprise Java, with more than 10,000 downloads per month. Seam integrates standard Java EE technologies with several nonstandard but interesting technologies into a consistent, unified programming model. These technologies include JSF, EJB3, JPA, Hibernate, Facelets, jBPM, JBoss Rules (Drools), iText, and more. Seam runs on almost all leading Java application servers, including but not limited to JBoss AS and Tomcat.

This book is the first comprehensive guide to Seam written by developers from the Seam team. We bring you the latest information on Seam, explain the rationales behind its design, and discuss alternative approaches within Seam. Based on our real-world experiences, we also give you tips and best practices on how to use Seam.

Of course, given the fast-evolving nature of Seam, the book will be playing catch-up with new Seam releases, which come out almost every month. This book covers Seam release 2.1.0. Subsequent releases of Seam should be at least compatible with 2.1.0 for the foreseeable future. For readers who want to stay on the bleeding edge, we maintain blogs for the book at www.michaelyuan.com/blog and www.solutionsfit.com/blog to bring you the latest updates on Seam. Come visit us there!

This book uses a series of example applications to illustrate how to write Seam applications. To download the source code for these sample applications, visit the book's web site at http://solutionsfit.com/seam.

# About the Authors

**M**ichael **Juntao Yuan** is cofounder of Ringful, LLC, a company that develops RESTful APIs for telephone voice and mobile messaging solutions. He contributes code to the Seam project and writes about Seam at www.michaelyuan.com/blog. Formerly technical product manager at Red Hat's JBoss division, Yuan is author of five books on software development.

**Jacob Orshalick** is an independent consultant and the owner of Focus IT Solutions, LLC. He has developed enterprise software solutions that span the retail, financial, media, and telecommunications industries. He specializes in developing enterprise Java solutions utilizing open source technologies and agile techniques. He is a committer to the Seam project, and you can find Jacob writing about Seam, Web Beans, and related Java EE technologies in his blog, www.solutionsfit.com/blog.

**Thomas Heute** was a contributor to the pre-JBoss Portal project before being hired by JBoss, Inc., in 2004. He started as a member of the JBoss Portal team but became a JBoss Seam coleader in 2005, with a plan to bring EJB3 closer to JSF (where it really should be). At the end of 2006, Thomas returned to the JBoss Portal team to work on a range of tasks.

# Acknowledgments

First of all, we would like to thank the entire JBoss Seam community for their great work. Like many other successful open source projects, Seam is a collaborative effort. It would have been impossible without a very active and dedicated user community. We have learned a great deal from Seam users on discussion forums, blogs, and mailing lists. Thanks, guys, and keep up the good work!

Gavin King, Seam's creator and lead developer, deserves special thanks. Seam would never exist if not for his vision, brilliance, and hard work. Gavin was very supportive of the book from the beginning. He patiently helped us with many of our newbie questions, reviewed the content, and offered encouragement along the way. Aside from Gavin, other Seam developers, including Norman Richards, Pete Muir, Emmanuel Bernard, Max Andersen, Shane Bryzak, James Williams, Christian Bauer, and Steve Ebersole, were also very helpful. Seam is truly a team effort in the spirit of Open Source.

We'd also like to thank the following people for reviewing early editions of this book and giving us great feedback: Ian White, Tony Herstell, Rich Rosen, Wes Boudville, Bil Lewis, Gregory Pierce, David Geary, Bruce Scharlau, Kito Mann, Daniel Brum, Chris Mills, Pete Muir, Srinivasan Raguraman, Ajay Gupta, and Chris Dempsey. Thank you all for the help!

Our editorial team at Prentice Hall was extremely professional and supportive throughout the process. Our editor, Greg Doench, and production staff, Anna Popick and John Fuller, put up with our numerous delays and guided us through the complex publishing process. Our production project managers, Alina Kirsanova and Dmitry Kirsanov, worked tirelessly to enhance the look of the chapters and ensure their accuracy. The book would not have been possible without their dedication.

Finally, and most importantly, we would like to thank our families for their love and support. They are truly the unsung heroes behind any achievement we might have.

# Part I

## Getting Started

In this part, we provide an overview of JBoss Seam and its key features and benefits. A simple Hello World example illustrates how Seam ties together the database, the web UI, and the transactional business logic to form an application. We discuss the JSF enhancements Seam and Facelets provide that make JSF one of the best web application frameworks around and ideal for Seam applications. For readers who do not want to waste time setting up common Seam/Java EE configuration files, we introduce a tool called seam-gen which generates projects with Eclipse and NetBeans IDE support. It's the best way to jump-start your Seam application.

# 1

# What Is Seam?

According to the Merriam-Webster dictionary, a *seam* is a "joining of two pieces by sewing, usually near the edge." When used in enterprise software development, the Seam Framework is one of the most successful integration frameworks that joins together multiple software components.

Integration is one of the hardest problems in enterprise application development. A multitier application is typically made up of many components, such as transactional services, security, data persistence, asynchronous messaging, UI rendering, etc. Those components are developed in different frameworks and libraries; they often have different programming models and scalability characteristics. The need to make those components work with each other has given rise to integration frameworks.

The Seam Framework sits on top of Java EE 5.0 to provide a consistent and easy-to-understand programming model for all components in an enterprise web application. It eliminates most of the boilerplate code and XML configuration from your applications. By solving the integration problem, Seam opens web developers to useful tools that were too hard to integrate into web applications before. For instance, with Seam, it is now trivial to write a web application that is driven by business processes and rules, or to write an AJAX data entry form that is directly validated against database constraints, or to trigger recurring offline events from web applications.

In this book, we show you how Seam can make development easier. We cover several web application examples to make our case. But before we get into concrete code examples, let's first explain what, exactly, Seam does and introduce its key design principles. This will help you better understand how Seam works in applications throughout the book.

---

**Requires Java 5**

As a Java EE 5 framework, Seam requires Java 5 and above to work. If you are using Java 6 and JBoss Application Server (AS), please make sure that you download the JBoss AS explicitly built for Java 6.

---

# 1.1   Integrating and Enhancing Java EE Frameworks

The core frameworks in Java EE 5.0 are EJB (Enterprise JavaBeans) 3.0 and JSF (JavaServer Faces) 1.2. EJB 3.0 (hereafter EJB3) converts Plain Old Java Objects (POJOs) into business service objects and database persistence objects. JSF is a Model-View-Controller (MVC) component framework for web applications. Most Java EE 5.0 web applications have both EJB3 modules for business logic and JSF modules for the web frontend. However, although EJB3 and JSF are complementary to each other, they are designed as separate frameworks, each with its own philosophy. For instance, EJB3 uses annotations to configure services, whereas JSF makes use of XML files. Furthermore, EJB3 and JSF components are not aware of each other at the framework level. To make EJB3 and JSF work together, you need artificial facade objects (i.e., JSF backing beans) to tie business components to web pages and boilerplate code (a.k.a. plumbing code) to make method calls across framework boundaries. Gluing those technologies together is part of Seam's responsibilities.

Seam collapses the artificial layer between EJB3 and JSF. It provides a consistent, annotation-based approach to integrate EJB3 and JSF. With a few simple annotations, the EJB3 business components in Seam can now be used directly to back JSF web forms or handle web UI events. Seam enables developers to use annotated POJOs for all application components. Compared with applications developed in other web frameworks, Seam applications are conceptually simple and require significantly less code (in both Java and XML) for the same functionality. If you are impatient, look at the Hello World example in Chapter 2 for a quick preview of how simple a Seam application can be.

Seam also makes it easy to accomplish tasks that were difficult in JSF. For instance, one of the major complaints about JSF is that it relies too much on HTTP POST. It is hard to bookmark a JSF web page and then get it via HTTP GET. Well, with Seam, generating a bookmarkable web page (i.e., a RESTful page, see Chapter 15) is very easy. Seam provides a number of JSF component tags and annotations that increase the "web friendliness" and web page efficiency of JSF applications. In Chapter 3, we will introduce various Seam JSF enhancements and the Facelets view framework for JSF. Then, in Part III, we will discuss specific topics such as end-to-end validation (Chapter 12) and custom exception pages (Chapter 17). In Chapter 24, we discuss how to use jBPM business processes to improve the JSF pageflow.

At the same time, Seam expands the EJB3 component model to POJOs (see Chapter 4) and brings the stateful context from the web tier to the business components (see Chapter 6). Furthermore, Seam integrates a number of other leading open source frameworks, such as jBPM, JBoss Rules (a.k.a. Drools), iText, and Spring. Seam not only wires them together, but also enhances these frameworks much like it does with the JSF + EJB3 combination.

Although Seam is rooted in Java EE 5.0, its applications are not limited to Java EE 5.0 servers. In fact, in this book, we show how Seam applications can be deployed on J2EE 1.4 application servers as well as plain Tomcat servers (see Chapter 4). That means you can obtain production support for your Seam applications today.

---

**1 + 1 > 2**

It would be a mistake to think of Seam as just another integration framework that wires various components together. Seam provides its own managed stateful context that allows the frameworks to deeply integrate via annotations, Expression Language (EL) expressions, etc. That level of integration comes from the Seam developers' intimate knowledge of the third-party frameworks. Read on to Section 1.2 for an example.

---

# 1.2  A Web Framework That Understands ORM

Object Relational Mapping (ORM) solutions are widely used in today's enterprise applications. However, most current business and web frameworks are not designed for ORM. They do not manage the persistence context over the entire web interaction lifecycle, from the moment the request comes in to when the response is fully rendered. That has resulted in all kinds of ORM errors, including the dreaded `LazyInitializationException`, and required ugly hacks such as the Data Transfer Object (DTO).

Seam was created by Gavin King, the inventor of the most popular ORM solution in the world, Hibernate. It was designed from the ground up to promote ORM best practices. With Seam, there are no more DTOs to write, lazy loading just works, and ORM performance can be greatly improved because the extended persistence context acts as a natural cache to reduce database roundtrips. Read more on this topic in Chapter 6.

Furthermore, since Seam integrates the ORM layer with the business and presentation layers, we can display ORM objects directly (see Chapter 13), use database validator annotations on input forms (see Chapter 12), and redirect ORM exceptions to custom error pages (see Chapter 17).

# 1.3   Supporting Stateful Web Applications

Seam was designed for stateful web applications. Web applications are inherently multiuser applications, and e-commerce applications are inherently stateful and trans-actional. However, most existing web application frameworks are geared toward stateless applications. You have to fiddle with the HTTP session objects to manage user states. That not only clutters your application with code that is unrelated to the core business logic, but also brings on an array of performance issues.

In Seam, all the basic application components are inherently stateful. They are much easier to use than the HTTP session because Seam declaratively manages their states. There is no need to write distracting state management code in a Seam application—just annotate the component with its scope, lifecycle methods, and other stateful properties, and Seam takes over the rest. Seam's stateful components also provide much finer control over user states than the plain HTTP session does. For instance, you can have multiple *conversations*, each consisting of a sequence of web requests and business method calls, in an HTTP session. For more on Seam's stateful components, refer to Chapter 6.

Furthermore, database caches and transactions can be automatically tied with the application state in Seam. Seam automatically holds database updates in memory and commits to the database only at the end of a conversation. The in-memory cache greatly reduces database load in complex stateful applications. Refer to Chapter 11 for more on conversation-based database transactions.

In addition to everything we've mentioned, Seam takes state management in web applications a big step further by supporting integration with the open source JBoss jBPM business process engine. You can now specify the workflows of different people in the organization (customers, managers, technical support, etc.) and use the workflows to drive the application instead of relying on the UI event handlers and databases. See Chapter 24 for more on Seam and jBPM integration.

**Declarative Contextual Components**

Each stateful component in Seam has a scope or context. For instance, a shopping cart component is created at the start of a shopping conversation and is destroyed at the end of the conversation when all items are checked out. Hence, this component lives in a conversation context. Your application simply declares this context via annotations on the component, and Seam automatically manages the component's creation, state, and removal.

Seam provides several levels of stateful contexts, ranging from a single web request to a multipage conversation, an HTTP session, or a long-running business process.

# 1.4 Web 2.0 Ready

Seam is fully optimized for Web 2.0 applications. It provides AJAX (Asynchronous JavaScript and XML, a technology to add interactivity to web pages) support in multiple ways, from drop-in JavaScript-less AJAX components (Chapter 19), to AJAX-enabling existing JSF components (Chapter 20), to a custom JavaScript library (Chapter 21) that provides direct access to Seam server components from the browser. Internally, Seam provides an advanced concurrency model to efficiently manage multiple AJAX requests from the same user.

A big challenge for AJAX applications is the increased database load. An AJAX application makes much more frequent requests to the server than its non-AJAX counterpart. If all those AJAX requests were to be served by the database, the database would not be able to handle the load. The stateful persistence context in Seam acts as an in-memory cache. It can hold information throughout a long-running conversation and thus help reduce the database roundtrips.

Web 2.0 applications also tend to employ complex relational models for data (e.g., a social network site is all about managing and presenting the relationships between users). For those sites, lazy loading in the ORM layer is crucial; otherwise, a single query could cascade to loading the entire database. As we discussed earlier, Seam is the only web framework today that supports lazy loading correctly for web applications.

# 1.5 POJO Services via Dependency Bijection

Seam is a *lightweight framework* because it promotes the use of Plain Old Java Objects (POJOs) as service components. No framework interfaces or abstract classes exist to "hook" components into the application. The question, of course, is, how do those POJOs interact with each other to form an application? How do they interact with container services (e.g., the database persistence service)?

Seam wires POJO components together using a popular design pattern known as *dependency injection* (DI). Under this pattern, the Seam framework manages the lifecycle of all the components. When a component needs to use another, it declares this dependency to Seam using annotations. Seam determines where to get this dependent component based on the application's current state and "injects" it into the asking component.

Expanding on the dependency injection concept, a Seam component A can also create another component B and "outject" the created component B back to Seam for other components, such as C, to use later.

This type of bidirectional dependency management is widely used in even the simplest Seam web applications (such as the Hello World example in Chapter 2). In Seam terms, we call this *dependency bijection*.

# 1.6  Convention over Configuration

The key design principle that makes Seam so easy to use is *convention over configuration*, also called *configuration by exception*. The idea is to have a set of common-sense default behaviors for the components (i.e., the convention). The developer needs to configure the component explicitly only when the desired behavior is not the default. For instance, when Seam injects component A as a property of component B, the Seam name of component A defaults to the recipient property name in component B. Many little things like that are true in Seam. Overall, the configuration metadata in Seam is much simpler than in competing Java frameworks. As a result, most Seam applications can be adequately configured with a small number of simple Java annotations. Developers benefit from reduced complexity and, in the end, fewer lines of code for the same functionality compared to competing frameworks.

# 1.7  Avoiding XML Abuse

As you have probably noticed, Java annotations play a crucial role in expressing and managing Seam configuration metadata. That is done by design to make the framework easier to work with.

In the early days of J2EE, XML was viewed as the holy grail of configuration management. Framework designers threw all kinds of configuration information, including Java class and method names, in XML files without much thought about the consequence to developers. In retrospect, that was a big mistake. XML configuration files are highly repetitive—they have to repeat information already in the code to connect the configuration to the code. Those repetitions make the application prone to minor errors; for example, a misspelled class name would show up as a hard-to-debug error at runtime. The lack of reasonable default configuration settings further compounds this problem. In fact, in some frameworks, the amount of boilerplate code disguised as XML might rival or even exceed the amount of actual Java code in the application. Among Java developers, this abuse of XML is commonly known as the "XML hell."

The enterprise Java community recognizes this problem and has successfully attempted to replace XML files with annotations in Java source code. EJB3 is an effort by the official Java standardization body to promote the use of annotations in enterprise Java components. EJB3 makes XML files completely optional, and it is definitely a step in the right direction. Seam adds to the EJB3 annotations and expands the annotation-based programming model to the entire web application.

Of course, XML is not entirely bad for configuration data. Seam designers recognize that XML is well suited to specifying web application pageflows or defining business process workflows. The XML file enables us to centrally manage the workflow for the entire application, as opposed to scattering the information around in Java source files. The workflow information has little coupling with the source code—and therefore, the XML files do not need to duplicate information already available in the code. For more details on this subject, see Section 24.5.

# 1.8 Designed for Testing

Seam was designed from ground up for easy testing. Since all Seam components are just annotated POJOs, they are easy to unit-test. You can just create instances of the POJOs using the regular Java new keyword and then run any methods in your testing framework (e.g., JUnit or TestNG). If you need to test interaction among multiple Seam components, you can instantiate those components individually and then set up their relationships manually (i.e., use the setter methods explicitly instead of relying on Seam's dependency injection features). In Chapter 26, we will see how to set up unit tests for your Seam applications and how to mock database service for the test cases.

Integration testing in Seam is perhaps even easier than unit testing. With the Seam Test framework, you can write simple scripts to simulate web user interaction, and then test the outcome. You can use the JSF Expression Language (EL) to reference Seam components in the test script just as you do on a JSF web page. Like unit tests, the integration tests run directly from the command line in the Java SE environment. There is no need to start the application server just to run the tests. Refer to Chapter 27 for more details.

# 1.9  Great Tools Support

Tools support is crucial for an application framework that focuses on developer productivity. Seam is distributed with a command-line application generator called seam-gen (Chapter 5). Seam-gen closely resembles the tools available in Ruby on Rails. It supports features such as generating complete CRUD applications from a database, quick developer turnaround for web applications via the edit/save/reload browser actions, testing support, and more.

But more importantly, seam-gen projects work out of the box with leading Java IDEs such as Eclipse and NetBeans. With seam-gen, you can get started with Seam in no time.

# 1.10  Let's Start Coding!

In a nutshell, Seam simplifies the developer overhead for Java EE applications and, at the same time, adds powerful new features beyond Java EE 5.0. Do not take our word for it, however. Starting with the next chapter, we will show you some real code examples to illustrate how Seam works.

You can download the source code for all example applications in the book from the book's web site at www.michaelyuan.com/seam.

# Seam Hello World

The most basic and widely used functionality of JBoss Seam is the glue between EJB3 and JSF. Seam allows seamless (no pun intended!) integration between the two frameworks through managed components. It extends the EJB3 annotated Plain Old Java Objects (POJOs) programming model to the entire web application. There's no more mandatory JNDI lookup, verbose JSF backing bean declarations, excessive facade business methods, or the pains of passing objects between tiers.

---

**Continue to Use Java EE Patterns in Seam**

In traditional Java EE applications, some design patterns, such as JNDI lookup, XML declaration of components, value objects, and business facade, are mandatory. Seam replaces those artificial requirements with annotated POJOs. However, you are still free to use those patterns if your Seam applications truly need them.

---

Writing a Seam web application is conceptually very simple. You only need to code the following components:

- Entity objects that represent the data model. These entity objects could be entity beans in the Java Persistence API (JPA, a.k.a. EJB3 persistence) or Hibernate POJOs. They are automatically mapped to relational database tables.

- JSF web pages that display the user interface. These pages capture user input via forms and display the data. The data fields on the page are mapped to the backend data model via the JSF Expression Language (EL).

- EJB3 session beans or annotated Seam POJOs that act as UI event handlers for the JSF web pages. They update the data model based on the user input.

Seam manages all these components and automatically injects them into the right pages or objects at runtime. For instance, when the user clicks a button to submit a JSF form, Seam automatically parses the form fields and constructs an entity bean. Then Seam passes the entity bean into the event handler session bean, which Seam also creates, for processing. You do not need to manage component lifecycles and relationships between components in your code. There is no boilerplate code and no XML file for dependency management.

In this chapter, we build a Hello World example to show how Seam glues together a web application. The example application works like this: The user can enter his or her name on a web form to say "hello" to Seam. After submitting the form, the application saves the name to a relational database and displays all the users who have said "hello" to Seam. The example project is in the `helloworld` folder in the source code download for this book.

To build the application, you must have Apache Ant 1.6+ (http://ant.apache.org) installed. First, edit the `build.properties` to point to your Seam and JBoss AS installation. Enter the `helloworld` directory and run the command `ant`. The build result is the `build/jars/helloworld.ear` file, which you can directly copy into your JBoss AS instance's `server/default/deploy` directory, or use the command `ant deploy` to do it. Now start JBoss AS; the application is available at `http://localhost:8080/helloworld/`.

---

**Install JBoss AS**

To run examples in the book, we recommend that you use JBoss AS 4.2.3 GA. You can download a ZIP distribution of JBoss AS from www.jboss.org/jbossas/downloads. Simply unzip the download file and you are done installing JBoss AS. Refer to Appendix A if you need further help on JBoss AS installation and application deployment.

---

You are welcome to use the sample application as a template to jump-start your own Seam projects (see Appendix B). Or, you can use the command-line tool seam-gen (see Chapter 5) to automatically generate project templates, including all configuration files. In this chapter, we do not spend much time explaining the details of the directory structure in the source code project. Instead, we focus on the code and configuration artifacts that a developer must write or manage to build a Seam application. This way, you can apply the knowledge to any project structure without being confined to our template.

**Source Code Directories**

A Seam application consists of Java classes and XML or text configuration files. In the book's example projects, the Java source code files are in the `src` directory, the web pages are in the `view` directory, and all configuration files are in the `resources` directory. For more details, see Appendix B.

# 2.1  Create a Data Model

The data model in the Hello World application is simply a `Person` class with `name` and `id` properties. The `@Entity` annotation tells the container to map this class to a relational database table, with each property a column in the table. Each `Person` instance corresponds to a row of data in the table. As Seam implements configuration by exception, the container simply uses the class name and property name for the table name and column name, correspondingly. The `@Id` and `@GeneratedValue` annotations on the `id` property indicate that the `id` column contains the primary key and that the application server automatically generates its value for each `Person` object saved into the database.

```
@Entity
@Name("person")
public class Person implements Serializable {

  private long id;
  private String name;

  @Id @GeneratedValue
  public long getId() { return id;}
  public void setId(long id) { this.id = id; }

  public String getName() { return name; }
  public void setName(String name) {
    this.name = name;
  }
}
```

The most important annotation in the `Person` class is the `@Name` annotation. It specifies the string name the `Person` bean should be registered by under Seam. In other Seam components (e.g., JSF web pages and session beans), you can reference the managed `Person` bean using the `person` name.

# 2.2  Map the Data Model to a Web Form

In the JSF page, we use the `Person` bean to back the form's input text field. The `#{person.name}` symbol refers to the `name` property on the Seam component named `person`, which is an instance of the `Person` entity bean as we just discussed. The `#{ ... }`

notation to reference Java objects is called JSF Expression Language (EL). It is widely used in Seam.

```
<h:form>
Please enter your name:<br/>
<h:inputText value="#{person.name}" size="15"/><br/>
<h:commandButton type="submit" value="Say Hello"
                 action="#{manager.sayHello}"/>
</h:form>
```

# 2.3   Handle Web Events

The `manager` component in Seam is the `ManagerAction` session bean, identified by the `@Name` annotation on the class. Notice that we use the `@Stateful` annotation here as Seam works best with stateful session beans (for details, refer to the end of this section). The `ManagerAction` class has a `person` field with the `@In` annotation.

```
@Stateful
@Name("manager")
public class ManagerAction implements Manager {

    @In
    private Person person;
```

The `@In` annotation tells Seam to assign the `person` component, which is composed from the JSF form data, to the `person` field (dependency injection) before executing any method in the session bean. You can specify an arbitrary name for the injected component in `@In(value="anyname")`; if no name is specified, as in our example, Seam just injects the component with the same type and same name as the receiving field variable.

When the user clicks on the **Say Hello** button, the `ManagerAction.sayHello()` method is triggered (EL notation `#{manager.sayHello}` links the UI event handler to the form submit button). It simply saves the injected `person` object to the database via the JPA `EntityManager`, which is injected via the `@PersistenceContext` annotation. Then, it searches the database for all `Person` objects, and stores the result in a `List <Person>` list named `fans`. The `fans` list is displayed on the page that comes up after you click on the **Say Hello** button.

```
@PersistenceContext
private EntityManager em;

public void sayHello () {
  em.persist (person);

  fans = em.createQuery("select p from Person p").getResultList();
}
```

It is important to note that the `fans` object must stay alive across two web pages. That is part of the reason for using a stateful session bean, as opposed to a stateless one, for `ManagerAction`.

# 2.4   Navigate to the Next Page

When the user clicks on the **Say Hello** button, the application should save the data and then navigate to the `list.jsp` page to display all fans in a list. The navigation rules are defined in the `WEB-INF/pages.xml` file in the web application WAR file (for more details, see Section 2.7). Below is the navigation rule for actions that happen on the `hello.jsp` page (i.e., the **Say Hello** button click). The rule is self-explanary.

```
<page view-id="/hello.jsp">
  <navigation from-action="#{manager.sayHello}">
    <redirect view-id="/list.jsp"/>
  </navigation>
</page>
```

---

**Seam Web Page Navigation**

The `pages.xml` file is a Seam-specific file that enhances the standard JSF navigation flow control. We will discuss more Seam enhancements to JSF in Chapter 3.

---

The `list.jsp` page has a JSF `dataTable` that iterates through the `fans` list and displays each `Person` object in a row. The `fan` symbol is the iterator for the `fans` list. Figure 2.1 shows the web page.

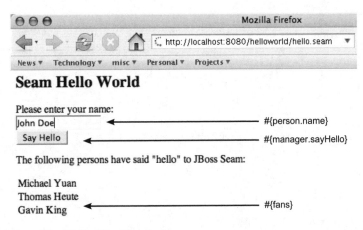

**Figure 2.1**     The Hello World web page

```
<h:dataTable value="#{fans}" var="fan">
  <h:column>
    <h:outputText value="#{fan.name}"/>
  </h:column>
</h:dataTable>
```

Now, wait, how can the web page reference the fans component via #{fans}? How does Seam know that the fans component maps to the ManagerAction.fans field? As you might have guessed, the ManagerAction component "outjects" its fans field to the fans component via an @Out annotation.

```
@Stateful
@Name("manager")
public class ManagerAction implements Manager {

  @Out
  private List <Person> fans;
```

# 2.5  EJB3 Bean Interface and Mandatory Method

We're almost done, except for one little thing. As you probably noticed, the ManagerAction bean class implements the Manager interface. To conform to the EJB3 session bean specification, we need an interface that lists all public methods in the bean, as well as a mandatory method annotated with @Remove. The following is the code for the Manager interface. Fortunately, it is easy to automatically generate this interface from any modern IDE tool.

```
@Local
public interface Manager {
  public void sayHello ();
  public void destroy ();
}

... ...

@Stateful
@Name("manager")
public class ManagerAction implements Manager {

  ... ...

  @Remove
  public void destroy () { }
}
```

That's all the code you need for the Hello World example. In the next two sections, we cover alternative ways to do things and the configuration of Seam applications. You can skip the rest of the chapter for now if you want to jump right into the code and customize the `helloworld` project for your own small database application.

# 2.6  More on the Seam Programming Model

Now we have rushed through the Hello World example application. But we have left off some important topics, such as alternative ways to do things and important features not covered by the previous code. In this section, we will go through those topics to help you gain a deeper understanding of Seam. If you are impatient, you can skip this section and come back later.

## 2.6.1  Seam Built-in Components

Aside from named application components (i.e., classes with `@Name` annotation), Seam maintains a set of built-in components providing access to the runtime context and infrastructure. The `@In` annotation injects Seam's built-in components, and the JSF EL enables you to reference Seam built-in components from a web page.

For instance, the Seam `FacesMessages` component provides access to the JSF messages (displayed by the `<h:messages>` tags) in the current JSF context. You can inject the `FacesMessages` component into any Seam component.

```
@Name("manager")
public class ManagerAction implements manager {

  @In
  Person person;

  @In
  FacesMessages facesMessages;

  public void sayHello () {

    try {
      // ... ...
    } catch (Exception e) {
      facesMessages.add("Has problem saving #{person.name}");
    }
    ... ...
  }
}
```

Another example is the Seam conversation list component, which gives the user an easy way to switch between workspaces. All you need is to reference the `#{conversationList}` component from the web page; see Chapter 9 for more details.

You can initialize and configure Seam built-in components in the `components.xml` file. We will discuss configuration files later in this chapter; for more elaborate component configuration examples, refer to Chapters 4 and 16.

## 2.6.2  Ease of Testing

As we mentioned in Chapter 1, Seam was built from ground up to enable easy and out-of-container testing. In the `helloworld` example project, we included two test cases, for unit testing and integrated JSF testing respectively, in the `test` folder. The Seam testing infrastructure mocks the database, JSF, Seam context, and other application server services in plain Java SE environment. Just run `ant test` to run those tests. To learn more about testing Seam applications, refer to Chapters 26 and 27.

## 2.6.3  Getter/Setter-Based Bijection

Hmm, what is "bijection"? As you might have guessed, it is a generic term to describe both dependency injection (`@In`) and outjection (`@Out`).

In the Hello World example, we demonstrated how to biject Seam components against field variables. You can also biject components against getter and setter methods. For instance, the following code would work just fine.

```
private Person person;
private List <Person> fans;

@In
public void setPerson (Person person) {
  this.person = person;
}

@Out
public List <Person> getFans () {
  return fans;
}
```

Although these getter/setter methods are trivial, the real value of bijection via getter/setter methods is that you can add custom logic to manipulate the bijection process. For instance, you can validate the injected object or retrieve the outjected object on the fly from the database.

## 2.6.4   Avoid Excessive Bijection

Dependency bijection is a very useful design pattern. However, as with any other design pattern, there is always a danger of overusing it. Too much dependency bijection can make the code harder to read because the developer has to figure out where each component is injected from. Too much bijection could also add performance overhead because the bijection happens at runtime.

In the Hello World example, there's a simple way to reduce and even eliminate the bijection: Just make the data components properties of the business component. This way, in the JSF pages, we will only need to reference the business component; no bijection is required to tie together the business and data components. For instance, we can change the `ManagerAction` class to the following:

```
@Stateful
@Name("manager")
public class ManagerAction implements Manager {

  private Person person;
  public Person getPerson () {return person;}
  public void setPerson (Person person) {
    this.person = person;
  }

  private List <Person> fans;
  public List<Person> getFans () {return fans;}

  ... ...
}
```

Then, on the web page, we reference the bean properties as follows:

```
<h:form>
Please enter your name:<br/>
<h:inputText value="#{manager.person.name}"/>
<br/>
<h:commandButton type="submit" value="Say Hello"
                 action="#{manager.sayHello}"/>
</h:form>
... ...
<h:dataTable value="#{manager.fans}" var="fan">
  <h:column>
    <h:outputText value="#{fan.name}"/>
  </h:column>
</h:dataTable>
```

The bottom line is that Seam is versatile when it comes to dependency management. It's generally a good practice to encapsulate a data component within its data access component. This is especially the case for stateful business components (see Section 7.1.2).

### 2.6.5  Accessing Database via the EntityManager

The Java Persistence API (JPA, a.k.a. EJB3 Entity Bean Persistence) `EntityManager` manages the mapping between relational database tables and entity bean objects. The `EntityManager` is created by the application server at runtime. You can inject an `EntityManager` instance using the `@PersistenceContext` annotation.

The `EntityManager.persist()` method saves an entity bean object as a row in its mapped relational table. The `EntityManager.query()` method runs an SQL-like query to retrieve data from the database as a collection of entity bean objects. Refer to the JPA documentation for more on how to use the `EntityManager` and the query language. In this book, we will only use the simplest queries.

By default, the `EntityManager` saves data to the embedded HSQL database. If you are running the application in JBoss AS on the local machine, you can open a GUI console for the HSQL database as follows: Go to `http://localhost:8080/jmx-console`, click on the `database=localDB,service=Hypersonic` MBean, and then click on the **Invoke** button under the `startDatabaseManager()` method. You can execute any SQL commands against the database from the console. If you want to use databases other than the HSQL with your Seam application, refer to Chapter 28.

## 2.7  Configuration and Packaging

Next, let's move on to configuration files and application packaging. You can actually generate almost all the configuration files and the build script via the seam-gen command-line utility (see Chapter 5), or you can simply reuse those in the sample application source project (see Appendix B). So if you want to learn Seam programming techniques first and worry about configuration and deployment later, that's fine. You can safely skip this section and come back later when you need it.

In this section, we focus on the Seam EJB3 component configuration. For Seam POJO configuration (and for potential deployment outside JBoss AS), see Chapter 4. Most Seam configuration files are XML files. But wait! Haven't we just promised that Seam would get you out of the XML hell in J2EE and Spring? Why does it have XML files at all? Well, as it turns out, XML files have some good uses. XML files are appropriate for deployment-time configuration (e.g., the root URL of the web application and the location of the backend database) because with them, you can make deployment-time changes without changing and recompiling the code. They're also good for gluing together different subsystems in the application server (e.g., to configure how JSF components interact with Seam EJB3 components), and they're good for presentation-related content (such as web pages and page navigation flow).

What we try to avoid is replicating information that already exists in the Java source code to XML files. We just need one place to express the information so that it is easier to maintain. As you will soon see, this simple Seam application has several XML configuration files. All of them are very short, and none repeats information that is already available in the Java code. In other words, no "XML code" exists in Seam.

Furthermore, most of the content in those XML files is fairly static, so you can easily reuse those files in your own Seam applications. Refer to Appendix B for instructions on how to use the sample application as a template for your own applications. We will use the next several pages to detail the configuration files and packaging structure of the sample application.

**JBoss AS 4.2.x and 5.x**

The information given in this section applies to deployment in JBoss AS 4.0.5. For JBoss AS 4.2.x and 5.x, the changes you need to make are described in Section 29.2.

Without further ado, let's look into how the Hello World example application is configured and packaged. To build a deployable Seam application for JBoss AS, we have to package all the Java classes and configuration files in an Enterprise Application aRchive (EAR) file. In this example, the EAR file is `helloworld.ear`. It contains three JAR files and two XML configuration files.

```
helloworld.ear
|+ app.war          // Contains web pages etc.
|+ app.jar          // Contains Seam components
|+ lib
    |+ jboss-seam.jar  // Required Seam library
    |+ jboss-el.jar    // Required Seam library
|+ META-INF
    |+ application.xml
    |+ jboss-app.xml
```

**Source Code Directories**

In the source code tree, the `resources/WEB-INF` directory contains the configuration files that go into `app.war/WEB-INF`, the `resources/META-INF` directory contains files that go into `app.jar/META-INF` and `helloworld.ear/META-INF`, and the `resources` directory root has files that go into the root directory of `app.jar`. See Appendix B for more details.

The `application.xml` file lists the JAR files in the EAR and specifies the root URL for this application.

```
<application>
  <display-name>Seam Hello World</display-name>

  <module>
    <web>
      <web-uri>app.war</web-uri>
      <context-root>/helloworld</context-root>
    </web>
  </module>

  <module>
    <ejb>app.jar</ejb>
  </module>

  <module>
    <java>lib/jboss-seam.jar</java>
  </module>

</application>
```

The `jboss-app.xml` file specifies the class loader for this application. Each EAR application should have a unique string name for the class loader. Here, we use the application name in the class loader name to avoid potential conflicts (see Appendix B for more on this).

```
<jboss-app>
  <loader-repository>
    helloworld:archive=helloworld.ear
  </loader-repository>
</jboss-app>
```

The `jboss-seam.jar` and `jboss-el.jar` files are the Seam library JAR files from the Seam distribution. They are placed in the EAR's default `lib` directory and automatically loaded onto the EAR's classpath. The `app.war` and `app.jar` files are built by us; let's look at them next.

## 2.7.1  The WAR File

The `app.war` file is a JAR file packaged according to the Web Application aRchive (WAR) specification. It contains the web pages as well as the standard JSF/Seam configuration files. You can also put JSF-specific library files in the `WEB-INF/lib` directory (e.g., `jboss-seam-ui.jar`, see Chapter 8).

```
app.war
|+ hello.jsp
|+ index.html
|+ WEB-INF
    |+ web.xml
    |+ pages.xml
    |+ faces-config.xml
    |+ components.xml
```

All Java EE web applications require the `web.xml` file. JSF uses it to configure the JSF controller servlet and Seam uses it to intercept all web requests. The configuration in this file is pretty standard.

```
<web-app version="2.4"
        xmlns="http://java.sun.com/xml/ns/j2ee"
        xmlns:xsi="..."
        xsi:schemaLocation="...">

  <!-- Seam -->
  <listener>
    <listener-class>
      org.jboss.seam.servlet.SeamListener
    </listener-class>
  </listener>

  <context-param>
    <param-name>
      javax.faces.STATE_SAVING_METHOD
    </param-name>
    <param-value>server</param-value>
  </context-param>

  <servlet>
    <servlet-name>Faces Servlet</servlet-name>
    <servlet-class>
      javax.faces.webapp.FacesServlet
    </servlet-class>
    <load-on-startup>1</load-on-startup>
  </servlet>

  <servlet-mapping>
    <servlet-name>Faces Servlet</servlet-name>
    <url-pattern>*.seam</url-pattern>
  </servlet-mapping>

</web-app>
```

The `faces-config.xml` file is a standard configuration file for JSF. Seam uses it to add the Seam interceptor into the JSF lifecycle.

```
<faces-config>
  <lifecycle>
    <phase-listener>
      org.jboss.seam.jsf.SeamPhaseListener
    </phase-listener>
  </lifecycle>
</faces-config>
```

The `pages.xml` file contains page navigation rules for multipage applications. We have discussed this file earlier in this chapter.

The `components.xml` file contains Seam-specific configuration options. It is also pretty much application-independent with the exception of the `jndi-pattern` property, which must include the EAR file's base name for Seam to access EJB3 beans by their full JNDI names.

```
<components ...>

  <core:init jndi-pattern="helloworld/#{ejbName}/local"
             debug="false"/>

  <core:manager conversation-timeout="120000"/>

</components>
```

## 2.7.2  The Seam Components JAR

The `app.jar` file contains all EJB3 bean classes (both entity beans and session beans), as well as EJB3-related configuration files.

```
app.jar
|+ Person.class        // entity bean
|+ Manager.class       // session bean interface
|+ ManagerAction.class // session bean
|+ seam.properties     // empty file but needed
|+ META-INF
   |+ ejb-jar.xml
   |+ persistence.xml
```

The `seam.properties` file is empty here but it is required. The Seam runtime searches for this file in all JAR files. If it is found, Seam would load the classes in the corresponding JAR file and process all the Seam annotations.

The `ejb-jar.xml` file contains extra configuration that can override or supplement the annotations on EJB3 beans. In a Seam application, it adds the Seam interceptor to all EJB3 classes. We can reuse the same file for all Seam applications.

```
<ejb-jar>
  <assembly-descriptor>
    <interceptor-binding>
      <ejb-name>*</ejb-name>
      <interceptor-class>
        org.jboss.seam.ejb.SeamInterceptor
      </interceptor-class>
    </interceptor-binding>
  </assembly-descriptor>
</ejb-jar>
```

The `persistence.xml` file configures the backend database source for the `EntityManager`. In this example, we just use the default HSQL database embedded into JBoss AS (i.e., the `java:/DefaultDS` data source). Refer to Chapter 28 for more details on this file and on how to use another database backend (e.g., MySQL).

```
<persistence>
  <persistence-unit name="helloworld">
    <provider>
      org.hibernate.ejb.HibernatePersistence
    </provider>
    <jta-data-source>java:/DefaultDS</jta-data-source>
    <properties>
      <property name="hibernate.dialect"
                value="org.hibernate.dialect.HSQLDialect"/>
      <property name="hibernate.hbm2ddl.auto"
                value="create-drop"/>
      <property name="hibernate.show_sql"
                value="true"/>
    </properties>
  </persistence-unit>
</persistence>
```

That's all the configuration and packaging a simple Seam application needs. We will cover more configuration options and library files as we move to more advanced topics in this book. Again, the simplest way to start your Seam application is not to worry about those configuration files at all and start from a ready-made application template (see Chapter 5 or Appendix B).

# 2.8  How Is This Simple?

That's it for the Hello World application. With three simple Java classes, a JSF page, and a bunch of largely static configuration files, we have a complete database-driven web application. The entire application requires fewer than 30 lines of Java code and no "XML code." However, if you are coming from a PHP background, you might be asking, "How is this simple? I can do that in PHP with less code!"

Well, the answer is that Seam applications are conceptually much simpler than those written in PHP or any other scripting language. The Seam component model enables you to add more functionality to the application in a controlled and maintainable manner. As you will soon see, Seam components make it a breeze to develop stateful and transactional web applications. The object-relational mapping framework (i.e., entity beans) enables you to focus on the abstract data model without having to deal with database-specific SQL statements.

In the rest of this book, we will discuss how to develop increasingly more complex applications using Seam components. In the next chapter, we will start by improving the Hello World example with Facelets and Seam UI libraries.

# 3

# Recommended JSF Enhancements

The Hello World example in Chapter 2 demonstrates how to build a Seam application with standard EJB3 and JSF. Seam chooses JSF as its web framework for many reasons. JSF is a standard technology in Java EE 5.0 and has a large ecosystem of users and vendors. All Java application servers support it. JSF is fully component-based and has a vibrant vendor community for components. JSF also has a powerful and unified expression language (EL, using the #{...} notation) that can be used in web pages, workflow descriptions, and component configuration files throughout the application. JSF also enjoys great support by visual GUI tools in leading Java IDEs.

However, JSF also has its share of problems and awkwardness. JSF has been criticized for being too verbose and too component-centric (i.e., not transparent to HTTP requests). Being a standard framework, JSF innovates more slowly than grassroots open source projects such as Seam itself and is therefore less agile when it comes to correcting design issues and adding new features. For these reasons, Seam works with other open source projects to improve and enhance JSF. For Seam applications, we strongly recommend that you use the following JSF enhancements:

- Use the Facelets framework for web pages. Write your web pages as Facelets XHTML files instead of JSP files. Facelets provides many benefits over the standard JSP in JSF; see Section 3.1.1 for more details.

- Use the Seam JSF component library for special JSF tags that take advantage of Seam-specific UI features, as well as Seam's extended EL for JSF.

- Set up Seam filters to capture and manage JSF redirects, error messages, debugging information, and so on.

Throughout the rest of the book, we assume that you already have these three JSF enhancements installed and enabled (see Section 3.3 for instructions). In Section 8.1.1, we explain how Seam supports lazy loading in JSF page rendering and expands the use of JSF messages beyond simple error messages. In Part III, we will cover integration of data components directly into the JSF web pages. Such direct integration allows Seam to add important features to JSF, including end-to-end validators (Chapter 12), easy-to-use data tables (Chapter 13), bookmarkable URLs (Chapter 15), and custom error pages (Chapter 17). In Part IV, we will discuss how to incorporate third-party AJAX UI widgets in Seam applications. In Section 24.5, we discuss how to use the jBPM business process to manage pageflows in JSF/Seam applications. This allows you to use EL expressions in page navigation rules and to have navigation rules that are dependent on the application state.

---

**JSF 2.0**

Many of the third-party JSF enhancements discussed in this chapter have made their way into the upcoming JSF 2.0 specification, so this chapter will help you with JSF 2.0 migration. Using Seam and the frameworks mentioned here, you can experience the JSF 2.0 productivity today!

---

In this chapter, we will first explore how those additional frameworks improve your JSF development experience. You will see how to develop applications with Facelets and Seam UI libraries. Then, in Section 3.3, we will list the changes you need to make in the Hello World example to support the Facelets and Seam UI components. The new example is in the `betterjsf` project in the book's source code bundle. Feel free to use it as a starting point for your own applications.

# 3.1  An Introduction to Facelets

JavaServer Pages (JSP) is the de-facto "view" technology in JavaServer Faces (JSF). In a standard JSF application, the web pages containing JSF tags and visual components are typically authored as JSP files. However, JSP is not the only choice for authoring JSF web pages. An open source project called Facelets (https://facelets.dev.java.net) allows you to write JSF web pages as XHTML files with significantly improved page readability, developer productivity, and runtime performance compared to equivalent pages authored in JSP. Although Facelets is not yet a Java Community Process (JCP) standard, we highly recommend that you use it in your Seam applications whenever possible.

## 3.1.1 Why Facelets?

First, Facelets improves JSF performance by 30 to 50 percent by bypassing the JSP engine and using XHTML pages directly as the view technology. By avoiding JSP, Facelets also avoids potential conflicts between JSF 1.1 and JSP 2.4 specifications, which are the specifications supported in JBoss AS 4.x (see the accompanying sidebar for details).

---

**The Potential Conflict between JSF and JSP**

In our Hello World example, we used JSP files (e.g., the `hello.jsp` file) to create the web pages in the JSF application. The JSP container processes those files at the same time they are processed by the JSF engine. That raises some potential conflicts between the JSP 2.0 container and JSF 1.1 runtime in JBoss AS 4.x. For a detailed explanation of the problems and examples, refer to Hans Bergsten's excellent article "Improving JSF by Dumping JSP" (www.onjava.com/pub/a/onjava/2004/06/09/jsf.html).

Those conflicts are resolved in JBoss AS 5.x, which supports JSP 2.1+ and JSF 1.2+. However, if you need to use JBoss 4.x for now, the best solution is to avoid JSP altogether and use Facelets instead.

---

Second, you can use any XHTML tags in Facelets pages. It eliminates the need to enclose XHTML tags and free text in the `<f:verbatim>` tags. These `<f:verbatim>` tags make JSP-based JSF pages tedious to write and hard to read.

Third, Facelets provides debugging support from the browser. If an error occurs when Facelets renders a page, it gives you the exact location of that error in the source file and provides context information around the error (see Section 17.5). It is much nicer than digging into a stack trace when a JSP/JSF error occurs.

Last, and perhaps most important, Facelets provides a template framework for JSF. With Facelets, you can use a Seam-like dependency injection model to assemble pages instead of manually including page header, footer, and sidebar components in each page.

---

**The Case for JSP**

If Facelets is this good, why do we bother to use JSP with JSF at all? Well, JSP is a standard technology in the Java EE stack, whereas Facelets is not yet a standard. That means JSP is supported everywhere, while Facelets might have integration issues with third-party JSF components. In the meantime, the JSP spec committee is certainly learning its lessons from Facelets. The next-generation JSPs will work a lot better with JSF.

---

## 3.1.2 A Facelets Hello World

As we discussed, a basic Facelets XHTML page is not all that different from the equivalent JSP page. To illustrate this point, we ported the Hello World sample application (see Chapter 2) from JSP to Facelets. The new application is in the betterjsf project. Below is the JSP version of the hello.jsp page:

```
<%@ taglib uri="http://java.sun.com/jsf/html" prefix="h" %>
<%@ taglib uri="http://java.sun.com/jsf/core" prefix="f" %>

<html>
<body>
<f:view>

<f:verbatim>
<h2>Seam Hello World</h2>
</f:verbatim>

<h:form>
<f:verbatim>
Please enter your name:<br/>
</f:verbatim>

<h:inputText value="#{person.name}" size="15"/><br/>
<h:commandButton type="submit" value="Say Hello"
                 action="#{manager.sayHello}"/>
</h:form>

</f:view>
</body>
</html>
```

Compare that with the Facelets XHTML version of the hello.xhtml page:

```
<html xmlns="http://www.w3.org/1999/xhtml"
      xmlns:ui="http://java.sun.com/jsf/facelets"
      xmlns:h="http://java.sun.com/jsf/html"
      xmlns:f="http://java.sun.com/jsf/core">
<body>

<h2>Seam Hello World</h2>

<h:form>
Please enter your name:<br/>
<h:inputText value="#{person.name}" size="15"/>
<br/>
<h:commandButton type="submit" value="Say Hello"
                 action="#{manager.sayHello}"/>
</h:form>

</body>
</html>
```

It is pretty obvious that the Facelets XHTML page is cleaner and easier to read than the JSP page since the XHTML page is not cluttered up with <f:verbatim> tags. The namespace declarations in the Facelets XHTML page conform to the XHTML standard. Other than that, however, the two pages look similar. All the JSF component tags are identical.

## 3.1.3   Use Facelets as a Template Engine

For most developers, the ability to use XHTML templates is probably the most appealing feature of Facelets. Let's see how it works.

A typical web application consists of multiple web pages with a common layout. They usually have the same header, footer, and sidebar menu. Without a template engine, you must repeat all those elements for each page. That's a lot of duplicated code with complex HTML formatting tags. Worse, if you need to make a small change to any of the elements (e.g., change a word in the header), you have to edit all pages. From all we know about the software development process, this type of copy-and-paste editing is very inefficient and error-prone.

The solution, of course, is to abstract out the layout information into a single source and thus avoid the duplication of the same information on multiple pages. In Facelets, the template page is the single source of layout information. The `template.xhtml` file in the Seam Hotel Booking example (the `booking` project in source code) is a template page.

```
<html xmlns="http://www.w3.org/1999/xhtml"
      xmlns:ui="http://java.sun.com/jsf/facelets"
      xmlns:h="http://java.sun.com/jsf/html">
<head>
   <title>JBoss Suites: Seam Framework</title>
   <link href="css/screen.css" rel="stylesheet" type="text/css" />
</head>
<body>

<div id="document">
  <div id="header">
    <div id="title">...</div>
    <div id="status">
      ... Settings and Log in/out ...
    </div>
  </div>
  <div id="container">
    <div id="sidebar">
      <ui:insert name="sidebar"/>
    </div>
    <div id="content">
      <ui:insert name="content"/>
    </div>
  </div>
  <div id="footer">...</div>
</div>
</body>
</html>
```

The `template.xhtml` file defines the layout of the page header, footer, sidebar, and main content area (Figure 3.1). Obviously, the sidebar and main content area have different content for each page, so we use the `<ui:insert>` tags as placeholders in the template. In each Facelets page, we tag UI elements accordingly to tell the engine how to fill the template placeholders with content.

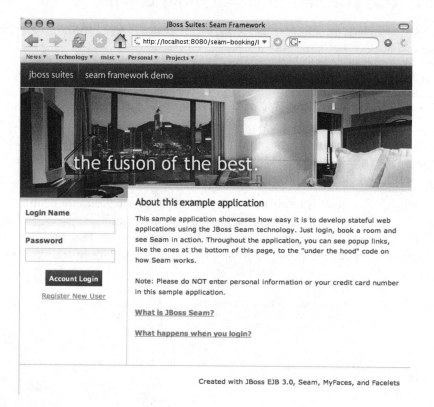

**Figure 3.1**    The template layout

---

**Multiple Template Pages**

Actually, we were not entirely accurate when we mentioned that the template is a "single" source for layout knowledge in an application. Facelets is flexible in managing template pages. In a Facelets application, you can have multiple template pages for alternative themes or for different sections of the web site. Yet, the basic idea of abstracting layout information to avoid duplicated code still applies.

---

**Extensive Use of CSS**

All pages in the Seam Hotel Booking example, including the `template.xhtml` page, are styled using CSS. We highly recommend using CSS in Seam/Facelet applications because it's concise and easy to understand. Even more importantly, CSS separates the styling from page content. With CSS, the web designer does not even need to understand the JSF/Seam symbols and tags in the page.

Of course, if you prefer to use XHTML tables to lay out your page, you can still do so in the `template.xhtml` file. Just make sure that you place the `<ui:insert>` tags in the right places within the nested tables.

Each Facelets page corresponds to a web page. It "injects" contents for the `<ui:insert>` placeholders into the template. Below is the `main.xhtml` page of the Seam Hotel Booking example application.

```
<ui:composition xmlns="http://www.w3.org/1999/xhtml"
                xmlns:ui="http://java.sun.com/jsf/facelets"
                xmlns:h="http://java.sun.com/jsf/html"
                xmlns:f="http://java.sun.com/jsf/core"
                template="template.xhtml">

  <ui:define name="content">
    <ui:include src="conversations.xhtml" />

    <div class="section">
      <h:form>
        <h1>Search Hotels</h1>
        ... ...
      </h:form>
    </div>

    <div class="section">
      <h:dataTable value="#{hotels}" ...>
        ... ...
      </h:dataTable>
    </div>

    <div class="section">
      <h1>Current Hotel Bookings</h1>
    </div>

    <div class="section">
      <h:dataTable value="#{bookings}" ...>
        ... ...
      </h:dataTable>
    </div>
  </ui:define>

  <ui:define name="sidebar">
    <h1>Stateful and contextual components</h1>
    <p>... ...</p>
  </ui:define>
</ui:composition>
```

At the beginning of the `main.xhtml` file, the code declares that the `template.xhtml` template is used to format the layout. The `<ui:define>` elements correspond to the `<ui:insert>` placeholders of the same names in the template. You can arrange those `<ui:define>` elements in any order, and at runtime, the Facelets engine renders the web pages according to the template.

## 3.1.4   Data List Component

One of the biggest omissions in the current JSF specification is that it lacks a standard component to iterate over a data list. The `<h:dataTable>` component displays a data list as an HTML table, but it is not a generic iteration component.

Facelets remedies this problem by providing a `<ui:repeat>` component to iterate over any data list. For instance, the following Facelets page snippet displays a list in a table-less format:

```
<ui:repeat value="#{fans} var="fan">
  <div class="faninfo">#{fan.name}</div>
</ui:repeat>
```

In Section 3.4.1 and Section 3.4.2, you will see that the Facelets `<ui:repeat>` component can be used in completely non-HTML environments.

In this section, we just scratched the surface of what Facelets can do. We encourage you to explore Facelets (https://facelets.dev.java.net/) and make the most out of this excellent framework.

# 3.2   Seam JSF Enhancements

Seam provides its own JSF enhancements that work with both Facelets XHTML and JSP pages. You can use Seam UI tags in your JSF view pages, use Seam's special extension to the JSF EL, and use the Seam filter to make Seam work better with the JSF URL redirecting and error handling mechanisms. Those Seam JSF components work with Seam framework features not yet discussed in the book. In this section, we will provide an overview of those enhancements but leave the details to later chapters of the book. Impatient readers can safely skip to Section 3.3 for instructions on how to install those Seam JSF components.

## 3.2.1   Seam UI Tags

The Seam UI tags give regular JSF UI components access to the Seam-managed runtime information. They help integrate Seam's business and data components more tightly with the web UI components. Seam UI tags can be roughly divided into the following categories:

**validation**  The Seam validation tags allow you to use Hibernate validator annotations on entity beans to validate JSF input fields. They also allow you to decorate an entire invalid (or valid) field when the validation fails. See Chapter 12 for more on using those components.

**conversation management**  A key concept in Seam is the arbitrarily long web conversation (see Chapter 8). Normally, the web pages in a conversation are connected via hidden fields in HTTP `POST` operations. But what if you want to click on a regular hyperlink and still stay in the same conversation? Seam provides tags that can generate conversation-aware hyperlinks. See Sections 8.3.6 and 9.2.2 for more.

**business process management**  Seam provides tags that can associate web page content with business processes in the background (see Chapter 24).

**performance**  The `<s:cache>` tag encloses page content that should be cached on the server. When the page is rendered again, the cached region is retrieved from the cache instead of being dynamically rendered (see Chapter 30).

**JSF replacement tags**  Some Seam tags are a direct replacement for JSF tags to fix certain deficiencies in JSF. Right now, the only such tag is `<s:convertDateTime>`, which fixes JSF's annoying default time zone problem.

**alternative display output**  In addition to the standard HTML output, Seam provides JSF tags that render PDF and email outputs based on Facelets templates. It also provides tags to render Wikitext snippets into HTML elements. Refer to Section 3.4 for more details on those alternative display technologies supported by the Seam tag library.

Later chapters cover the use of these Seam UI tags when we discuss specific Seam features related to them. Here, we use the `<s:convertDateTime>` tag as an example to demonstrate how Seam UI tags are used. The `<s:convertDateTime>` tag replaces JSF's converter tag, `<f:convertDateTime>`, to convert the backend `Date` or `Time` objects to formatted output/input strings in the server's local time zone. The JSF tag is insufficient because it converts the time stamp to the UTC time zone by default. The sensible default time zone in the Seam tag makes life a lot easier for developers. To use the Seam UI tags in a web page, you need to declare the Seam taglib namespace as follows:

```
<html xmlns:ui="http://java.sun.com/jsf/facelets"
      xmlns:h="http://java.sun.com/jsf/html"
      xmlns:f="http://java.sun.com/jsf/core"
      xmlns:s="http://jboss.com/products/seam/taglib">

  ... ...

  The old hello date is:<br/>
```

```
<h:outputText value="#{manager.helloDate}">
<s:convertDateTime/>
</h:outputText>

Please enter a new date:<br/>
<h:inputText value="#{manager.helloDate}">
<s:convertDateTime/>
</h:inputText>
```

```
</html>
```

## 3.2.2  Seam JSF EL Enhancement

Chapter 2 showed that the JSF #{ . . . } EL notation is highly useful. However, in standard JSF EL, the "property" (value expression) and "method" (method expression) on the backend component are the same. As a result, the EL method expression cannot take any call arguments. For instance, the name property on the person component is expressed as follows:

```
<h:inputText value="#{person.name}" size="15"/>
```

The event handler method sayHello() on the manager component is written the same way, as shown below, and therefore cannot take any call arguments. All the objects the method operates on must be injected into the component before the method is called.

```
<h:commandButton type="submit"
                 value="Say Hello"
                 action="#{manager.sayHello}"/>
```

With the Seam EL extension, you can now call any component method with the () to improve readability:

```
#{component.method()}
```

The method can now take call arguments as well. So, with the following example, you no longer need to inject the person component into the manager component. That reduces the need for dependency injection and makes the application easier to read.

```
<h:commandButton type="submit"
                 value="Say Hello"
                 action="#{manager.sayHello(person)}"/>
```

Here is the new ManagerAction class with the new sayHello() method:

```
@Stateless
@Name("manager")
public class ManagerAction implements Manager {

   private Person person;
```

```
@Out
private List <Person> fans;

@PersistenceContext
private EntityManager em;

public void sayHello (Person p) {
  em.persist (p);
  fans = em.createQuery("select p from Person p").getResultList();
}
}
```

The enhanced EL allows multiple call arguments separated by commas. If the backend method takes a `String` argument, you can pass it directly in the EL as follows:

```
... action="#{component.method('literal string')}"/>
```

The new Seam JSF EL makes your code more readable and more elegant. Use it!

## 3.2.3 Use EL Everywhere

Seam not only expands the syntax of JSF EL but also makes the EL available beyond JSF web pages. In a Seam application, you can use JSF expressions to substitute static text in configuration files (Section 9.2.1), test cases (Chapters 26 and 27), JSF messages (Section 8.1.2), and jBPM processes (Chapter 24).

The expanded use of JSF EL greatly simplifies application development.

## 3.2.4 Seam Filter

Seam provides a very powerful servlet filter. The filter does additional processing before the web request is processed by JSF and after the web response is generated. It improves integration between Seam components and JSF.

- The filter preserves the conversation context during JSF URL redirects. That allows the Seam default conversation scope to span from the request page to the redirected response page (Chapter 8).

- It captures any uncaught runtime errors and redirects to custom error pages or the Seam debug page, if necessary (Chapter 17).

- It provides support for the file upload JSF component in Seam UI.

- It allows any non-JSF servlet or JSP page to access Seam components via the Seam `Component` class.

See Section 3.3 for how to install the Seam filter in your `web.xml`.

### 3.2.5  Stateful JSF

Perhaps the most important feature of Seam is that it is a stateful application framework. The stateful design has great implications for JSF. For instance, it enables much tighter integration between JSF and ORM solutions such as Hibernate (Section 6.1) and allows JSF messages to propagate across different pages (Section 8.1.2). Throughout the rest of this book, we will cover how Seam's stateful design improves web application development.

# 3.3  Add Facelets and Seam UI Support

To support the Facelets and Seam UI frameworks, you must first bundle the necessary library JAR files in the application. Three JAR files go into the `app.war` archive's `WEB-INF/lib` directory because they contain tag definitions. Facelets requires the `jsf-facelets.jar` file; Seam needs the `jboss-seam-ui.jar` and `jboss-seam-debug.jar` files. An additional JAR file, `jboss-el.jar`, goes into the EAR file `mywebapp.ear` to support the JSF Expression Language (EL) in both the web module (`app.war`) and the EJB3 module (`app.jar`).

```
mywebapp.ear
|+ app.war
    |+ web pages
    |+ WEB-INF
        |+ web.xml
        |+ faces-config.xml
        |+ other config files
        |+ lib
            |+ jsf-facelets.jar
            |+ jboss-seam-ui.jar
            |+ jboss-seam-debug.jar
|+ app.jar
|+ lib
    |+ jboss-el.jar
    |+ jboss-seam.jar
|+ META-INF
    |+ application.xml
    |+ jboss-app.xml
```

To use Facelets and Seam's enhancements to JSF EL, you need to load a special view handler in the `faces-config.xml` file, which is located in the `WEB-INF` directory in the `app.war` (or in the `resources/WEB-INF` directory in the project source). The view handler renders HTML web pages from Facelets template and pages. This is the relevant snippet from the `faces-config.xml` file:

```
<faces-config>
 ... ...
  <application>
   <view-handler>
     com.sun.facelets.FaceletViewHandler
   </view-handler>
  </application>
<faces-config>
```

In a Facelets application, we typically use the `.xhtml` filename suffix for web pages since they are now XHTML files, not JSP pages. We have to tell the JSF runtime about this change in the `web.xml` file (in the same directory as the `faces-config.xml` file):

```
<web-app>
 ... ...
  <context-param>
    <param-name>javax.faces.DEFAULT_SUFFIX</param-name>
    <param-value>.xhtml</param-value>
  </context-param>
</web-app>
```

Finally, let's set up the Seam filter and resource servlet in the same `web.xml` file. The `SeamFilter` provides support for error pages, JSF redirects, and file upload. The Seam resource servlet provides access to images and CSS files in `jboss-seam-ui.jar`, which are required by Seam UI components. The resource servlet also enables direct JavaScript access to Seam components (Chapter 21).

```
<web-app>
 ... ...
  <servlet>
    <servlet-name>Seam Resource Servlet</servlet-name>
    <servlet-class>
      org.jboss.seam.servlet.ResourceServlet
    </servlet-class>
  </servlet>

  <servlet-mapping>
    <servlet-name>Seam Resource Servlet</servlet-name>
    <url-pattern>/seam/resource/*</url-pattern>
  </servlet-mapping>

  <filter>
    <filter-name>Seam Filter</filter-name>
    <filter-class>
      org.jboss.seam.web.SeamFilter
    </filter-class>
  </filter>

  <filter-mapping>
    <filter-name>Seam Filter</filter-name>
    <url-pattern>/*</url-pattern>
  </filter-mapping>

</web-app>
```

# 3.4  PDF, Email, and Rich Text

So far, we have discussed the JSF enhancements provided by Facelets and the `jboss-seam-ui.jar` library. Those are important usability and integration features required by almost all Seam web applications. In this section, we discuss several additional UI features Seam provides. To use those features, you need to bundle more library JAR files in your application and provide extra configuration as described below. You can choose and mix the UI feature sets you want in the application while keeping its footprint and configuration complexity to a minimum.

## 3.4.1  Generate PDF Reports

The Facelets XHTML files generate HTML web pages by default. However, a real-world web application sometimes needs to generate PDF output for printer-ready documents such as reports, legal documents, tickets, receipts, etc. The Seam PDF library leverages the open source iText toolkit to generate PDF documents. Here is a simple Facelets file, `hello.xhtml`, which renders a PDF document:

```
<p:document xmlns:p="http://jboss.com/products/seam/pdf"
            title="Hello">
  <p:chapter number="1">
    <p:title>
      <p:paragraph>Hello</p:paragraph>
    </p:title>
    <p:paragraph>Hello #{user.name}!</p:paragraph>

    <p:paragraph>The time now is

      <p:text value="#{manager.nowDate}">
        <f:convertDateTime style="date" format="short"/>
      </p:text>

    </p:paragraph>
  </p:chapter>

  <p:chapter number="2">
    <p:title>
      <p:paragraph>Goodbye</p:paragraph>
    </p:title>
    <p:paragraph>Goodbye #{user.name}.</p:paragraph>
  </p:chapter>
</p:document>
```

While the `hello.xhtml` file has the `xhtml` suffix, it is really an XML file with Seam PDF UI tags. When the user loads the `hello.seam` URL, Seam generates the PDF document and redirects the browser to `hello.pdf`. The browser then displays the `hello.pdf` file in its PDF reader plugin or prompts the user to save the PDF file. By passing the `pageSize` HTTP parameter to the URL, you can specify the page size of the generated PDF document. For instance, the `hello.seam?pageSize=LETTER` URL produces a letter-sized `hello.pdf` document. Valid `pageSize` options also include `A4`, `LEGAL`, and others.

You can use any JSF EL expressions in the `xhtml` page; these EL expressions are resolved on the fly when the PDF document is rendered, just as are EL expressions on web pages. You can also use JSF converters to control text formatting, the `<f:facet>` tag to control table formatting, or the Facelets `<ui:repeat>` tag to render a list or table from dynamic data. See the Seam Reference Documentation (http://seamframework.org/ Documentation) for more details on the tags.

To use the Seam PDF tags, you need to include the `jboss-seam-pdf.jar` and `itext.jar` files in the `WEB-INF/lib` directory of your WAR application archive.

```
mywebapp.ear
|+ app.war
    |+ web pages
    |+ WEB-INF
        |+ web.xml
        |+ faces-config.xml
        |+ other config files
        |+ lib
            |+ jsf-facelets.jar
            |+ jboss-seam-ui.jar
            |+ jboss-seam-debug.jar

            |+ jboss-seam-pdf.jar

            |+ itext.jar
|+ app.jar
|+ lib
    |+ jboss-el.jar
    |+ jboss-seam.jar
|+ META-INF
    |+ application.xml
    |+ jboss-app.xml
```

Then, you need to configure the PDF-related Seam component in the `components.xml` file. The `useExtensions` property indicates that the `hello.seam` URL should redirect to the `hello.pdf` URL. If the `useExtensions` property is set to `false`, the redirection would not happen and the web application would serve PDF data directly to the browser from a `.seam` URL, which could cause usability problems in some browsers.

```
<components xmlns:pdf="http://jboss.com/products/seam/pdf"
            xmlns:core="http://jboss.com/products/seam/core">

  <pdf:documentStore useExtensions="true"/>

  ... ...

</components>
```

Finally, you need to set up servlet filters for the `.pdf` files. Those filters are only needed when you have the `useExtensions` property set to `true` in the `components.xml` configuration we've just seen.

```
<web-app ...>

... ...

<filter>
  <filter-name>Seam Servlet Filter</filter-name>
  <filter-class>
    org.jboss.seam.servlet.SeamServletFilter
  </filter-class>
</filter>

<filter-mapping>
  <filter-name>Seam Servlet Filter</filter-name>
  <url-pattern>*.pdf</url-pattern>
</filter-mapping>

<servlet>
  <servlet-name>
    Document Store Servlet
  </servlet-name>
  <servlet-class>
    org.jboss.seam.pdf.DocumentStoreServlet
  </servlet-class>
</servlet>

<servlet-mapping>
  <servlet-name>
    Document Store Servlet
  </servlet-name>
  <url-pattern>*.pdf</url-pattern>
</servlet-mapping>
</web-app>
```

The Seam PDF library supports generating digitally signed PDF documents. The public key configuration, however, is beyond the scope of this book. See the Seam Reference Documentation and iText documentation for more details.

## 3.4.2  Template-Based Email

Sending email from your web application is not hard—but it can be a messy task. The standard JavaMail API requires developers to embed the email messages as literal strings inside Java code. That makes it very difficult to write rich email (i.e., HTML email with elaborate text formatting and embedded images), and makes it nearly impossible for non-developers to design and compose the email messages. The lack of design and branding in email messages is a major weakness in many web applications.

In Seam, we provide a template-based approach to handling email. A business person or a page designer writes the email as a web page. Here is an example email template page `hello.xhtml`:

```
<m:message xmlns="http://www.w3.org/1999/xhtml"
           xmlns:m="http://jboss.com/products/seam/mail"
           xmlns:h="http://java.sun.com/jsf/html">
  <m:from name="Michael Yuan" address="myuan@redhat.com"/>
  <m:to name="#{person.firstname} #{person.lastname}">
    #{person.address}
  </m:to>
  <m:subject>Try out Seam!</m:subject>
  <m:body>
  <p>Dear #{person.firstname},</p>
  <p>You can try out Seam by visiting
  <a href="http://labs.jboss.com/jbossseam">
    http://labs.jboss.com/jbossseam
    </a>.</p>
  <p>Regards,</p>
  <p>Michael</p>
  </m:body>
</m:message>
```

When a web user needs to send out the `hello.xhtml` message, he or she clicks on a button or a link to invoke a Seam backing bean method to render the `hello.xhtml` page. Below is an example method to send the `hello.xhtml` email. The message recipient is dynamically determined at runtime via the `#{person.address}` EL expression. Similarly, you can dynamically determine the sender address or any content in the message via EL expressions.

```
public class ManagerAction implements Manager {

  @In(create=true)
  private Renderer renderer;

  public void send() {
    try {
      renderer.render("/hello.xhtml");
      facesMessages.add("Email sent successfully");
    } catch (Exception e) {
      facesMessages.add("Email sending failed: " + e.getMessage());
    }
  }
}
```

If a message has multiple recipients, you can insert multiple `<m:to>` tags using the Facelets `<ui:repeat>` tag. You can also use the Facelets `<ui:insert>` tag to compose messages from a template.

To use the Seam email support tags, you need to bundle the `jboss-seam-mail.jar` file in the `WEB-INF/lib` directory of your WAR archive.

```
mywebapp.ear
|+ app.war
   |+ web pages
   |+ WEB-INF
      |+ web.xml
      |+ faces-config.xml
      |+ other config files
      |+ lib
         |+ jsf-facelets.jar
         |+ jboss-seam-ui.jar
         |+ jboss-seam-debug.jar

         |+ jboss-seam-mail.jar
|+ app.jar
|+ lib
   |+ jboss-el.jar
   |+ jboss-seam.jar
|+ META-INF
   |+ application.xml
   |+ jboss-app.xml
```

Then, you need to configure an SMTP server to actually send the email. That is done via the Seam `mailSession` component in `components.xml`. You can specify the host name, port number, and login credentials for the SMTP server. Here is an example SMTP configuration:

```
<components xmlns="http://jboss.com/products/seam/components"
            xmlns:core="http://jboss.com/products/seam/core"
            xmlns:mail="http://jboss.com/products/seam/mail">

    <mail:mailSession host="smtp.example.com"
                      port="25"
                      username="myuan"
                      password="mypass" />

    ... ...

</components>
```

## 3.4.3  Display Rich Text

A community-oriented web application often needs to display user-contributed content (e.g., forum posts, comments etc.). Here, a big issue is how to allow rich text formatting in user-contributed content. Allowing the web user to submit arbitrary HTML-formatted text is out of the question, as raw HTML is insecure and prone to various cross-site scripting attacks.

One solution is to use a WYSIWYG rich text editor widget to capture user input. The widget transforms its content to sanitized HTML when the form is submitted to the server. Refer to Section 21.3.2 for more on this subject.

Another solution, which we cover here, is to provide the web users with a small set of non-HTML markup tags they can use to format the content. When the application displays the content, it automatically converts the markup to HTML tags. A popular non-HTML text markup language is Wikitext which is widely used on wiki community sites (e.g., the http://wikipedia.org site). The Seam `<s:formattedText>` UI component converts Wikitext to HTML formatted text. For instance, suppose that the `#{user.post}` Seam component contains the following text:

```
It's easy to make *bold text*, /italic text/,
|monospace|, -deleted text-, super^scripts^,
or _underlines_.
```

The UI element `<s:formattedText value="#{user.post}"/>` would produce the following HTML text on the web page:

```
<p>
It's easy to make <b>bold text</b>,
<i>italic text</i>, <tt>monospace</tt>
<del>deleted text</del>, super<sup>scripts</sup>,
or <u>underlines</u>.
</p>
```

Support for the `<s:formattedText>` tag is already included in the `jboss-seam-ui.jar` file. But it depends on the ANTLR (ANother Tool for Language Recognition, see www.antlr.org) parser to process the Wikitext grammar. In order to use the `<s:formattedText>` tag, you need to bundle the ANTLR JAR in your WAR archive:

```
mywebapp.ear
|+ app.war
    |+ web pages
    |+ WEB-INF
        |+ web.xml
        |+ faces-config.xml
        |+ other config files
        |+ lib
            |+ jsf-facelets.jar
            |+ jboss-seam-ui.jar
            |+ jboss-seam-debug.jar

            |+ antlr-x.y.z.jar
|+ app.jar
|+ lib
    |+ jboss-el.jar
    |+ jboss-seam.jar
|+ META-INF
    |+ application.xml
    |+ jboss-app.xml
```

With the ANTLR parser, Seam can potentially support other markup languages beyond the Wikitext. For instance, it might one day support sanitized HTML (i.e., HTML text with all potential security loopholes removed), BBCode (widely used in online forms), and others. Refer to Seam documentation for the latest updates on this subject.

# 3.5  Internationalization

JSF in general provides very good support for internationalization. To support the proper local encoding of web pages, you just need to select the default encoding for the XHTML pages. A safe choice would be to use UTF-8 encoding:

```
<?xml version="1.0" encoding="UTF-8"?>
... ...
```

However, an issue in JSF is that it does not always submit the POST or GET data in the proper encoding format. To fix this, you can setup the following filter in components.xml to enforce UTF-8 encoding in HTTP requests.

```
<web:character-encoding-filter encoding="UTF-8"
                               override-client="true"
                               url-pattern="*.seam" />
```

Another important aspect of JSF is its ability to select different locales for localized strings in the UI. In Seam, you can define the locales supported by your application in components.xml.

```
<international:locale-config default-locale="en"
                            supported-locales="en fr de"/>
```

Then, we can offer the user to select the correct locale for the UI via standard JSF mechanisms.

```
<h:selectOneMenu value="#{localeSelector.localeString}">
  <f:selectItems value="#{localeSelector.supportedLocales}"/>
</h:selectOneMenu>
<h:commandButton action="#{localeSelector.select}"
                 value="#{messages['ChangeLanguage']}"/>
```

The localized strings are defined in message bundles in the app.war/WEB-INF/classes directory. For example, the en (English) locale strings are defined in the messages_en.properties file.

# Seam without EJB3

**J**Boss Seam was originally designed to be a framework on top of Java EE 5.0—to bridge the gap between JSF and EJB3. However, Seam is highly flexible and can stand on its own. In fact, Seam has no hard dependency on either JSF or EJB3. In Seam, any POJO with an `@Name` annotation can be turned into a managed component. We can build Seam applications solely from POJOs. Such applications can be deployed in any J2EE 1.4 application server, as well as in plain Tomcat servers.

In this chapter, we modify the `betterjsf` example to use a POJO instead of an EJB session bean to handle data access and business logic. The resulting example is `hellojpa`. POJOs are clearly simpler and require less runtime infrastructure than EJBs. However, there are still trade-offs in not using EJBs. We will discuss those trade-offs at the end of this chapter.

## 4.1  A Seam POJO Example

A Seam POJO component is simpler than the corresponding EJB3 session bean. No interface needs to be implemented, and the only required annotation is `@Name` to give it a Seam name.

```
@Name("manager")
public class ManagerPojo {

  ... ...

}
```

As we discussed before, the `@PersistenceContext` annotation makes the EJB3 container inject an `EntityManager` object. As we no longer have an EJB3 container here, we just inject a Seam-managed JPA `EntityManager` using the Seam `@In` annotation. It works the same way as the EJB3 container-managed `EntityManager`. Here is the complete code for the `ManagerPojo` class:

```
@Name("manager")
public class ManagerPojo {

  @Out
  private List <Person> fans;

  @In
  private EntityManager em;

  public void sayHello (Person p) {
    em.persist (p);
    fans = em.createQuery("select p from Person p").getResultList();
  }

}
```

# 4.2  Configuration

To deploy an application outside the EJB3 container, we need to configure Seam to take over some of the essential services that the EJB3 container handles for us. In this section, we demonstrate how to configure the `hellojpa` POJO application for deployment in the J2EE 1.4-compatible profile of JBoss AS, as well as in plain Tomcat.

Here, we focus on the difference between Seam POJO and EJB3 configuration. You can change any Seam EJB3 application from session beans to POJOs and then perform the changes highlighted here to make it deployable in J2EE.

First, you need to set up the persistence context and the `EntityManager` to use in a non-EJB3 environment. In the `persistence.xml` file (in `app.jar/META-INF/`), you must specify a cache provider and a mechanism to look up the transaction manager—the EJB3 container automatically does that for session beans, but we are dealing with POJOs here. Below is the example `persistence.xml` for deployment inside JBoss AS. We look up the JBoss JTA transaction manager to use with the Seam-managed `EntityManager`.

```
<persistence>
  <persistence-unit name="helloworld" transaction-type="JTA">
    <provider>
      org.hibernate.ejb.HibernatePersistence
    </provider>

    <jta-data-source>
      java:/DefaultDS
    </jta-data-source>
```

```
    <properties>
      <property name="hibernate.dialect"
                value="org.hibernate.dialect.HSQLDialect"/>
      <property name="hibernate.hbm2ddl.auto"
                value="create-drop"/>
      <property name="hibernate.show_sql"
                value="true"/>
      <property name="hibernate.cache.provider_class"
                value="org.hibernate.cache.HashtableCacheProvider"/>
      <property name="hibernate.transaction.manager_lookup_class"
          value="org.hibernate.transaction.JBossTransactionManagerLookup"/>
    </properties>
  </persistence-unit>
</persistence>
```

To deploy Seam POJOs on non-JBoss application servers, you only need to customize the `persistence.xml` file for the particular application server. Typically, you need to change the JNDI binding for the data source, the Hibernate dialect for the database, and, most importantly, the transaction manager lookup class. For instance, for deployment on WebLogic, you would need the `WeblogicTransactionManagerLookup` class.

The configuration is slightly different if you want to deploy on a plain Tomcat server. Tomcat does not have a JTA transaction manager. So, you have to use a `RESOURCE_LOCAL` transaction, and there is no transaction manager lookup class. Below is an example `persistence.xml` configuration for Tomcat:

```
<persistence>
  <persistence-unit name="helloworld"
                    transaction-type="RESOURCE_LOCAL">

    <provider>
      org.hibernate.ejb.HibernatePersistence
    </provider>

    <non-jta-data-source>
      java:comp/env/jdbc/TestDB
    </non-jta-data-source>

    <properties>
      <property name="hibernate.dialect"
                value="org.hibernate.dialect.HSQLDialect"/>
      <property name="hibernate.hbm2ddl.auto"
                value="create-drop"/>
      <property name="hibernate.show_sql"
                value="true"/>
      <property name="hibernate.cache.provider_class"
                value="org.hibernate.cache.HashtableCacheProvider"/>
    </properties>
  </persistence-unit>
</persistence>
```

**Tomcat Database Hookup**

Since Tomcat does not come bundled with an embedded database, we need to explicitly configure the `java:comp/env/jdbc/TestDB` data source in the `persistence.xml` listed above. This is covered in Section 28.5 and in the example application `tomcatjpa`.

Next, for Seam to build an `EntityManager` and inject it into the POJO, we must bootstrap it in the `components.xml` file. The `core:entity-manager-factory` component scans the `persistence.xml` file and instantiates the persistence unit named `helloworld` (see the previous code listing). Then the `core:managed-persistence-context` component builds an `EntityManager` from the `helloworld` persistence unit. The `EntityManager` is named `em`. That ensures that the `@In (create=true) EntityManager em;` statement in `ManagerPojo` works because it injects the `EntityManager` named `em` to the field variable with the same name. Since the application has no EJB3 components, you do not need to specify the `jndiPattern` attribute on the `core:init` component.

```
<components ...>

  <core:init debug="true"/>

  <core:manager conversation-timeout="120000"/>

  <core:entity-manager-factory name="helloworld"/>

  <core:managed-persistence-context name="em"
    entity-manager-factory="#{helloworld}"/>

</components>
```

Any other EJB3-specific configuration, such as `ejb-jar.xml` and the `jndi-pattern` property in `components.xml`, is not needed.

# 4.3  Packaging

For J2EE 1.4 deployment, you can always package your application in EAR format as we did in Section 2.7. However, as our `hellojpa` POJO application does not have any EJB components, we can package it in a simple WAR file. In a WAR file, you put all the framework JAR files, as well as `app.jar` containing the application POJO classes and `persistence.xml`, in the `WEB-INF/lib` directory. Here is the packaging structure of the `hellojpa.war` file for deployment in JBoss AS 4.2.3 GA:

```
hellojpa.war
|+ index.html
|+ hello.xhtml
|+ fans.xhtml
|+ ... ...
```

```
|+ WEB-INF
   |+ lib
      |+ jboss-seam.jar
      |+ jboss-seam-el.jar
      |+ jboss-seam-ui.jar
      |+ jboss-seam-debug.jar
      |+ jsf-facelets.jar
      |+ app.jar
         |+ META-INF
            |+ persistence.xml
         |+ ManagerPojo.class
         |+ Person.class
         |+ seam.properties
   |+ web.xml
   |+ faces-config.xml
   |+ components.xml
   |+ jboss-web.xml
   |+ pages.xml
```

### JAR Files for Other Application Servers

The library JARs we listed here in `hellojpa.war` are for JBoss AS deployment. If you plan to deploy your WAR file in a non-JBoss application server or in an older version of JBoss AS 4, you will probably need more dependency JARs. For instance, for JBoss AS 4.2.0 deployment, you will need to bundle the Hibernate 3 JARs; for WebLogic AS 9.2 deployment, you need the JSF RI JARs, the Apache Commons JARs, and several other third-party JARs. Refer to the `jpa` example in the Seam official distribution for the necessary JARs for different application servers.

The `jboss-web.xml` file replaces the `jboss-app.xml` in the EAR file to configure the scoped class loader and root URL context. The `jboss-web.xml` file is not required but is nice to have when multiple applications are deployed on the same server. Here is an example `jboss-web.xml` file:

```
<jboss-web>
  <context-root>/hellojpa</context-root>
  <class-loading java2ClassLoadingCompliance="false">
    <loader-repository>
      jpa:loader=jpa
      <loader-repository-config>
        java2ParentDelegation=false
      </loader-repository-config>
    </loader-repository>
  </class-loading>
</jboss-web>
```

The `jboss-web.xml` file is obviously a JBoss-specific configuration file. The application works fine without it, and the root URL then just defaults to the WAR filename. For other application servers, refer to their manuals to find out how to configure equivalent options.

# 4.4 POJO Trade-Offs

Now, we have seen how to turn EJB3 session beans into Seam POJOs with simpler code and more flexible deployment options. Shall we just get rid of EJBs and use POJOs in all cases? Well, the answer is no. POJOs have fewer features than EJB3 components because POJOs cannot use the EJB3 container services. Examples of EJB3 services that you lose in non-EJB3 Seam POJOs include:

- No support exists for declarative method-level transactions in POJOs. Instead, you can configure Seam to demarcate a database transaction from the moment the web request is received until the response page is rendered. See Section 11.2 for more details.

- Seam POJOs cannot be message-driven components.

- No support for @Asynchronous methods exists.

- No support for container-managed security exists.

- No transaction- or component-level persistence context exists. All persistence contexts in Seam POJOs are "extended" (see Section 8.1.1 for more details).

- No integration into the container's management architecture (e.g., JMX console services) exists.

- No Java remoting (RMI) into Seam POJO methods exists.

- Seam POJOs cannot be @WebService components.

- No JCA integration exists.

In addition, EJB3 session beans are a standardized component model that would allow other application modules, not just Seam, to access your business and persistence logic. If your application has a significant subsystem outside of the Seam-based web module, you are probably better off using EJB3 session beans to improve code reusability.

For the above reasons, most of the example applications in the rest of the book are still implemented with EJB3. But it would be easy to convert them to POJOs. For instance, example application jpa is the POJO version of example integration, which is used from Chapter 12 to Chapter 15; the tomcatjpa example is the Tomcat deployable version of the jpa example with all the necessary data source hookups (see Section 28.5).

# 5

# Rapid Application Development Tools

In the previous two chapters, we saw that Seam applications are very easy to code but there are several configuration files to manage. To be fair, the configuration files are simple (no "XML code"); moreover, they are about 90% the same across different projects. Still, the developers need to keep track of them. That is where development tools can really help!

Seam-gen is a rapid application generator shipped with the Seam distribution. With a few command-line operations, seam-gen generates an array of artifacts for Seam projects. In particular, we often use seam-gen to do the following:

- Automatically generate an empty Seam project with common configuration files, a build script, and directories for Java code and JSF view pages
- Automatically generate complete Eclipse and NetBeans project files for the Seam project
- Reverse-engineer entity bean objects from relational database tables
- Generate template files for common Seam components

The command-line script-based approach allows seam-gen to work in any development environment, using much the same successful approach that Ruby on Rails took. Unlike Ruby on Rails, however, seam-gen also works with IDEs—in particular, it provides excellent integration support for Eclipse and NetBeans. In this chapter, we will show how to start a project with seam-gen.

# 5.1   Prerequisites

Apache Ant 1.6+ is required for seam-gen. In fact, all the build scripts in this book's examples require Apache Ant. Please download Ant and install it from http://ant.apache.org, if you have not yet done so.

Seam-gen generates code and configuration fiies for deployment in JBoss Application Server 4.2.x (see Appendix A for installation instructions). It does not work with J2EE 1.4 or plain Tomcat deployment options (see Chapter 4). Note that you can use the generated project with other J2EE or Java EE 5 application servers by making a few manual changes to the project configuration. Use of other application servers is covered in Chapter 29 and at www.seamframework.org/Documentation/ ServersAndContainers.

Seam-gen projects use Facelets (see Section 3.1) as the view framework. You must author your JSF web pages in XHTML files.

# 5.2   A Quick Tutorial

The `seam` (Linux, Unix, and Mac) and `seam.bat` (Windows) scripts in the Seam distribution are the main scripts for seam-gen. On a Linux/Unix machine, you might need to adjust the permissions of the `seam` file to make it executable from the command line (i.e., execute `chmod +x seam`).

In the rest of this section, we will go through the steps of using seam-gen to generate and build the complete `betterjsf` example application we discussed in Chapter 3.

## 5.2.1   Setting Up Seam-gen

First, you need to tell seam-gen about the project you will be generating. Just type the following in your Seam distribution's root directory:

```
seam setup
```

The script asks you a few questions about the project, such as the project name, JBoss AS location, Eclipse workspace, and database server. The following is an example conversation. You can simply press **Enter** to accept the default value in the square brackets for each question.

```
setup:
     [echo] Welcome to seam-gen :-)
     [input] Enter your Java project workspace (the directory that
             contains your Seam projects) [C:/Projects] [C:/Projects]
c:/projects/seamgen
```

```
    [input] Enter your JBoss home directory [C:/Program Files/
            jboss-4.2.2.GA] [C:/Program Files/jboss-4.2.2.GA]
C:/oss/jboss-4.2.2.GA
    [input] Enter the project name [myproject] [myproject]
helloseamgen
     [echo] Accepted project name as: helloseamgen
    [input] Do you want to use ICEFaces instead of RichFaces [n]
            (y, [n])
n
    [input] skipping input as property icefaces.home.new has already
            been set.
    [input] Select a RichFaces skin [blueSky] ([blueSky], classic,
            ruby, wine, deepMarine, emeraldTown, japanCherry, DEFAULT)
classic
    [input] Is this project deployed as an EAR (with EJB components)
            or a WAR (with no EJB support) [ear] ([ear], war)
ear
    [input] Enter the Java package name for your session beans
            [com.mydomain.helloseamgen] [com.mydomain.helloseamgen]
book.helloseamgen
    [input] Enter the Java package name for your entity beans
            [book.helloseamgen] [book.helloseamgen]
book.helloseamgen
    [input] Enter the Java package name for your test cases
            [book.helloseamgen.test] [book.helloseamgen.test]
book.helloseamgen.test
    [input] What kind of database are you using? [hsql] ([hsql],
            mysql, oracle, postgres, mssql, db2, sybase,
            enterprisedb, h2)
hsql
    [input] Enter the Hibernate dialect for your database
            [org.hibernate.dialect.HSQLDialect]
            [org.hibernate.dialect.HSQLDialect]

    [input] Enter the filesystem path to the JDBC driver jar
            [../lib/hsqldb.jar] [../lib/hsqldb.jar]

    [input] Enter JDBC driver class for your database
            [org.hsqldb.jdbcDriver] [org.hsqldb.jdbcDriver]

    [input] Enter the JDBC URL for your database [jdbc:hsqldb:.]
            [jdbc:hsqldb:.]

    [input] Enter database username [sa] [sa]

    [input] Enter database password [] []

    [input] Enter the database schema name (it is OK to leave
            this blank) [] []

    [input] Enter the database catalog name (it is OK to leave
            this blank) [] []

    [input] Are you working with tables that already exist in
            the database? [n] (y, [n])
n
    [input] Do you want to drop and recreate the database tables
            and data in import.sql each time you deploy? [n]
            (y, [n])
y
```

Listed below are some tips on how to answer the seam-gen questions. Many of the choices deal with the database server. For beginners, it is fastest to start with the embedded HSQL database inside JBoss AS; for other database options, when you are ready to test or deploy the application, refer to Chapter 28.

- The *Java project workspace* is really an Eclipse term. If you do not use Eclipse, you should simply enter a directory where you want to store your Seam projects. You can have multiple Seam projects coexist in the same workspace. If you enter a relative path here, the directory will be created under the `seam-gen` directory.

- The *JBoss home directory* is the directory where you installed the JBoss AS.

- The *project name* is the name of your project. The generated project directory will have the same name as the project name. The build script builds the application to `projectname.jar`, `projectname.war`, and `projectname.ear` files.

- It is assumed that you will use either JBoss RichFaces or ICEfaces for your project. It is not required that you use either of these technologies, but this selection will automate the configuration for use with your project. With RichFaces you have a selection of skins. These are essentially themes providing a look-and-feel for your application. To choose a skin, refer to http://livedemo.exadel.com/richfaces-demo/index.jsp.

- You can choose whether you want to build an EAR archive or a WAR archive for your application. We recommend the EAR archive for most scenarios since it provides EJB3 support in JBoss AS. The WAR archive can be used if your application uses Seam POJOs instead of EJB3 session beans and you plan to deploy the application in a J2EE 1.4 server. Notice that the WAR file generated by seam-gen is not deployable on plain Tomcat. Refer to Chapter 4 for Tomcat deployment instructions.

- The *Java package names* are used for later seam-gen code generation tasks, such as generating the entity beans from database tables, generating forms and actions, etc. If you do not plan to use seam-gen for those tasks, the package names do not matter; just accept the default value. Even if you do use seam-gen to generate some skeleton classes later, you can easily change the package name by hand or via refactoring support in an IDE, so don't worry too much here.

- The database type selection enables you to choose a relational database to go with your application. For deployment inside the JBoss AS, just accept the default `hsql`, which is the embedded HSQL database in JBoss AS which maps to JNDI name `java:/DefaultDS` by default. Of course, for production applications, you would probably choose a more robust database server, such as MySQL. To learn more about production databases, refer to Chapter 28.

- The *Hibernate dialect* choice depends on your database choice. For the default HSQL, it is `org.hibernate.dialect.HSQLDialect`; for MySQL, it is `org.hibernate.dialect.MySQLDialect`. Note that you have to enter the full

Hibernate class name. Refer to the Hibernate documentation for more on database dialects.

- The *JDBC driver* choice depends on the database of choice. For the default HSQL, the driver is already bundled in JBoss AS, so just enter an empty line here. For MySQL or other databases, you must download the appropriate JBDC driver and enter the path to the JAR file here.

- The *JDBC driver class* is the JDBC driver class for the database you choose. For the default HSQL, it is `org.hsqldb.jdbcDriver`; for MySQL, it is `com.mysql.jdbc.Driver`. Again, refer to you JDBC documentation if you are using another database.

- The *JDBC URL* tells the application how to connect to your particular database. For the default HSQL, it is `jdbc:hsqldb:.`; for MySQL, it is `jdbc:mysql://host:3306/dbname`, where `dbname` refers to the database name.

- The *database username* and *password* are specific to your database server. For the default HSQL, the username is simply `sa` and the password is empty.

- The *database schema* and *catalog* names are used for reverse-engineering database tables into entity beans. We do not use those features here.

- The last two questions ask you how you want to manage the database tables by controlling how the `hbm2ddl` attribute in the Hibernate persistence engine is set. If you are in development mode, you probably should answer `y` to the last question. It sets `hbm2ddl` to `create-drop` (i.e., tables are created when the application is deployed and dropped when undeployed). If you answer `n` to the last question and `y` to the second to last, `hbm2ddl` is set to `update`. Otherwise, `hbm2ddl` is set to `validate`.

The answers to the `seam setup` questions are stored in the `seam-gen/build.properties` file. You can edit the file directly if you need to change some settings but do not wish to go through all the questions again.

## 5.2.2 Generating a Skeleton Application

To generate the skeleton application template with configuration files and a build script, simply run the following command in the Seam distribution directory:

```
seam new-project
```

A new project directory is now created in your Eclipse workspace. The directory name is the same as your project name. In our case, we get the `C:/projects/seamgen/helloseamgen` directory with the following initial structure. As you can see, the project directory layout is very similar to the book's example applications (see Appendix B) and the official Seam example applications. The directory also contains support files for NetBeans and Eclipse IDE integration, which we will discuss later in this chapter.

```
helloseamgen
|+ .classpath                              // Eclipse support
|+ .settings                               // Eclipse support
|+ exploded.launch                         // Eclipse support
|+ helloseamgen.launch                     // Eclipse support
|+ debug-jboss-helloseamgen.launch         // Eclipse support
|+ .project                                // Eclipse support
|+ nbproject                               // NetBeans support
|+ hibernate-console.properties            // Hibernate Tools support
|+ seam-gen.properties                     // Properties defined in setup
|+ build.properties                        // JBoss Home, etc.
|+ build.xml                               // Build script
|+ bootstrap                               // Seam Test support
|+ lib                                     // Library JARs
|+ src                                     // Java source code
|+ view                                    // Facelets XHTML files
|+ resources                               // Configuration files
```

---

**The Project Name**

The example project here is `helloseamgen`, but we will use `projectname` to refer to a generic project name generated by seam-gen.

---

The `src` folder in the above listing is divided into three source types: `src/main`, `src/hot`, and `src/test`. These source types are defined as follows:

`src/main`  All classes included in this `src` directory will be deployed in the application classpath, and are considered static (not hot-deployable). JPA entities should always be placed in this directory.

`src/hot`  This is a special `src` directory that should include the classes you want to hot-deploy during development. To find out what classes can be hot-deployed and how to enable this feature, see Section 5.2.5.

`src/test`  All test classes are included in this `src` directory. Seam-gen uses TestNG as the testing framework. JUnit can be substituted if you prefer, but TestNG is required for using Seam Test.

Each seam-gen project is completely self-contained. You can build, test, and deploy the application without any referencing or linking to any JAR files outside of the project directory.

To try the skeleton application, just enter the `projectname` directory and type `ant`. It should build the `projectname.ear` file in the `dist` directory and then deploy it to your JBoss AS. Start JBoss AS and point your browser to `http://localhost:8080/projectname/`; you should see a nice welcome page.

## 5.2.3 Understand the Profiles

Borrowing a page from Ruby on Rails' playbook, seam-gen supports the concept of *profiles*. The idea is that the application will probably need different database settings for the development, test, and production phases. So, the project provides alternative database configuration files for each of the three scenarios. In the `resources` directory, there are the following database configuration files:

```
projectname
|+ ... ...
|+ resources
   |+ projectname-dev-ds.xml
   |+ projectname-prod-ds.xml
   |+ import-dev.sql
   |+ import-prod.sql
   |+ import-test.sql
   |+ components-dev.properties
   |+ components-prod.properties
   |+ components-test.properties
   |+ ... ...
   |+ META-INF
      |+ persistence-dev.xml
      |+ persistence-prod.xml
      |+ persistence-test.xml
      |+ ... ...
```

The `*dev*` files are database configuration files for the development phase (i.e., the `dev` profile). When an EAR or WAR archive is built for the `dev` profile, the `persistence-dev.xml` and `import-dev.sql` files are packaged in the archive as `persistence.xml` and `import.sql` files. The `projectname-dev-ds.xml` file is copied to the server's `deploy` directory as `projectname-ds.xml` to configure the development HSQL database.

At development time, you probably want to use the embedded HSQL database and a simple set of imported data for quick turnaround. Below is an example `projectname-dev-ds.xml` file. It just maps the embedded HSQL data source to JNDI name `projectnameDatasource`, which is essentially the same as the default `java:/DefaultDS` already available in JBoss AS.

```xml
<datasources>

  <local-tx-datasource>
    <jndi-name>projectnameDatasource</jndi-name>
    <connection-url>jdbc:hsqldb:.</connection-url>
    <driver-class>
      org.hsqldb.jdbcDriver
    </driver-class>
    <user-name>sa</user-name>
    <password></password>
  </local-tx-datasource>

</datasources>
```

Similarly, the `*prod*` files are for production time configuration (the `prod` profile). When the project is first generated, the `*prod*` files are the same as the `*dev*` files. They are all generated based on your answers in `seam setup`. You should probably modify the `*prod*` files to use a real production database such as MySQL; refer to Chapter 28 for details.

The `*test*` files contain the database configuration for out-of-the-container tests. It typically uses an HSQL database bootstrapped by the test runner; refer to Part VI for details.

To change the build profile for the project, you can either execute the build command with the profile specified as `seam -Dprofile=[profile] [target]`, or edit the `build.xml` file and change the value of the `profile` property:

```
<project ...>

  <!-- development (default) -->
  <property name="profile" value="dev" />
  <!-- production
    <property name="profile" value="prod" />
  -->
  <!-- test
    <property name="profile" value="test" />
  -->

</project>
```

You may note that the seam-gen project uses a wildcard attribute to determine the value of the `debug` attribute:

```
<core:init debug="@debug@" />
```

Wildcard values are determined at runtime based on the settings in a `components.properties` file definition. Any attribute can use a wildcard as long as the wildcard name is surrounded by the @ symbols (e.g., `@myWildCard@`). This can be quite useful for swapping out `components.xml` attributes based on deployment environment and is considered a best practice. Similar to the seam-gen approach of using environment-specific `persistence.xml` definitions, a `components.properties` file is defined for each environment:

```
resources
|+ components-dev.properties
|+ components-prod.properties
|+ components-test.properties
... ...
```

Each of the `components.properties` files specified above is generated as part of your project with reasonable defaults. As before, the appropriate profile is selected based on the profile chosen (i.e., `dev`, `test`, or `prod`).

Swapping the `debug` attribute based on environment is an obvious example demonstrating the usefulness of this approach. In addition, when configuring your own custom components, this approach allows settings to be altered based on profile. For example, let's say we have an IP address and port for a service we are accessing. This IP address and port can change based on environment, making the configuration a perfect candidate for the wildcard approach.

## 5.2.4  Developing the Application

Now it's time to fill out the skeleton template with Java code, XHTML pages, and application-specific configuration. For the `helloseamgen` example, it's quite simple. First, copy everything from the `betterjsf` project's `view/` directory to the corresponding directory in the `helloseamgen` project. The seam-gen project is set up to support Facelets as the view framework (see Section 3.1).

Now we can simply place the source files into the `src/main` folder created by seam-gen. Copy the `ManagerAction`, its interface `Manager`, and the `Person` entity to the `src/main` folder. These classes will now be compiled and deployed as part of the application classpath.

As we spend most of the book explaining how to develop Seam applications, we do not get into details of the `helloseamgen` example here. Interested readers should read Chapters 2 and 3.

To run complex examples in seam-gen, you need a little more than moving over the `src/` and `view/` contents. For instance, to run the Natural Hotel Booking example (see Chapter 8), you should copy the `resources/WEB-INF/navigation.xml`, `resources/WEB-INF/pages.xml`, and `resources/import.sql` files to the seam-gen project as well. Make sure that you answer `y` to the last question in seam-gen setup so that the demo application properly initializes the database tables.

## 5.2.5  Building and Deploying

Building and deploying the application is a simple matter of executing the command `ant` in the project directory. In this section, we discuss how to build and deploy the EAR archive. If you selected to build a WAR archive during `seam setup`, the packaging structure would be slightly different but the process is the same.

The `ant` command compiles all the Java classes; packages the classes, XHTML files, and configuration files together in `dist/projectname.ear`, which, in turn, contains `projectname.jar` and `projectname.war`; and deploys `projectname.ear` into JBoss AS. The `projectname.ear` application uses the data source (i.e., database connection) defined in the `resources/projectname-ds.xml` file, so the `*-ds.xml` file is also deployed into JBoss AS.

**Deploying into JBoss AS**

To deploy `projectname.ear` and `projectname-ds.xml` in JBoss AS, you just need to copy those two files to the `$JBOSS_HOME/server/default/deploy` directory.

If you just want to build the `projectname.ear` file but do not want to deploy it, run the `ant archive` task.

The `build.xml` script can also build and deploy the application in the "exploded" format. An exploded archive is a directory that contains the same content as the archive file. The exploded `projectname.jar/war/ear` archives are created in the `exploded-archives` directory in your project. The Ant task `ant explode` deploys the exploded `projectname.ear` to JBoss AS. In general, exploded deployment is the preferred deployment approach during development.

Exploded deployment allows changes to any XHTML file or the `pages.xml` file to be redeployed without an application restart. In order to enable incremental hot deployment, you must set Seam and Facelets into debug mode. By default, an seam-gen application is debug-enabled in the `dev` profile. The following line in `components.xml` configures debug mode for both Seam and Facelets:

```
<core:init debug="true" />
```

The benefit of exploded deployment is that it supports incremental changes to the application without restarting the JBoss AS every time you make a change. If you make any changes to the XHTML files or `pages.xml` file, a restart is not required. However, changes to entities or EJB components will require a restart. This can be accomplished by executing the `ant restart` task which copies only the changed files to the exploded archives in JBoss AS, and updates the timestamp on the `application.xml` file to make JBoss AS redeploy the updated application. You can then see your updated application by refreshing your browser.

**Fast Turnaround through Incremental Redeployment with POJOs**

While EJB components and entities require a restart of the application, Seam supports a very fast edit/compile/test cycle through incremental redeployment of POJOs placed in the `src/hot` folder. Seam provides a special class loader that will automatically load changes to these classes when they are deployed to the `WEB-INF/dev` directory. There are some limitations to this approach:

- EJB3 beans and entities do not apply, although the former may be supported in future releases.
- Components defined by `components.xml` are not supported.
- Classes outside the `WEB-INF/dev` directory cannot access these classes.

- Seam debug must be enabled, as discussed above, and `jboss-seam-debug.jar` must be included in `WEB-INF/lib` (included by default for a seam-gen project).

- The Seam filter must be configured in `web.xml` (included by default for a seam-gen project).

A seam-gen application has all the necessary library JARs for JBoss AS deployment. That includes all the RichFaces, Drools (see Chapter 18), and jBPM support JARs (see Chapter 24), but it does not include Hibernate and other JARs that might be needed for deployment on other application servers (see Chapter 4).

### 5.2.6 Running Test Cases

As discussed previously, in a seam-gen project, you put test classes and TestNG configuration files in the `src/test` directory. The TestNG configuration files must be named `*Test.xml`. You can learn more about the Seam testing frameworks in Part VI.

To run those tests, execute the `ant test` task. The test results are available in the `testng-report` directory. Note that these tests are executed by spooling up the Seam Test framework. Seam-gen is by far the easiest (and recommended) approach to setting up Seam Test for use with your project.

If you are trying to replicate the book's example application in a seam-gen project, you can copy everything from the example's `test` directory to the seam-gen project's `src/test` directory, and then rename the `testng.xml` file to `HelloWorldTest.xml`.

# 5.3 Working with IDEs

Seam-gen projects work well with leading Java IDEs. In particular, seam-gen provides built-in support for the open source NetBeans and Eclipse IDEs. As you will see, Eclipse users enjoy extensive Seam support thanks to JBoss Tools (www.jboss.org/tools). While JBoss Tools is not required, it is recommended, as its features will aid in Seam development. For those who wish to use Eclipse without JBoss Tools, basic Eclipse support will be covered first, followed by JBoss Tools support.

### 5.3.1 NetBeans

A seam-gen project has an `nbproject/project.xml` file which defines a NetBeans project. You can open the project by selecting the project directory in NetBeans' **Open Project** wizard. Figure 5.1 shows what a seam-gen project looks like in NetBeans. All the Java source files in the `src` directory are ready for NetBeans introspection. The files under the `view` and `resources` directories are also available in the project along with the `build.xml`. You can open any of the Java source, XHTML, and XML files in the NetBeans editor. NetBeans automatically performs syntax highlighting and syntax checking. You can also use NetBeans's built-in visual wizards to edit those files (e.g., `web.xml`).

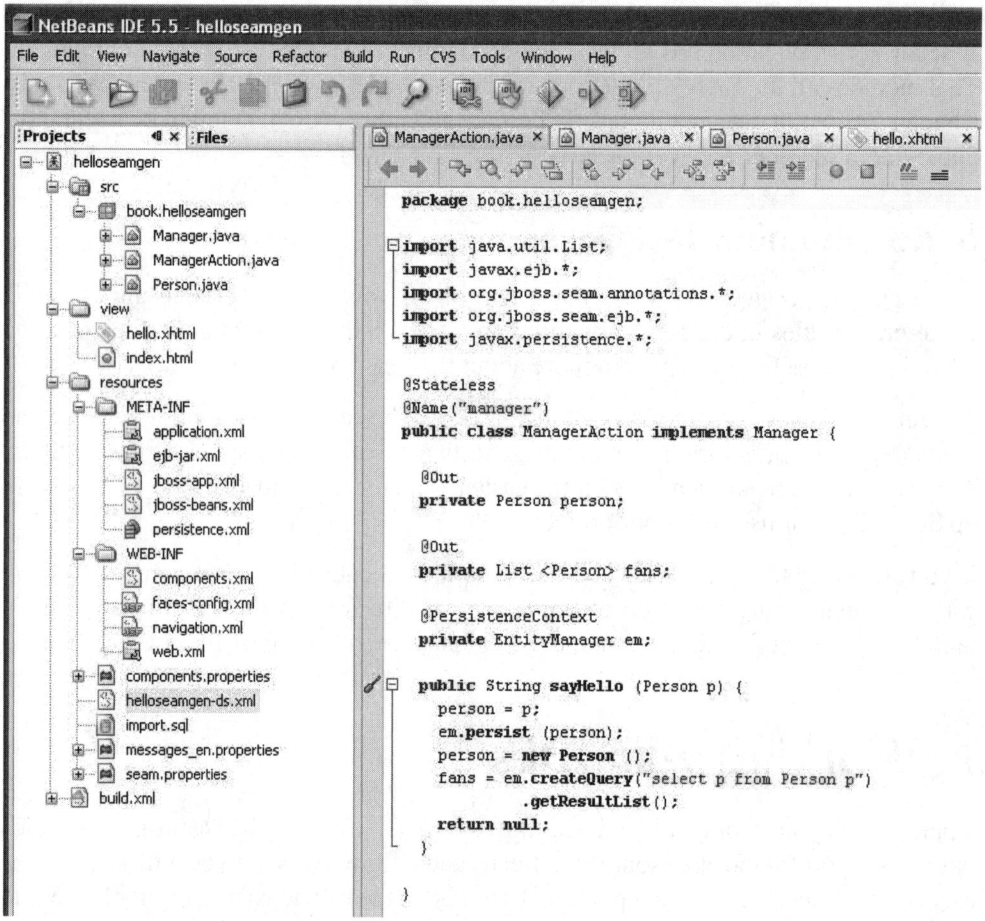

**Figure 5.1**      The seam-gen project in NetBeans

---

**Editor Support for Facelets XHTML Files**

We recommend the NetBeans Facelets support module (must be snapshot 04 or newer) because it provides tag completion, syntax checking, formatting, and other support for editing Facelets XHTML files in the NetBeans editor. You can download the module from https://nbfaceletssupport.dev.java.net.

If you do not have the Facelets module installed, your Facelets XHTML file will open as either a regular text file or a regular XHTML file without Facelets tag support.

---

To compile, build, and deploy the project, you can right-click on the project name and select the **Deploy Project** menu item (see Figure 5.2; sometimes it is labeled **Redeploy Project**). When the application is deployed and running, you can make changes to any of the files in the project, save it, and call **Deploy Project** to push only the changed files to the server. You can immediately see the effect by refreshing the web browser.

**Figure 5.2**    **Build** and **Deploy** action menu items for the project

Now, you probably noticed a **Debug Project** item in the project pop-up menu. Yes, you can use the NetBeans debugger to debug Seam applications—but you face some limitations: You cannot set breakpoints or watches inside EJB3 session bean components. The reason is that Seam generates a runtime proxy to invoke session bean methods, and that confuses the debugger. However, you can debug Seam POJO components (see Chapter 4) and entity beans. Of course, if your session bean makes calls to other objects, you can set breakpoints and watches in those objects.

To debug an application, you must first run the application server's JVM in debugging mode on port 8787 (see the accompanying sidebar). You can then set breakpoints and watches in the source code editor, build the application, and deploy it. Right-click on the project and select the **Debug Project** menu item to launch the debugger. Now you can use a web browser to access the deployed application. When you hit the breakpoint, the application pauses (i.e., the browser waits) and NetBeans displays the current debug information. Figure 5.3 shows the IDE display when the debugger reaches a breakpoint in an UI event handler method in a Seam POJO.

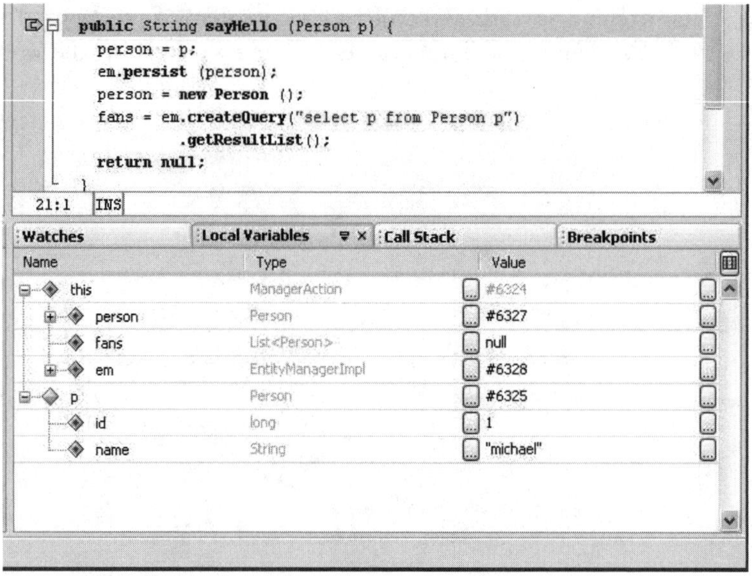

**Figure 5.3**     Debugging a Seam POJO

### Running JBoss AS in Debugging Mode

On Windows, edit the `bin/run.bat` file and uncomment the following line (a single line):

```
set JAVA_OPTS=-Xdebug -Xrunjdwp:transport=
dt_socket,address=8787,server=y,suspend=y %JAVA_OPTS%
```

On Unix/Linux/Max OS X, you need to manually add the following line to the `bin/run.sh` script (a single line):

```
JAVA_OPTS="-Xdebug -Xrunjdwp:server=y,transport=
dt_socket,address=8787 $JAVA_OPTS"
```

If you are running debugger on a port other than 8787, or if you are debugging a JVM on a remote machine, you should alter the `nbproject/debug-jboss.properties` file in the seam-gen project accordingly:

```
jpda.host=localhost
jpda.address=4142
jpda.transport=dt_socket
```

With excellent Facelets/JSF support and built-in debugging, NetBeans is a great choice for Seam applications—although, as you will see in the following sections, Seam also enjoys direct support in Eclipse thanks to JBoss Tools.

## 5.3.2 Eclipse

To open the seam-gen project in Eclipse, start Eclipse with the workspace set to the workspace directory you entered in the `seam setup` task. Then, choose **File > Import > Existing Projects into Workspace** to import the project. In the wizard, browse to the directory containing the project, as shown in Figure 5.4, and click **Finish**.

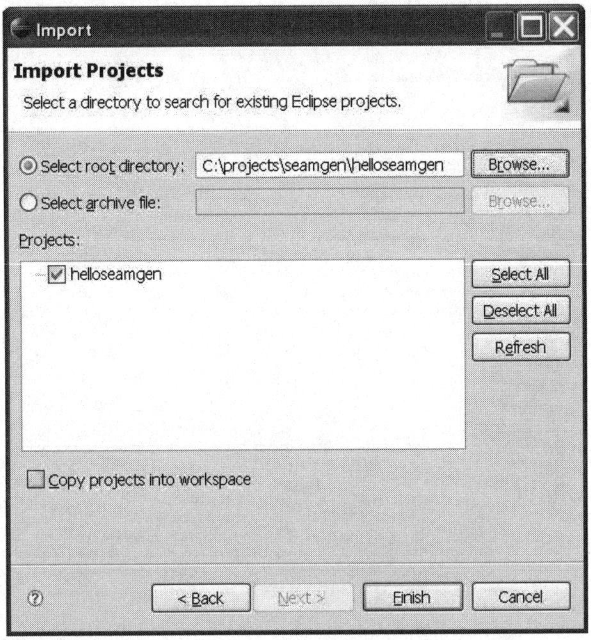

**Figure 5.4**    Importing a seam-gen project into Eclipse

The project opens (Figure 5.5). You can add Java source files to the `src/main`, `src/hot`, and `src/test` directories, and add Facelets XHTML pages into the `view` directory. You can also edit the configuration files in the `resources` directory. You have to scroll to see the `view` and `resources` directories.

Like NetBeans, Eclipse can attach its debugger to a running application server; refer to the NetBeans section for connection parameters. The Ant launch configuration provided by seam-gen ensures that deployment is a snap by generating the exploded archive and deploying it to your local JBoss instance. Each time a modification is detected, the build copies the modified files to the exploded archive, ensuring quick turnaround time between changes.

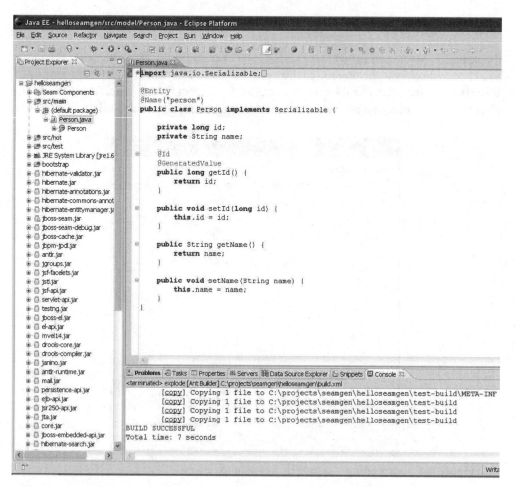

**Figure 5.5**     The seam-gen project imported into Eclipse

## 5.3.3  JBoss Tools and JBoss Developer Studio

It is not required, but recommended that you install the JBoss Tools (www.jboss.org/tools) plugin to enable direct Eclipse support of your Seam projects. This plugin can be installed from the JBoss Tools update site at http://download. jboss.org/jbosstools/updates/stable. Note that the plugin requires Eclipse 3.3. Another option is JBoss Developer Studio which requires a subscription at www.jboss.com/ products/devstudio. JBoss Developer Studio provides a certified Eclipse bundle including JBoss Tools. The following section applies to both JBoss Tools and JBoss Developer Studio.

The steps in the previous section describe how to import a seam-gen project into Eclipse. Once imported, the first step is to initialize the project as a Seam project. First, right-click on the project and access the **Properties** menu. Under **Properties**, select **Seam Settings** which will display the settings for your Seam project (Figure 5.6).

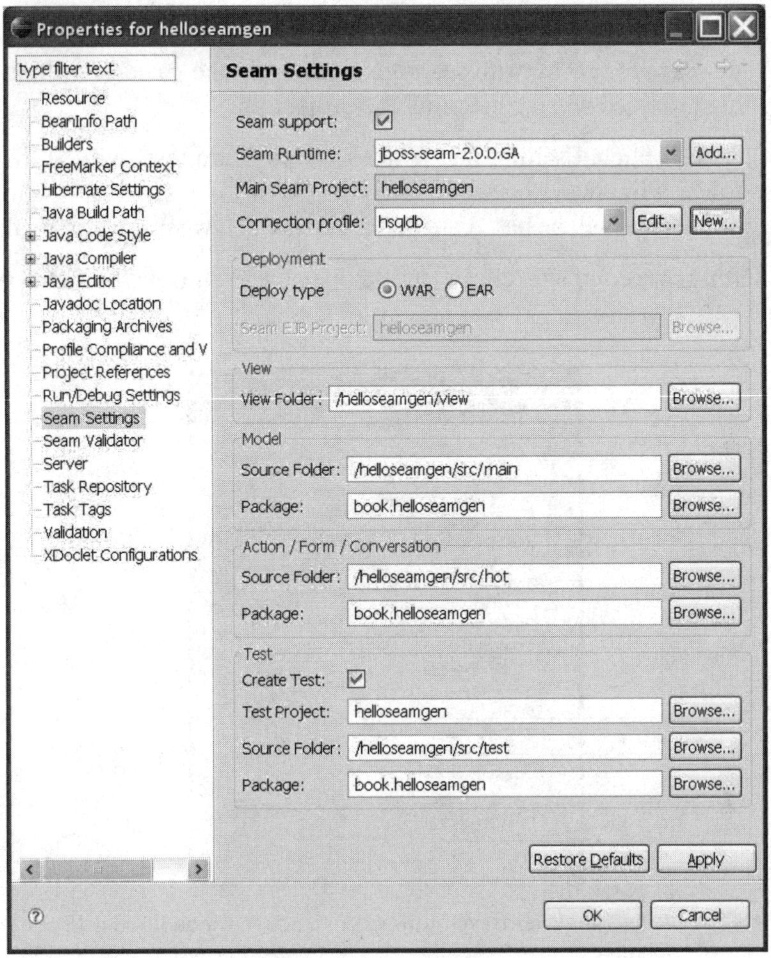

**Figure 5.6**     Configuring a project with the JBoss Tools Seam nature

The following points will guide you through these configuration settings.

**Seam Runtime**     The **Seam Runtime** should be configured to the home directory of your locally installed Seam distribution. Simply select **Add ...** and browse to the appropriate directory. The runtime should now appear in the drop-down for selection.

**Deployment**     This will be based on the type of Seam project you created when running seam-gen. Simply select the appropriate option.

**View**     Ensure that this is set to the `view` folder generated by seam-gen.

**Model**   The source folder will always be set to `$project.name/src/main` by seam-gen, but the package will be based on the setting provided when generating the project.

**Action / Form / Conversation**   The source folder will always be set to `$project.name/src/hot` with seam-gen, but again the package will be based on the setting provided when generating the project.

**Test**   This is an optional setting that defines where Seam tests will be located. The source folder will always be set to `$project.name/src/test` with seam-gen, but again, the package will be based on the value provided when generating the project.

Once the settings are complete, click **OK** and open the **Web Development** perspective (Figure 5.7).

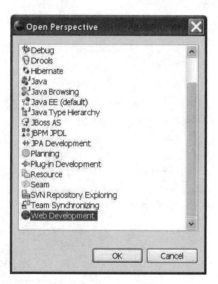

**Figure 5.7**     Select the **Web Development** perspective for additional JBoss Tools features.

This perspective provides a number of new features. First, let's look at the `hello.xhtml` page of the generated project (Figure 5.8).

Without deploying the application, you can get a preview of the page. The preview is automatically updated to reflect changes made to `hello.xhtml`. In addition, as mentioned previously, the changes to the page will be automatically copied to the exploded server deployment, allowing the changes to be immediately viewed on the server as well.

Seam components within the project are automatically registered with the IDE. The **Seam Components** tab lists all Seam components within the project with their respective scopes. This can be useful for quickly resolving scoping issues (Figure 5.9).

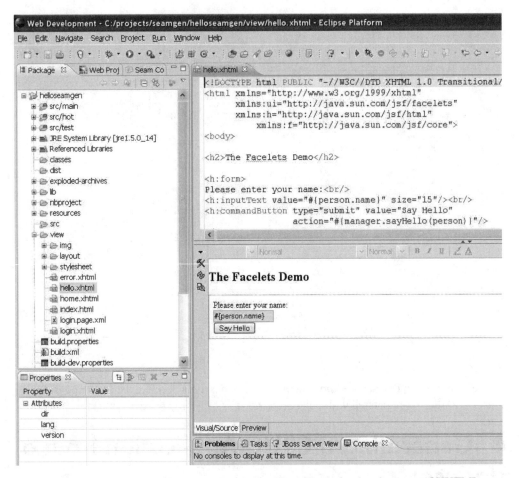

**Figure 5.8** The **Preview** pane provided by JBoss Tools for development of XHTML pages

In addition to all of these features, wizards are provided for generation of actions, components file, conversations, entities, forms, entities from an existing database, pageflow, and a completely new project. Simply select a wizard in **New > Seam**.

---

**Autocompletion with EL Expressions**

With JBoss Tools, not only do you get the tag completion offered by NetBeans, but you can simply press **CTRL+space** in an EL expression (just as you would in a standard class definition) and components as well as their methods will be completed for you. This is one of the most useful features provided by JBoss Tools as all Seam components are automatically registered for completion.

---

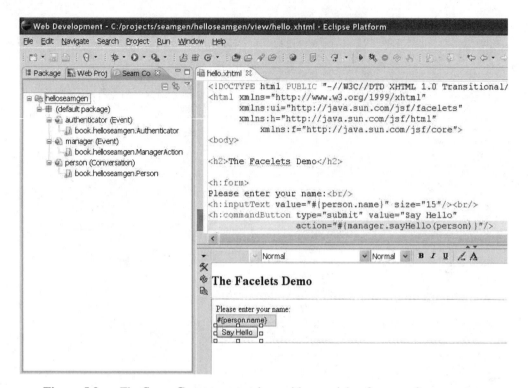

**Figure 5.9**     The **Seam Components** tab provides a quick reference of components registered within the project.

# 5.4   Generating a CRUD Application from a Database

The seam-gen utility can reverse-engineer a complete Create, Retrieve, Update, and Delete (CRUD) web application from existing tables in a database. This feature is similar to what Ruby on Rails offers, only more powerful. When you execute the `seam generate-entities` command, seam-gen reads the table schema from the database and generates the following artifacts:

- EJB3 entity beans that map to the tables. Each table has a corresponding bean with the same name as the table name. The associations and relationships between the tables are properly generated in the entity bean classes. Refer to Hibernate or JPA documentation on how relational associations are expressed in the entity objects via annotations. All the `NOT NULL` constraints on data columns are also translated into Hibernate validators (see Chapter 12).

- Seam POJOs to access the database. Those Data Access Objects (DAOs) are based on Seam's built-in CRUD component framework (see Chapter 16). Each generated entity bean has a corresponding DAO. The DAO provides methods for CRUD operations using the `EntityManager`. In Chapter 4, we explain how to use the `EntityManager` from Seam POJOs.

- Facelets XHTML files for presentation. Each table has a corresponding XHTML file to search and display rows in the table, an XHTML file to display a row of data, and an XHTML file to edit a selected row or create a new row. For each "edit" XHTML file, there is also a `*.page.xml` file to define page parameters so that RESTful URLs can be supported for those view files (see Chapter 15).

The `seam generate-entities` task is really powerful and fun to use. Try it on one of your databases and see how well it works!

# 5.5 Seam-gen Command Reference

Now that we have discussed how to use seam-gen, let's review the available commands (Table 5.1). This will serve as a handy reference while using seam-gen in practice.

**Table 5.1** Seam-gen Commands

| Command | Description |
|---|---|
| `seam setup` | Configures seam-gen for your environment: JBoss AS installation directory, Eclipse workspace, and database connection. |
| `seam new-project` | Creates a new deployable Seam project based on the configuration settings provided in the setup. |
| `seam -D[profile] deploy` | Deploys the new project you've created with the configuration specific to the given `[profile]`, i.e., `dev`, `test`, or `prod`. |
| `seam new-action` | Creates a simple web page with a stateless action method. Generates a Facelets page and component for your project. |
| `seam new-form` | Creates a form with an action. |
| `seam generate-entities` | Generates an application from an existing database. Just make sure your setup points to the appropriate database. |
| `seam generate-ui` | Generates an application from existing JPA/EJB3 entities placed into the `src/model` folder. |
| `seam restart` | Restarts the application on the server instance. |

Seam-gen provides a rapid application generator capable of generating an array of artifacts for Seam projects. Seam-gen will help you get started quickly with Seam and will continue to aid you in rapidly developing enterprise-ready Seam applications.

# Part II

## Stateful Applications Made Easy

**A** key innovation in Seam is the declarative management of POJO-based stateful components. In this part, we explain why stateful components are crucial for today's database-driven web applications. We show how the components are constructed and how their lifecycles are managed. We cover useful features such as multiple conversations in an HTTP session and multiple independent workspaces for a single user. Finally, we discuss how to perform database transactions for Seam conversations.

# 6

# An Introduction to Stateful Framework

In Part I, we demonstrated how Seam simplifies Java EE 5.0 application development by integrating annotated EJB3 session beans (Chapter 2) into JSF. However, as you learn more about Seam, you will realize that the simple Java EE 5.0 integration just barely scratches the surface of what Seam can do. The real jewel of Seam is its support for sophisticated application state management that is not available in any other web application framework today. That is what we mean when we call Seam the next generation web application framework.

The state management facilities in Seam are independent of JSF or EJB3. That makes Seam useful in a variety of environments. For instance, Chapter 21 discusses how to use client JavaScript to access Seam objects directly. Those AJAX UI examples work outside of the JSF framework yet they can still take advantage of Seam's stateful components.

Since state management is such a crucial feature in Seam, we dedicate this short chapter to explaining why you should seriously consider using it in your applications. Here, we will focus on the concepts; you will see ample code examples in the next several chapters.

## 6.1 Correct Usage of ORM

Consider that Seam was invented by Gavin King of the Hibernate ORM (Object-Relational Mapping) framework fame. It is not surprising that one of the primary goals of Seam was to facilitate work with ORM solutions—and a stateful framework is key to the correct usage of an ORM solution.

One of the chief challenges of ORM is to bridge the paradigm rift between the object world and the relational world. A key concept here is *lazy loading*. When the framework loads an object from the relational database, it does not necessarily load all its associated objects. To understand lazy loading, let's look at an example. Below is a code snippet from a typical data model: A `Teacher` object can be associated with a number of `Student` objects; each `Student` object can be associated with a number of `Assignment` objects, etc.

```
@Entity
public class Teacher implements Serializable {

    protected Long id;
    protected String name;
    protected List <Student> students;

    // getter and setter methods
}

@Entity
public class Student implements Serializable {

    protected Long id;
    protected List <Assignment> assignments;

    // getter and setter methods
}

@Entity
public class Assignment implements Serializable {
    // ... ...
}
```

If the ORM framework loads all associated `Student` and `Assignment` objects when it loads a `Teacher` object (this is known as *eager loading*), it would issue two SQL `JOIN` commands and might end up loading a sizable chunk of the database into this single object. Of course, when the application actually *uses* the `Teacher` object, it might not use the `students` property at all. It might just change the teacher's name and save the object right back to the database. Eager loading is a huge waste of resources in this case.

The ORM framework deals with this problem by lazy loading the `Teacher` object—that is, not loading any of the `Student` objects initially at all. Then, when the application calls `Teacher.getStudents()` explicitly, it goes back to the database to load the `students` list.

So far, so good. But the real problem arises when the data access layer of the web application is stateless. For instance, let's look at how data is loaded in the very popular Spring framework. When an HTTP request comes in, it is dispatched to Spring's Hibernate integration template and Hibernate lazy-loads the `Teacher` object, which is returned to the web presentation layer. Now, if the web page displays a list of student names associated with the teacher, the web presentation layer will need to lazy-load the `students` list as it renders the page. But here is the problem: Since Spring is a stateless framework, it destroys the persistence context when the `Teacher` object is passed back to the presentation layer in preparation for the next stateless data query. As far as Spring is concerned, the data loading is done. If the web presentation layer attempts to lazy-load associated objects after Spring returns, an exception will be thrown. In fact, this lazy loading exception is one of the most often encountered Hibernate exceptions of all time.

To avoid the nasty lazy loading exceptions, developers have to work around the framework using hacks such as Data Transfer Objects (DTOs) or messing with the database queries or schema.

With a stateful framework like Seam, this lazy loading problem is solved once and for all. By default, a Seam component keeps the persistence context valid from the time when an HTTP request is submitted to the time when the response page is fully rendered (Section 8.1.1). If needed, you can configure your Seam component to keep the persistence context valid across an entire HTTP session or even beyond. Seam can do that because it is stateful and remembers which request/response cycle or HTTP session it is associated with.

So, in a Seam application, we can focus our attention and effort on working with objects rather than messing with data queries or massaging the database schema. We can pass entity objects (i.e., EJB3 entity beans) directly across the business layer and the presentation layer without the need to wrap them in DTOs. Those are significant productivity gains from the simple fact that Seam finally allows us to use ORM the "correct" way.

---

**In the Relational World . . .**

The lazy loading versus eager loading problem does not exist in the relational world since you can always tweak your `JOIN` statement to select only the data you know the application would actually use. In the object world, however, there is no concept of "join" (those are objects, not relational tables, after all). This problem represents a fundamental rift between the two worlds.

---

# 6.2 Better Performance

A nice side effect of keeping the persistence context valid beyond a single stateless method call is improved database performance. We already know that lazy loading results in better database performance, but we are talking about *another* performance improvement in a somewhat opposite direction: the reduction of database roundtrips.

A major performance problem with database-driven web applications is that many of those applications are *chatty*. A chatty web application saves information to the database whenever the user changes anything, as opposed to queueing database operations and executing them in a batch. Since a roundtrip to the database, potentially over the network, is much slower than a method call inside the application server, it slows down the application significantly.

For instance, a shopping cart application can save every item of an order into the database as the user adds products into the cart. But then, if the user abandons the shopping cart, the application would have to clean up the database. Wouldn't it be much better if the orders were never saved into the database in the first place? The application should only save orders in a batch when the user checks out the shopping cart.

Before Seam, application developers had to develop sophisticated caching mechanisms to hold the database updates for each user session in memory. With the extended persistence context in Seam, you get all that for free! A stateful Seam component can stay valid across several web pages (such as a web wizard or a shopping cart). It is known as a *long-running conversation* in Seam. The component only dirty-checks objects and flushes changes to the database from its persistence context at the end of the conversation.

All of this is accomplished with no explicit API calls or elaborate XML files. Just a few annotations on your component class would do the trick. Refer to Section 8.2 for the exact syntax for defining a long-running conversation and Section 11.2 for details on how such batch database updates work.

---

**But I Heard Stateful Frameworks Are Not Scalable . . .**

To be fair, the argument has its merits: The more state data you have, the more work the server must do to replicate it to other nodes in a cluster environment (see Chapter 30). However, the argument is only true if Seam requires you to manage substantially more state data than other stateless frameworks. In fact, in most so-called stateless architectures, the application simply puts all the state data in an HTTP session, which requires the exact same amount of work in clusters as the equivalent state data managed by Seam. Seam does not necessarily increase your stateful data; it just makes your existing state data a lot easier to manage.

Furthermore, the HTTP session approach is prone to memory leaks (see later in this chapter). Once there is a memory leak, the scalability of the stateless approach using HTTP session would be much worse than Seam.

---

# 6.3　Better Browser Navigation Support

Before Seam, almost all web application frameworks saved the per-user application state in HTTP sessions. It works fine until the user clicks on the browser's **Back** button or simply opens up another browser window or tab for the same application. Why? Because the view displayed in the browser is now out of sync with the application state on the server!

---

**What Is an HTTP Session**

The HTTP protocol used in web applications is fundamentally stateless. Each HTTP request is independent of other requests. In order to distinguish requests from different users, the server will generate a unique session ID for each user and ask the user (i.e., the web browser) to embed the ID in all subsequent HTTP requests. The web browser can choose to append the ID at the end of the request URL or embed it in the `Cookie` field of the HTTP header. On the server side, each session ID is associated with an `HttpSession` object, which holds the application state data as properties. This setup allows the server to provide stateful services to each individual user. Session-scoped Seam components have the same lifecycle as the `HttpSession` object in the servlet container.

---

In the case of the browser **Back** button, the displayed page might come from the browser cache, not reflecting the current state on the server. For instance, the user might click on **Back** after having added an item to the shopping cart—and get the impression that the item is now properly removed from the cart.

In the case of multiple browser windows or tabs, the problem is that you might do something in one window that is not reflected in the other since the second window has not been manually refreshed. For instance, the user might open two browser windows at the checkout screen, start checking out in window #1 but then change her mind and go to window #2 to abort the shopping cart. The user would then leave, knowing that the last action she did was to abort the cart—while the server would have a different record.

Those kinds of things can really cause trouble in your web application. You cannot blame the user since she only responds to what she sees in the browser. In many cases, an application would simply throw up an error to prevent this from happening. Web application developers go to great lengths to prevent confusion—but still, web applications are much less intuitive than desktop applications because of such erratic behavior.

Seam is a perfect fit for such applications due to its stateful design. Inside a Seam conversation, you can go back to any previous page and have the server state automatically restored. For example, you can go back, click on a different button, and have the process started in another direction (see Section 8.2). Seam also provides an independent context (i.e., workspace, Chapter 9) for each browser window or tab. In case of a shopping cart application, you can check out two shopping carts independently in parallel in two browser tabs.

Of course, the best news is that Seam does all the above out-of-the-box. The correct browser behaviors come free with Seam stateful conversations. All you need to do is add a few annotations to define where the conversation starts and ends.

# 6.4  Fewer Memory Leaks

It is a common myth that Java applications are free of memory leaks simply because of the garbage collector in the JVM. In fact, server-side Java applications have memory leaks all the time! The biggest source of potential memory leaks is the HTTP session.

Prior to Seam, HTTP session was the only place to store the application state, so developers have put all kinds of user-related objects into HTTP session. However, since we do not want our users to login too often, we typically set the HTTP session to expire after a long time. That means all the objects in the session are not garbage-collected in a long time, potentially after the user is already long gone. The symptom of such memory leak is that the application eats up more and more memory as more users access the site but it does not free the memory as the users leave. Eventually, the site crashes due to insufficient memory. Such oversized HTTP sessions also have major implications in clustered environments where the HTTP session data must be replicated between server nodes.

Traditionally, web application developers had to monitor objects in the HTTP session very closely and remove any objects that are no longer needed. That is extra work for the developer; worse, programming errors tend to happen when developers need to track complex state objects.

Seam takes the pain out of manual memory management in HTTP sessions. Since each Seam component can be associated with a *conversation*, which is defined as a series of web pages and user actions in a session (e.g., a multipage shopping cart checkout process is a conversation), it can be automatically removed from the session and garbage-collected once the user completes the conversation (e.g., confirms an order). Since defining a Seam conversation is very easy and can be incorporated into the business logic (see Section 8.2), Seam could greatly cut down memory leak bugs in complex applications.

# 6.5  High Granularity Component Lifecycle

The reduction of memory leaks is just one benefit from a deeper change Seam introduces to the application component infrastructure: Seam provides multiple stateful contexts beyond the HTTP session and thus makes stateful object management much easier. As we have already seen, the conversation context has a shorter lifecycle than the HTTP session context, and is therefore less prone to memory leaks.

A web application is inherently stateful. Most of the so-called "stateless" web frameworks rely on the HTTP session in the view layer (in servlet or JSP container) or on the static application scope to maintain the application state. By making stateful components first-class constructs in the framework, Seam supports stateful contexts of finer granularity and longer lifecycle than HTTP sessions and/or the static application scope. Here is a list of stateful contexts in Seam:

**stateless**   Components in this context are completely stateless and do not hold any state data of their own.

**event**   This is the narrowest stateful context in Seam. Components in this context maintain their state throughout the processing of a single JSF request.

**page**   Components in this context are tied to a specific page. You can have access to these components from all events emitted from that page.

**conversation**   In Seam, a conversation is a series of web requests to accomplish a certain task (e.g., to check out the shopping cart). Components tied to a conversation context maintain their state throughout the conversation. The conversation context is the most important context in Seam; it is discussed in more detail in Chapter 8.

**session**   Components in the session context are managed in an HTTP session object. They maintain their state until the session expires. You can have multiple conversations in a session.

**business process**   This context holds stateful components associated with a long-running business process managed in the JBoss jBPM (Business Process Manager) engine. While all the previously discussed contexts manage stateful components for a single web user, the business process components can span across several users. We will explore this in more detail in Chapter 24.

**application**   This is a global context that holds static information. There is no concept of web users in this context.

Of all those contexts, the conversation context is the most important and most widely used.

# 6.6   Reducing Boilerplate Code

With stateless frameworks, there is an artificial gap between the web presentation layer and the business logic layer of the application. The web presentation layer is always stateful thanks to the HTTP session object. The business layer, however, is stateless and has to wipe the slate clean after each service request. As a result, you need all kinds of "wrapper objects" to move data from one layer to the next. For instance, you may need to explicitly wrap objects for the following occasions:

- To transport complex database query results (the DTOs, which we discussed earlier)

- To embed data objects into display components (i.e., to build JSF `DataModel` components)

- To propagate exceptions (e.g., data validation errors, transaction errors, etc.) from the business layer to the presentation layer

Those wrapper objects amount to boilerplate code since their existence is solely needed to make the frameworks happy. Seam breaks the artificial barrier between the web presentation layer and the stateless business layer. It is now possible to share important state information between the two layers without extra code. With a few annotations, you can transparently wrap objects. We already noted that DTOs are largely unnecessary in Seam applications. In this book, we will cover how to transparently generate JSF `DataModel` (Chapter 13), how to associate Hibernate validators (using database validation annotation) with user input fields (Chapter 12), and how to redirect to any custom error page upon an exception (Chapter 17). To give you a taste of what Seam is capable of, let's look at an example of Hibernate validator. You can use annotations to specify the validation constraints you need for each database field.

```
@Entity
@Name("person")
public class Person implements Serializable {

    ... ...

    @NotNull
    @Email
    // Or, we can use
    // @Pattern(regex="^[\w.-]+@[\w.-]+\.[a-zA-Z]{2,4}$")
    public String getEmail() { return email; }

    // ... ...
}
```

Then, on the user input page, you simply place the `<s:validate/>` tag in the input fields mapping to the entity bean fields.

```
<h:inputText id="email" value="#{person.email}">
  <s:validate/>
</h:inputText>
```

The input field is now automatically validated, in the same way as it would be validated by a regular JSF input validator. It saves you the trouble of writing a separate JSF validator for the input field. For more details on how validation works, refer to Chapter 12.

Furthermore, Seam's declarative approach eliminates the boilerplate code associated with state management itself. In other frameworks, state management usually involves a lot of boilerplate code. For instance, to manage objects in an HTTP session, you often have to retrieve the HTTP session object and then put/get application objects into/from it. In Seam, the boilerplate code is completely eliminated by annotations. For instance, you can simply declare an application object as an object of the SESSION scope, and it will automatically be placed in the HTTP session. When you reference this object by its Seam name, Seam automatically gets it from the HTTP session.

```
@Name("manager")
@Scope (SESSION)
public class ManagerAction implements Manager {
  // ... ...
}
```

As we mentioned, Seam extends this annotation approach to conversations and other stateful contexts as well. State management has never been so easy and powerful at the same time.

Once you get used to the Seam approach to state management, you will probably find that today's stateless architectures are very awkward and hard to use. It is time to deprecate the stateless architecture!

# Thinking in Components

In Chapter 6, we discussed the benefits of automatic state management in Seam. We mentioned that the stateful context of *conversation* is probably the most important for most web application developers. However, the conversation context may also be a little difficult to grasp for beginners. To make the learning curve as gentle as possible, let's start from the stateful context everyone is already familiar with—the HTTP session context. In this chapter, we describe how a Seam stateful component is declared, constructed, and managed.

To illustrate how a stateful component works, we refactor the Hello World example from Chapter 2 into a stateful three-page application. The `hello.xhtml` page displays the form to enter your name. After you click on the **Say Hello** button, the application checks whether the name matches the "firstname lastname" pattern. If it does, the application saves your name to the database and forwards the browser to the `fans.xhtml` page. If not, it displays the `warning.xhtml` page asking you to confirm the name you just entered. You can now confirm the name or go back to the `hello.xhtml` page to edit it. If you do confirm, the name is saved to the database and the `fans.xhtml` page is shown. The `fans.xhtml` page displays the name you just entered and all the names in the database. Figure 7.1 shows the application in action. The source code for this example is in the `stateful` directory of the source code bundle.

## 7.1  Stateful Components

In applications such as `stateful`, the backend components must maintain their state across multiple pages. For instance, the `person` component is referenced on all three

**Figure 7.1**    The three-page stateful Hello World

web pages. It must retain its value across multiple HTTP page requests so that all pages for the same user can display the same `person`.

```
< -- Snippet from hello.xhtml -->
Please enter your name:<br/>
<h:inputText value="#{person.name}" size="15"/>
... ...

< -- Snippet from warning.xhtml -->
<p>You just entered the name
<i>#{person.name}</i>
... ...

< -- Snippet from fans.xhtml -->
<p>Hello,
<b>#{person.name}</b></p>
... ...
```

Similarly, the `manager` component must track whether the user has already confirmed that he or she wants to input an "invalid" name, because the `manager.sayHello()` method is invoked directly or indirectly on both `hello.xhtml` and `warning.xhtml` pages. The outcome of the method (i.e., which page to display next) depends on the `confirmed` field variable inside `manager`. All pages must access the same object instance when they reference the `manager` component.

```
public class ManagerAction implements Manager {

    @In @Out
    private Person person;

    private boolean confirmed = false;
    private boolean valid = false;

    // ... ...

    // Called from the hello.xhtml page
    public void sayHello () {
      if (person.getName().matches("^[a-zA-Z.-]+ [a-zA-Z.-]+")
          || confirmed) {

        em.persist (person);
        confirmed = false;
        find ();
        valid = true;
        person = new Person ();

      } else {
        valid = false;
      }
    }

    // Called from the warning.xhtml page
    public void confirm () {
      confirmed = true;
      sayHello ();
    }
}
```

Experienced web developers know that we probably need to store the `person` and `manager` objects inside the HTTP session to retain states across page requests from the same user. That is exactly what we are going to do here (in fact, we store proxies of those Seam components in the HTTP session, but that is functionally equivalent to storing those components themselves). Seam allows us to declaratively manage the HTTP session, and thereby eliminate the boilerplate code for getting objects into/out of it. Seam also supports lifecycle methods in stateful components, which allow us to properly instantiate and destroy those components with minimal effort.

**Beyond HTTP Session**

Stateful management is a core feature in Seam. Seam supports several stateful contexts apart from the HTTP session, which truly distinguishes it from previous generations of web frameworks. In this example, we discuss the HTTP session scope since it is already a familiar concept for most web developers. We will discuss additional Seam stateful contexts later in this chapter, and then in Chapters 8 and 24.

## 7.1.1 Stateful Entity Bean

To declare the `person` component in the session context, all we need is to annotate the entity bean class with the `@Name` annotation. All the injection and outjection of this component will automatically happen in the session context thanks to the `@Scope` annotation.

```
import static org.jboss.seam.ScopeType.SESSION;

... ...

@Entity
@Name("person")
@Scope(SESSION)
public class Person implements Serializable {
  // ... ...
}
```

By default, entities are bound to the `CONVERSATION` context which we will cover later. By specifying `@Scope`, we override this default behavior and ensure that the `person` component is created in the `SESSION` context.

**Limitations of Entity Beans as Seam Components**

Entities are generally bound explicitly in Java code; only when an entity is implicitly created by Seam will it be managed as a Seam component. In addition, bijection and context demarcation are disabled for entity bean components. This limits their usefulness as Seam components, but improves their testability. Since entities generally contain the business logic of the application, they should remain easily testable without dependency on complex components.

## 7.1.2 Stateful Session Bean

Similarly, the `manager` component is an EJB3 stateful session bean in the session context. Since the `manager` component is stateful, it can expose its state as properties to the JSF web pages. To illustrate this point, we use the `manager.fans` property to represent the list of Seam fans who said "hello." This way, we no longer need to outject the `fans` variable (see Section 2.6.4).

```
@Stateful
@Name("manager")
@Scope(SESSION)
public class ManagerAction implements Manager {
  private List <Person> fans;

  public List <Person> getFans() {
    return fans;
  }

  // ... ...
}
```

Again, notice the use of the @Name and @Scope annotations. As with entity beans, stateful session beans have a default scope of CONVERSATION, so we have to explicitly change the scope to SESSION.

---

**Seam POJO Component**

If we use a Seam POJO component to replace the EJB3 session bean here (see Chapter 4), we would not need the @Stateful annotation on the POJO. Seam POJO components by default have the most limiting stateful scope. As you will see in Chapter 8, POJOs have a default scope of EVENT if @Scope is not specified.

---

In the fans.xhtml page, you can just reference the stateful manager component.

```
<h:dataTable value="#{manager.fans}" var="fan">
  <h:column>
    #{fan.name}
  </h:column>
</h:dataTable>
```

---

**How to Decouple Seam Components**

The stateful session bean component integrates data and business logic in the same class. In this example, we saw that the fans list is now a property in the manager component and no longer needs to be outjected.

But what about the person data field in the ManagerAction class? Should we make it a property of the manager component as well (i.e., #{manager.person}, see Section 2.6.4)? Well, we could do that but we decided not to. The reason is that we'd like to decouple the person component from the manager component. This way, we can update the person value without involving the manager. The person and manager can have different scopes and lifecycles. Also, we do not need to create a person instance in the ManagerAction constructor (the instance is created by Seam and then injected).

The moral is that you can choose the level of coupling between stateful components in Seam. With stateful session beans and bijection, you have the ultimate flexibility to achieve the optimal coupling between components in the application.

---

# 7.2   Managing Stateful Components

Now that we know how to define components, let's take a look at some of the patterns for controlling the lifecycle of a Seam component. These patterns allow you to control the creation, destruction, and even visibility of a component within the Seam context.

## 7.2.1   Stateful Component Lifecycle

One of the challenges when using stateful components is to make sure that the component has the proper state when it is created. For instance, in our example, a user might load the `fans.xhtml` page as the first page in the session to see who has said "hello." A `manager` component would be created for this user session. However, since the `sayHello()` method has never been invoked on this component, the `manager.fans` property will be `null` even if there are people in the database. To fix this problem, we need to run the database query right after the `manager` component is created. In a stateful Seam component, any method marked with the `@Create` annotation will be executed right after the component creation. Here is the fix we need for `manager` to behave correctly:

```
@Stateful
@Name("manager")
@Scope(SESSION)
public class ManagerAction implements Manager {

  private List <Person> fans;

  @Create
  public void find () {
    fans = em.createQuery("select p from Person p").getResultList();
  }

  // ... ...
}
```

---

**Why Not Use the Class Constructor?**

The class constructor is called before the component object is created, while a `@Create` method is called after the component creation. The constructor would not have access to injected Seam objects such as the `EntityManager`.

---

If you can customize the creation of a Seam component, you can, of course, customize its destruction as well. A method annotated with `@Destroy` is invoked by Seam when the component is removed from the context (e.g., in the case of an HTTP session timeout for the `manager` component in this example). You can implement this method to handle the component removal event (e.g., to save the current bean state to a database at the timeout). For stateful session beans, you will also need a method annotated with `@Remove` to let the container know which method to invoke when removing the bean object from the memory. In most common scenarios, the same bean method is annotated with both `@Remove` and `@Destroy` annotations.

In fact, the `@Remove`-annotated method is mandatory for stateful session beans. In our example, we just let the `manager` component expire with the HTTP session and leave the `@Remove` method empty.

```
@Stateful
@Name("manager")
@Scope(SESSION)
public class ManagerAction implements Manager {
  // ... ...

  @Remove @Destroy
  public void destroy() {}
}
```

**Seam POJO Component**

If we use a Seam POJO component to replace the EJB3 session bean here (see Chapter 4), we will not need the empty `@Remove` `@Destroy` method in the POJO. Such method is mandated by the EJB3 specification.

Component creation is dependent on where the component is requested from. When a component is requested from EL, it will always be created by Seam if it is not found in the context. This is not the case for bijection. When specifying `@In` for a component, by default Seam will attempt to retrieve the component from the context, but will not create the component if it does not exist.

```
// ... ...

@In(create=true) Manager manager;

// ... ...
```

Note that we specify `create=true` in the listing above. This controls, on a case-by-case basis, whether the component will be created if it does not exist. If you want to ensure that the component is always created at injection time, you can annotate the component with `@AutoCreate`.

```
@Stateful
@Name("manager")
@Scope(SESSION)
@AutoCreate
public class ManagerAction implements Manager {
  // ... ...
```

**Component Install Precedence**

At this point, you may be wondering what happens if we have two Seam components named `manager`. Seam allows you to control which component is used through install precedence. The `@Install` annotation specifies which component should be used if two components of the same name are found. This annotation is placed at the top of the component as shown below:

```
@Stateful
@Name("manager")
@Scope(SESSION)
@Install(precedence=APPLICATION)
public class ManagerAction implements Manager {
  // ... ...
```

This is quite useful for providing mock objects in test cases (Chapter 26), swapping components based on deployment environment, or generating your own framework components to reuse in varying contexts. The precedence can be specified by using one of the constants provided in the `org.jboss.seam.annotations.Install` annotation or by specifying your own integer value; the component with the higher precedence value always wins.

## 7.2.2  Factory Methods

A `@Create`-annotated method is handy for a stateful session bean. But what about the `fans` variable from Chapter 2? It does not have an associated class. If we outject the `fans` variable in this example, instead of using the `manager.fans` property, can we still initialize it at creation time?

The answer is yes. That is what the `@Factory` annotation is for. Below is the `ManagerAction` class refactored to outject the `fans` variable:

```
@Stateful
@Name("manager")
@Scope(SESSION)
public class ManagerAction implements Manager {
  // ... ...

  @Out (required=false)
  private List <Person> fans;

  @Factory("fans")
  public void find () {
    fans = em.createQuery("select p from Person p").getResultList();
  }
  ... ...
}
```

When the user loads `fans.xhtml` at the beginning of a session, Seam looks for the `fans` variable in the context. Since Seam cannot find `fans`, it calls the method annotated with `@Factory("fans")` which constructs and outjects the `fans` variable.

The @Out(required=false) is used here because the manager factory component must first be constructed before the fans factory method can be called. So, when the factory component is constructed, there is no valid value for the fans variable, and the default bijection annotations might therefore complain. In general, you should use the required=false bijection attribute if you are bijecting and factorying the same component in the same class.

Factory methods may also directly set variables into the context by returning a value rather than void. This second type of factory method is generally useful for stateless factory components. When using this factory method approach, it is recommended to specify the scope that the component is intended to be set into. This is especially true when using stateless components, as you can see in the listing below. As with outjection, the scope will default to the scope of the factory component.

```
@Stateless
@Name("personFactory")
public class PersonFactoryImpl implements PersonFactory {
  // ... ...

  @Factory(value="fans", scope=ScopeType.CONVERSATION)
  public List<Person> loadFans() {
    return em.createQuery("select p from Person p").getResultList();
  }
}
```

This pattern is commonly known as the *factory method pattern* and is attributed to the classic book, *Design Patterns* (Gamma, Helm, Johnson, & Vlissides, 1994). As you will see throughout our book, Seam has made it simple to use well-known design patterns in your daily development. Table 7.1 describes the available @Factory attributes.

**Table 7.1** @Factory Attributes

| Attribute | Description |
|-----------|-------------|
| value | Specifies a name for the context variable created by the factory method for reference within the context. Note that this name should be unique. |
| scope | Defines the scope (or context) the variable will be placed into by the container when created. Only applicable to factory methods that return a value. |
| autoCreate | Specifies that this factory method should be automatically called whenever the variable is asked for through injection, even if @In does not specify create=true. Note that an EL request will always result in the factory method being called if the value is not found in the context. |

Factory methods are very useful for one-time creation of a variable by components that have no further part to play in the lifecycle of the value. Next, we'll discuss the manager component pattern which allows a component to manage the lifecycle of a variable while remaining invisible to clients.

## 7.2.3 Manager Components

The factory method pattern creates a variable in the context when it is requested and its context value is `null`. Once the variable is created, the `@Factory` method plays no further role in the lifecycle of the variable. To gain fine-grained control over the value of a contextual variable, the *manager component pattern* can be used. A manager component is any component with a method annotated with `@Unwrap`. The annotated method is invoked each time the variable is requested.

```java
@Stateful
@Name("fans")
@Scope(SESSION)
public class FansRegistryImpl implements FansRegistry {
   // ... ...

   private List<Fans> fans;

   @Unwrap
   public List<Person> getFans() {
      if(fans == null)
         fans = em.createQuery("select p from Person p").getResultList();
      return fans;
   }
}
```

Notice that in this case, we name our component `fans`. The `FansRegistry` is unknown to clients requesting a `fans` instance. The `getFans()` method is invoked to return the `fans` value each time it is requested from the context. Now, imagine we want to track new fans and immediately make the changes available to the context. This is quite simple with the manager pattern.

```java
@Stateful
@Name("fans")
@Scope(SESSION)
public class FansRegistryImpl implements FansRegistry {
   // ... ...

   @In(required=false) Person fan;
   private List<Person> fans;

   @Create
   public void initFans() {
      fans = em.createQuery("select p from Person p").getResultList();
   }

   @Observer("newSeamFan")
   public void addFan() {
      fans.add(fan);
   }

   @Observer("fanSpreadsWord")
   public void addFans(List<Person> moreFans) {
      fans.addAll(moreFans);
   }
```

```
    @Unwrap
    public List<Person> getFans() {
      return fans;
    }
  }
```

The @Unwrap method ensures that every request for the fans instance returns an updated result based on events that have occurred within the context. Here, event listeners are used in conjunction with the manager pattern to manage the state of the fans instance. This is common with the manager pattern. The @Observer annotation will be discussed in depth in Chapter 14.

# 7.3 Configuring Components through XML

In addition to the annotations we've discussed, it is possible to define Seam components through XML. As we said previously, one of the goals of Seam is to reduce XML configuration, but there are some situations when component definition through annotations is not an option:

- When a class from a library outside of your control is to be exposed as a component
- When the same class is being configured as multiple components

In addition, you may want to configure into a component some values that could be changed by environment—for example, IP addresses, ports, etc. In any of these cases, we can use XML to configure the component through the components namespace. Components defined through XML are declared in the components.xml file we discussed in Chapter 5. The following example demonstrates how we could configure the ManagerAction component with a new authors attribute:

```
    @Stateful
    public class ManagerAction implements Manager {

      // ... ...

      private List<Person> authors;

      public void setAuthors(List<Person> authors) {
        this.authors = authors;
      }

      public List<Person> getAuthors() {
        return this.authors;
      }

      // ... ...
    }
```

The following listing demonstrates configuration of the `ManagerAction` using the components namespace, `http://jboss.com/products/seam/components`:

```xml
<?xml version="1.0" encoding="UTF-8"?>
<components xmlns="http://jboss.com/products/seam/components"
            xmlns:xsi="http://www.w3.org/2001/XMLSchema-instance"
            xsi:schemaLocation="http://jboss.com/products/seam/components
                http://jboss.com/products/seam/components-2.1.xsd">
  <component name="manager" scope="session" class="ManagerAction">
    <property name="authors">
      <value>#{author1}</value>
      <value>#{author2}</value>
    </property>
  </component>

  <component name="author1" class="Person">
    <property name="name">
      Michael Yuan
    </property>
  </component>

  <component name="author2" class="Person">
    <property name="name">
      Jacob Orshalick
    </property>
  </component>
</components>
```

Here, we configure the `ManagerAction` with two `authors`. Multiple `<value>` elements can be used to configure a collection of objects. The `authors` are initialized as `Person` instances and injected through EL expressions. It's easy to reference components or values through EL.

---

**Simplify Your Component Configuration by Using Namespaces**

Seam makes component configuration simpler by using the `@Namespace` annotation. Just create a file named `package-info.java` in the package where your components live:

```java
@Namespace(value="http://solutionsfit.com/example/stateful")
package com.solutionsfit.example.stateful;

import org.jboss.seam.annotations.Namespace;
```

Now we can reference the namespace and simplify our `components.xml` configuration:

```xml
<components xmlns="http://jboss.com/products/seam/components"
            xmlns:hello="http://solutionsfit.com/example/stateful">
  ... ...
  <hello:manager-action name="manager" scope="session">
  ... ...
```

Note that component and attribute names are specified in hyphenated form when using namespaces. To gain the benefits of autocompletion and validation, a schema can be created to represent your components; a custom schema can import the components namespace to reuse the defined component types.

---

# 7.4 Page Navigation Flow

In the Hello World example in previous chapters, we showed how to manage simple navigation flows via `pages.xml`. The `pages.xml` file can integrate with stateful components to manage complicated navigation flows based on the current state of the web application. The listing below shows the navigation rules in `pages.xml` for the stateful sample application in this chapter.

```
<page view-id="/hello.xhtml">
  <navigation from-action="#{manager.sayHello}">
    <rule if="#{manager.valid}">
      <redirect view-id="/fans.xhtml"/>
    </rule>
    <rule if="#{!manager.valid}">
      <redirect view-id="/warning.xhtml"/>
    </rule>
  </navigation>
</page>

<page view-id="/warning.xhtml">
  <navigation from-action="#{manager.confirm}">
    <redirect view-id="/fans.xhtml"/>
  </navigation>
</page>

<page view-id="/fans.xhtml">
  <navigation from-action="#{manager.startOver}">
    <redirect view-id="/hello.xhtml"/>
  </navigation>
</page>
```

Pay special attention to the navigation rules for the `hello.xhtml` page. The next page to navigate to is determined by the `#{manager.valid}` value. If the input name is not valid and the user has not confirmed the invalid name, `#{manager.valid}` would be `false` and we redirect to `warning.xhtml`.

The deep root of stateful components in the Seam framework makes it possible to integrate state objects into navigation flows based on business processes as well. We will cover these advanced use cases later in Section 24.5.

# 8

Conversations

In the previous chapter, we discussed session-scoped stateful Seam components. In most web frameworks, the application state is completely managed in the `HttpSession` object, so the session scope is the only stateful scope. However, for most applications, the session scope is too coarsely grained for effective state management. We already covered most of the reasons in Chapter 6. Let's quickly recap the key points here:

- To manage complex application state in an HTTP session, you must write a lot of code to manually shuffle objects into and out of the session. If you forget to save a modified state object back into the session, the application will exhibit hard-to-debug behavior errors at runtime.

- A single timeout parameter controls the HTTP session. Objects in a session have no notion of a lifecycle. As a result, the HTTP session is a major source of memory leaks in web applications when developers forget to manually clean out objects from a long-running session.

- The state objects in the HTTP session have no notion of scope. They are shared among all browser windows or tabs in the same user session. That makes web applications behave unexpectedly when the user opens multiple browser tabs for the same application. You can read more about this problem in Chapter 9.

Seam sets out to solve those HTTP session shortcomings by implementing declarative state management and finely grained stateful scopes. With declarative state management, there is no more need to programmatically track objects in the HTTP session. You saw declarative state management in action in the last chapter. In this chapter, we focus on the most important stateful scope in Seam: the conversation scope.

# 8.1   What Is a Conversation?

Simply put, a conversation is a state container, just like the `HttpSession`, but providing immense benefits over the HTTP session as it allows multiple concurrent state containers for a single user. The concept of a conversation is the core of the Seam framework; whether you specify conversation handling or not, a conversation is always in progress during a request.

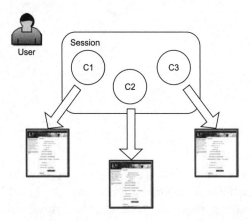

**Figure 8.1**   Multiple conversations in a single user session when using Seam

In Seam, a conversation refers to any user action—a unit of work—that takes several pages to complete (Figure 8.1). A web wizard or a shopping cart are obvious examples of conversations. However, each request/response cycle is also a conversation because it involves two pages: the form page submitted as request and the response page. Multiple conversations can exist in the same HTTP session. As mentioned before, Seam's conversation model supports multiple concurrent conversations, and each can be contained inside its own browser window or tab (see Chapter 9). In addition, Seam database transactions can be tied to conversations (see Chapter 11).

Since conversations are such a core concept in Seam, let's see how they work.

## 8.1.1   The Default Conversation Scope

Stateful session beans by default (i.e., if you omit the `@Scope` annotation on the component class) have a conversation scope. The default conversation scope is synonymous with a temporary conversation. A temporary conversation is started at the beginning of a request and ends once the response is fully rendered (temporary conversations are discussed in Section 8.2.2). Thus, a component with default conversation scope spans only two pages: It is instantiated when the first page is submitted and destroyed after the response page is fully rendered. Consider the following stateful session bean class:

```
@Stateful
@Name("manager")
public class ManagerAction implements Manager {

  @In @Out
  private Person person;

  private String mesg;

  @PersistenceContext (type=EXTENDED)
  private EntityManager em;

  public String sayHello () {

    // save person
    // update mesg

  }

  @Remove @Destroy
  public void destroy() {}

  public String getMesg () {
    return mesg;
  }

  public void setMesg (String mesg) {
    this.mesg = mesg;
  }
}
```

When the user submits the form, the `ManagerAction` object is instantiated with the user input captured in its `person` property. JSF invokes the `sayHello()` method as the UI event handler. The `sayHello()` method saves the `person` object to the database and updates the `mesg` property. Now, on the response page, we display the `mesg` to inform the user that `person` has been successfully saved to the database. After the response page is completely rendered, the `ManagerAction` component is removed from the stateful context and garbage-collected.

Notice that the `ManagerAction` object stays valid after the `sayHello()` method executes so that the `mesg` property can propagate back to the response page; that is a major difference between Seam and stateless frameworks. In addition, we gave the `EntityManager` an `EXTENDED` type, which allows it to lazy-load more data from the database as needed when the `sayHello()` method exists (see a discussion of lazy loading in Section 6.1).

**HTTP GET Request**

An HTTP `GET` request also breaks out a new conversation. Components associated with this conversation last for only one page; they are destroyed after the `GET` response page is rendered. One exception is if the conversation ID is sent along with the `GET` request as part of the URL; this will be discussed in Sections 8.3.6 and 9.2.2.

**Redirect**

In JSF, you can choose to redirect the response page to its own URL instead of using the request page's URL. With a Seam filter (see Section 3.2.4), Seam conversation components can live until the redirect page is fully rendered.

**Seam JavaBean Component**

Note that the conversation scope is not the default scope for JavaBean components (i.e., non-EJB components). JavaBean components are by default bound to the event context, so if you intend to scope a JavaBean component to the conversation context, `@Scope(ScopeType.CONVERSATION)` must be specified. The event context will essentially clear your state after each request. This can be an initial source of confusion when developing in a non-EJB environment. Refer to Chapter 4 for more on Seam JavaBean components.

## 8.1.2  Displaying JSF Messages

Besides correct ORM lazy loading, the Seam default conversation scope helps improve JSF by expanding JSF support for error messages.

One of the most useful features in JSF is its message facility. When an operation fails, the JSF backing bean method can add a message to the JSF context and return `null`. The JSF runtime can then redisplay the current page with error messages added to the page. In Seam, this operation is simplified because you can directly inject a `FacesMessages` object into a Seam component. Thus, you can easily add JSF error messages from a Seam event handler using the `FacesMessages.add()` method. You can add global JSF messages or messages to JSF components with specific IDs. The error message is displayed wherever on the page there is a `<h:messages>` tag. With Seam, you can even use EL expressions in the messages, for example:

```
@Name("manager")
@Scope(ScopeType.CONVERSATION)
public class ManagerAction implements manager {

  @In
  Person person;

  @In
  FacesMessages facesMessages;

  public String sayHello () {

    try {
    // ... ...
    } catch (Exception e) {
      facesMessages.add("Oops, had a problem saving #{person.name}");
      return null;
    }
    return "fans";
  }
}
```

With plain JSF, if the operation succeeds, the message system cannot display the "success message" on the next page. That is because the next page is out of the current JSF request context (as with lazy-loaded entity objects) and often requires a redirect. But in Seam, the next page is still within the default conversation scope, so Seam can easily display a success message through the JSF message system as well. This is a great enhancement to JSF. Here is an example of how to add a success message to a Seam UI event handler:

```
@Name("manager")
@Scope(ScopeType.CONVERSATION)
public class ManagerAction implements Manager {

  @In
  Person person;

  @In
  FacesMessages facesMessages;

  public String sayHello () {
    // ... ...

    facesMessages.add("#{person.name} said hello!");

    return "fans";
  }
}
```

The default conversation scope should suffice for many web interactions. But the power of the conversation concept is that it can be easily expanded to handle more than two pages. Seam provides a very clever mechanism to declaratively manage stateful components across a series of related pages (such as a wizard or a shopping cart). These types of conversations are referred to as *long-running conversations*. In the rest of the chapter, we will discuss how to manage long-running conversations within an application.

# 8.2 Long-Running Conversations

In a web application, a long-running conversation usually consists of a series of web pages that the user must go through to accomplish a task. The application data generated from the task is permanently committed to the database at the end of the conversation. For instance, in an e-commerce application, the checkout process is a conversation, consisting of a page for order confirmation, a page for billing information, and a final page for the confirmation code.

## 8.2.1 Introducing the Hotel Booking Example

This chapter introduces the Natural Hotel Booking example, which is a variation of the Seam Hotel Booking example which ships with the Seam distribution and demonstrates the use of Seam for making hotel reservations. State management can be difficult when developing such applications, but these examples demonstrate how the Seam conversation model makes it simple.

The Natural Hotel Booking example in this book demonstrates alternative approaches to conversation management and more advanced conversation topics. The `booking` project can be found in the book's source code bundle; it has the same directory setup as the Hello World examples in the previous chapters (see Appendix B for the application template).

---

**More about the Natural Hotel Booking Example**

This chapter will only cover the basics of the Natural Hotel Booking example to explain the navigation approach to conversation management. The Natural Hotel Booking example also demonstrates the use of natural conversations which will be covered in Section 9.3.

---

Figures 8.2 to 8.6 show a conversation in action with the Natural Hotel Booking example. On the `main.xhtml` page, the user clicks the **Find Hotels** button which loads the hotels matching the provided criteria. You can then click on any of the **View Hotel** links in the search results list. This will begin a long-running conversation allowing you to view the hotel details on the `hotel.xhtml` page. Clicking on the **Book Hotel** button initializes a hotel booking transaction based on the selected hotel and loads the `book.xhtml` page to enter the booking dates and credit card information. Click on the **Proceed** button to load the confirmation page, `confirm.xhtml`. Click the **Confirm** button to confirm the booking and end the conversation. Seam then loads the `confirmed.xhtml` page to display the confirmation number.

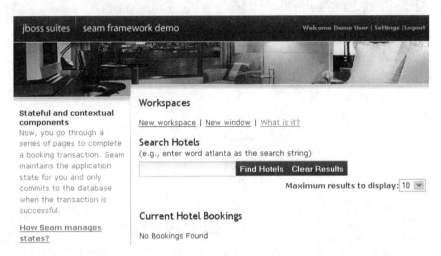

**Figure 8.2**    `main.xhtml`: Click on **Find Hotels** to display the hotels matching the selected search criteria.

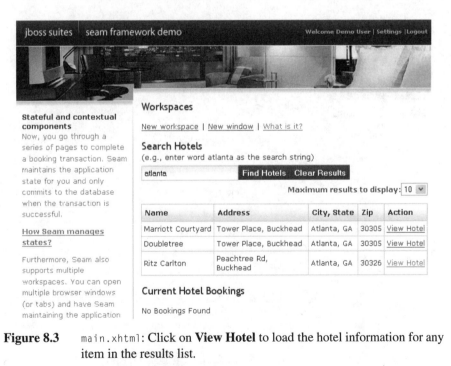

**Figure 8.3**    `main.xhtml`: Click on **View Hotel** to load the hotel information for any item in the results list.

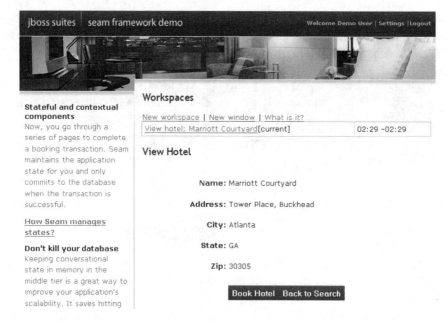

**Figure 8.4** `hotel.xhtml`: Click on the **Book Hotel** button to start a booking conversation.

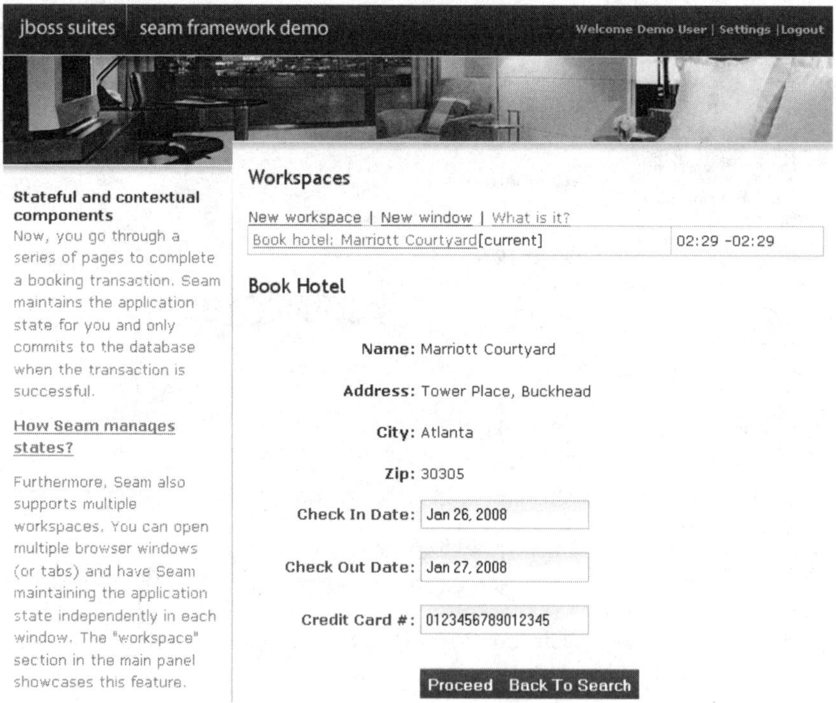

**Figure 8.5** `book.xhtml`: Enter dates and a 16-digit credit card number.

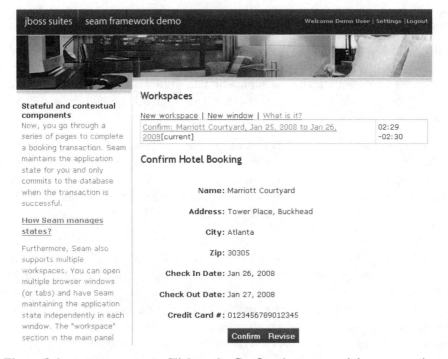

**Figure 8.6** `confirm.xhtml`: Click on the **Confirm** button to end the conversation.

---

**The Back Button Just Works**

Within a conversation, you can use the browser's **Back** button to navigate to any preceding page; the application state then reverts to that page. For instance, from the `confirmed.xhtml` page, you can click the **Back** button several times to go back to the `main.xhtml` page. From there, you can select another hotel and book it. No "invalid state" error is thrown. You can back into an interrupted conversation or a finished conversation. The incomplete bookings are not saved to the database, and no booking is saved twice by accident. Further in this chapter and in Chapter 9, we include sidebars to discuss various **Back** button scenarios that are hard to deal with in pre-conversation web frameworks.

---

The current hotel selection, reservation dates, and the credit card number are all associated with the conversation. Stateful objects that hold that data have conversational scope. They are automatically created when the conversation starts and destroyed when the conversation ends. You do not need to manage them in a long-running HTTP session. As you will see in Chapter 9, you can even have multiple concurrent conversations in the same session. Let's take a look at the lifecycle of a conversation; then, we will dig into the code and see how this lifecycle can be managed.

# 8.2.2  The Lifecycle of a Long-Running Conversation

The lifecycle of a conversation may seem complex at first—but once you get the hang of it, it is actually quite simple. Let's take a look at the lifecycle states of a conversation during a user's interaction with the application. In Figure 8.7, the filled circle indicates the initial state, while a hollow circle containing a smaller filled circle indicates an end state.

As shown in Figure 8.7, a conversation essentially has two main states, temporary and long-running. A temporary conversation is started on every request unless a previous long-running conversation is being resumed. This means that even if your application does not explicitly specify conversation handling, a conversation will be initialized for the request. This provides a number of benefits that we discussed in Section 8.1.1.

The lifespan of a temporary conversation is a single request; however, a temporary conversation is promoted to long-running if you tell Seam to begin a long-running conversation. A simple way to do this is by annotating an action method with @Begin (see Section 8.3.3). By promoting a conversation to long-running, you are telling Seam that you want the conversation to be maintained between requests. Thus, our conversation and all variables maintained in its state container will be stored by Seam once the request completes. This conversation can then be resumed upon subsequent requests.

---

**Page Scope versus Conversation Scope**

As we mentioned, the lifespan of a temporary conversation is a single request. This means that the conversation and all state maintained in it will be destroyed at the end of the request. Thus, if you want to maintain state across requests, especially across a number of views, a long-running conversation should be started. If you simply want to maintain state within a single view across requests, consider the PAGE context. The Natural Hotel Booking example demonstrates the use of the PAGE scope in the HotelSearchingAction.

---

A conversation is resumed based on the conversation ID that is sent along with the request. The conversation ID is either sent with the form or through a query parameter in the URL string. Either way, Seam recognizes this variable and resumes the conversation state if the conversation still exists. If the conversation does not exist and is required, Seam handles this situation gracefully by redirecting the user to a configurable view-id. This configuration option is discussed further in Section 8.3.4.

A long-running conversation is destroyed in one of three ways, as shown in Figure 8.7. The most logical approach is telling Seam when to end a long-running conversation. This can be done by annotating an action method with @End (see Section 8.3.5). When Seam is told to end the conversation, it demotes the conversation back to a temporary conversation.

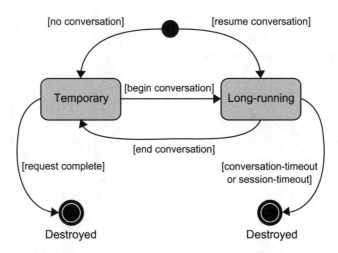

**Figure 8.7** The two main lifecycle states of a conversation, temporary and long-running

This means that Seam will destroy the conversation once the request completes. This is a good idea, as our conversation state is maintained until the end of the request. This allows us to tell the user about the action that was just performed (see Section 8.1.2).

## 8.2.3 Conversation Timeout

Telling Seam to end a long-running conversation makes sense—but is not always feasible. For example, a user may invoke an action that begins a conversation but close the window, or navigate to another section of the application without invoking the action that tells Seam to end the long-running conversation. Seam provides two types of timeouts for this scenario. The first timeout is the most obvious—the session timeout. Session timeout will destroy all long-running conversations for the user's session as all conversations are maintained within the session. A less obvious timeout is the conversation timeout.

A long-running conversation is marked for timeout when it becomes a background conversation. In Figure 8.8, we show the two states a long-running conversation can be in. Each time a conversation is resumed, it is switched to the foreground state. Remember, a conversation is resumed when a user request sends its matching conversation ID. A foreground conversation only times out when the session times out. Any other conversation in the user session is in the background state when it is resumed.

A background conversation is susceptible to both the session timeout and the conversation timeout. Section 8.3.5 provides the configuration details for setting the `conversation-timeout`. On each request, the foreground conversation is determined (which could even be a temporary conversation), and all background

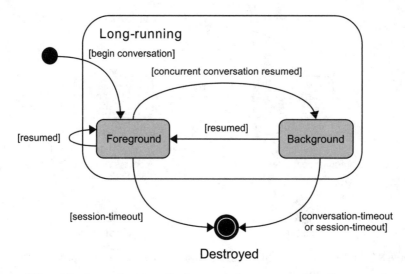

**Figure 8.8**     The two sub-states of a long-running conversation: foreground and background

conversations are checked for timeout according to the last time they were resumed. If the time since the background conversation was last resumed is greater than the configured `conversation-timeout` period, the conversation is destroyed and the event `org.jboss.seam.conversationTimeout` is raised. For a tutorial guiding you through different `conversation-timeout` scenarios, see Section 9.4.

Now that some background has been provided on the concepts behind the Seam conversation model, let's see how we can manage long-running conversations in practice.

# 8.3   Managing Long-Running Conversations

Long-running conversations are managed declaratively within an application. Managing conversations through annotations and through `pages.xml` will be discussed in the following sections. In Section 8.3.6 we will discuss how conversations can be managed through links. Regardless of how you choose to manage your long-running conversations, the semantics of the conversation lifecycle we discussed in Section 8.2.2 remain the same; only the definition of the boundaries of the conversation differs.

## 8.3.1   The Annotation Approach

The Seam Hotel Booking example that ships with Seam uses the annotation approach (i.e., adds `@Begin` to declaratively indicate that a conversation is started when the `HotelBookingAction.selectHotel()` method is invoked). The following listing demonstrates this approach:

```
@Stateful
@Name("hotelBooking")
@Restrict("#{identity.loggedIn}")
public class HotelBookingAction implements HotelBooking
{
  // attribute definitions for maintaining stateful context
  // ... ...

  @Begin
  public void selectHotel(Hotel selectedHotel) {
    // initialize the conversation state
  }

  // ... ...

  @End
  public void confirm() {
    // handle business rules associated with confirmation
    // and, if valid, persist booking
  }

  @End
  public void cancel() {
    // handle any conversation cleanup
  }
  // ... ...
}
```

Annotations are one approach to manage the conversation context. Notice that we also placed an @End on some methods to destroy the conversation when that method executes. This is not required as we could simply allow our conversation to time out, which we discussed previously.

## 8.3.2  The Navigation Approach

In the Natural Hotel Booking example, included with the book examples, the HotelBookingAction bean is the long-running conversation component; the following listing shows its structure:

```
@Stateful
@Name("hotelBooking")
@Restrict("#{identity.loggedIn}")
public class HotelBookingAction implements HotelBooking
{
  // attribute definitions for maintaining stateful context
  // ... ...

  public String selectHotel(Hotel selectedHotel)
  {
    // initialize the conversation context for the hotel to book

    return "selected";
  }

  // ... ...
```

```
public String confirm() throws InventoryException {
    // handle business rules associated with confirmation
    // if valid, persist booking and return confirmed outcome

    return "confirmed";
}

public String cancel() {
    // handle any conversation cleanup and return cancel outcome

    return "cancel";
}
// ... ...
}
```

You will quickly notice some key differences between the implementations. First, nowhere are annotations provided to manage the conversations. Instead, the conversation is managed within the pages.xml definition.

```
<page view-id="/main.xhtml" ... >
  <navigation>
    <rule if-outcome="selected">
      <begin-conversation join="true" ... />
      <redirect view-id="/hotel.xhtml" />
    </rule>
  </navigation>
</page>

<page view-id="/confirm.xhtml" ...>
  ... ...
  <navigation>
    <rule if-outcome="confirmed">
      <end-conversation/>
      <redirect view-id="/confirmed.xhtml" />
    </rule>
    ... ...
  </navigation>
</page>
```

Notice that we have defined the beginning and end points of the conversation based on user navigation. This often makes sense if the conversation encompasses a well-defined set of pages in your application (e.g., a wizard).

---

**Which Approach Should I Use?**

This is generally up to personal preference, but from experience, the navigation approach tends to lead to more maintainable code. The navigation approach provides clear boundaries for the conversation based on user navigation, instead of trying to relate conversation boundaries to page components that the user interacts with. The remainder of the chapter will discuss both approaches within the context of the Seam Hotel Booking (annotation) and Natural Booking (navigation) examples so you can make an informed decision based on your application requirements.

---

## 8.3.3 Beginning a Long-Running Conversation

When a `@Begin` method is invoked, as demonstrated in the Seam Hotel Booking example, Seam creates a bean instance that is associated with the temporary conversation we discussed before. The bijections occur at this time, based on the current context. Once the method executes, if a `void` return type has been specified for the method or a non-null `String` is returned, the temporary conversation is promoted to long-running. This means that any component or value that has been added to the temporary conversation, including our newly instantiated instance, will be part of the long-running conversation. In addition, any outjections from our component will by default be scoped to the conversation context unless specified otherwise.

In the Seam Hotel Booking example, the `HotelBookingAction.selectHotel()` method is invoked when the user clicks on the **View Hotel** link on the `main.xhtml` page to start the conversation.

```
<h:column>
  <f:facet name="header">Action</f:facet>
  <s:link id="viewHotel" value="View Hotel"
          action="#{hotelBooking.selectHotel(hot)}" />
</h:column>
```

The `@Begin selectHotel()` method initializes the conversation state. It receives the selected hotel from the EL expression and populates the stateful variable `hotel`, which is outjected to the Seam context under the name `hotel`. Since we have not specified a context for outjection, the conversation context will be assumed as our component is scoped to the conversation.

```
@Stateful
@Name("hotelBooking")
@Restrict("#{identity.loggedIn}")
public class HotelBookingAction implements HotelBooking
{
  @PersistenceContext(type=EXTENDED)
  private EntityManager em;

  @In
  private User user;

  @In(required=false) @Out
  private Hotel hotel;

  // ... ...

  @Begin
  public void selectHotel(Hotel selectedHotel)
  {
    hotel = em.merge(selectedHotel);
  }

  // ... ...
}
```

---

### Using the `EntityManager.merge()` Operation

The `merge()` operation executed in the `selectHotel()` method is required to ensure that the `Hotel` is associated with our `PersistenceContext`. In Chapter 11, we will discuss how to better manage entities in the conversation by using Seam-managed transactions and a Seam-managed persistence context (SMPC).

---

As demonstrated in the Natural Hotel Booking example, the `<begin-conversation/>` tag offers an alternative approach to beginning a long-running conversation. Since we have embedded this tag in a navigation rule for `main.xhtml`, a long-running conversation is started when the user is redirected to `hotel.xhtml`. Again, our `HotelBookingAction` component is instantiated by Seam when invoked and the bijections occur, but the conversation is promoted to long-running based on navigation rather than invocation of the component.

```
<page view-id="/main.xhtml" ... >
  <navigation>
    <rule if-outcome="selected">
      <begin-conversation ... />
      <redirect view-id="/hotel.xhtml" />
    </rule>
  </navigation>
</page>

<page view-id="/hotel.xhtml" ...
    conversation-required="true" ...>
  ... ...
  <navigation>
    ... ...
    <rule if-outcome="cancel">
      <end-conversation/>
      <redirect view-id="/main.xhtml" />
    </rule>
  </navigation>
</page>

<page view-id="/confirm.xhtml" ...
    conversation-required="true" ...>
  ... ...
  <navigation>
    <rule if-outcome="confirmed">
      <end-conversation/>
      <redirect view-id="/confirmed.xhtml" />
    </rule>
    ... ...
  </navigation>
</page>
```

The tag `<end-conversation/>`, when encountered, specifies that a conversation should end. Notice that we have specified navigation rules for when the conversation should be ended. If the user has navigated to the `confirm.xhtml` page and invokes the action `HotelBookingAction.confirm()`, the returned `confirmed` result will end the conversation and redirect the user to `confirmed.xhtml`.

---

**Constraining Navigation through jPDL Pageflow**

The navigation approach can be further improved via pageflows using jPDL in your `pages.xml`. By constraining the flow of navigation, you can ensure state consistency regardless of user actions. For further information, see Section 24.5.

---

**Natural Conversations**

You probably noticed that we elided some of the definitions in our `pages.xml` configuration above. The Natural Booking example uses the new Natural Conversations feature provided by Seam 2. We will return to this `pages.xml` definition in Section 9.3 to discuss this feature in depth.

---

## 8.3.4 Inside the Conversation

When you are inside a conversation, you can call any bean method to manipulate the stateful data in the conversation context. For instance, the `hotel.xhtml` page displays the contents of the `hotel` component in the conversation context. If you click on the **Book Hotel** button in the Seam Hotel Booking example or the Natural Hotel Booking example, Seam invokes the `bookHotel()` method to create a new `Booking` object from the current `hotel` instance.

```
<div class="section">
  <div class="entry">
    <div class="label">Name:</div>
    <div class="output">#{hotel.name}</div>
  </div>
  <div class="entry">
    <div class="label">Address:</div>
    <div class="output">#{hotel.address}</div>
  </div>
  ... ...
</div>

<div class="section">
  <h:form>
    <fieldset class="buttonBox">
      <h:commandButton action="#{hotelBooking.bookHotel}"
                       value="Book Hotel" class="button"/>
      <h:commandButton action="#{hotelBooking.cancel}"
                       value="Back to Search" class="button"/>
    </fieldset>
  </h:form>
</div>
```

The `bookHotel()` method creates a new `Booking` object for this conversation. This `Booking` object has default reservation dates and is displayed on the `booking.xhtml` page for you to edit.

```
@Stateful
@Name("hotelBooking")
@Restrict("#{identity.loggedIn}")
public class HotelBookingAction implements HotelBooking {

    @In(required = false) @Out(required=false)
    private Hotel hotel;

    @In(required=false)
    @Out(required=false)
    @Valid
    private Booking booking;

    // ... ...

    public String bookHotel()
    {
        booking = new Booking(hotel, user);
        Calendar calendar = Calendar.getInstance();
        booking.setCheckinDate( calendar.getTime() );
        calendar.add(Calendar.DAY_OF_MONTH, 1);
        booking.setCheckoutDate( calendar.getTime() );

        return "book";
    }
    // ... ...
}
```

All of the bean methods in `HotelBookingAction` are designed to be invoked in the context of a long-running conversation. However, in real life, there is no guarantee of that. The user might load the `book.seam` page first and then click on the **Confirm Hotel** button. Since no valid conversation context exists here, the application would fail. To avoid this, we specify `conversation-required="true"` in our `pages.xml` definition.

```
<page view-id="/hotel.xhtml" ...
      conversation-required="true" ... >
  ... ...
</page>

<page view-id="/book.xhtml" ...
      conversation-required="true" ... >
  ... ...
</page>

<page view-id="/confirm.xhtml" ...
      conversation-required="true" ... />
  ... ...
</page>
```

Now, if the page is accessed outside of an active long-running conversation, the application should redirect to the `no-conversation-view-id` page which is also specified in `pages.xml`.

```
<pages no-conversation-view-id="/main.xhtml"
       login-view-id="/home.xhtml">
... ...
```

This is also why you are forwarded to `main.xhtml` when you move back to a conversation page, after the conversation has ended, and click on a button on that page. The `no-conversation-view-id` can also be specified at the `page` level in your configuration.

As you probably noticed, there is no difference between the two conversation management approaches when inside a long-running conversation. The semantics of a conversation remain the same regardless of the approach, only the definition of the boundaries of the conversation will differ.

## 8.3.5 Ending a Long-Running Conversation

In the Seam Hotel Booking example, there are two `@End` methods for two possible endpoints of the conversation. The `confirm()` method is invoked after the user creates a reservation and clicks on the **Confirm** button on the `confirm.xhtml` page. Before the conversation ends, the `confirm()` method saves the `booking` object into the database.

```
@Name("hotelBooking")
@Restrict("#{identity.loggedIn}")
public class HotelBookingAction implements HotelBooking {

  // ... ...

  @In(required=false)
  @Out(required=false)
  private Booking booking;

  // ... ...

  @End
  public void confirm()
  {
    em.persist(booking);
    facesMessages.add("Thank you, #{user.name}, " +
      "your confirmation number for #{hotel.name} is #{booking.id}");
    log.info("New booking: #{booking.id} for #{user.username}");
    // ... ...
  }

  @End
  public void cancel() {}
}
```

As before, ending the conversation depends on the outcome of your method. If the return type is `String` rather than `void`, a `null` return value will not end the long-running conversation and will return the user to the previous view.

This behavior is very useful for validation. Suppose the user enters some information in the final form of your wizard and clicks **Submit**. If a validation error occurs, we would not want to throw away all the previously entered information. Instead, we simply add a `FacesMessage` and return `null`. This will return the user to the view where the issue occurred, display the error message, and maintain our conversation state.

For example, we could process the credit card information, provided by the user during booking, on confirmation and notify the user of any issues.

```
// ... ...

@End
public String confirm()
{
  if(processCredit())
  {
    em.persist(booking);
    facesMessages.add("Thank you, #{user.name}, " +
      "your confirmation number for #{hotel.name} is #{booking.id}");
    log.info("New booking: #{booking.id} for #{user.username}");

    return "confirmed";
  }

  FacesMessages.add("There was an issue with " +
    "processing your credit card.  Better call the bank!");

  return null;
}

public boolean processCredit()
{
  // perform credit card processing tasks and
  // return result
}

// ... ...
```

If credit card processing fails, the user is returned to `confirm.xhtml` with a message about the credit issue. The conversation is still in progress, so the user has a chance to revise the credit card information or resolve the issue with the bank before proceeding.

```
<h:form>
  <fieldset>
    <div class="entry">
      <div class="label">Name:</div>
      <div class="output">#{hotel.name}</div>
    </div>

    ... Hotel and reservation details ...
```

```
    <div class="entry">
      <div class="label"> </div>
      <div class="input">
        <h:commandButton value="Confirm"
                         action="#{hotelBooking.confirm}"
                         class="button"/>
        <h:commandButton value="Revise"
                         action="back" class="button"/>
      </div>
    </div>
  </fieldset>
</h:form>
```

Similarly, in our Natural Booking example, we showed the <end-conversation/> tag. The confirmed result, returned by the confirm() method, ends the conversation. Before returning the confirmed navigation constant, the confirm() method reduces the hotel room inventory from the database to reflect the booking. (In fact, the two database operations must be performed in an atomic transaction to ensure database integrity; that is the topic for Chapter 11.) Unless the confirmed navigation constant is returned, the conversation will continue to allow the user to resolve any issues with the booking.

```
public class HotelBookingAction implements HotelBooking, Serializable {

  // ... ...
  public String confirm() throws InventoryException {
    if (booking==null || hotel==null) return "main";

    em.persist(booking);
    hotel.reduceInventory();

    if (hotel.getId() == 1)
      throw new RuntimeException("Simulated DB error");

    if(bookingList != null)
      bookingList.refresh();

    return "confirmed";
  }

  public String cancel() {
    return "cancel";
  }
  // ... ...
}
```

---

**Reduce Database Roundtrips**

In a complex application, you might need to perform multiple database operations in a conversation. We recommend that you cache all database updates as in-memory objects in the conversation and then synchronize them to the database at the end of the conversation. That helps reduce database roundtrips and preserve database integrity (see Chapter 11 for more details).

---

The `cancel()` method, on the other hand, is called when the user wants to end the conversation without booking anything. Whether the method is annotated with `@End` or returns a navigation constant which ends the conversation through `pages.xml`, the conversation is demoted to temporary and cleaned from memory once the redirect to `main.xhtml` is complete. Should you wish to clean up the conversation context before the redirect occurs, Seam provides the `beforeRedirect` attribute which can be specified as `@End(beforeRedirect="true")` or as `<end-conversation before-redirect="true"/>`.

---

**Using the Back Button to Back into an Ended Conversation**

After you complete a conversation by calling the `@End` method or through a navigation rule in `pages.xml`, you can still use the **Back** button to return to any page in the ended conversation. However, if you click on any link or button on the page, you will be redirected to `main.xhtml` because a valid conversation context no longer exists for that page.

---

In a Seam application, the conversational state is tied to the business logic. That is, all possible methods to exit the conversation should be tagged with `@End` or have an associated navigation rule that ends the conversation. It is therefore unlikely that a user would exit a conversation without an ending being invoked. But what if the user abandons the current conversation and loads a new site or conversation with a manual HTTP `GET` request? Or, what if we simply make a coding error and forget to tag an exiting method with `@End` or create an associated navigation rule? In those cases, the current conversation times out when a preset conversation timeout is reached or when the current HTTP session times out.

You can set the global conversation timeout in the `components.xml` configuration file (see Appendix B). The unit is milliseconds.

```
<components ...>
  ... ...
  <core:manager conversation-timeout="120000"/>
</components>
```

At first glance, you may relate the conversation timeout to the session timeout—but, as we saw in Section 8.2.3, they are actually quite different. Alternatively, you can specify a timeout for each individual conversation in the `pages.xml` configuration file (see Chapter 9 and Section 24.5).

As we discussed earlier in this chapter, an abandoned conversation is a potential risk of a memory leak. Fortunately, it is not nearly as error-prone as manually managing the HTTP session. In addition, the Seam user can actually go back to the abandoned conversation to pick up where he or she left off using the conversation switcher (see Chapter 9) or simply using the browser's **Back** button.

# 8.3.6 Links and Buttons

So far, our conversation has been driven by a series of button clicks (i.e., regular HTTP POST operations). That is because Seam uses hidden form fields in those POST requests to maintain the conversation context for the user. If you click on a regular link in the middle of a conversation, the browser issues a simple HTTP GET request to get the page, and the current conversation context is lost; Seam then simply starts a new conversation following the link (see Chapter 9 for multiple concurrent conversations for the same user session). Still, sometimes we want to use hyperlinks to navigate inside a conversation. For instance, we might want to allow the user to right-click on the link and open the subsequent pages in a separate browser tab or window.

An obvious solution is to use the <h:commandLink> component instead of <h:commandButton> in JSF. However, the JSF <h:commandLink> is not really a regular link. When you click on it, JSF uses JavaScript to post the request back to the server. This breaks the normal right-click behavior of links. To fix this problem with JSF links, Seam provides its own conversation-aware link component: <s:link> (see Chapter 3 for more on how to install and use Seam UI tags).

---

**The <h:outputLink> Component**

The JSF <h:outputLink> component renders a regular link in the browser. This is not very useful in a Seam conversation because you cannot attach event handler methods to an <h:outputLink>, but this tag is actually very useful when initiating natural conversations as you will see in Section 9.3.

---

In the following example, we declare the s: namespace prefix for the Seam tags:

```
<html xmlns="http://www.w3.org/1999/xhtml"
      xmlns:h="http://java.sun.com/jsf/html"
      xmlns:f="http://java.sun.com/jsf/core"
      xmlns:s="http://jboss.com/products/seam/taglib">
```

With the namespace prefix declared, it is easy to use the <s:link> tag to build links in your conversation. You can specify an event handler method for the link or give a direct JSF view-id as the link destination. The rendered link maintains the conversational context and behaves like a regular HTML link.

```
<s:link view-id="/login.xhtml" value="Login"/>
<s:link action="#{login.logout}" value="Logout"/>
```

The <s:link> component does more than just provide HTML links for navigating inside conversations. You can actually control the conversation from the links. For instance, if you click on the following link, Seam leaves the current conversation when the main.xhtml page is loaded, just as a regular HTTP GET request would do. The propagation attribute can take other values, such as begin and end, to force the beginning or ending of the current conversation.

```
<s:link view-id="/main.xhtml" propagation="none"
        value="Abandon Conversation" />
```

**Bookmarks**

Another implication of using HTTP POST is that it is difficult to place bookmarks on POST result pages. In fact, it is fairly easy to build bookmarkable pages in Seam applications; see Chapter 15.

The <s:link> component actually has richer conversation management capabilities than the plain JSF <h:commandButton>, which simply propagates the conversation context between pages. What if you want to exit, begin, or end a conversation context from a button click? You need the Seam <s:conversationPropagation> tag. The following example shows a button that exits the current conversation context:

```
<h:commandButton action="main" value="Abandon Conversation">
  <s:conversationPropagation type="none"/>
</h:commandButton>
```

**Warning on the Use of Conversation Propagation in Links and Buttons**

It is recommended that you limit the use of conversation propagation for links or buttons to simply choosing whether or not to propagate the current conversation. As we have seen, propagating a conversation is as simple as ensuring that the conversationId is sent with the request. Propagation of none leaves the current conversation by not passing the conversationId. Potential maintenance difficulties can arise when beginning or ending a conversation in a link or a button, as this does not provide a clear delineation of conversational boundaries.

# 8.4  New Frontiers

You have seen how the Seam conversation model simplifies stateful application development. But Seam goes far beyond simplifying the development of traditional web applications.

The fully encapsulated conversation components enable us to tie the user experience and the application's transactional behavior with conversations. That has opened new frontiers in web application development. Seam makes it possible to develop advanced web applications that are too complex or even impossible for older web frameworks. We cover some of those new scenarios in Chapters 9 and 11.

# 9

# Workspaces and Concurrent Conversations

As we discussed in the previous chapter, you can have multiple conversations in an HTTP session. It's easy for a user to have several *consecutive* conversations in a session. For instance, in the Hotel Booking example, you can book several hotels in a row, with each booking in its own conversation. But what makes Seam truly unique is its support for multiple *concurrent* conversations in a session. These concurrent conversations can each run in a separate browser window or tab. This gives rise to the concept of a *workspace*. In this chapter, we will discuss what a Seam workspace is and how to work with workspaces in your web application. Again, we will use the Natural Hotel Booking example application in the `booking` source project.

## 9.1 What Is a Workspace?

A workspace is a common concept in desktop applications. For instance, in a word processor or spreadsheet program, each document is a workspace. In an IDE, each project is a workspace. You can make a change in one workspace without affecting other workspaces. In general, a workspace is a set of self-contained application contexts.

However, most of today's web applications do not support workspaces. The reason is that most web applications manage all their application contexts via HTTP sessions. An HTTP session does not have the granularity required to differentiate between browser windows. To better understand this, let's revisit the Natural Hotel Booking application. Let's open two browser tabs and select different hotels to book in each of those tabs. For instance, imagine that you first select the Marriott San Francisco hotel in tab 1. Then you select the Ritz Carlton Atlanta hotel in tab 2 and click **Book Hotel**. Now, go back to tab 1 and click on the **Book Hotel** button there too. Which hotel will be booked? You can see the process in Figures 9.1 and 9.2.

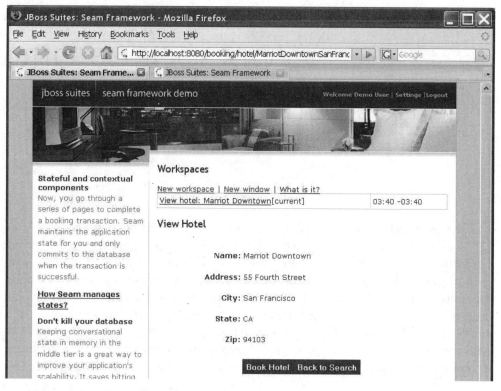

**Figure 9.1**    Step 1: Load the Marriott San Francisco hotel in tab 1.

If the application were based on an older-generation web framework which saves state in the HTTP session, you would end up booking the Ritz Carlton Atlanta hotel. The reason is that the Ritz hotel in tab 2 was most recently put into the HTTP session, and the button action in either tab 1 or tab 2 would therefore perform the booking operation on that hotel. An HTTP session-based web application does not properly support multiple browser windows or tabs; those workspaces interfere with each other via the shared application state.

Seam, on the other hand, was designed from the ground up to support stateful application contexts. Seam web applications automatically support workspaces by default. So, in our Seam Hotel Booking example, the **Book Hotel** button in each browser tab works

**Figure 9.2**  Step 2: Load the Ritz Carlton Atlanta hotel in tab 2 and click on **Book Hotel**.

as expected—the button in tab 1 always books the Marriott hotel, and the button in tab 2 always books the Ritz hotel, no matter what order they're invoked in (see Figure 9.3). The conversations in each window are completely independent, although all conversations are tied to the same user. The best way to understand the workspace concept is to try it yourself. Open several browser windows or tabs and load the `hotel.xhtml` page in each of them. You can then book different hotels in parallel in all windows.

Seam always injects the appropriate hotel and booking instances based on the current workspace, as shown in Figure 9.4.

In addition, you may notice that the user instance is shared across workspaces. The user instance is scoped to the session, as shown in the following listing. Session scope is always shared among workspace instances, so only variables global to the user's session should be maintained in this scope.

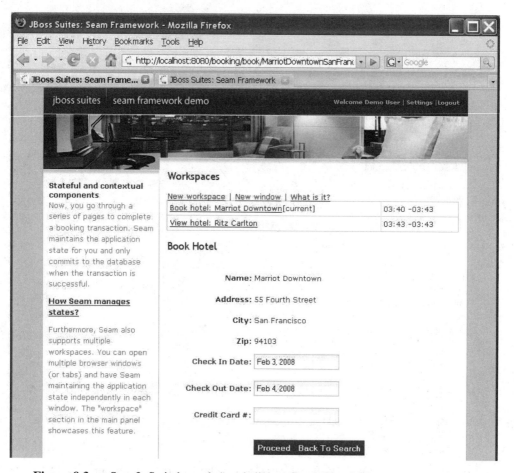

**Figure 9.3**    Step 3: Switch to tab 1 and click on **Book Hotel**. The application books
the Marriott San Francisco hotel. This makes sense, but only Seam, with
its support for multiple workspaces, can do this easily.

```
@Entity
@Name("user")
@Scope(SESSION)
@Table(name="Customer")
public class User implements Serializable
{
   ... ...
```

In a Seam application, a workspace maps one-to-one to a conversation, so a Seam
application with multiple concurrent conversations has multiple workspaces. As we
discussed in Section 8.3.4, a user starts a new conversation via an explicit HTTP GET
request. Thus, when you open a link in a new browser tab or manually load a URL in
the current browser tab, you start a new workspace. Seam then provides you a method
for accessing the old workspace/conversation (see Section 9.2.1).

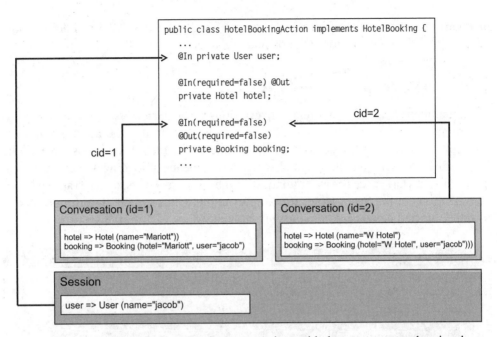

```
public class HotelBookingAction implements HotelBooking {
    ...
    @In private User user;

    @In(required=false) @Out
    private Hotel hotel;

    @In(required=false)
    @Out(required=false)
    private Booking booking;
    ...
}
```

cid=2

cid=1

**Conversation (id=1)**

hotel => Hotel (name="Mariott"))
booking => Booking (hotel="Mariott", user="jacob")

**Conversation (id=2)**

hotel => Hotel (name="W Hotel")
booking => Booking (hotel="W Hotel", user="jacob")))

**Session**

user => User (name="jacob")

**Figure 9.4**  A group of concurrent conversations with the same user, each uniquely identifiable by ID

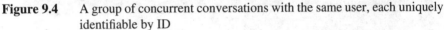

### The Back Button Works across Conversations and Workspaces

If you interrupt a conversation via an HTTP `GET` request (e.g., by manually loading the `main.xhtml` page in the middle of a conversation), you can then go back to the interrupted conversation. When you are backed to a page inside an interrupted conversation, you can simply click on any button and resume the conversation as if it had never been interrupted.

As we discussed in Section 8.3.4, if the conversation has ended or timed out by the time you try to return to it, Seam handles this gracefully by redirecting you to a `no-conversation-view-id` page (see Section 9.2.2) which is configurable in your `pages.xml`. This ensures that, regardless of back-buttoning, the user's experience remains consistent with the server-side state.

## 9.2  Workspace Management

Seam provides a number of built-in components and features that facilitate workspace and concurrent conversation management. The following sections will explore the features provided by Seam to help you manage workspaces in your applications. Section 9.2.1 will discuss the workspace switcher which provides a simple way to allow users to swap between workspaces. In Section 9.2.2, we will demonstrate how you can maintain a workspace even across GET requests. Finally, Section 9.2.3 will discuss how Seam allows the conversation ID to be manipulated.

## 9.2.1  Workspace Switcher

Seam maintains a list of concurrent conversations in the current user session in a component named #{conversationList}. You can iterate through the list to see the descriptions of the conversations, their start times, and their last access times. The #{conversationList} component also provides a means of loading any conversation in the current workspace (browser window or tab). Figure 9.5 shows an example list of conversations in the Seam Hotel Booking example. Click on any description link to load the selected conversation in the current window.

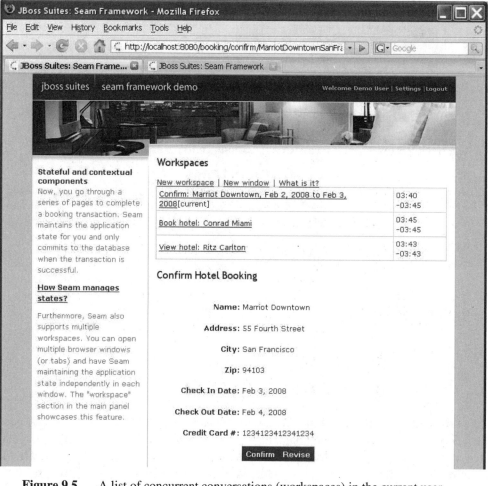

**Figure 9.5**    A list of concurrent conversations (workspaces) in the current user session

Below is the JSF page code behind the workspace switcher. It is in the `conversations.xhtml` file in the example source code.

```
<h:dataTable value="#{conversationList}" var="entry">
  <h:column>
    <h:commandLink action="#{entry.select}"
                   value="#{entry.description}"/>
    <h:outputText value="[current]"
                  rendered="#{entry.current}"/>
  </h:column>

  <h:column>
    <h:outputText value="#{entry.startDatetime}">
      <f:convertDateTime type="time" pattern="hh:mm"/>
    </h:outputText>
    -
    <h:outputText value="#{entry.lastDatetime}">
      <f:convertDateTime type="time" pattern="hh:mm"/>
    </h:outputText>
  </h:column>
</h:dataTable>
```

The `#{entry}` object iterates through conversations in the `#{conversationList}` component. The `#{entry.select}` property is a built-in JSF action for loading the conversation `#{entry}` in the current window. Similarly, the `#{entry.destroy}` JSF action destroys that conversation. What's interesting is the `#{entry.description}` property, which contains a string description of the current page in the conversation. How does Seam figure out the "description" of a page? That requires another XML file.

The `WEB-INF/pages.xml` file in the `app.war` archive file (it is the `resources/WEB-INF/pages.xml` file in the source code bundle) specifies the page descriptions. This `pages.xml` file can also be used to replace the `WEB-INF/navigation.xml` file for jBPM-based pageflow configuration (see Section 24.5 for more details). You can learn more about `pages.xml` in Chapter 15. Here is a portion of the content of the `pages.xml` file in the Natural Hotel Booking example:

```
<pages>
  ... ...
  </page>
  <page view-id="/book.xhtml" timeout="600000" ... >
    <description>
      Book hotel: #{hotel.name}
    </description>
    ... ...
  </page>
  <page view-id="/confirm.xhtml" timeout="600000" ... >
    <description>
      Confirm: #{booking.description}
    </description>
    ... ...
  </page>
</pages>
```

We can reference Seam components by name in the `pages.xml` file which is very useful for displaying the description of a conversation.

---

**Why Is the Conversation List Empty or Missing an Entry?**

A conversation is only placed into the `#{conversationList}` component if a page description has been provided. This is often a source of confusion for first-time users, so if you are unsure as to why your conversation is not appearing in the `conversationList`, check your `pages.xml` configuration.

---

The conversation switcher shown in Figure 9.5 displays conversations in a table. Of course, you can customize how the table looks. But what if you want a switcher in a drop-down menu? The drop-down menu takes less space on a web page than a table, especially if you have many workspaces. However, the `#{conversationList}` component is a `DataModel` and cannot be used in a JSF menu, so Seam provides a special conversation list to use in a drop-down menu, which has a structure similar to the data table.

```
<h:selectOneMenu value="#{switcher.conversationIdOrOutcome}">
  <f:selectItems value="#{switcher.selectItems}"/>
</h:selectOneMenu>
<h:commandButton action="#{switcher.select}"
                 value="Switch"/>
<h:commandButton action="#{switcher.destroy}"
                 value="Destroy"/>
```

## 9.2.2  Carrying a Conversation across Workspaces

As we discussed earlier, Seam creates a new workspace for each HTTP `GET` request. By definition, the new workspace has its own fresh conversation. So, what if we want to do an HTTP `GET` and still preserve the same conversation context? For instance, you might want a pop-up browser window to share the same workspace/conversation as the current main window. That's where the Seam conversation ID comes into play.

If you look at the URLs of the Seam Hotel Booking example application, every page URL has a `cid` URL parameter at the end. This `cid` stays constant within a conversation. For instance, a URL could look like this: `http://localhost:8080/booking/hotel.seam?cid=10`.

To `GET` a page without disrupting the current conversation, you can append the same `cid` name/value pair to your HTTP `GET` URL.

Appending the `cid` value to an URL can be risky. What if you pass in a wrong value for the `cid` parameter? Will the application just throw an error? As a protection, you can configure the `pages.xml` file to set a default page to forward to when the URL has an unavailable `cid` value.

```
<pages no-conversation-view-id="/main.xhtml" ...>
  ... ...
  <page view-id="/confirm.xhtml" conversation-required="true">
  ... ...
</pages>
```

---

**Requiring a Conversation for the View**

Notice the attribute `conversation-required` specified in the above listing for the `/hotel.xhtml` `view-id`. As we discussed in Chapter 8, this attribute requires that a long-running conversation be in progress when `hotel.xhtml` is accessed by the user. This ensures that if the user has entered a URL directly or bookmarked a page that is not directly accessible, the user will be redirected to an appropriate location.

---

Of course, manually entering the `cid` parameter is not a good idea. So, to go back to the original question of opening the same workspace in a new window, you need to dynamically render a link with the right parameter already in place. The following example shows you how to build such a link. The Seam tags nested in `<h:outputLink>` generate the right parameters in the link.

```
<h:outputLink value="hotel.seam" target="_blank">
  <s:conversationId/>
  <s:conversationPropagation propagation="join"/>
  <h:outputText value="Open New Tab"/>
</h:outputLink>
```

---

**Use the `<s:link>` Tag**

You can also use the Seam `<s:link>` tag, discussed in Section 8.3.6, to open new browser windows or tabs within the same conversation. Using the `<s:link>` tag is generally the recommended approach to achieve this behavior.

---

## 9.2.3 Managing the Conversation ID

As you have probably noted by now, the conversation ID is the mechanism Seam uses to identify the current long-running conversation. Thus, a unique conversation ID must be sent with the request, either through `GET` or `POST`, to resume a long-running conversation. In order to make this a little less verbose, Seam enables you to customize the `cid` parameter. The name of that parameter is configured in the `components.xml` file. Here is our configuration in the Hotel Booking example to use the `cid` name for the parameter:

```
<components ...>
  ... ...
  <core:manager conversation-timeout="120000"
              concurrent-request-timeout="500"
              conversation-id-parameter="cid" />
  ... ...
</components>
```

If you don't configure this, Seam uses the verbose `conversationId` name by default. The `conversation-timeout` value shown here is discussed in Sections 8.2.3 and 9.4.

By default, Seam automatically increases the conversation ID value by one for each new conversation. The default setting is good enough for most applications, but it can be improved for applications that have many workspaces. The number is not very informative, and it is hard to remember which workspace is in what state by looking at the ID numbers. Furthermore, if you have many workspaces opened in tabs, you might open two different workspaces to perform the same task, and that can get confusing very quickly.

In the next section, we will discuss natural conversations—the feature Seam provides to customize the conversation IDs. Natural conversations allow your conversation IDs to be meaningful and user-friendly.

# 9.3  Natural Conversations

Managing the conversation ID is not difficult, but it is simply a number fabricated by Seam. It would be nice if a conversation could be identified by something more meaningful to the developers and users alike. Seam 2 addresses this by supporting natural conversations.

Natural conversations provide a more natural way of identifying the current conversation among workspaces (or concurrent conversations). This feature allows you to configure a unique identifier for the entity involved in the conversation that will be used to identify the conversation itself. Thus, in the Seam Hotel Booking example, it would be nice to identify conversations based on the hotel being booked (e.g., `MarriottCourtyardBuckhead`). This identifier is meaningful not only to you as a developer but also to the users of your application.

Using natural conversations, it is quite easy to get user-friendly URLs and simple redirecting to existing conversations. User-friendly URLs are generally a recommended practice in today's web world. They allow users to navigate by simply altering the URL and to get an idea of what they are currently viewing from the URL. For example, if my URL reads `http://natural-booking/book/MarriottCourtyardBuckhead`, it is quite obvious that I am trying to book a room at the Marriott Courtyard Buckhead.

Such a URL requires the use of natural conversations in conjunction with URL rewriting (which will be discussed later in this chapter).

The following sections will discuss how to use natural conversations in practice and provide an introduction into URL rewriting with Seam.

---

**Natural Conversations versus Explicit Synthetic Conversation IDs**

If you have used pre-Seam 2 releases, you may be familiar with explicit synthetic conversation IDs. Explicit synthetic conversation IDs are now deprecated; use natural conversations instead.

---

## 9.3.1 Beginning a Natural Conversation via Links

Seam provides excellent support for GET parameters to enable your application to use RESTful URLs (see Chapter 15). This feature can also be used to achieve a simple approach to natural conversations. Simply by linking to /hotels.seam? hotelId=MarriottCourtyardBuckhead, we can use the hotelId to initialize our hotel instance and populate our natural conversation identifier. This approach is used in the following link from hotels.xhtml:

```
... ...
<h:outputLink value="#{facesContext.externalContext.requestContextPath}
                     /hotel.seam?hotelId=#{hot.hotelId}">
   View Hotel
</h:outputLink>
... ...
```

The above fragment outputs a standard HTML link to the /hotel.seam view. The query string specified as hotelId=#{hot.hotelId} is used to initialize the hotel instance and subsequently will be used to identify the conversation (which we will discuss shortly). The expression #{facesContext.externalContext.requestContextPath} prepends the current context root to the link, as an <h:outputLink> does not perform this task for us.

Now that we have a link to our initial conversation page, we need to define our natural conversation in pages.xml.

```
<conversation name="Booking"
              parameter-name="hotelId"
              parameter-value="#{hotel.hotelId}" />
```

This definition specifies a natural conversation named Booking. This name is used to identify the participants in the natural conversation. The parameter-name and parameter-value define the parameter that will be used to uniquely identify a conversation instance. You must ensure that the EL expression evaluates to value when the conversation is initialized.

Now that we have defined our natural conversation, the pages that participate in it must be listed.

```
<page view-id="/hotel.xhtml" conversation="Booking"
      login-required="true" timeout="300000">
  ... ...
  <param name="hotelId"
    value="#{hotelBooking.hotelId}" />
  <begin-conversation join="true" />
  ... ...
</page>

<page view-id="/book.xhtml" conversation="Booking"
      conversation-required="false" login-required="true"
      timeout="600000">
  ... ...
</page>

<page view-id="/confirm.xhtml" conversation="Booking"
      conversation-required="true" login-required="true"
      timeout="600000">
  ... ...
</page>
```

You may notice that the portions of our page definition that we elided in Chapter 8 are now shown. The conversation attribute is set to the name of the natural conversation the page participates in. In our example, the Booking conversation is specified. Thus, the hotel.xhtml, book.xhtml, and confirmed.xhtml pages all participate in the conversation.

Note the use of <param> in the hotel.xhtml definition. This <param> sets the hotelId for the hotel to be viewed into the hotelBooking instance. This value of the attribute can then be used by the HotelBookingAction to initialize the hotel in the conversation context. This can be easily achieved through a @Factory method in the HotelBookingAction.

```
@Stateful
@Name("hotelBooking")
@Restrict("#{identity.loggedIn}")
public class HotelBookingAction implements HotelSearching
{
  // ... ...

  @Out(required=false)
  private Hotel hotel;

  // ... ...
```

```
@Factory(value="hotel")
public void loadHotel()
{
  // loads hotel into the conversation based on the RESTful id
  hotel = (Hotel) em.createQuery("select h from " +
          "Hotel h where hotelId = :identifier")
          .setParameter("identifier", hotelId).getSingleResult();
}
// ... ...
```

Notice that the @Factory method is defined for the hotel variable. This means that when Seam requests the hotelId from the #{hotel.hotelId} expression specified in our natural conversation definition, our hotel instance will be appropriately instantiated. In addition, the combination of the <param> and the @Factory method now allows our page to be bookmarked by a user.

---

**Defining a Unique Key for Your Natural Conversation**

You may notice that the unique key used to identify the hotel, MarriottCourtyard-Buckhead, is not the primary key. The primary key can be used, but often it is not meaningful to users of your application. Instead, you can define a custom key to identify your entity, but this key must be unique.

---

## 9.3.2 Redirecting to a Natural Conversation

So far we have provided a way to meaningfully identify our conversation through a GET request—but what if we need to perform a redirect to start a natural conversation? This can be accomplished by making a few adjustments to our Natural Hotel Booking example. First, we can define an action for the HotelBookingAction that accepts a hotel instance for booking.

```
@Stateful
@Name("hotelBooking")
@Restrict("#{identity.loggedIn}")
public class HotelBookingAction implements HotelBooking
{
  @PersistenceContext(type=EXTENDED)
  private EntityManager em;

  @In(required=false) @Out
  private Hotel hotel;

  // ... ...

  public String selectHotel(Hotel selectedHotel)
  {
    hotel = em.merge(selectedHotel);

    return "selected";
  }
  // ... ...
```

Note that the @Factory method we used previously has been replaced by an action that accepts a selected Hotel instance and merges that instance with the @PersistenceContext. Now we can define a navigation rule to redirect the user to hotel.xhtml when a hotel is selected from main.xhtml.

```
... ...
<page view-id="/main.xhtml" login-required="true">
  <navigation>
    <rule if-outcome="selected">
      <redirect view-id="/hotel.xhtml" />
    </rule>
  </navigation>
</page>

<page view-id="/hotel.xhtml" conversation="Booking"
      login-required="true" timeout="300000">
  <description>View hotel: #{hotel.name}</description>
  <begin-conversation join="true" />
... ...
```

We begin the conversation just as before, but no longer require the specification of a request parameter. Again, Seam uses the named conversation to determine the natural conversation ID when beginning the natural conversation. In the main.xhtml view, the <h:outputLink> used previously is changed to a <h:commandLink> to invoke the newly defined action:

```
... ...
<h:commandLink id="viewHotel"
               action="#{hotelSearching.selectHotel(hot)}"
               value="View Hotel"/>
  <s:conversationName value="Booking" />
</h:commandLink>
... ...
```

The <s:conversationName value="Booking"/> UI component must be provided to ensure that a natural conversation is resumed if the same hotel is selected. Due to the timing of processing for conversation propagation specified in navigation rules, the use of this component is required in this case. By specifying this component, Seam ensures that if a natural conversation is already in progress for this hotel selection, it will be resumed.

## 9.3.3  Resuming a Natural Conversation

So far, the main drawback of this approach is that in both cases, when a hotel is selected on main.xhtml, while the same conversation is resumed, selecting that hotel again would return us to the initial page of the conversation (i.e., the hotels.xhtml view). This is because we have essentially hard-coded the navigation into our application by using an <h:outputLink> or a navigation rule in pages.xml.

It may be more useful to return the user back to the point in the natural conversation where he or she left off. As the Natural Hotel Booking example demonstrates, when a user selects **View Hotel** for a specific hotel in the `main.xhtml` view, this results in a natural conversation associated with the selected `hotel`. If a natural conversation is already in progress for the selected hotel, the user is returned to the point in the booking where he or she left off. This can be accomplished through interaction with the core API.

```
@Stateful
@Name("hotelBooking")
@Restrict("#{identity.loggedIn}")
public class HotelBookingAction implements HotelBooking
{
  // ... ...

  public String selectHotel(Hotel selectedHotel)
  {
    ConversationEntry entry =
      ConversationEntries.instance()
        .getConversationEntry("Booking:"
          + selectedHotel.getHotelId());

    if(entry != null)
    {
      entry.select();
      return null;
    }

    hotel = em.merge(selectedHotel);

    return "selected";
  }

  // ... ...
```

Notice the check that is performed prior to initiating the conversation context. The `ConversationEntries` component provided by Seam allows us to check for an existing `ConversationEntry` associated with the selected `hotel` instance. If a `ConversationEntry` is found, we simply select that entry, which switches to that conversation, just as we saw with the conversation switcher previously. The user is returned to the point in the conversation where he or she left off.

This approach also avoids the requirement to specify the `s:conversationName` component in the **View Hotel** link. As we check for the `ConversationEntry` programmatically, we are assured that the conversation will be resumed appropriately if it is found.

## 9.3.4  Rewriting to User-Friendly URLs

As already mentioned, natural conversations allow you to create URLs that are navigable and meaningful. So far, we saw URLs that are somewhat meaningful, but still lack the desired navigability. By using URL rewriting, we can satisfy both of these requirements.

Seam implements a very simple approach to configurating navigable URLs. First, you need to add the following snippet to your `components.xml` file to enable URL rewriting:

```
<web:rewrite-filter view-mapping="*.seam"/>
```

The `view-mapping` parameter must match the servlet mapping defined for the Faces Servlet in your `web.xml` file. If this parameter is not specified, the rewrite filter will assume the pattern `*.seam`.

Once configured, we can specify how URLs should be rewritten per page in the `pages.xml` file. The Natural Hotel Booking example demonstrates this:

```
<page view-id="/hotels.xhtml">
  <rewrite pattern="/hotels/{hotelId}" />
  ... ...
</page>
```

Note that the `pattern` definition specifies the `hotelId` query parameter we saw previously as part of the URL. The above pattern converts the following URL, `/hotels.seam?hotelId=MarriottCourtyardBuckhead`, to something much more navigable: `/hotels/MarriottCourtyardBuckhead`.

---

**URL Rewriting Can Be Used for Any `GET` Request**

URL rewriting is not specific to natural conversations and can be quite useful for RESTful URLs (see Chapter 15). The above configuration could also be applied to any page in your application that requires a "pretty" URL.

---

# 9.4  Workspace Timeout

We discussed the `conversation-timeout` previously, but now we will revisit the conversation timeout to see how it relates to user experience. At first glance, most developers relate `conversation-timeout` to session timeout where any conversation will simply time out after the configured conversation timeout period (see Section 8.2.3). As you will quickly notice during testing, this is not the case. The conversation timeout is best explained through interaction with a Seam application. Try the following configuration in the `components.xml` of the Seam Hotel Booking example:

```
... ...

<core:manager conversation-timeout="60000" />

... ...
```

Since the `conversation-timeout` is measured in milliseconds, the above configuration sets it to 1 minute. Now, in `web.xml`, set the session timeout to 5 minutes:

```
... ...

<session-config>
  <session-timeout>5</session-timeout>
</session-config>

... ...
```

In the `destroy()` method of the `HotelBookingAction`, add the following line:

```
// ... ...
@Destroy @Remove
public void destroy()
{
   log.info("Destroying HotelBookingAction...");
}
// ... ...
```

This will log a message when the conversation ends and the `HotelBookingAction` is destroyed. Deploy the `booking` example to your local JBoss instance and start up a conversation. This can be accomplished by logging in, navigating to the hotels listing, and selecting a hotel for booking. At this point, wait for 1 minute; nothing happens. Now wait 4 more minutes and the expected message is displayed. The conversation timed out along with the session.

Why didn't our conversation time out as configured? This is because the `conversation-timeout` only affects background conversations. The foreground conversation will only time out when the session times out. As we discussed in Section 8.2.3, the foreground conversation is simply the conversation that the user last interacted with; a background conversation is any other conversation in the user's session. Thus, in our previous scenario, the foreground conversation timed out with the session as expected.

Let's try another approach. Perform the same steps as before to go to the booking screen. Now, open a new window and perform the same steps. We now have a foreground conversation and a background conversation in progress. Again, wait 1 minute. Nothing happened. If you wait 4 more minutes, both conversations will time out. So what is going on here—I thought we had a background conversation? We did, but Seam only checks the conversation timeout on each request. Thus, if I interact with the foreground conversation after 1 minute, the background conversation will time out. Try it: Perform the same steps, wait 1 minute, and then click on the window of the foreground conversation—and you will see the log message.

This is a very desirable behavior. Essentially, when a user leaves his or her desk for a period of time and comes back, if the session is still active it would be desirable to maintain the state the user was previously in—the foreground conversation state of the current workspace. All other background conversations or workspaces are left to time out after the configured `conversation-timeout` period, which reduces the overall memory consumption. This enables a developer to worry less about memory usage and cleaning up state and more about developing the business logic. That's why we're here, right?

---

**Why Not Poll for the `conversation-timeout`?**

You may be asking at this point, why doesn't the `conversation-timeout` use polling? As we said, you must interact with the foreground conversation to cause the background conversations to time out after the `conversation-timeout` period.

Imagine that the user had many windows open and leaves his or her desk. Whichever window the user clicks upon return becomes the foreground conversation, timing out any other background conversations. This gives the user a chance to resume the conversation he or she chooses, not the one the developer chooses.

---

You may have noticed in the previous listings that each web page in the conversation can also have a `timeout` value; if a background conversation is idle for too long, the conversation automatically expires. Note that the `page timeout` overrides the global `conversation-timeout` for this page. If a `page timeout` is not specified, the conversation simply times out according to the configured global `conversation-timeout`.

```
<pages>
  ... ...
  <page view-id="/hotel.xhtml" timeout="300000" ... >
    ... ...
  </page>
  <page view-id="/book.xhtml" timeout="600000" ... >
    ... ...
  </page>
  <page view-id="/confirm.xhtml" timeout="600000" ... >
    ... ...
  </page>
</pages>
```

In the configuration shown in the previous listing, the timeout for `hotel.xhtml` is 5 minutes, while the timeout for `book.xhtml` and `confirm.xhtml` is 10 minutes. This seems reasonable, as the user may view multiple hotels prior to making a decision to book, which would quickly become background conversations. We can time out the conversations associated with simply viewing the hotel much more quickly than the booking conversation, as the user is more likely to resume a conversation in the process of booking.

# 9.5  Desktop Features in a Stateless Web

Workspaces and conversations are key concepts in Seam, setting Seam apart from previous generations of stateless web frameworks. It's easy to develop multiworkspace web applications using the rich set of Seam annotations and UI tags. However, web pages in a Seam conversation are typically not bookmarkable because they are tied together by HTTP POST requests with a lot of hidden field data. In the next chapter, we will discuss how to build bookmarkable RESTful URLs into your Seam application.

# 10

Nested Conversations

In previous chapters we have discussed a number of the features provided by the Seam conversation model. Long-running conversations provide a great mechanism for maintaining consistency of state in an application. Unfortunately, simply beginning and ending a long-running conversation is not always enough. In certain situations, multi-window operation and using the **Back** button can still result in inconsistencies between what the user sees and what the reality of the application's state is.

Although we've managed to segregate state within the HTTP session, there may be scenarios where the simple conversation model results in the same issues we faced with the HTTP session. This chapter will discuss the need for nested conversations through another variation of the Seam Hotel Booking example, the Nested Hotel Booking example. The nestedbooking project can be found in the book's source code bundle. The Nested Hotel Booking example has the same directory setup as the Hello World and Natural Hotel Booking examples in the previous chapters (see Appendix B for the application template).

## 10.1  Why Are Nested Conversations Needed?

In the booking example we discussed in Chapters 8 and 9, we might add a new requirement. Suppose a user can not only book hotels but, when booking a hotel, certain rooms may be available depending on the booking dates selected. In addition, the hotels would like us to provide in-depth descriptions of the rooms to entice users to upgrade their

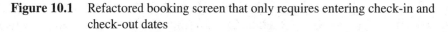

**Figure 10.1**  Refactored booking screen that only requires entering check-in and
check-out dates

room preferences. This would require inserting additional screens in our booking wizard.
Selecting a hotel for booking is shown in Figure 10.1.

The **Select Room** button then sends the user to a list of available rooms, as shown in
Figure 10.2.

The user can select any available room which will now appear as part of the booking
package. Suppose the user opens another window with the room selection screen. In
that screen, the user selects the **Wonderful Room** and proceeds to the confirmation
screen. In the other window, the user decides to see what it would be like to live the
high life, selects the **Fantastic Suite** for booking, and again proceeds to confirmation.
After reviewing the total cost, the user remembers that his or her credit card is near its
limit! The user then returns to the window showing **Wonderful Room** and selects
**Confirm**. Sounds familiar?

Being within a long-running conversation does not protect us from multiwindow operation within that conversation. Just as with the HTTP session, if a conversation variable
changes, that change affects all windows operating within the same conversation context.
As a result, the user may be charged for a room upgrade that was not intended, leading
to some serious credit card fees due to exceeding the credit limit and a nasty phone call
to customer service.

**Nesting conversations**

Nested conversations allow the application to capture a consistent continuable state at various points in a user interaction, thus insuring truly correct behavior in the face of backbuttoning and workspace management.

**How Seam manages continuable state**

Seam provides a container for context state for each nested conversation. Any contextual variable in the outer conversations context will not be overwritten by a new value, the value will simply be stored in the new context container. This allows the previous value to be retrieved should the outer conversation continue.

**Room Preference**

Rooms available for the dates selected: Sep 30, 2007 –Oct 1, 2007

| Name | Description | Per Night | Action |
|------|-------------|-----------|--------|
| Wonderful Room | One king bed. Desk. Cable/satellite TV with pay movies and DVD player. CD player. Coffee/tea maker and minibar. Hair dryer. Iron/ironing board. In-room safe. Complimentary newspaper. | $450.00 | Select |
| Spectacular Room | One king bed. Desk. Cable/satellite TV with pay movies and DVD player. CD player. Coffee/tea maker and minibar. Hair dryer. Iron/ironing board. In-room safe. Complimentary newspaper. | $600.00 | Select |
| Fantastic Suite | One king bed. Desk. Cable/satellite TV with pay movies and DVD player. CD player. Coffee/tea maker and minibar. Hair dryer. Iron/ironing board. In-room safe. Complimentary newspaper. | $1,000.00 | Select |

Revise Dates

**Workspaces**

| Room Preference: W Hotel [current] | 02:47 –02:48 |
|---|---|

**Figure 10.2**    Additional room selection screen allowing the user to select a room for booking

# 10.2  Continuing the Conversation

Seam's conversation model provides a simplified approach to continuations. If you are familiar with the concept of a continuation server, you are aware of the capabilities they provide, including seamless **Back** button operation and automatic state management. A user session has many continuations, which are simply snapshots of state during execution and can be reverted to at any time. If you are not familiar with this concept, do not worry—Seam makes it easy.

The simple conversation model we discussed before is only part of the equation. In Seam, you also have the ability to nest conversations. A conversation is simply a state container, as we saw in Chapter 8. Each booking occurs in its own conversation. As we saw before, based on the conversation ID, or `cid` for short, the appropriate hotel and booking will be injected each time the `HotelBookingAction` is accessed.

## 10.2.1  Understanding the Nested Conversation Context

Nesting a conversation provides a state container that is stacked on top of the state container of the original, or parent, conversation. You can view this as a concept similar to the relationship between a conversation and the HTTP session. Any objects changed in the nested conversation's state container will not affect the objects accessible in the parent conversation's state container.

This allows each nested conversation to maintain its own unique state, as shown in Figure 10.3. As noted in previous chapters, when Seam performs a lookup of the `roomSelection` object, it looks at the current conversation determined by the `cid`. Thus, the appropriate `roomSelection` is injected based on the user's conversation context. In addition, the appropriate hotel and booking instances will also be injected, based on the outer conversation. Let us see how this impacts our interaction scenario.

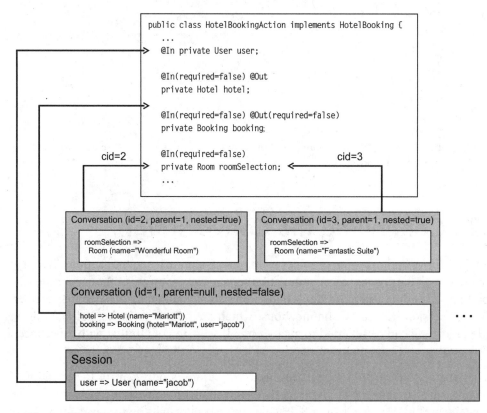

**Figure 10.3**   A conversation with two nested conversations. Each nested conversation has its own unique state as well as access to the parent conversation's state.

In the previous example, when the user reaches the **Book Hotel** screen, the application is operating within a long-running conversation. A click on the **Select Room** button shows the list of available rooms. Once a room is selected, a conversation is nested. Thus, regardless of whether the user opens multiple windows, the state is unique for each room selection. The appropriate nested conversation is restored unaffected by a `roomSelection` made in any other nested conversation.

Note that if Seam does not find the requested object in the nested conversation, it will seek out the object in the parent conversation, as shown in Figure 10.3 with the `hotel` and `booking` instances. Since Seam cannot find these objects in the nested conversation state container, it will traverse the `conversationStack`, which will be discussed further in Section 10.3, to retrieve the object instances. Thus, both conversations, `cid=2` and `cid=3`, share the `hotel` and `booking` instances as they are nested within the same parent conversation. If these objects are not found in the `conversationStack`, Seam will traverse the remaining contextual scopes as usual.

---

**The "Read-Only" Parent Conversation Context**

The parent conversation's context is *read-only* within a nested conversation, but because objects are obtained by reference, changes to the objects themselves will be reflected in the outer context. This means that if in the previous example we outject an object in the nested conversation named `hotel`, this object would only be accessible in the nested conversation. The `hotel` reference in the parent conversation remains the same.

As Seam looks in the current conversation context for a value before looking in the parent, the new reference will always be applicable in the context of the nested conversation or any of its children. However, because context variables are obtained by reference, changes to the state of the object itself will impact the parent conversation. Thus, changing the internal state of parent conversation variables within a nested conversation is not recommended as the parent and all nested conversations will be impacted.

---

Now that we know how the nested conversation context works, let's look at how nested conversations can be managed in practice.

## 10.2.2 Nesting Conversations

We have seen what nested conversations provide and discussed the semantics of a nested conversation context, but how difficult can it be to achieve this magic? The following listing contains the `RoomPreferenceAction` which allows the user to select a `Room` in the `rooms.xhtml` view:

```
@Stateful
@Name("roomPreference")
@Restrict("#{identity.loggedIn}")
public class RoomPreferenceAction implements RoomPreference
{
  @Logger private Log log;

  @In private Hotel hotel;

  @In private Booking booking;

  @DataModel(value="availableRooms")
  private List<Room> availableRooms;

  @DataModelSelection(value="availableRooms")
  private Room roomSelection;

  @In(required=false, value="roomSelection")
  @Out(required=false, value="roomSelection")
  private Room room;

  @Factory("availableRooms")
  public void loadAvailableRooms()
  {
    this.availableRooms =
      this.hotel.getAvailableRooms(
        booking.getCheckinDate(), booking.getCheckoutDate());

    log.info("Retrieved #0 available rooms", availableRooms.size());
  }

  public BigDecimal getExpectedPrice()
  {
    log.info("Retrieving price for room #0", room.getName());

    return booking.getTotal(room);
  }

  @Begin(nested=true)
  public String selectPreference()
  {
    log.info("Room selected");

    this.room = this.roomSelection;

    return "payment";
  }

  public String requestConfirmation()
  {
    // All validations are handled through the s:validateAll,
    // so checks are already performed.
    log.info("Request confirmation from user");

    return "confirm";
  }
```

```
@End(beforeRedirect=true)
public String cancel()
{
  log.info("ending conversation");

  return "cancel";
}

@Destroy @Remove
public void destroy() {}
}
```

As you can see, when the user selects a room, we nest a conversation. By using Seam's
`@DataModel` and `@DataModelSelection`, which are discussed in Chapter 13, we are
able to simply outject the `room` back to the nested conversation context once it is selected.
The user is then sent to the payment screen through a navigation rule defined in
`pages.xml`. When rendering the payment screen, the new `roomSelection` instance is
retrieved from the nested conversation context. Similarly, when the confirmation screen
is displayed, the `roomSelection` will be retrieved from the context, as shown in
Figure 10.4.

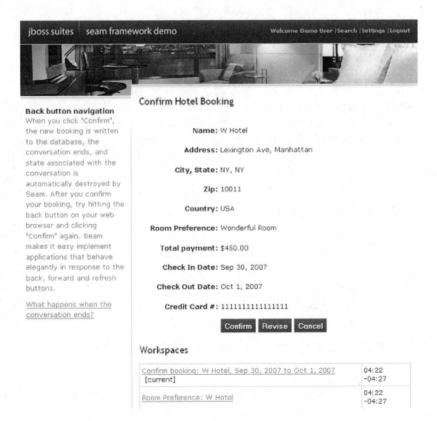

**Figure 10.4** The `roomSelection` being displayed on the `payment.xhtml view-id`

---

**Bijection with Nested Conversations**

Note that we only inject the `hotel` and `booking` values from the conversation context. Outjection is not necessary here, as these attributes are already present in the parent conversation context. This makes them available for injection in the nested conversation.

---

If the user confirms booking, the correct `roomSelection` will always be found for the current conversation regardless of multiwindow operation.

You may then ask, what happens once the user has confirmed the booking for the `hotel` and `roomSelection`? What if the user then goes back to the **Wonderful Room** and confirms? We end the entire conversation stack when the user confirms a booking. As before, Seam recognizes that the conversation has ended and redirects the user to the `no-conversation-view-id`, as shown in the following listing. The conversation stack is described in the next section.

```
<pages no-conversation-view-id="/main.xhtml"
  login-view-id="/home.xhtml" />
... ...
```

# 10.3   The Conversation Stack

When a nested conversation is started, the semantics are essentially the same as beginning a normal long-running conversation except that a nested conversation will be pushed onto the conversation stack. As mentioned previously, nested conversations have access to their outer conversation's state, but setting any variables in a nested conversation's state container will not impact the parent conversation. In addition, other nested conversations can exist concurrently, stacked on the same outer conversation, allowing independent state for each.

The conversation stack is essentially what you would expect—a stack of conversations. The top of the stack is the current conversation. If the conversation is nested, its parent conversation would be the next element in the stack, and so on until the root conversation is reached. The root conversation is the conversation where the nesting began; it has no parent conversation. Let's look at the details of managing the conversation stack.

## 10.3.1   Managing the Conversation Stack

Nesting a conversation can be accomplished in the same way as beginning a general long-running conversation which we discussed in Chapter 8. As you saw in our previous listing, nesting simply requires the addition of the `nested` attribute.

- With the *annotation approach*, a nested conversation starts if the method return type is `void` or the method does not return `null`. Simply annotate a method with `@Begin(nested=true)`.

- With the *navigation approach*, specified in `pages.xml`, a nested conversation starts when a `view-id` is accessed. Simply specify `<begin-conversation nested="true"/>` in your page definition.

- With the *view approach*, a nested conversation starts when a link is selected. Specify `propagation="nest"` inside your `<s:link>` tag.

Once started, a nested conversation is pushed onto the `conversationStack`. In our Nested Hotel Booking example, execution of the `RoomPreferenceAction.selectPreference()` action would result in a nested conversation.

```
@Stateful
@Name("roomPreference")
@Restrict("#{identity.loggedIn}")
public class RoomPreferenceAction implements RoomPreference
{
  // ... ...

  @Begin(nested=true)
  public String selectPreference()
  {
    // Seam takes care of everything for us here.  We don't have
    // to do anything other than send the appropriate outcome to
    // forward to the payment screen.
    log.info("Room selected");

    return "payment";
  }

  // ... ...

  @End(beforeRedirect=true)
  public String cancel()
  {
    log.info("ending conversation");

    return "cancel";
  }

  // ... ...
}
```

The stack would consist of the parent long-running conversation and its nested conversation, as we saw in Figure 10.3. Figure 10.3 also shows a concurrent nested conversation that would result from the user **Back**-buttoning to the `rooms.xhtml` page and selecting a different room. If an @End is encountered, as in `RoomPreferenceAction.cancel()`, the `conversationStack` is popped, meaning that the outer conversation will be resumed effectively reverting the state back to the outer conversation's state container.

The current `conversationStack` is determined based on the current long-running conversation. Figure 10.5 shows two concurrent `conversationStacks` for conversations `cid=3` and `cid=4`. If the current conversation is `cid=4`, encountering an `@End` would pop `cid=4` off of the stack and destroy the conversation. Our current conversation would now be `cid=2` and all state for `cid=4` would now be destroyed. Figure 10.6 shows the result of popping the `conversationStack`.

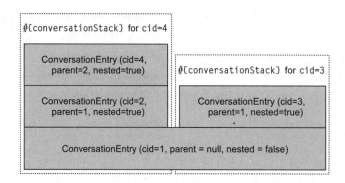

**Figure 10.5**   The `conversationStack` components for two concurrent conversation stacks (`cid=3` and `cid=4`)

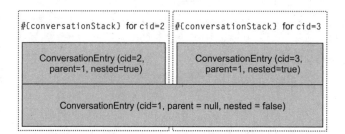

**Figure 10.6**   The `conversationStack` components after popping the `conversationStack` for `cid=4`

When a conversation is nested, the conversation that it is nested within is called its parent conversation. A conversation that has no parent is the root conversation. Thus, in our previous figures, the parent of conversation `cid=4` is `cid=2`. Both conversations `cid=2` and `cid=3` have the same parent, `cid=1`. The `cid=1` has no parent, therefore it is the root conversation that all other conversations have been nested within.

Note that by ending a conversation you end all conversations up the `conversationStack` from it. You may remember that the same behavior applies to the relationship between the HTTP session and conversations. In our figure, if we were to end the conversation `cid=2`, this would result in both `cid=2` and `cid=4` being destroyed and `cid=1` being resumed. In addition, we can end the root, `cid=1`, and thereby end all nested conversations (which will be discussed further shortly).

The Nested Hotel Booking example demonstrates popping the conversation stack as well as ending the root conversation. If the user is on the `payment.xhtml` view and selects **Revise Room**, the action `roomUpgrade.cancel()` is annotated with `@End(beforeRedirect=true)`, as shown previously in the `RoomPreferenceAction`. This ends the nested conversation by popping it off the `conversationStack`, clearing all of the nested conversation's state, and effectively reverting back to the outer conversation. Specifying `beforeRedirect=true` ensures that when the next view is rendered, the outer conversation state will be effective.

When the user confirms the booking, we must end the entire `conversationStack`. Once the booking is complete, any state associated with the booking is no longer needed. Simply by ending the root conversation, we can clear out all conversation state. This can be accomplished declaratively by specifying `@End(root=true)`:

```
// ... ...

@End(root=true)
public void confirm()
{
  // On confirmation, we set the room preference in the booking.
  // The room preference will be injected based on the nested
  // conversation we are in.
  booking.setRoomPreference(roomSelection);

  em.persist(booking);
  facesMessages.add("Thank you, #{user.name}, your " +
    "confirmation number for #{hotel.name} is #{booking.id}");
  log.info("New booking: #{booking.id} for #{user.username}");
  events.raiseTransactionSuccessEvent("bookingConfirmed");
}

// ... ...
```

When the user submits the booking, the root conversation is ended, which effectively ends the entire `conversationStack`. You can also end the `conversationStack` using the navigation approach in `pages.xml`:

```
<page view-id="/confirm.xhtml" ... ...>
  <description>Confirm: #{booking.description}</description>

  <navigation>
    <rule if-outcome="confirmed">
      <end-conversation root="true" />
      <redirect view-id="/confirmed.xhtml" />
    </rule>
    ... ...
</page>
```

This is also quite useful for exception handling, as we can easily end the `conversationStack` should an exception occur:

```
<exception class="javax.persistence.PersistenceException">
  <end-conversation root="true" />
  <redirect view-id="/generalError.xhtml">
    <message>Database access failed</message>
  </redirect>
</exception>
```

In this case, if the conversationStack only contains the current conversation, then the current conversation will be ended. This makes the directive safe to use in the case of exceptions.

## 10.3.2  Displaying Breadcrumbs

The conversationStack can be retrieved in EL through the #{conversationStack} expression. The conversationStack contains a list of ConversationEntry instances, just as we saw with the conversationList component in Section 9.2.1. This is especially useful for displaying breadcrumbs.

As a conversation is nested for sub-conversation states, it may make sense to display a "breadcrumb trail" of conversations. In our Nested Hotel Booking example, it may be nice to see that we have selected a hotel and a room and are now in the process of confirming our booking. We could easily accomplish this by using the following listing in our included conversation.xhtml:

```
<ui:repeat value="#{conversationStack}" var="entry">
  <h:outputText value="  |  "/>
  <h:commandLink value="#{entry.description}" action="#{entry.select}"/>
</ui:repeat>
```

As before, the description of the ConversationEntry is set in pages.xml (see Section 9.2.1).

## 10.3.3  Nested Conversation Timeout

At this point you may be wondering how nested conversations impact conversation timeout. This is actually quite simple. The conversationStack associated with the current foreground conversation is not susceptible to the conversation-timeout. Thus, if our foreground conversation is a nested conversation, each ConversationEntry in its conversationStack is in the foreground as well. If we resume a conversation down the stack, that is, a parent conversation, then the nested conversation becomes a background conversation. To review the difference between foreground and background conversations, see Sections 8.2.3 and 9.4.

If you look back at Figure 10.5, you will note that if cid=4 is the foreground conversation, cid=2 and cid=1 are also in the foreground. On the other hand, cid=3 is a background conversation. Even though it shares a common parent with the foreground conversation, it is not part of the current `conversationStack`. Similarly, if `cid=2` is the foreground conversation, then `cid=1` is also in the foreground, whereas `cid=3` and `cid=4` are background conversations as they are not part of the current `conversationStack`.

# 10.4 Fine-Grained State Management

Seam offers a very attractive approach to state management through its simple conversation model, but nested conversations provide the flexibility necessary to address complicated state management scenarios. With nested conversations, state management can not only be segregated within the HTTP session, but can be segregated further, if required by your application, to achieve fine-grained state management.

# 11

## Transactions and Persistence

**T**ransactions are an essential feature for database-driven web applications. In each conversation, we typically need to update multiple database tables. If an error occurs in the database operation (e.g., a database server crashes), the application needs to inform the user, and all the updates this conversation has written into the database must be rolled back to avoid partially updated (i.e., corrupted) records. In other words, all database updates in a conversation must happen inside an atomic operation. Transactions enable you to do exactly that.

In a Seam application, we typically assemble and modify database entity objects throughout a conversation. At the end of the conversation, we commit all those entity objects into the database. For instance, in the Natural Hotel Booking example (the booking project in the source code bundle), the HotelBookingAction.confirm() method at the end of the conversation (i.e., the method with the @End annotation) uses a single transaction to save the booking object in the database and then deduct the hotel room inventory from the database.

```
public class HotelBookingAction implements HotelBooking, Serializable {
  @End
  public String confirm() throws InventoryException {
    if (booking==null || hotel==null)
      return "main";
    em.persist(booking);
    hotel.reduceInventory();
    if (bookingList!=null)
      bookingList.refresh();
      return "confirmed";
  }
  // ... ...
}
```

If anything goes wrong, the entire transaction fails and the database remains unchanged. The user then receives an error message instead of a confirmation number.

Seam provides the features necessary to achieve this transactional behavior even in the context of long-running conversations which include user's think time. Throughout this chapter, we will discuss how to achieve atomic conversations through the core Seam features: Seam-managed transactions and Seam-managed persistence contexts.

# 11.1  Seam-Managed Transactions

Transactions are enabled by default for all EJB3 session bean methods in an EJB3 application, so you don't need to do anything special to put the `confirm()` method under a transaction. The transaction manager is started when an event handler thread starts (e.g., when the `confirm()` method is invoked). The transaction manager commits all the updates to the database at the end of the thread. Since the transaction manager tracks the thread, it manages the event handler method and all the nested method calls from inside the event handler.

If any database operation in the `confirm()` method fails and throws a `RuntimeException`, the transaction manager rolls back all database operations. For instance, if the hotel inventory reduction operation fails due to a database connection error, the booking save operation, which already executed, would be canceled as well. The database is returned to the state before the conversation, and Seam displays an error message instead of the confirmation number (see Figure 11.1). We discuss how to display a custom error page for the `RuntimeException` in Section 17.4; if you do not set up the custom error page, the server just displays the error stack trace in JBoss's standard error page.

The stack trace displayed in Figure 11.1 does not show the root cause of `RuntimeException` because the root exception has been wrapped and rethrown from the JSF and Seam runtime. Unfortunately, our generic error page has made debugging harder, as you now have to look into the server log file to see the complete stack trace of the exception. Custom error pages, specifically tailored to each exception, can improve the application usability in this case (Section 17.4).

While standard EJB container-managed transactions are valuable, they have a few key disadvantages.

- It would be desirable to scope all write operations in a request to a single transaction even among loosely coupled components. Many components could potentially be invoked independently from the web layer.

- Applications operating outside of an EJB environment cannot take advantage of EJB container-managed transactions. It would be great to achieve the benefits of EJB container-managed transactions in a POJO environment.

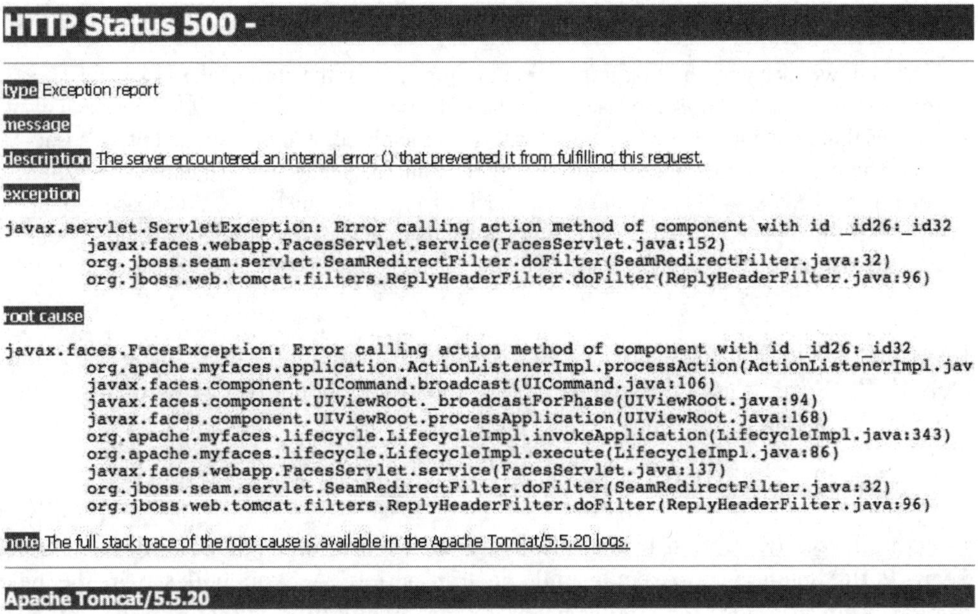

HTTP Status 500 -

**type** Exception report

**message**

**description** The server encountered an internal error () that prevented it from fulfilling this request.

**exception**

```
javax.servlet.ServletException: Error calling action method of component with id _id26:_id32
        javax.faces.webapp.FacesServlet.service(FacesServlet.java:152)
        org.jboss.seam.servlet.SeamRedirectFilter.doFilter(SeamRedirectFilter.java:32)
        org.jboss.web.tomcat.filters.ReplyHeaderFilter.doFilter(ReplyHeaderFilter.java:96)
```

**root cause**

```
javax.faces.FacesException: Error calling action method of component with id _id26:_id32
        org.apache.myfaces.application.ActionListenerImpl.processAction(ActionListenerImpl.jav
        javax.faces.component.UICommand.broadcast(UICommand.java:106)
        javax.faces.component.UIViewRoot._broadcastForPhase(UIViewRoot.java:94)
        javax.faces.component.UIViewRoot.processApplication(UIViewRoot.java:168)
        org.apache.myfaces.lifecycle.LifecycleImpl.invokeApplication(LifecycleImpl.java:343)
        org.apache.myfaces.lifecycle.LifecycleImpl.execute(LifecycleImpl.java:86)
        javax.faces.webapp.FacesServlet.service(FacesServlet.java:137)
        org.jboss.seam.servlet.SeamRedirectFilter.doFilter(SeamRedirectFilter.java:32)
        org.jboss.web.tomcat.filters.ReplyHeaderFilter.doFilter(ReplyHeaderFilter.java:96)
```

**note** The full stack trace of the root cause is available in the Apache Tomcat/5.5.20 logs.

Apache Tomcat/5.5.20

**Figure 11.1** The `RuntimeException` error page

Seam addresses both these issues through Seam-managed transactions. When used with JSF, the Seam transaction manager runs two transactions for each web request/response cycle. The first transaction spans from the start of the `RESTORE_VIEW` phase to the end of the `INVOKE_APPLICATION` phase. The second transaction is started prior to the `RENDER_RESPONSE`.

Since write operations, in practice, should be scoped to the `INVOKE_APPLICATION` phase, this allows you to group database write operations into a single atomic transaction. Should a write operation fail, regardless of the component, the entire transaction fails ensuring atomicity of the request. In addition, prior to rendering the response, you will know if an issue occurred during execution of the transaction. The user can then be notified appropriately about the issue, be it a database connection issue, a constraint violation, or an exception that results in a rollback (which will be discussed further in Section 11.1.2).

The second transaction ensures that database operations in the `RENDER_RESPONSE` phase are executed within a transaction. Read operations are common in this phase; lazy associations may be fetched for display, or `@Factory` methods could be triggered by the view.

**The Scope of the First Transaction**

You may wonder why the first transaction is scoped from the start of the RESTORE_VIEW to the INVOKE_APPLICATION phase rather than just the INVOKE_APPLICATION phase. This ensures that all database operations, regardless of the phase, will be included in a transaction. There are a number of scenarios that could result in execution of a database operation prior to the INVOKE_APPLICATION phase, such as @Factory methods, a database lookup while setting a page parameter, etc. This allows us to ensure that all database operations execute within the context of a transaction.

If you are using EJBs, to ensure that your session bean methods are managed appropriately by the Seam transaction manager, you must include the following configuration in your components.xml file:

```
<transaction:ejb-transaction />
```

In addition to EJB session beans, the Seam transaction manager also allows simple Seam POJO methods to execute under a transaction. As you will see in the next section, Seam provides the similar behavior for your POJOs as that provided by EJB container-managed transactions.

**Seam-Managed Transactions Are Enabled by Default**

Seam 2 differs from previous versions of Seam in that Seam-managed transactions are now enabled by default. While this reduces boilerplate configuration for the general Seam usage, you can disable this behavior by placing the following in your components.xml:

```
<core:init transaction-management-enabled="false"/>

<transaction:no-transaction />
```

# 11.1.1  Transactional Attributes

In EJB3 session beans, you can set the transaction attribute for any method using the @TransactionAttribute annotation. For instance, you can start a new transaction in the middle of a call stack or exclude any particular method from the current transaction. Refer to the EJB3 documentation for more. Transaction attributes can also be configured at the component level by placing the annotation at the top of the class.

In EJB3, by default all session bean methods are REQUIRED to participate in a transaction. REQUIRED indicates that if the calling client is associated with a transaction, your bean will participate in that transaction. If the calling client is not associated with a transaction, the container will begin a new transaction and attempt to commit that transaction on completion of method execution.

Methods of a Seam POJO are also managed by the Seam transaction manager by default (see Chapter 4). POJO components have `@Transactional(SUPPORTS)` behavior by default, but this behavior can be customized through use of the `@Transactional` annotation. Note that, as the Seam transaction manager scopes two transactions across a request/response cycle, the default setting ensures that your POJOs will execute in a transaction when invoked. As with EJBs, the `@Transactional` annotation can be used at the class or method level to alter transaction attributes. Do not use the `@Transactional` annotation with EJB3 session beans, use the `@TransactionAttribute` annotation instead.

The `@Transactional` annotation specifies transaction types similar to those provided by EJBs through the `TransactionPropagationType` enumeration, listed in Table 11.1.

**Table 11.1** Transactional Propagation Types

| Type | Description |
|------|-------------|
| REQUIRED | The default `TransactionPropagationType` if the `@Transactional` annotation is placed on the POJO. As with the EJB3 `REQUIRED` attribute, indicates that if the calling client is associated with a transaction, your POJO will participate in that transaction. If the calling client is not associated with a transaction, the container will begin a new transaction and attempt to commit that transaction on completion of method execution. |
| SUPPORTS | The default `TransactionPropagationType` if the `@Transactional` annotation is *not* placed on a POJO component. This attribute indicates that if the calling client is associated with a transaction, the POJO will participate in that transaction; otherwise, no transaction is started. |
| MANDATORY | Requires a POJO method to be invoked within the context of an active transaction. Throws an `IllegalArgumentException` if not invoked within the context of a transaction. |
| NEVER | Indicates that a POJO method should *never* be invoked within the context of an active transaction. Throws an `IllegalArgumentException` if invoked within the context of a transaction. |

For both EJB and POJO environments, the default transactional behavior provided by Seam is very useful and should suffice for most applications. The default behavior ensures that both EJB's and POJO's methods execute within the context of a transaction and atomicity is ensured in a request even across loosely coupled components. The additional transactional attributes supported by Seam simply provide a finer granularity of control for more complex transactional scenarios regardless of application environment. In the following section we will discuss how to control transactional behavior further by forcing a transaction rollback.

# 11.1.2   Forcing a Transaction Rollback

In a Java application, a `RuntimeException` or an unchecked exception indicates an unexpected runtime error (e.g., a network problem or database crash). By default, the transaction is automatically rolled back only when an unchecked exception is thrown.

However, that is not enough. Transactions are much more useful if we can tell the transaction manager to roll a transaction back when certain conditions occur in the application. Seam provides a simple way to forcefully roll back a transaction while remaining compliant with the EJB3 specification: exceptions.

## 11.1.2.1   Rolling Back Transactions via Checked Exceptions

You can choose to roll back the transaction when a certain checked exception is thrown. For instance, you could throw checked exceptions to indicate a logic error in the application (e.g., the reserved hotel is not available). The trick is to tag the checked exception class with the `@ApplicationException(rollback=true)` annotation. The following is the code for the `InventoryException`, which is used to indicate that the hotel has no rooms available:

```
@ApplicationException(rollback=true)
public class InventoryException extends Exception {
  public InventoryException () { }
}
```

The `Hotel.reduceInventory()` method could throw this exception:

```
@Entity
@Name("hotel")
public class Hotel implements Serializable {
  // ... ...

  public void reduceInventory () throws InventoryException {
    if (inventory > 0) {
      inventory--;
      return;
    } else {
      throw new InventoryException ();
    }
  }
}
```

---

**Inventory Reduction**

In a real-world hotel booking application, we would reduce the hotel room inventory by the booking dates and room type. In this example, we simply reduce the available number of rooms for the booked hotel. That is, of course, oversimplified. But then, the Seam Hotel Booking example is meant only as an example. For instance, we do not even have a daily rate for each hotel and do not calculate a total bill amount at the end of the conversation.

---

When an `InventoryException` is thrown from `Hotel.reduceInventory()` in the `HotelBookingAction.confirm()` method, the booking transaction is rolled back when the method aborts. Seam then displays an error message page to the user. Again, in Section 17.3, we discuss how to display a custom error page for this particular exception.

# 11.2  Atomic Conversation (Web Transaction)

A Seam/EJB3 transaction is tied to a Java thread. It can manage operations only within a method call stack. It flushes all updates to the database at the end of each call stack. This behavior has two problems in a web conversation:

- First, it can be inefficient to make multiple roundtrips to the database in a conversation when all the updates are closely related.

- Second, when a certain operation in the conversation fails, you must manually roll back the already-committed transactions in the conversation to restore the database to its state prior to the conversation.

A much better way is for the application to hold all database updates in memory and flush them all at once at the end of the conversation. If an error occurs in any step in the conversation, the conversation just fails without affecting the database. From the database point of view, the entire conversation either succeeds or fails—i.e., this is an atomic conversation. The atomic conversation behavior is also referred to as a *web transaction*. Seam makes it easy to implement atomic conversations. In the following sections, we discuss how this can be achieved with Seam in both POJO and EJB environments.

## 11.2.1  Managing the Persistence Context

As you have seen in many examples already, it is very simple to load an entity in JPA through an injected `EntityManager` instance. JPA can be used in both Java SE (POJO) and Java EE 5 (EJB) environments, although as you will see, Seam greatly simplifies usage of JPA in both environments. When using Seam in a Java SE (POJO) environment, there is no container to manage the persistence context lifecycle for you. In addition, even if you are using a persistence context in an EJB environment, the rules associated with propagation of the persistence context across components are complex and error-prone. When using a Seam-managed persistence context, these issues can be alleviated.

Using Seam-managed transactions in conjunction with a Seam-managed persistence context (also referred to as an SMPC), we can achieve the goal of atomic conversations. So you may be asking, why are these additional features required when we have already discussed how conversational behavior can be achieved? Essentially, we would like to not only maintain state within our conversation, but also maintain a persistence context tied to that conversation. This allows us to alleviate common issues with stateless architectures, including:

- `LazyInitializationExceptions` when retrieving entity associations. If you have worked with web applications long enough, you are likely familiar with this issue and may have used the *open session in view* pattern to work around the problem. Seam avoids this issue altogether while side-stepping the disadvantages of this pattern.

- Loosely coupled components can easily share the same persistence context and participate in the same transaction. We would certainly want a set of operations for a request to utilize the same context to avoid consistency and isolation issues, essential to achieving ACID (Atomicity, Consistency, Isolation, Durability) transactions. In addition, including all write operations in the same transaction is a way to ensure atomicity.

There are several approaches to the problem, but essentially, to achieve the goal of a web transaction, state must be maintained across requests while still ensuring atomicity. One approach is to maintain a persistence context scoped to an atomic transaction. This approach is common to pre-EJB3/Seam applications. Entities are then loaded by a persistence provider that is initialized for the purpose of a single atomic transaction and is destroyed once the transaction completes. Once the persistence provider is destroyed, entities become detached (i.e., they are no longer managed by a persistence provider).

Detached entities are then updated through the course of the conversation. Once the conversation completes, the entities are merged with a persistence provider, effectively persisting the changes to the entity if the transaction commits successfully. While this approach is simple to achieve, and probably familiar, the main drawback is that if you attempt to lazily load entity associations, you will receive a `LazyInitializationException` because the original persistence provider is no longer available to load the entity associations when they are requested.

Figure 11.2 represents this approach graphically in a simplified manner, using components from the Nested Hotel Booking example. As you can see, the `Hotel` instance is loaded from a persistence provider that is scoped to a single atomic transaction. Once the transaction completes, the persistence provider is destroyed. You will notice that when the next request is processed, the `HotelBookingAction` attempts to invoke `Hotel.getRooms()`, a lazy association. Depending on the ORM implementation, this step may vary, but essentially, through some form of interception, an attempt is made to load the association. Since the persistence provider is no longer available, we obviously have an issue.

This issue has been a common complaint for Hibernate users, and maybe you are grumbling about this experience as you read this. Not to fear, Seam resolves this issue by allowing you to scope a persistence context to the conversation, allowing entities to

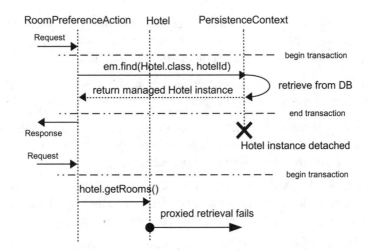

**Figure 11.2**    Loading a `Hotel` instance with a persistence provider scoped to a single atomic transaction

remain managed until the conversation is completed. In addition, Seam ensures that loosely coupled components participate in the same transaction to ensure atomicity as managed entities are updated.

---

**Extended Persistence Contexts in EJB3**

EJB3 addressed the issue of transaction-scoped persistence providers by introducing the extended persistence context that is scoped to the lifetime of a stateful session bean. You will learn more about the extended persistence context in the next section.

---

## 11.2.2  Seam-Managed Persistence Contexts

When JPA is used within an EJB environment, an extended persistence context can be associated with a stateful session bean. An extended persistence context provides a persistence context that lives between requests and is scoped to a stateful component. The Nested Hotel Booking example demonstrates use of an extended persistence context.

```
@Stateful
@Name("hotelBooking")
@Restrict("#{identity.loggedIn}")
public class HotelBookingAction implements HotelBooking
{
  @Logger
  private Log log;

  @PersistenceContext(type=EXTENDED)
  private EntityManager em;
  // ... ...
```

As you can see, the persistence context is created and injected by the container and scoped to the lifecycle of the `HotelBookingAction`. Thus, when the proxied retrieval in Figure 11.2 occurs, the persistence context is still available.

Now our entities will remain managed between requests, which is great. However, the EJB3 approach has several shortcomings:

- What if our application does not operate in an EJB environment? Unfortunately, without the container around to manage the lifecycle of the persistence context, we have to resort to other, less desirable approaches.

- As we mentioned previously, it can be tricky to ensure that the persistence context is shared between loosely coupled components due to the propagation rules defined by EJB3. Refer to the EJB3 specification for more details.

- EJB3 does not include the concept of manual flushing. As you will soon see, manual flushing is critical to achieving atomic conversations when using an extended persistence context.

A Seam-managed persistence context (SMPC) is available for use in both environments and removes these issues altogether. An SMPC is initialized and maintained by Seam throughout the course of a long-running conversation. Your conversational components are each injected with the same SMPC instance, and SMPCs are usable in a non-EJB environment.

With all these benefits, you are probably scanning the remainder of the chapter for the code required to achieve this. Not to worry, we cover this in the next section.

## 11.2.2.1  Configuration of a Seam-Managed Persistence Context

A Seam-managed persistence context is quite simple to configure in your `components.xml` file. Using our booking example, we could configure an SMPC as follows:

```
... ...
<persistence:managed-persistence-context name="entityManager"
    auto-create="true"
    persistence-unit-jndi-name="java:/EntityManagerFactories/bookingData"/>
```

You must also configure an `EntityManagerFactory` instance in your `persistence.xml` file for the `bookingData` JNDI name. You can refer to the examples provided with the book or the JPA documentation to achieve this. Once this configuration is complete, you can simply inject a Seam-managed persistence context (i.e., an `EntityManager` injected via `@In`, see Chapter 4) and specify the transactional behavior for a conversation in the `@Begin` annotation. The SMPC defined above can be injected as follows:

```
... ...
@In EntityManager entityManager;
... ...
```

You can also customize the name of the SMPC through the `name` attribute in your `components.xml` configuration. When Seam initializes an instance of the SMPC, it is stored in the current conversation context which ensures that all other conversational components will receive the same instance. In addition, by maintaining this instance in the conversational context, the lifetime of the persistence context is appropriately scoped to the lifetime of the conversation.

## 11.2.2.2 Manually Flushing the Persistence Context

Once we have configured a persistence context scoped to the conversation, the final step is configuring manual flushing. JPA does not define the concept of manual flushing, but instead provides an approach described in Section 11.2.3. By default, a JPA persistence context is configured for `AUTO` commit mode. This means that each time a transactional method is executed, any updates to an entity during execution will be persisted once the transaction is successfully committed. This is an issue, since we only want to commit entity changes once the conversation completes. We can achieve this by manually flushing the persistence context.

Setting the `flushMode` attribute to `MANUAL` stops the transaction manager from flushing any updates to the database at the end of each transaction. The database updates are cached in the `EntityManager` throughout the entire conversation. Then, in the `@End` method, you call `EntityManager.flush()` to send the updates to the database all at once.

One approach to achieve this when using an EJB container with Hibernate is to specify a `@PersistenceProperty` in your `@PersistenceContext` definition:

```
@Stateful
@Name("hotelBooking")
@Restrict("#{identity.loggedIn}")
public class HotelBookingAction implements HotelBooking
{
  @PersistenceContext(
    type = PersistenceContext.EXTENDED,
    properties = @PersistenceProperty(
      name="org.hibernate.flushMode", value="MANUAL")
  )
  private EntityManager em;

  @Begin(join=true)
  public String find() {
    // ... ...
  }

  // ... ...
```

While this approach is attractive due to its declarative nature, it still suffers from two disadvantages: An EJB environment is required, and it does not achieve simple persistence context propagation. Seam provides an approach that is usable in both EJB and POJO environments while keeping our persistence context scoped to the conversation. Note that this approach requires Hibernate to be the underlying ORM provider. The following is an example Seam POJO to show how this is done:

```java
public class HotelBookingPojo implements Serializable {
  // ... ...
  @In private EntityManager em;

  @Begin(join=true, flushMode=MANUAL)
  public String find() {
    // ... ...
  }

  public String bookHotel() throws InventoryException {
    // ... ...
    hotel.reduceInventory ();
  }

  @End
  public String confirm() {
    // ... ...
    em.persist(booking);
    em.flush();
  }
}
```

As you would expect, this is also achievable via `pages.xml`. The following code snippet demonstrates this approach:

```xml
<page view-id="/main.xhtml" ... >
  ... ...
  <navigation>
    <rule if-outcome="edit">
      <begin-conversation flush-mode="manual" />
      <redirect view-id="/editBooking.xhtml" />
    </rule>
  </navigation>
</page>
```

Making changes to persisted entities becomes a breeze. For example, suppose a user wants to modify a previously submitted booking. This could be accomplished as follows:

```java
public class BookingEditorAction implements BookingEditor {
  // ... ...
  @In EntityManager entityManager;
  // ... ...

  @Begin(flushMode=MANUAL)
  public void retrieve() {
    booking = em.find(Booking.class, selectedBookingId);
  }
```

```
// Actions to make modifications to booking
// ... ...

@End
public submit() {
  em.flush();
}

}
```

As you can see, we never call the `merge()` operation. By simply invoking the `flush()` operation, any changes made to the `booking` during the course of the conversation are automatically persisted. Should the user abandon the conversation, or if an issue occurs during interaction, the conversation simply ends or times out (see Section 8.2.3). The persistence context is destroyed along with the conversation, as it is scoped to the conversation, thereby clearing the changes from memory.

---

**Default `flushMode` Configuration**

Seam provides the ability to specify `MANUAL` as the default `flushMode` configuration. This reduces what is generally boilerplate configuration in most Seam applications. Simply place the following in your `components.xml` definition:

```
<core:manager default-flush-mode="MANUAL" />
```

Now, each time a conversation is started, the `flushMode` is set to `MANUAL`.

---

## 11.2.2.3 Concurrency Control

A conversation includes the user's think time and may encompass a relatively long period of time. It is therefore entirely possible that another user could load the same entities and make changes to them before the conversation completes. Since changes are not committed until the end of the conversation, it is possible for a conflict to occur. This conflict could result in loss of data since an `UPDATE` from the current conversation may include stale data. Using ORM features such as `dynamicUpdate` reduces this risk, but does not eliminate it. How can we resolve this issue? JPA includes an optimistic locking scheme that allows you to address this scenario.

Optimistic locking achieves concurrency control by being optimistic—that is, assuming that conflicts occur rarely. Optimistic locking allows you to either ensure that the first commit wins or, using a more sophisticated strategy, provide the user a chance to merge conflicting changes. If you include a `version` attribute in your `@Entity`, JPA will automatically increment this version each time an update is made. Thus, JPA can easily determine whether the version number has changed since the object was loaded. The following code shows a `version` attribute added to the `Booking` class:

```
@Entity
@Name("booking")
public class Booking implements Serializable
{
  @Version
  @Column(name="OBJ_VERSION")
  private int version;
  // ... ...
}
```

With a `version` attribute, if a version conflict occurs, the `EntityManager` throws a `javax.persistence.OptimisticLockException`. You can use this exception to send a message to the user through the exception handling provided by Seam, as described in Section 17.4. A more sophisticated approach could catch the exception and redisplay the changes to the user with the conflicts noted.

---

**Optimistic Locking with Legacy Schemas**

You may notice that the JPA approach requires an additional column. While this is entirely reasonable for a new schema, this is often not possible when working with legacy schemas. ORM providers, such as Hibernate, support extensions to achieve optimistic locking with legacy schemas.

---

## 11.2.3  One Transaction per Conversation

Another alternative is to disable the transaction manager on all methods except for the `@End` method. Since this approach requires method-level transaction demarcation, it can be used only on EJB3 session bean components with an EJB3-managed `EntityManager` (i.e., an `EntityManager` injected via `@PersistenceContext`).

This method is not as outrageous as it might sound. The transaction manager is not flushing anything to the database before the end of the conversation, so there is nothing to "roll back" if an error occurs. In the `@End` method, the data is automatically flushed to the database in a properly managed transaction. This is done by declaring all non-transactional methods in a conversation with the `@TransactionAttribute` annotation. Consider this example:

```
public class HotelBookingAction implements HotelBooking, Serializable {

  // ... ...

  @PersistenceContext (type=EXTENDED)
  private EntityManager em;

  @Begin(join=true)
  @TransactionAttribute(TransactionAttributeType.NOT_SUPPORTED)
  public String find() {
    // ... ...
  }
```

```
@TransactionAttribute(TransactionAttributeType.NOT_SUPPORTED)
public String bookHotel() throws InventoryException {
   // ... ...
   hotel.reduceInventory ();
}

@End
@TransactionAttribute(TransactionAttributeType.REQUIRED)
public String confirm() {
   // ... ...
   em.persist (booking);
}
}
```

Since this approach uses only standard EJB3 annotations, it works in all EJB3-compliant application servers. While it does not provide the elegance of the SMPC approach, it does provide the advantage of vendor independence.

---

**Autocommit Mode**

Note that this approach relies on the use of autocommit mode for any queries executed in nontransactional methods. This is an inherent risk, as it has a number of potentially error-prone consequences. This should be considered carefully when designing an application using this approach.

---

# Part III

## Integrating Web and Data Components

Seam makes life easier for web developers by acting as the "glue" between the web UI and the backend data model. It provides annotations to streamline the communication between the UI and model, and thereby reduces the amount of redundant information in the application's source code. As a side effect, Seam fixes some of the most nagging problems in JSF development. In this part, we introduce these powerful Seam UI tags, annotations, and ready-to-use components. We show how to enhance the JSF validator infrastructure with Hibernate validators, how to expose data collections directly as JSF data tables, how to build bookmarkable URLs, how to manage custom error pages and debug pages, how to write simple CRUD database applications with ready-made Seam components, and how to secure your applications with Seam Security.

# 12

# Validating Input Data

$\mathbf{A}$ key value proposition of Seam is the unification of EJB3 and JSF component models. Through the unified components, we can use EJB3 entity beans to back data fields in JSF forms, as well as use EJB3 session beans as JSF UI event handlers. But Seam does much more than that. Seam enables us to develop data components that have UI-related "behaviors." For instance, entity beans can have validators that behave like JSF validators.

In this chapter, we cover the Seam-enhanced end-to-end validators that take advantage of Hibernate validator annotations on entity beans as well as Seam UI tags (see Section 3.2). We refactor the stateful Hello World example to show how to use this Seam feature. The new application is in the `integration` directory in the source code bundle. We use the Integration application in the next two chapters as well.

---

**AJAX Validators**

In this chapter, we cover only the "standard" method of validation via form submission. In Part IV, we discuss how to create AJAX-based validators. Still, the Seam annotations and tags discussed in this chapter are highly relevant for AJAX-based validators as well.

---

# 12.1  Form Validation Basics

Form data validation is a task that almost every web application must implement. For example, the Integration application has four data fields on the `hello.xhtml` page, and all of them need to be validated before the `person` object can be saved into the database.

In particular, the name must conform to a "Firstname Lastname" pattern with no non-alphabetical characters, the age must be between 3 and 100, the email address must contain only one @ and other legitimate email characters, and the comment must be shorter than 250 characters. If validation fails, the page redisplays with all the data you already entered and with the problem fields highlighted with images and error messages. Figures 12.1 and 12.2 show what happens when you try to submit a web form with invalid data.

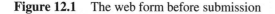

**Figure 12.1**   The web form before submission

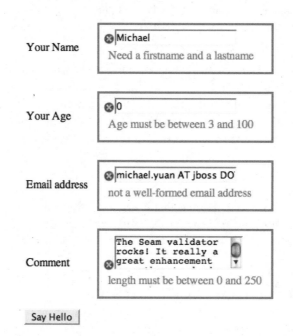

**Figure 12.2**   Validation errors in the web form

**Validating on the Server**

The built-in form validation mechanism in Seam validates the user input data on the server side. You should always validate your data on the server because a malicious user can tamper with any client-side validation mechanisms, such as JavaScripts in the browser.

Form validation sounds easy, but in reality, it can be a nuisance to implement. The web application must manage the validation conditions, handle multiple roundtrips between the browser and the server, and partially update the entry form for alerts. It could easily take several hundred lines of code to implement such validation in previous-generation web frameworks. In Seam, on the other hand, all it takes is a couple of annotations and JSF tags.

**Validation in the Seam Hotel Booking Example**

In the Seam Hotel Booking example application, the register.xhtml form is backed by the User entity bean and is validated by Hibernate validators, so you can use it as an example as well.

# 12.2 Validation Annotations on Entity Beans

Since all JSF forms in Seam are backed by EJB3 entity beans, the first thing we do is annotate the validation constraints directly on the entity bean fields. The following is what the Person entity bean looks like in the example project:

```
public class Person implements Serializable {

  ... ...

  @NotNull
  @Pattern(regex="^[a-zA-Z.-]+ [a-zA-Z.-]+",
    message="Need a firstname and a lastname")

  public String getName() { return name; }
  public void setName(String name) {
    this.name = name;
  }

  // @Min(value=3) @Max(value=100)
  @NotNull
  @Range(min=3, max=100, message="Age must be between 3 and 100")
  public int getAge() { return age; }
  public void setAge(int age) { this.age = age; }
```

```
// @Pattern(regex="^[\w.-]+@[\w.-]+\.[a-zA-Z]{2,4}$")
@NotNull
@Email
public String getEmail() { return email; }
public void setEmail(String email) {
  this.email = email;
}

@Length(max=250)
public String getComment() { return comment; }
public void setComment(String comment) {
  this.comment = comment;
}
}
```

---

**Don't Repeat Yourself**

Seam validator annotations are specified on entity bean properties, but they are enforced all the way from the JSF form to the database fields. You only need to specify the validation conditions once in the entire application. No duplicated configuration is necessary for the presentation and database layers.

---

These validation annotations have self-explanatory names. Each data property can have multiple annotations. Each annotation can take a `message` attribute, which holds the error message to display on the web form if this validation condition fails. If the `message` attribute is missing, a default error message is used. The following is a list of validation annotations supported by Seam out of the box:

- `@Length(max=,min=)` applies to a `String` property to check that the string length is in the specified range.

- `@Max(value=)` applies to a numeric property (or a string representation of a numeric value) to check that the property value is less than the specified `max` value.

- `@Min(value=)` applies to a numeric property (or a string representation of a numeric value) to check that the property value is greater than the specified `min` value.

- `@NotNull` applies to any property to check that the property is not `null`.

- `@Past` applies to a `Date` or `Calendar` property to check that the date is in the past.

- `@Future` applies to a `Date` or `Calendar` property to check that the date is in the future.

- `@Pattern(regex="regexp", flag=)` applies to a `String` property to check that the string matches the regular expression. The `flag` attribute specifies how the matching should be done (e.g., whether to ignore case).

- `@Range(max=,min=)` applies to a numeric property (or a string representation of a numeric value) to check that the property value is inside the given range.

- `@Size(max=,min=)` applies to a `Collection` or `Array` property to check that the number of elements in the property is inside the given range.

- `@Email` applies to a `String` property to check whether the string conforms to the email address format.

- `@Valid` applies to any property. It performs validation recursively on the associated objects. If the object is a `Collection` or an `Array`, the elements are validated recursively. If the object is a `Map`, the value elements are validated recursively.

If you need custom validation conditions in your applications, you can also implement your own validator annotations. Refer to the documentation for more details.

---

**Hibernate Validators**

Seam validator annotations are the same as Hibernate validator annotations. The error messages can easily be internationalized (see the Hibernate annotations documentation for details). The EJB3 entity bean implementation in JBoss is based on the Hibernate framework. Seam links the validators on an entity bean to UI elements on the corresponding JSF form.

---

# 12.3  Triggering the Validation Action

By default, the entity bean validation process is triggered by database operations. The entity bean objects are validated right before they are saved into the backend database. When the `EntityManager` tries to save an invalid entity object, Seam throws a `RuntimeException`, which could lead to an error page or a generic HTTP 500 error (see Chapter 17).

However, for web form validation, we want the validation to happen immediately after the form is submitted, before even the event handler method is invoked or any database operation occurs. If the validation fails, we want to display an error message on the form, with all input data still in the fields, instead of being redirected to a special error page. In this section, we discuss how to trigger Hibernate validator actions by form submission; in Section 12.4, we discuss how to display the error messages.

To trigger validator actions at the time of form submission, you need to insert the Seam `<s:validate/>` tag inside the input data field elements. When the form is submitted, Seam validates tagged data fields using the corresponding validators on the backing entity bean object. If the validation fails, Seam redisplays the form with error messages (see Section 12.4). The following listing shows an example for the `integration` example project:

```
<h:form>
  ... ...

  <h:inputText value="#{person.name}">
    <s:validate/>
  </h:inputText>
  ... ...
  <h:inputText value="#{person.age}">
    <s:validate/>
  </h:inputText>
  ... ...
  <h:inputText value="#{person.email}">
    <s:validate/>
  </h:inputText>
  ... ...
  <h:inputTextarea value="#{person.comment}">
    <s:validate/>
  </h:inputTextarea>

  <h:commandButton type="submit" value="Say Hello"
                   action="#{manager.sayHello}"/>
</h:form>
```

---

**Using Seam UI Tags**

As we discussed in Chapter 3, you need to bundle the `jboss-seam-ui.jar` file in your `app.war` file's `WEB-INF/lib` directory to use the Seam UI tags.

---

The `<s:validate/>` tag enables you to specify each input field to be validated. But in most cases, we want to validate all fields in a form, and in that case the `<s:validate/>` tags may become too verbose. Instead, we can enclose multiple fields in a `<s:validateAll>` tag. For instance, the following code is equivalent to the previous listing:

```
<h:form>
  ... ...

  <s:validateAll>
    <h:inputText value="#{person.name}"/>
    ... ...
    <h:inputText value="#{person.age}"/>
    ... ...
    <h:inputText value="#{person.email}"/>
    ... ...
    <h:inputTextarea value="#{person.comment}"/>
  </s:validateAll>

  <h:commandButton type="submit" value="Say Hello"
                   action="#{manager.sayHello}"/>
</h:form>
```

### Validation in the UI Event Handler

Alternatively, you can omit the Seam validation tags and specify the validation actions on the session bean that handles the form submission button. With this approach, you do not need the `jboss-seam-ui.jar` file (unless you have other Seam UI tags in the application). In most applications, however, we strongly recommend that you use validator tags.

To trigger validation in a Seam session bean, you need two annotations. The `@Valid` annotation validates the `person` object injected from the JSF web form. The `@IfInvalid(outcome=REDISPLAY)` annotation tells the **Say Hello** button's event handler to redisplay the current page with error messages if the injected `person` object is invalid.

```
public class ManagerAction implements Manager {

  @In @Out @Valid
  private Person person;
  ... ...
  @IfInvalid(outcome=REDISPLAY)
  public String sayHello () {
    em.persist (person);
    find ();
    return "fans";
  }
  ... ...
}
```

# 12.4 Displaying Error Messages on the Web Form

As we discussed earlier, when the validation fails, we want to redisplay the form with the input data intact and error messages displayed for each invalid field. You can do this in two ways: with the standard JSF error display or with the enhanced Seam decorator approach. The Seam decorator is slightly more complex but offers much richer UI features.

Since the `<s:validate/>` tag incorporates the Hibernate validator as a JSF validator for the form, we can use the standard JSF mechanism to display the error messages for each invalid input field. This is done by adding a JSF `message` element for each input field. Those `message` elements render the error messages in case of a validation failure. Make sure that the `for` attribute on the `message` tag matches the input field's `id` attribute.

```
<s:validateAll>
  <h:inputText id="name" value="#{person.name}"/>
  <h:message for="name" />

  ... ...

</s:validateAll>
```

However, the problem with the standard JSF validation messages is that they are not very flexible. Although you can assign CSS classes to customize the look of the error message itself, you cannot alter the appearance of the input field that contains the invalid input. For instance, in plain JSF, you cannot add an image in front of the invalid field, and you cannot change the size, font, color, or background of the invalid field. The Seam decorator enables you to do all this, and it gets rid of the id/for nuisance.

To use a Seam decorator, you need to define how the decorator behaves using specially named JSF facets. The beforeInvalidField facet defines what to display in front of the invalid field; afterInvalidField facet defines what to display after the invalid field; the <s:message> tag shows the error message for the input field; and the aroundInvalidField facet defines a span or div element that encloses the invalid field and the error message. You also can use the aroundField facet (not shown in the example here) to decorate the appearance of valid (or initial) input fields.

```
<f:facet name="beforeInvalidField">
  <h:graphicImage styleClass="errorImg" value="error.png"/>
</f:facet>
<f:facet name="afterInvalidField">
  <s:message/>
</f:facet>
<f:facet name="aroundInvalidField">
  <s:span styleClass="error"/>
</f:facet>
```

Then, simply enclose each input field in a pair of <s:decorate> tags. The result is shown in Figure 12.2.

```
... Set up the facets ...

<s:validateAll>
  ... ...

  <s:decorate>
    <h:inputText value="#{person.name}"/>
  </s:decorate>
  ... ...
  <s:decorate>
    <h:inputText value="#{person.age}"/>
  </s:decorate>
  ... ...
  <s:decorate>
    <h:inputText value="#{person.email}"/>
  </s:decorate>
  ... ...
  <s:decorate>
    <h:inputTextarea id="comment" value="#{person.comment}"/>
  </s:decorate>

  ... ...
</s:validateAll>
```

There is no more messing around with the `id` and `for` attributes as we did with the JSF message tags, because the `<s:message>` tag "knows" which input field it is associated with through the parent `<s:decorate>` tag.

You can also customize the Seam decorators on a per-input-field basis. For instance, if the `name` input field needs a different highlight, we can customize it as follows:

```
<s:decorate>
  <f:facet name="beforeInvalidField">
    <h:graphicImage src="anotherError.gif"/>
  </f:facet>
  <f:facet name="afterInvalidField">
    <s:message styleClass="anotherError"/>
  </f:facet>
  <f:facet name="aroundInvalidField">
    <s:span styleClass="error"/>
  </f:facet>

  <h:inputText value="#{person.name}"/>
</s:decorate>
```

Seam's `<s:validate>` and `<s:decorate>` tags greatly simplify form validation in the web tier. We highly recommend that you take advantage of them.

# 12.5  Using JSF Custom Validators

As we discussed, a great benefit of the Seam validator is minimizing repetitive configuration in the presentation and database layers. In some cases, however, validation is needed only in the presentation layer. For instance, we might want to make sure that the user enters a valid credit card number for the transaction, but the credit card number might not even get saved in the database when the transaction is finished. In this situation, you can also use plain JSF validators in Seam applications.

JSF only supports a couple simple validators out of the box, but third-party JSF component libraries provide plenty of custom validators. For instance, the following example shows the use of the Apache Tomahawk validator for credit card numbers. Refer to the Tomahawk documentation for how to install the component library.

```
<h:outputText value="Credit Card Number" />
<s:decorate>
  <h:inputText id="creditCard" required="true"
               value="#{customer.creditCard}">
    <t:validateCreditCard />
  </h:inputText>
</s:decorate>
```

You can use the `<s:decorate>` tags to enhance the error message display for any JSF custom validators as well.

# Clickable Data Tables

**B**esides the validated entity objects, another example of a Seam behavioral data component is the clickable data table. A regular JSF data table displays a list of data objects, with each row showing the contents of an object. A clickable data table has additional action columns; each such column contains buttons or links that enable you to operate on the entity data object corresponding to each row.

For instance, the `fans.xhtml` page in the Integration example application contains a clickable data table (Figure 13.1). The table displays all persons in the database, with each row representing a person. Each row also contains a clickable button that allows you to delete the person represented by the row. In a general clickable data table, you can have multiple action buttons or links for each row.

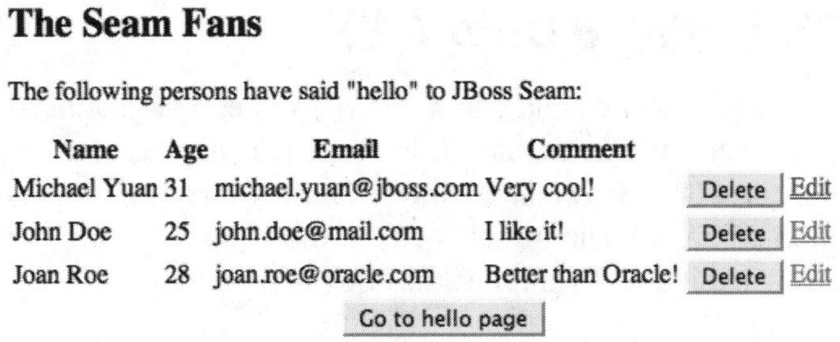

### The Seam Fans

The following persons have said "hello" to JBoss Seam:

| Name | Age | Email | Comment | | |
|------|-----|-------|---------|--------|------|
| Michael Yuan | 31 | michael.yuan@jboss.com | Very cool! | Delete | Edit |
| John Doe | 25 | john.doe@mail.com | I like it! | Delete | Edit |
| Joan Roe | 28 | joan.roe@oracle.com | Better than Oracle! | Delete | Edit |

Go to hello page

**Figure 13.1**　Clickable data table on the `fans.xhtml` page

In the Hotel Booking example application (the `booking` project), the `main.xhtml` page displays a clickable data table containing all previous reservations that you booked along with the buttons to delete any of those reservations (Figure 13.2).

**Current Hotel Bookings**

| Name | Address | City, State | Check in date | Check out date | Confirmation number | Action |
|------|---------|-------------|---------------|----------------|---------------------|--------|
| Conrad Miami | 1395 Brickell Ave | Miami, FL | Apr 11, 2006 | Apr 12, 2006 | 3 | Cancel |
| W Hotel | Lexington Ave, Manhattan | NY, NY | Apr 11, 2006 | Apr 12, 2006 | 2 | Cancel |
| Marriott Courtyard | Tower Place, Buckhead | Atlanta, GA | Apr 11, 2006 | Apr 12, 2006 | 1 | Cancel |

**Figure 13.2**    Clickable data table on the `main.xhtml` page in the Hotel Booking example

For clarity and simplicity, in this chapter we use the Integration example to illustrate the implementation of a clickable data table.

# 13.1   Implementing a Clickable Data Table

In plain JSF, clickable tables are difficult to implement because there is no clean way to associate the row ID with the event handlers for the action buttons in that row. Seam, however, provides two very simple ways to implement those highly useful clickable tables.

## 13.1.1   Displaying a Data Table

The JSF page to display a clickable data table is simple. You just need a regular JSF `<h:dataTable>` UI element. The `<h:dataTable>` element iterates over a Java `List`-typed component with the `@DataModel` annotation. The following listing shows the code in the Integration example. The `@DataModel` turns the `fans` component into a JSF `DataModel` object, and it already implies the `@Out` annotation.

```
public class ManagerAction implements Manager {
  ... ...

  @DataModel
  private List <Person> fans;

  @DataModelSelection
  private Person selectedFan;
```

```
@Factory("fans")
public void findFans () {
  fans = em.createQuery("select p from Person p").getResultList();
}

... ...
}
```

Each property in the `Person` bean is presented in its own column of the table. The **Delete** buttons also occupy their own column and all have the same event handler method, #{manager.delete}. We explain how the #{manager.delete} method works in the next two sections.

```
<h:dataTable value="#{fans}" var="fan">
  <h:column>
    #{fan.name}
  </h:column>
  <h:column>
    #{fan.age}
  </h:column>
  <h:column>
    #{fan.email}
  </h:column>
  <h:column>
    #{fan.comment}
  </h:column>
  <h:column>
    <h:commandButton value="Delete" action="#{manager.delete}"/>
  </h:column>
</h:dataTable>
```

In this example, the **Delete** button is a <h:commandButton>. We can also render an action link for each row in a clickable table with the JSF <h:commandLink> or the Seam <s:link> component—those link components can take Seam event handler methods in the action attribute. Seam's <s:link> is recommended because it supports the expected browser behavior such as the right-click pop-up menu (see Section 8.3.6 for more details).

Still, with all rows having the same button event handler, how does the #{manager.delete} method know which `Person` object to operate on? You can either inject the selected object to the #{manager} component or use Seam's extended EL to reference the selected object.

## 13.1.2 Injecting Selected Object into an Event Handler

We define a `selectedFan` field in the `ManagerAction` class and annotate it with the `@DataModelSelection` annotation. When you click on a button or link in any row in the clickable table, Seam injects the `Person` object represented by that row into the `selectedFan` field before invoking the event handler method. Finally, we implement the event handler for the **Delete** button on each row. The event handler merges the injected `Person` object into the current persistence context and deletes it from the database.

```
public class ManagerAction implements Manager {
  ... ...

  @DataModel
  private List <Person> fans;

  @DataModelSelection
  private Person selectedFan;

  ... ...

  public String delete () {
    Person toDelete = em.merge (selectedFan);
    em.remove( toDelete );
    findFans ();
    return null;
  }
}
```

The merge is needed because the `ManagerAction` component has the default conversation scope: The component and its persistence context are destroyed when the data table is completely rendered. So, when the user clicks on a data table button or link, a new `ManagerAction` component is constructed for the new conversation. The `selectedFan` object is out of the new persistence context and therefore needs to be merged.

---

**Merging Data Objects into Persistence Context**

If we manage data objects in a long-running conversation, there is less need to merge the persistence context from time to time.

---

## 13.1.3  Using Extended EL in a Data Table

The injection via `@DataModelSelection` decouples the presentation from the event handler. It is the standard JSF way of doing things. However, with the Seam's extended EL (see Section 3.2.2), there is a simpler alternative. You can directly reference the object in the selected row:

```
<h:dataTable value="#{fans}" var="fan">
  <h:column>
    #{fan.name}
  </h:column>
  ... ...
  <h:column>
    <h:commandButton value="Delete" action="#{manager.delete(fan)}"/>
  </h:column>
</h:dataTable>
```

In the `ManagerAction` class, you need a `delete()` method that takes the `Person` argument:

```
public class ManagerAction implements Manager {
  ... ...

  @DataModel
  private List <Person> fans;

  ... ...

  public String delete (Person selectedFan) {
    Person toDelete = em.merge (selectedFan);
    em.remove( toDelete );
    findFans ();
    return null;
  }
}
```

The clickable data table is an excellent example of the tight integration between data and UI components in Seam applications.

# 13.2  Seam Data-Binding Framework

The `@DataModel` and `@DataModelSelection` annotations are just concrete use cases of the Seam data-binding framework, which provides a generic mechanism for turning any data objects into JSF UI components and capturing the user input on these components. For instance, the `@DataModel` annotation simply turns a `Map` or `Set` into a JSF `DataModel` component, and the `@DataModelSelection` annotation passes in any selection the user made on the `DataModel`.

The generic data-binding framework enables third-party developers to extend Seam and write custom annotations to give UI behaviors to arbitrary data model objects. For instance, one might write an annotation to expose an image as a map widget on the web page and capture the user selection as a location on the map. The data-binding framework opens the door for some extremely interesting use cases from the community.

The data-binding framework is an advanced topic which requires knowledge of the internal workings of Seam and JSF. This is a little beyond the scope of this book; in this section, we just give a brief overview of different components in the framework and leave interested readers to investigate the Seam source code themselves.

The `DataBinder` and `DataSelector` interfaces in the `org.jboss.seam.databinding` package define the methods you have to implement for your own data binding classes. The `DataModelBinder` and `DataModelSelector` classes in the same package provide example implementations. Then, in the `@DataModel` and `@DataModelSelection` annotations, we simply pass control to those implementation classes.

```
@Target({FIELD, METHOD})
@Retention(RUNTIME)
@Documented
@DataBinderClass(DataModelBinder.class)
public @interface DataModel {
  String value() default "";
  ScopeType scope() default ScopeType.UNSPECIFIED;
}

@Target({FIELD, METHOD})
@Retention(RUNTIME)
@Documented
@DataSelectorClass(DataModelSelector.class)
public @interface DataModelSelection {
  String value() default "";
}
```

For more details on the implementation of the `DataModelBinder` and `DataModelSelector` classes, refer to the Seam source code.

# 14

Decoupling Components
Using Events

UI frameworks commonly use events to decouple web and data components. Events allow components to react to changes in the model or in other components without creating a direct dependency between the two. Seam is no different; it provides a simple approach to using events in your application through an implementation of the *observer pattern*.

This chapter will discuss the Seam approach to the observer pattern. As you will see, Seam makes it simple to use this powerful pattern to decouple your components by communicating events across contexts. First, let's take a look at some background on the observer pattern.

## 14.1  The Observer Pattern

The observer pattern is a commonly used pattern in software design, especially with user interface development. This pattern describes an event model where a number of observers are interested in a state change or an event associated with a specific subject. A change or event within the subject triggers notification of each observer, allowing the observers a chance to respond—either updating based on the change or performing some action. This model is also referred to as *publish-subscribe*. In general, implementation of this pattern requires creating some well-known interfaces and their concrete implementations.

As you can see in Figure 14.1, any number of observers can attach to a subject, when interested in a change or event notification, effectively registering the observer with the subject. This pattern allows loose coupling between a subject and its observers, as a subject does not need to know the details of its observers or their interests. To learn more about the observer pattern, refer to the design classic *Design Patterns* (Gamma et al., 1994).

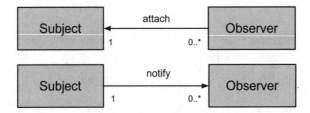

**Figure 14.1**    A simple representation of the observer pattern where the observer attaches or registers with a subject and the subject notifies the observer of a change or an event

Let us take a look at an example implementation of this pattern to gain a deeper understanding. The Rewards Booking example allows users to earn rewards from hotel bookings. If a user chooses to participate in the awards program upon registration, awards accrue on each booking. Earning rewards is essentially a side effect of booking a hotel. Therefore, we can loosely couple the logic to earn rewards to the logic that creates a booking.

There are two components involved in the implementation, the `HotelBookingAction` and the `RewardsManager`. In order to allow the `RewardsManager` to receive notifications when a hotel is booked, we can create a `BookingObserver` interface.

```
public interface BookingObserver {
   public void notifyBookingEvent(Booking booking);
}
```

The `RewardsManager` can now implement this interface to execute the reward accrual logic when a booking is placed by a user:

```
@Name("rewardsManager")
@Scope(ScopeType.CONVERSATION)
public class RewardsManager implements BookingObserver {
  // ... ...

  public void notifyBookingEvent(Booking booking) {
    this.accrueRewards(booking);
  }

  // ... ...
}
```

The `HotelBookingAction` must now provide a method to allow an `Observer` to attach or register with the subject. In addition, a list of observers must be maintained to ensure that the subject knows who needs to be notified when the booking event occurs.

```
@Stateful
@Name("hotelBooking")
@Restrict("#{identity.loggedIn}")
public class HotelBookingAction implements HotelBooking
{
  // ... ...
  List<BookingObserver> bookingObservers =
    new ArrayList<BookingObserver>();

  public void addBookingObserver(BookingObserver observer) {
    bookingObservers.add(observer);
  }
  // ... ...
}
```

Now we can notify observers when a hotel booking is confirmed by looping through and invoking the notifyBookingEvent() methods:

```
@Stateful
@Name("hotelBooking")
@Restrict("#{identity.loggedIn}")
public class HotelBookingAction implements HotelBooking
{
  List<BookingObserver> bookingObservers =
    new ArrayList<BookingObserver>();
  // ... ...

  public void confirm()
  {
    // ... ...
    notifyBookingEventObservers(booking);
  }

  public void notifyBookingEventObservers(Booking booking) {
    for(BookingObserver observer : bookingObservers) {
      observer.notifyBookingEvent(booking);
    }
  }
  // ... ...
}
```

We now know how to implement the pattern, but what issues might we encounter with the implementation? Consider the following:

- This pattern defeats the DRY (Don't Repeat Yourself) principle taught to us by *The Pragmatic Programmers* (Andrew Hunt and Dave Thomas, 1999). Obviously, the logic to register and notify observers would be repeated in all places where we want to implement this pattern. Much of the repetition could be resolved through abstraction, but it still requires creating an unnatural class hierarchy.

- When does the RewardsManager component register with the HotelBookingAction? This is an inherent problem as these components may be created at different times. In our example, while the RewardsManager is a conversational component, it may exist in conversations where the HotelBookingAction does not exist.

- Another issue is a subject with a broader scope than the observer. In this case, the reference maintained to the observing component can lead to *scope impedance* with the observing component outliving its intended scope as the subject still holds a reference to the component. While this issue can be resolved through some workarounds, it is certainly not an optimal solution.

Seam makes it simple to use the observer pattern through annotations and/or XML configuration with no custom implementation required. Let us take a look at how easy it is to use this pattern with Seam.

# 14.2   Component-Driven Events

Seam defines an event model that allows Seam components to easily register for and send notification events. Seam uses this pattern heavily in its internals to provide notifications of Seam component events. This allows you to specify custom behaviors in reaction to Seam components' execution. These events are discussed throughout the book as the corresponding components are covered. In the following sections we will discuss how to raise your own custom events and how to observe events with Seam.

## 14.2.1   Raising Events Declaratively

Seam allows you to raise your own custom events, making it simple to implement the subject of the observer pattern. Seam components can raise events declaratively through annotations, XML configuration, or programmatically. The annotation approach and the XML approach are declarative, making them least invasive, but they also provide the least flexibility. The annotation approach is as simple as annotating a method with @RaiseEvent. In line with the semantics of other Seam annotations (see Chapter 8), the event is only raised if the method returns successfully. A successful return indicates that no exception is thrown and the method either has a void return type or does not return null.

```
@Stateful
@Name("hotelBooking")
@Restrict("#{identity.loggedIn}")
public class HotelBookingAction implements HotelBooking
{
    // ... ...

    @RaiseEvent("newBooking")
    public void confirm()
    {
        // execute confirmation logic
    }
}
```

The string specified in the `@RaiseEvent` annotation provides the name for the event. As you will see in the next section, any observers interested in this event will specify this string to identify the appropriate subject. The `confirm()` method is also tied to a navigation rule in our `pages.xml` configuration. This provides the option to raise the event through XML configuration as well. Instead of specifying the `@RaiseEvent` annotation on the `confirm()` method directly, we can place the event in the navigation rule.

```
... ...

  <page view-id="/confirm.xhtml" conversation-required="true">

    <description>Confirm booking: #{booking.description}</description>

      <navigation from-action="#{hotelBooking.confirm}">
        <raise-event type="newBooking" />
        <redirect view-id="/main.xhtml"/>
      </navigation>
  </page>

... ...
```

The `type` in this case specifies a string that identifies the event. As before, observers will use this string to identify the event they are interested in. In this case, the event will always be raised when the navigation rule is fired. Another option is to raise an event each time a page is accessed. In our example, we could raise an event when rewards are accessed by a user for auditing purposes:

```
... ...

  <page view-id="/rewards/*">
    <description>Rewards Summary</description>
    <raise-event type="rewardsAccessed" />
    ... ...
  </page>

... ...
```

In our Rewards Booking example, it is important for the `RewardsManager` component to know the `Booking` instance to determine rewards. There are two options here. Given that Seam provides context when invoking components through bijection, we can easily retrieve the booking instance from the context. Simply annotating a `Booking` member variable with `@In` will ensure that Seam provides the `Booking` instance from the current context. Each of the declarative approaches described above would require using bijection to retrieve this instance.

Yet another option, as demonstrated in the Rewards Booking example, is passing the `Booking` instance as an event object. This requires the programmatic approach to raising events by using the `Events` API. The following listing demonstrates this approach:

```
@Stateful
@Name("hotelBooking")
@Restrict("#{identity.loggedIn}")
public class HotelBookingAction implements HotelBooking
{
  @In private Events events;

  @In(required=false)
  @Out(required=false)
  private Booking booking;

  // ... ...

  public void confirm()
  {
    // ... ...

    events.raiseEvent("newBooking", booking);

    // ... ...
  }
}
```

Note that we inject the `Events` component into the `HotelBookingAction`. As with
other Seam components, the `Events` component can also be retrieved through a static
`instance` method: `Events.instance()`. In Section 14.2.3, we will discuss this API in
depth and see how each method impacts event processing, but first let's take a look at
how we can observe events.

---

**Event Constants for Simplified Refactoring and Maintenance**

While it is simple to use strings to specify events in both the subject and the observer, it
is often useful to define event names as constants. The `Identity` component in the Seam
security model follows this pattern (see Chapter 18). It is quite simple to specify these
event constants through `static final String` definitions. These constants can then be
specified in observers to avoid dependencies on string definitions. This simplifies refactoring
and maintenance as constants can be easily identified using your favorite IDE.

---

## 14.2.2  Observing Events

As mentioned previously, each event is given a name. Observing components register
for events by specifying the event name through annotations or XML. This declarative
approach makes it simple to create observers without using any custom interfaces or
class extensions. The annotation approach simply requires that you specify the `@Observer`
annotation on the component, specifying the name of the event. The Rewards Booking
example demonstrates this approach in the `RewardsManager` component by observing
the `newBooking` event.

```
@Name("rewardsManager")
@Scope(ScopeType.CONVERSATION)
public class RewardsManager {
  // ... ...

  @Observer("newBooking")
  public void accrueRewards(Booking booking)
  {
    // execute rewards accrual logic
  }
}
```

Note that we specified `Booking` as a parameter accepted by the `accrueRewards()` method. As shown previously, this parameter is passed as an event object through the `Events` API. The `@Observer` annotation also provides an additional attribute allowing a component to be created when the event is triggered. If you specify `@Observer(value="newBooking", create=true)` and if the `RewardsManager` component did not exist in the current conversation context when the event was triggered, the component would be created by Seam and the `accrueRewards()` method would be invoked. This is very useful for stateless event processing components.

Event observers can also be registered through XML. This requires creating a file in the `WEB-INF` folder named `events.xml`. This approach keeps all defined event observers in a single location but provides no type safety.

```
<events>
  <event type="newBooking">
    <action expression="#{rewardsManager.accrueRewards(booking)}"/>
  </event>
<events>
```

When using Seam, it is quite simple to specify event observers without custom implementation. In addition, Seam manages the details of registering and notifying components, thereby avoiding the scope impedance issues we discussed previously. Let's now take a look at how we can achieve more fine-grained control over event processing through the `Events` API.

## 14.2.3  Event Processing and the Events API

Event processing in Seam is performed through the `Events` component. The `Events` API provides some insight into how events are processed and how we can have more fine-grained control over event processing.

`raiseEvent(String type, Object... parameters)`
> Raises a synchronous event. In other words, the event is processed by observers as soon as it is raised and control is not returned to the application until all observers finish. Annotating a component method with the `@RaiseEvent` annotation or specifying an event through XML results in invocation of this method.

`raiseAsynchronousEvent(String type, Object... parameters)`
> Raises an asynchronous event to be processed immediately. In other words, the event is processed by observers as soon as it is raised, but the processing occurs asynchronously, immediately handing control back to the component that raised the event.

`raiseTimedEvent(String type, Schedule schedule, Object... parameters)`
> Raises an asynchronous event to be processed according to a `Schedule`. The `Schedule` allows the exact timing of the event to be controlled either by a delay or by a specific date and time.

`raiseTransactionCompletionEvent(String type, Object... parameters)`
> Raises an asynchronous event to be processed immediately once the transaction completes, whether the transaction is successful or not.

`raiseTransactionSuccessEvent(String type, Object... parameters)`
> Raises an asynchronous event to be processed immediately once the transaction completes, only if the transaction completes successfully. The event will be effectively ignored should the transaction fail.

Synchronous events are processed as part of the main thread of execution. Control is transferred to the `Events` component which invokes each registered event `@Observer`. This means that, once a component raises an event through the `@RaiseEvent` annotation, either through XML or through the `raiseEvent()` method, the main thread of execution will cease until all observers complete processing. You should therefore always consider the time of execution for event observers. Long-running event observers will certainly impact response time when using synchronous events. If execution time of observers is a concern, you may consider raising an asynchronous event. Figure 14.2 demonstrates how the `newBooking` event, raised when a booking is confirmed, would be processed as a synchronous event.

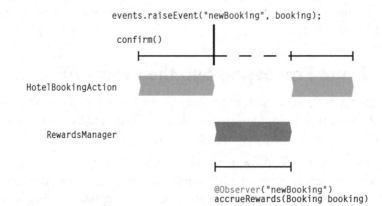

**Figure 14.2**   Processing the `newBooking` event as a synchronous event with the `Events` API

All asynchronous events are scheduled with the registered `org.jboss.seam.async.` `dispatcher` instance. The `Dispatcher` component is discussed in depth in Chapter 31. The most important feature of asynchronous events is that they immediately transfer control back to the main thread of execution. The event observers are executed in parallel to the main thread of execution, either immediately or according to a specified `Schedule`. Figure 14.3 demonstrates how the `newBooking` event would be processed as an asynchronous event.

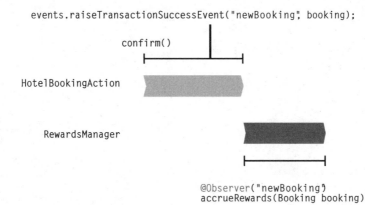

events.raiseTransactionSuccessEvent("newBooking", booking);

confirm()

HotelBookingAction

RewardsManager

@Observer("newBooking")
accrueRewards(Booking booking)

**Figure 14.3**  Processing the `newBooking` event as an asynchronous event tied to the success of a transaction through the `Events` API

Note that Figure 14.3 demonstrates invocation of the `raiseTransactionSuccessEvent`. This event would be processed once the `confirm()` method completes and the transaction commits successfully. For our example, a transaction success event makes sense. It is not necessary to immediately process the logic of accruing rewards as the main goal of the action is to book a hotel stay. Thus, we can perform this operation asynchronously, allowing the booking to complete and the user to be immediately notified. In addition, from a business perspective, if an exception occurs while processing the rewards, we would not want to roll back the booking. Once the booking transaction completes, we can kick off the accrue rewards logic asynchronously in a separate transaction.

---

**Event Notification between Contexts**

We now know how to raise and observe events—but, when an event is triggered, how does Seam determine who to notify? Event notification is performed similarly to bijection. Essentially, Seam searches the context for components observing the triggered event and notifies those components. This means that a Seam component can observe events from any context. Be careful not to hold onto references in broader-scoped components in order to avoid scope impedance issues. Bijection automatically disinjects (nulls references to) any attributes annotated with `@In`, but event objects should never be held onto.

---

# 15

# Bookmarkable Web Pages

**O**ne of the loudest criticisms of JSF (as well as other component-based web frameworks) is its reliance on HTTP `POST` requests. JSF uses HTTP `POST` to match user actions (e.g., button clicks) to UI event handler methods on the server side (i.e., in Seam's stateful session beans). It also uses hidden fields in HTTP `POST` requests to keep track of the user's conversational state.

In an HTTP `POST` request, the URL does not contain the complete query information about the request. It is impossible to bookmark a web page dynamically generated from an HTTP `POST`. However, in many web applications, it is highly desirable to have bookmarkable web pages (a.k.a. RESTful URLs, where REST stands for Representational State Transfer). For instance, on an e-commerce web site, you probably want to display product information via URLs such as `http://mysite.com/product.seam?pid=123`; on a content site, you probably want to display articles via URLs such as `http://mysite.com/article.seam?aid=123`. The chief benefit of the bookmarkable URLs is that they can be saved for later access and emailed to someone (i.e., they can be bookmarks).

In plain JSF, bookmarkable pages are somewhat difficult to construct: When the page is loaded from an HTTP `GET`, it is cumbersome to pass request parameters to backing beans and then automatically start bean method to process the parameters and load page data. However, with Seam, this barrier is easy to overcome. In this chapter, we discuss two approaches: using Seam page parameters and using request parameter injection with component lifecycle methods.

The example application is in the `integration` project in the source code bundle. It works like this: After users enter their names and messages on the `hello.seam` page, you can load any individual's personal details and comments via the `http://localhost:8080/integration/person.seam?pid=`*n* URL, where *n* is the unique ID of that individual. You can then make changes to any of the details and submit them back to the database (see Figure 15.1).

**Edit Michael Yuan**

Your name: Michael Yuan

Your age: 31

Email: michael.yuan@jboss

Comment: Very cool!

Update

**Figure 15.1**    The bookmarkable edit page with individual person information in the Integration example

---

**When to Use Bookmarkable URLs**

We believe that bookmarkable URLs and `POST` URLs both have their places. For instance, you probably do not want the user to bookmark a temporary page inside a conversation, such as a credit card payment submission page. In that case, a nonbookmarkable `POST` page is more appropriate.

---

# 15.1   Using Page Parameters

The easiest way to pass HTTP `GET` request parameters to backend business components is to use Seam page parameters. Each Seam web page can have from zero to several page parameters, which are HTTP request parameters bound to properties on the backend components.

Seam page parameters are defined in the `pages.xml` file in the `app.war/WEB-INF/` directory. You have already seen this file early on in this book, where we used it to manage the pageflow. But it does much more than pageflow. In the following example, when the `person.xhtml` page is loaded, the HTTP `GET` request parameter `pid` is converted to a `Long` value and bound to the `#{manager.pid}` property. Notice that we can use JSF EL and the converter here, although the `pages.xml` file is not a JSF web page; this is the power of Seam's expanded use of JSF EL.

```
<pages>

  <page view-id="/person.xhtml">
    <param name="pid" value="#{manager.pid}"
          converterId="javax.faces.Long"/>
  </page>

</pages>
```

So, when you load a URL such as `person.seam?pid=3`, Seam automatically invokes the `ManagerAction.setPid(3)` method. In the setter method, we initialize the `person` object and outject it.

```
@Stateful
@Name("manager")
public class ManagerAction implements Manager {

  @In (required=false) @Out (required=false)
  private Person person;

  @PersistenceContext (type=EXTENDED)
  private EntityManager em;

  Long pid;

  public void setPid (Long pid) {
    this.pid = pid;

    if (pid != null) {
      person = (Person) em.find(Person.class, pid);
    } else {
      person = new Person ();
    }
  }

  public Long getPid () {
    return pid;
  }

  ... ...
}
```

### The Bijection Values Are Not Required

The `@In` and `@Out` annotations on the `person` field have the `required=false` attribute. When the `ManagerAction.setPid()` method is called, the `person` component does not have a valid value. In fact, we construct the `person` object in the setter and then outject it.

Of course, if you set `@In(required=false)`, Seam could also inject a `null` value for `person` when you invoke any event handler method in the `ManagerAction` component. If there is an event handler method which does not provide a valid `person` object to outject (e.g., the `ManagerAction.delete()` method), you must set the `@Out(required=false)` as well.

Using similar techniques, you can have multiple page parameters bound to the same or different backend components on the same page. This `person.xhtml` page displays the editing form with the outjected `person` component:

```
<s:validateAll>

<table>
  <tr>
    <td>Your name:</td>
    <td>
      <s:decorate>
        <h:inputText value="#{person.name}"/>
      </s:decorate>
    </td>
  </tr>

  <tr>
    <td>Your age:</td>
    <td>
      <s:decorate>
        <h:inputText value="#{person.age}"/>
      </s:decorate>
    </td>
  </tr>

  <tr>
    <td>Email:</td>
    <td>
      <s:decorate>
        <h:inputText value="#{person.email}"/>
      </s:decorate>
    </td>
  </tr>

  <tr>
    <td>Comment:</td>
    <td>
      <s:decorate>
        <h:inputTextarea value="#{person.comment}"/>
      </s:decorate>
    </td>
  </tr>

</table>

</s:validateAll>

<h:commandButton type="submit" value="Update"
                 action="#{manager.update}"/>
```

When you click on the **Update** button, the `person` object corresponding to the `pid` is updated. Many readers find this puzzling: When we first loaded the `person.xhtml` page via HTTP `GET`, we explicitly gave the `pid` parameter. Why don't we need to explicitly pass the `pid` in an HTTP `POST` request associated with the **Update** button submission (e.g., as a hidden field in the form or as an `f:param` parameter for the **Update** button)?

After all, the `person` and `manager` components are both in the default conversation scope (Section 8.1.1); they have to be constructed anew when the form is submitted. So how does JSF know which `person` you want to update? As it turns out, the page parameter has a `PAGE` scope (Section 6.5). When you submit the page, it always submits the same `pid` parameter from which the page is originally loaded. This is a very useful and convenient feature.

---

**Page Action**

When the page is loaded, the page parameter automatically triggers the setter method on the backend property it binds to. Seam takes this concept one step further: You can trigger any backend bean method at page load time in the `pages.xml` file. That is called page action. If the page action method is annotated with `@Begin`, the HTTP `GET` request for the page starts a long-running conversation. Furthermore, you can specify page actions that are executed only when a JSF EL condition is met. Here are two examples of page actions:

```
<pages>
  <page view-id="/foo.xhtml">
    <action execute="#{barBean.startConv}"/>
  </page>

  <page view-id="/register.xhtml">
    <action if="#{validation.failed}" execute="#{register.invalid}"/>
  </page>

  ... ...

</pages>
```

---

The Seam page parameters are an elegant solution for bookmarkable pages. You will see them used again in Chapter 16.

# 15.2  The Java-Centric Approach

Page parameters are not the only solution for bookmarkable pages. For one thing, a lot of developers dislike putting application logic in XML files. The `pages.xml` file can also get too verbose in some cases. For instance, you might have the same HTTP request parameter on multiple pages (e.g., `editperson.seam?pid=x`, `showperson.seam?pid=y`, etc.), or have multiple HTTP request parameters for the same page. In either case, you then have to repeat very similar page parameter definitions in the `pages.xml` file.

Furthermore, the page parameter does not work correctly if the page is loaded from a servlet, which is the case for some third-party JSF component libraries. Those libraries use their own special servlets to do more processing or rendering of the page; for an example, see Section 19.4.

To resolve these issues, Seam provides a mechanism for processing HTTP request parameters in a "pure Java" way. This is more involved than the page parameter approach, but the benefit is that you can add your own custom logic at more points.

## 15.2.1   Obtaining Query Parameters from an HTTP GET Request

Our first challenge is to pass the HTTP GET query parameters to the business component that provides the contents and supports actions for the page. Seam provides a @RequestParameter annotation to make this happen. The @RequestParameter annotation is applied to a string variable in a Seam component. When the component is accessed at runtime, the current HTTP request parameter matching the variable name is automatically injected into the variable. For instance, we could have the following code in the ManagerAction stateful session bean to support URLs such as person.seam?pid=3. Notice that the HTTP request parameter is a String object, but the injected value is a Long type. Seam converts the String to a Long during injection. Of course, you can inject a String value and convert it yourself.

```
@Stateful
@Name("manager")
public class ManagerAction implements Manager {

  @RequestParameter
  Long pid;

  // ... ...
}
```

Whenever a method (e.g., a UI event handler, a property accessor, or a component lifecycle method) inside the ManagerAction class is accessed, Seam first injects the request parameter pid into the field variable with the same name. If your request parameter and field variable have different names, you must use the value argument in the annotation. For instance, the following code injects the pid request parameter into the personId field variable:

```
@RequestParameter (value="pid")
  Long personId;
```

## 15.2.2   Loading Data for the Page

Getting the request query parameter is only the first step. When the person.seam?pid=3 page is loaded, Seam has to actually retrieve the person's information from the database. For instance, the person.xhtml page simply displays data from the person component. So how do we instantiate the person component with the pid parameter at the HTTP GET?

### 15.2.2.1 The @Factory Method

As we discussed in Section 7.2.2, we can use a factory method to initialize any Seam component. The factory method for the `person` component is located in the `ManagerAction` bean. Seam calls `ManagerAction.findPerson()` when it instantiates the `person` component. The factory method uses the injected `pid` to retrieve the `Person` object from the database.

```
@Stateful
@Name("manager")
public class ManagerAction implements Manager {

  @In (required=false) @Out (required=false)
  private Person person;

  @PersistenceContext (type=EXTENDED)
  private EntityManager em;

  @RequestParameter
  Long pid;

  ... ...

  @Factory("person")
  public void findPerson () {
    if (pid != null) {
      person = (Person) em.find(Person.class, pid);
    } else {
      person = new Person ();
    }
  }

}
```

In summary, the whole process works like this: When the user loads the `person.seam?pid=3` URL, the `person.xhtml` page is processed and Seam finds it necessary to instantiate the `person` component to display data on the page. Seam injects the `pid` value into the `ManagerAction` object and then calls the `ManagerAction.findPerson()` factory method to build and outject the `person` component. The page is then displayed with a `person` component.

### 15.2.2.2 The @Create Method

The `person` component can be constructed with a factory method. But what if the page data comes from a business component? For instance, the page could display data from `#{manager.person}` instead of `#{person}`. In this case, we need to initialize the `person` property in the `manager` component when Seam instantiates the `manager` component. According to Section 7.2.1, we can do it via the `@Create` lifecycle method in the `ManagerAction` class:

```
@Stateful
@Name("manager")
public class ManagerAction implements Manager {

    @RequestParameter
    Long pid;

    // No bijection annotations
    private Person person;

    @PersistenceContext(type=EXTENDED)
    private EntityManager em;

    public Person getPerson () {return person;}
    public void setPerson (Person person) {
        this.person = person;
    }

    @Create
    public String findPerson() {
        if (pid != null) {
            person = (Person) em.find(Person.class, pid);
        } else {
            person = new Person ();
        }
    }

    // ... ...
}
```

---

**Event Handler Methods**

The @Factory and @Create methods can also be used as UI event handler methods in regular JSF HTTP POST operations. They also can use the injected HTTP request parameter if the POST request has such parameters (see Section 15.2.3).

---

# 15.2.3  Further Processing from the Bookmarked Page

Without the PAGE-scoped page parameter, we must include the HTTP request parameter in all subsequent requests. For instance, the person.xhtml page loads the manager and person components only in the default conversation scope (see Section 8.1.1), so the components expire when the page is fully rendered. When the user clicks on the **Say Hello** button to edit the person's information, a new set of manager and person components must be constructed for the new conversation. Thus, the JSF POST for the **Say Hello** button submission must also include the pid parameter. The pid is injected into the ManagerAction class, which uses it to build the person component before the event handler method ManagerAction.sayHello() is invoked. To do that, we use a hidden field in the form:

```
<h:form>
<input type="hidden" name="pid" value="#{person.id}"/>

<s:validateAll>
 ... ...
</s:validateAll>

<h:commandButton type="submit" value="Update"
                 action="#{manager.update}"/>
</h:form>
```

If you annotate the @Factory or @Create methods with the @Begin annotation, you can start a long-running conversation from a bookmarked page. For instance, in an e-commerce web site, you can start a shopping cart conversation when the user loads a bookmarked product page with a productId. The REST-loaded product component stays available throughout the conversation until the user checks out or aborts the shopping session. There is no need to load the product component again from the productId as long as the conversation stays valid.

---

**The Hidden Field Hack**

The hidden field in the web form is really a hack. We do not recommend it because it may confuse code maintainers in the future. If you need a hidden field to make your RESTful page work, you are probably better off injecting the page parameter via the pages.xml file instead of using the @RequestParameter. However, in Section 19.4 we will see that this hack is sometimes necessary with third-party JSF component libraries.

---

# 15.3  RESTful Web Services

Using annotations, Seam goes beyond simple RESTful web pages. It can turn any POJO method into a RESTful web service. Seam integrates with the RESTEasy library to support standard web service annotations defined in the JAX-RS specification (JSR-311). The idea is that you can annotate any POJO method specifying a URL path. An HTTP GET request to that URL would retrieve the result in serialized XML format. For instance, the following listing shows how to make the #{manager.findPerson} method a web service:

```
@Stateful
@Name("manager")
@Path("/manager")
public class ManagerAction implements Manager {

  ... ...

  @PersistenceContext(type=EXTENDED)
  private EntityManager em;
```

```
@GET
@Path("/person/{personId}")
@ProduceMime("application/xml")
public String findPerson(@PathParam("personId") int pid) {
  person = (Person) em.find(Person.class, pid);
  String result = "<person>";
  result = result + "<name>" + person.getName() + "</name>";
  result = result + "<age>" + person.getAge() + "</age>";
  result = result + "<email>" + person.getEmail() + "</email>";
  result = result + "<comment>" + person.getComment() + "</comment>";
  result = result + "</person>";
  return result;
}

// ... ...
}
```

When the user does an HTTP GET to /seam/resource/rest/manager/person/123, the server would return an XML string that presents the Person entity object with id equal to 123. Here, we serialized the Person object by hand, but it is easy to see how you can use a ready-made XML serializer for this work.

All these @Path, @GET, @PathParam, and @ProduceMime annotations are JAX-RS annotations. Here, Seam automatically wires up the entity manager, transaction, and other server resources for the web service.

The URL prefix to the web service (/seam/resource/rest) is required by Seam. In the components.xml file, you can customize the rest prefix to version your web services. Please see the Seam RESTEasy documentation for more details (http://docs.jboss.com/seam/2.1.1.GA/reference/en-US/html/webservices.html).

To use RESTEasy with Seam, you need to include the RESTEasy library JARs, jaxrs-api.jar and jboss-seam-resteasy.jar, in your EAR or WAR file's library classpath.

Seam provides great REST support for JSF applications. This is one of the most compelling reasons to use Seam with JSF.

# The Seam CRUD
# Application Framework

**W**ithout Seam, a plain JSF application has at least four layers: the UI pages, the backing beans for the page data and event handlers, the session beans for business and data access logic, and the entity beans for the data model. Seam has eliminated the artificial gap between JSF backing beans and EJB3 session beans. But there's more. Seam comes with a built-in framework for Create, Retrieve, Update, and Delete (CRUD) data operations. With this framework, we can make JSF applications even simpler by reusing much of the standard event handler methods. For small projects, we can even completely eliminate the need for session beans. Too good to be true? Well, read on . . .

The Seam CRUD application framework essentially provides prepackaged Data Access Objects (DAOs). Let's start this chapter with a brief introduction to DAOs.

## 16.1  Data Access Objects (DAOs)

One of the most useful design patterns in enterprise Java is the Data Access Object (DAO) pattern. DAOs typically support CRUD operations on the ORM entity objects. In Seam applications, a DAO is an EJB3 session bean or a Seam POJO component holding reference to a managed `EntityManager` object.

In many small database-driven applications, the CRUD data access logic is the business logic. The web UI simply provides the user access to the database. In a JSF CRUD application, web pages reference DAOs directly to operate on the data. For those applications, the backend programming primarily consists of coding the DAOs. For instance, in the series of Hello World examples we have seen so far in this book, the `ManagerAction` session bean primarily functions as a DAO for the `Person` entity bean.

In large enterprise applications, the main benefit of the DAO pattern is that it abstracts out the data access logic from the business logic. The business components contain only the domain-specific business logic and no API calls specific to data access (e.g., no `EntityManager` references). This way, the business components are more portable and lightweight by being less attached to the underlying frameworks. That is certainly a good thing from an architectural point of view.

On the other hand, DAOs are highly repetitive—they are largely the same for each entity class and therefore ideal for code reuse. Seam provides an application framework with built-in generic DAO components. You can develop simple CRUD web applications in Seam without writing a single line of business logic code. Read on and we will show you how.

The example application in this chapter is in the `crud` project in the book's source code bundle. In terms of functions, the `crud` example is roughly equivalent to the Integration example used in the previous chapters.

# 16.2  Seam CRUD DAOs Are POJOs

A DAO is only responsible for data access and does not need any other EJB3 container services, which means we should be able to use Seam POJOs instead of EJB3 session beans. The benefits of Seam POJOs are that they are simpler than EJB3 session beans and can be deployed on the older J2EE 1.4 application servers, but they do need a little extra configuration (see Chapter 4). If you use seam-gen (Chapter 5) to generate your configuration files, the POJO settings are enabled by default. If you write your own configuration files based on the Hello World examples, you need to pay attention to a few places. The idea here is to bootstrap a Seam-managed `EntityManager` for the DAO POJOs because the POJOs cannot directly use the EJB3-managed `EntityManager`.

In the `persistence.xml` file in `app.jar/META-INF`, you need to register the persistence context unit under a JNDI name unique to your application:

```
<persistence>
  <persistence-unit name="helloworld">
    ... ...
    <properties>
      ... ...
      <property name="jboss.entity.manager.factory.jndi.name"
                value="java:/crudEntityManagerFactory"/>
    </properties>
  </persistence-unit>
</persistence>
```

Then, in the `components.xml` file in `app.war/WEB-INF`, you need to define the Seam-managed `EntityManager` component so that it can be injected into Seam POJO components:

```
<components ...>
  ... ...
  <core:managed-persistence-context name="em"
    persistence-unit-jndi-name="java:/crudEntityManagerFactory"/>
  ... ...
</components>
```

That's it for the `EntityManager` configuration. The Seam DAO components themselves are also defined in the `components.xml` file. Let's check out how they work next.

# 16.3   A Declarative Seam DAO Component

A useful feature of Seam DAO components is that they can be declaratively instantiated in the Seam `components.xml` file, so you do not even need to write any data access code. Let's look at an example for the `Person` entity bean adopted from previous examples. Since the DAO now manages the entity bean, you no longer need the `@Name` annotation on the entity bean:

```
@Entity
public class Person implements Serializable {

  private long id;
  private String name;
  private int age;
  private String email;
  private String comment;

  ... Getter and Setter Methods ...
}
```

To instantiate a DAO component for the `Person` entity bean, all you need is an `entity-home` element in `components.xml`. The DAO component can be referenced in JSF pages or injected into other Seam components via the Seam name `personDao`. The `#{em}` references the Seam-managed `EntityManager` we defined in the previous section; the DAO uses this `EntityManager` to manage the `Person` object.

```
<components ... xmlns:fwk="http://jboss.com/products/seam/framework" ...>
  ... ...
  <fwk:entity-home name="personDao" entity-class="Person"
                   entity-manager="#{em}"/>
  ... ...
</components>
```

You can now reference the `Person` instance that `personDao` manages via `#{personDao.instance}`. The following is an example JSF page that uses the DAO to add a new `Person` object to the database:

```
<s:validateAll>
<table>
  <tr>
    <td>Your name:</td>
    <td>
      <s:decorate>
        <h:inputText value="#{personDao.instance.name}"/>
      </s:decorate>
    </td>
  </tr>
  ... ...
</table>
</s:validateAll>
<h:commandButton type="submit" value="Say Hello"
                 action="#{personDao.persist}"/>
```

The pages.xml file provides a mechanism to navigate to the next page when the user clicks on the button. We have discussed page navigation before and will not repeat it here.

## 16.3.1  Using Simpler Names for the Entity Object

Using #{personDao.instance} to reference the managed Person instance in the DAO is not as elegant as using #{person}, as we did in the previous example. Fortunately, the component factory in Seam makes it very easy to map #{personDao.instance} to #{person}. Just add the factory element in the components.xml file as follows:

```
<components ... xmlns:fwk="http://jboss.com/products/seam/framework" ...>
  ... ...
  <factory name="person" value="#{personDao.instance}"/>
  <fwk:entity-home name="personDao" entity-class="Person"
                   entity-manager="#{em}"/>
  ... ...
</components>
```

You can now use #{person} to back the data fields on the page and #{personDao} to back the actions on the #{person} data.

```
<s:validateAll>
<table>
  <tr>
    <td>Your name:</td>
    <td>
      <s:decorate>
        <h:inputText value="#{person.name}"/>
      </s:decorate>
    </td>
  </tr>
  ... ...
</table>
</s:validateAll>
<h:commandButton type="submit" value="Say Hello"
                 action="#{personDao.persist}"/>
```

## 16.3.2  Retrieving and Displaying an Entity Object

A CRUD application typically uses HTTP GET request parameters to retrieve entity objects for a page. The DAO must receive the HTTP request parameters, query the database, and make the retrieved entity object available for the page. In Chapter 15, we discussed how to bind the HTTP request parameter to backend components. In the Seam DAO objects, all you need is to bind the HTTP request parameter to the DAO's id property.

For instance, in the crud example application, we want to load individual persons via URLs such as person.seam?pid=3. You can use the following element in the app.war/WEB-INF/pages.xml file to accomplish this:

```
<pages>
  <page view-id="/person.xhtml">
    <param name="pid" value="#{personDao.id}"
           converterId="javax.faces.Long"/>
  </page>
</pages>
```

Now, when you load the person.seam?pid=3 URL, the DAO automatically retrieves the Person object with an ID equal to 3. You can then reference the entity object via the JSF EL expression #{person}.

## 16.3.3  Initializing a New Entity Instance

When a new DAO is created, it instantiates its managed entity object. If the id property in the DAO is not set, it just creates a new entity object using the entity bean's default constructor. You can initialize the newly created entity object in the entity-home component. The new-instance property allows Seam to inject an existing entity object, which is also created in the components.xml as a component, into the DAO. The following is an example; notice that the property values in the newPerson component can also be JSF EL expressions.

```
<fwk:entity-home name="personDao"
                 entity-class="Person"
                 entity-manager="#{em}"
                 new-instance="#{newPerson}"/>

<component name="newPerson" class="Person">
  <property name="age">25</property>
</component>
```

## 16.3.4  Success Messages

As we discussed in Section 8.1.2, Seam enhances the JSF messaging system enabling it to display a success message after an operation. In the entity-home component, you can customize the success messages for the CRUD operations. You can then simply use an `<h:message>` component on any page to display a message. This is a great time saver in simple CRUD applications.

```
<fwk:entity-home name="personDao"
                 entity-class="Person"
                 entity-manager="#{em}">
  <fwk:created-message>
    New person #{person.name} created
  </fwk:created-message>
  <fwk:deleted-message>
    Person #{person.name} deleted
  </fwk:deleted-message>
  <fwk:updated-message>
    Person #{person.name} updated
  </fwk:updated-message>
</fwk:entity-home>
```

---

**Handling Failures**

Obviously, no success messages are sent to the JSF messaging system when the CRUD operation fails. In this case, we can redirect to a custom error page (see Chapter 17).

---

# 16.4  Queries

Data querying is a key feature in database-driven applications. The Seam application framework provides query components in addition to the basic CRUD DAO components. You can use a query component to declare queries in `components.xml` without writing a single line of Java code.

The declarative approach to data queries helps us manage all queries in a central location and allows the Java code to reuse queries. It is a proven approach similar to the `NamedQuery` in Hibernate or Java Persistence API.

For instance, the following element defines a Seam query component named `fans`. When the query is executed, it retrieves all `Person` objects from the database.

```
<components ...>

  ... ...

  <fwk:entity-query name="fans"
        entity-manager="#{em}"
        ejbql="select p from Person p"/>

</components>
```

On a JSF web page, you can execute the query and reference its result list via `#{fans.resultList}`:

```
<h:dataTable value="#{fans.resultList}" var="fan">
  <h:column>
    <f:facet name="header">Name</f:facet>
    #{fan.name}
  </h:column>
  <h:column>
    <f:facet name="header">Age</f:facet>
    #{fan.age}
  </h:column>
  <h:column>
    <f:facet name="header">Email</f:facet>
    #{fan.email}
  </h:column>
  <h:column>
    <f:facet name="header">Comment</f:facet>
    #{fan.comment}
  </h:column>
  <h:column>
    <a href="person.seam?pid=#{fan.id}">Edit</a>
  </h:column>
</h:dataTable>
```

You can use the `WHERE` clause to constrain the query results in the `ejbql` property. However, you cannot use parameterized query constraints because no Java code explicitly calls the `Query.setParameter()` method at runtime. To use dynamic queries, you must declaratively bind user input to the query, as we discuss in the next section.

## 16.4.1 Dynamic Queries

Static database queries are useful. But in real-world applications, most queries are dynamically constructed from user input. For instance, the user might search for all persons under age 35 who have a `redhat.com` email address.

Dynamic querying binds user input values (search criteria) to placeholders in the constraint clause of the query. The query API in the `EntityManager` enables you to place parameters (i.e., the placeholders) into the query string and then use the `setParameter()` method to set the parameter value at runtime before the query is executed. The Seam query component enables you to do similar things.

The Seam query component is defined in `components.xml`, so we can declaratively bind user input to query constraints. For that, we use the JSF EL to capture user input in `components.xml`. For instance, let's assume that you have a `#{search}` component that backs the input fields on the search query page. The age constraint in the query is bound to `#{search.age}` and the email constraint is bound to `#{search.email}`. The following is the corresponding query example in the `components.xml` file:

```
<fwk:entity-query name="fans"
                  entity-manager="#{em}"
                  ejbql="select p from Person p"
                  order="name">
  <fwk:restrictions>
    <value>age < #{search.age}</value>
    <value>lower(email) like lower('%' + #{search.email})</value>
  </fwk:restrictions>
</fwk:entity-query>
```

Although it is possible to bind any JSF EL expression to the query constraint, the most common pattern is to use an example entity component to capture the user input. It provides a more structured way to manage the data fields. In the following example, we use the `order` property to order the query results:

```
<component name="examplePerson" class="Person"/>

<fwk:entity-query name="fans"
                  entity-manager="#{em}"
                  ejbql="select p from Person p"
                  order="name">
  <fwk:restrictions>
    <value>age < #{examplePerson.age}</value>
    <value>lower(email) like lower('%'+#{examplePerson.email})</value>
  </fwk:restrictions>
</fwk:entity-query>
```

The web page for the query form and the results list follows. Notice that the form submission button for the page is not bound to any backend event handler method; it simply submits the user input search criteria to the `#{search}` component. When JSF renders the `#{fans}` component later on the page, Seam invokes the query with the parameters in the `#{search}` component, as shown earlier.

```
<h:form>
Search filters:<br/>
Max age:
<h:inputText value="#{examplePerson.age}"/>
Email domain:
<h:inputText value="#{examplePerson.email}"/>
<h:commandButton value="Search" action="/search.xhtml"/>
</h:form>

<h:dataTable value="#{fans.resultList}" var="fan">
  <h:column>
    <f:facet name="header">Name</f:facet>
    #{fan.name}
  </h:column>
  <h:column>
    <f:facet name="header">Age</f:facet>
    #{fan.age}
  </h:column>
  <h:column>
    <f:facet name="header">Email</f:facet>
    #{fan.email}
  </h:column>
```

```
<h:column>
  <f:facet name="header">Comment</f:facet>
  #{fan.comment}
</h:column>
<h:column>
  <a href="person.seam?pid=#{fan.id}">Edit</a>
</h:column>
</h:dataTable>
```

## 16.4.2 Displaying Multipage Query Results

If your query returns a long list of results, you usually want to display those results across multiple pages with links to navigate between pages. The Seam query component has built-in support for paged data tables. First, you specify how many result objects you want to display on each page via the `max-results` property:

```
<fwk:entity-query name="fans"
                  entity-manager="#{em}"
                  ejbql="select p from Person p"
                  order="name"
                  max-results="20"/>
```

Then on the JSF page, you use the `firstResult` HTTP request parameter to control the part of the result set to display. The `firstResult` parameter is automatically injected into the query component (i.e., `fans`) when the page loads, and no more coding is needed. For instance, the URL `fans.seam?firstResult=30` for the following page displays query result objects numbered 30 to 49:

```
<h:dataTable value="#{fans.resultList}" var="fan">
  <h:column>
    <f:facet name="header">Name</f:facet>
    #{fan.name}
  </h:column>
  ... ...
</h:dataTable>
```

The `entity-query` component also provides built-in support for pagination links. That makes it easy to add **Next/Prev/First/Last** links on the results page:

```
<h:dataTable value="#{fans.resultList}" var="fan">
  <h:column>
    <f:facet name="header">Name</f:facet>
    #{fan.name}
  </h:column>
  ... ...
</h:dataTable>

<a href="fans.seam?firstResult=0">First Page</a>

<a href="fans.seam?firstResult=#{fans.previousFirstResult}">
  Previous Page
</a>
```

```
<a href="fans.seam?firstResult=#{fans.nextFirstResult}">
  Next Page
</a>
<a href="fans.seam?firstResult=#{fans.lastFirstResult}">
  Last Page
</a>
```

The static HTML pagination links appear even if the query result fits in one page; for multiple page results, all of them appear even if the user is already on the first or last page. A better approach is to use Seam's <s:link> component to render the links (see Section 3.2.1). This way, you can control when the pagination links are rendered. Consider this example:

```
<h:dataTable value="#{fans.resultList}" var="fan">
  <h:column>
    <f:facet name="header">Name</f:facet>
    #{fan.name}
  </h:column>
  ... ...
</h:dataTable>

<s:link view="/fans.xhtml"
        rendered="#{fans.previousExists}"
        value="First Page">
  <f:param name="firstResult" value="0"/>
</s:link>

<s:link view="/fans.xhtml"
        rendered="#{fans.previousExists}"
        value="Previous Page">
  <f:param name="firstResult" value="#{fans.previousFirstResult}"/>
</s:link>

<s:link view="/fans.xhtml"
        rendered="#{fans.nextExists}"
        value="Next Page">
  <f:param name="firstResult" value="#{fans.nextFirstResult}"/>
</s:link>

<s:link view="/fans.xhtml"
        rendered="#{fans.nextExists}"
        value="Last Page">
  <f:param name="firstResult" value="#{fans.lastFirstResult}"/>
</s:link>
```

With the Seam CRUD framework, you can write an entire database application declaratively. However, if you are not comfortable with coding in XML, you can also extend the Seam POJO classes behind the entity-home and entity-query components to accomplish the same tasks; refer to the Seam Reference Documentation for details.

# 17

# Failing Gracefully

Like input validation, error handling is a very important aspect of a web application, but it is hard to do right. Without proper error handling, uncaught exceptions in the application (e.g., a `RuntimeException` or a transaction-related exception) would propagate out of the web framework and cause a generic "Internal Server Error" (HTTP error code 500). The user would see a page full of technical jargon and a partial stack trace of the exception itself (see Figure 17.1). That is certainly unprofessional. Instead, we should try to fail gracefully and display a nice custom error page for the user.

With the tight integration between business components and presentation components, Seam makes it easy to convert any business-layer exception into a custom error page. In this chapter, we will go back to the `booking` example discussed in Chapters 8 to 11 to show how errors from transactions are handled.

Before we discuss the Seam approach, we'll present a quick overview on the standard error handling mechanism in Java EE and discuss why it is insufficient.

## 17.1  Why Not Standard Servlet Error Pages?

Java EE (the servlet specification) uses a standard mechanism for handling servlet or JSP exceptions. Using the `error-page` element in `web.xml`, you can redirect to a custom error page upon any exception or HTTP error code. The following is an example that redirects to `/error.html` when an uncaught error is thrown from the application or to `/notFound.html` when an HTTP 404 error is encountered.

**HTTP Status 500 -**

**type** Exception report

**message**

**description** The server encountered an internal error () that prevented it from fulfilling this request.

**exception**

```
javax.servlet.ServletException: Error calling action method of component with id _id26:_id32
        javax.faces.webapp.FacesServlet.service(FacesServlet.java:152)
        org.jboss.seam.servlet.SeamRedirectFilter.doFilter(SeamRedirectFilter.java:32)
        org.jboss.web.tomcat.filters.ReplyHeaderFilter.doFilter(ReplyHeaderFilter.java:96)
```

**root cause**

```
javax.faces.FacesException: Error calling action method of component with id _id26:_id32
        org.apache.myfaces.application.ActionListenerImpl.processAction(ActionListenerImpl.jav
        javax.faces.component.UICommand.broadcast(UICommand.java:106)
        javax.faces.component.UIViewRoot._broadcastForPhase(UIViewRoot.java:94)
        javax.faces.component.UIViewRoot.processApplication(UIViewRoot.java:168)
        org.apache.myfaces.lifecycle.LifecycleImpl.invokeApplication(LifecycleImpl.java:343)
        org.apache.myfaces.lifecycle.LifecycleImpl.execute(LifecycleImpl.java:86)
        javax.faces.webapp.FacesServlet.service(FacesServlet.java:137)
        org.jboss.seam.servlet.SeamRedirectFilter.doFilter(SeamRedirectFilter.java:32)
        org.jboss.web.tomcat.filters.ReplyHeaderFilter.doFilter(ReplyHeaderFilter.java:96)
```

**note** The full stack trace of the root cause is available in the Apache Tomcat/5.5.20 logs.

**Apache Tomcat/5.5.20**

**Figure 17.1**    An uncaught exception from the Seam event handler method

```
<web-app>
  ... ...
  <error-page>
    <exception-type>
      java.lang.Throwable
    </exception-type>
    <location>/error.html</location>
  </error-page>

  <error-page>
    <error-code>
      404
    </error-code>
    <location>/notFound.html</location>
  </error-page>

</web-app>
```

However, a problem with this approach is that the JSF servlet wraps around the exception from the business layer and throws a generic `ServletException` instead, before the server captures the exception and redirects to the error page. So, in the `exception-type` tag, you cannot accurately specify the actual exception in the business layer. Some people would just capture a very generic `java.lang.Throwable` and redirect to a generic error page. That is not satisfactory because you would probably want to display different error messages for different error causes and present remedy action choices to the user.

In the JSP world, there's a workaround: You can simply redirect to a JSP error page. From that page, you can access the JSP built-in variable `exception`. Then, you can programmatically drill down to the root cause of the exception and display the appropriate message. Unfortunately, the `exception` variable does not work properly in JSF-rendered JSP pages or Facelets XHTML pages.

Seam provides a much better solution—with it, you can integrate the error page directly into your existing JSF view. Better yet, Seam enables you to declare whether the exception should end the current conversation if it was thrown from inside a long-running conversation.

# 17.2   Setting Up the Exception Filter

Seam uses a servlet filter to capture uncaught exceptions and then render the appropriate custom error page (or error code). Make sure that the following elements are present in your `app.war/WEB-INF/web.xml` file (see Section 3.3):

```
<web-app ...>
  ... ...
  <filter>
    <filter-name>Seam Filter</filter-name>
    <filter-class>
      org.jboss.seam.web.SeamFilter
    </filter-class>
  </filter>

  <filter-mapping>
    <filter-name>Seam Filter</filter-name>
    <url-pattern>/*</url-pattern>
  </filter-mapping>

</web-app>
```

With the Seam `filter` properly set up, you can now specify custom error pages for exceptions in one of the two ways: For application-defined exceptions, you can use annotations, and for system or framework exceptions, you can use the `pages.xml` file. We will discuss both approaches in this chapter.

# 17.3   Annotating Exceptions

If your application throws its own exceptions, you can use three kinds of annotations to tell Seam what to do when the annotated exception is uncaught.

The `@Redirect` annotation instructs Seam to display the error page specified in the `viewId` attribute when this exception is thrown. The `end` attribute specifies whether this exception ends the current long-running conversation; by default, the conversation does not end. The following example was taken from the Hotel Booking sample application (Chapter 11). This exception is thrown when the requested hotel is not available. It rolls back the database transaction but does not end the conversation, enabling the user to click the browser **Back** button to go back and select another hotel to book.

```
@ApplicationException(rollback=true)
@Redirect(viewId="/inventoryError.xhtml")
public class InventoryException extends Exception {

    public InventoryException () { }

}
```

The error page `inventoryError.xhtml` is just a regular JSF view page (Figure 17.2). Notice that it still has access to the conversation-scoped components (i.e., `#{hotel}`) and the user can use the **Back** button to book another hotel in the same conversation.

```
<ui:composition ... template="template.xhtml">

  <ui:define name="content">
    <div class="section">
      <h1>Insufficient Inventory</h1>
      <p>The <b>#{hotel.name}</b> hotel
      in #{hotel.city} does not have any rooms left.
      Please use your browser's BACK button to
      go back and book another hotel!</p>
    </div>
  </ui:define>
... ...
</ui:composition>
```

**Custom Error page**

Transactional exceptions would rollback all database updates that already happened in this transaction. This is a good way to preserve the database integrity.

You can configure error pages for each exception via the @Render annotation on the exception class. Or, you can specify a general error page for a system eception in exceptions.xml

**Insufficient Inventory**

The **Swissotel** hotel in Sydney does not have any rooms left. Please use your browser's BACK button to go back and book another hotel!

**Figure 17.2**   The error page showing unavailable room inventory

**No Stack Trace**

Notice that we do not display the exception stack trace in the custom error page. You should never display the stack trace on a production web site. If you are debugging the application and want to see the stack trace, you can enable Seam debugging (Section 3.3) and go to /debug.seam.

The @HttpError annotation causes Seam to send an HTTP error code back to the browser when the annotated exception propagates out of the Seam runtime. The message attribute provides the HTTP message to be sent to the browser, and the end attribute specifies whether the current long-running conversation should end here.

```
@HttpError(errorCode=404, end=true)
public class SomeException extends Exception {
  ...
}
```

# 17.4  Using pages.xml for System Exceptions

The annotation approach applies only to application-defined exceptions. Of course, that is inadequate because many runtime errors are system- or framework-level exceptions. For instance, when a database connection error occurs, the application throws a RuntimeException, which is not defined by the application and, therefore, cannot be annotated.

In a Seam application, you can configure how to deal with system or framework exceptions via the pages.xml file we discussed earlier in the book (see, e.g., Section 15.1). This file should be packaged in the app.war file's WEB-INF directory together with web.xml, components.xml, etc. As with annotations, we can redirect to a custom JSF page, send an HTTP error code, and end the current long-running conversation when such exceptions are thrown.

The following pages.xml is from the Hotel Booking sample application. It configures custom error pages for the RuntimeException and other system exceptions. When Seam redirects to an error page, it sends along a JSF message that can be displayed via an <h:messages/> UI element on the error page.

```
<pages>

  ... Page actions and parameters ...

  <exception class="javax.persistence.EntityNotFoundException">
    <http-error error-code="404"/>
  </exception>
```

```
<exception class="javax.persistence.PersistenceException">
  <end-conversation/>
  <redirect view-id="/generalError.xhtml">
    <message>Database access failed</message>
  </redirect>
</exception>

<exception class="java.lang.RuntimeException">
  <redirect view-id="/generalError.xhtml">
    <message>Unexpected failure</message>
  </redirect>
</exception>
```

```
</pages>
```

When a `RuntimeException` is thrown from the application, Seam redirects to the `/generalError.xhtml` page with the JSF error message, but without ending the current long-running conversation. The `generalError.xhtml` page is as follows; Figure 17.3 shows it in a browser.

```
<ui:composition ...>

  <ui:define name="content">
    <div class="section">
      <h1>General</h1>
      <p>The following general error has occurred</p>

      <p><h:messages/></p>

      <p>Please come back and try again! Thanks.</p>
    </div>
  </ui:define>

  <ui:define name="sidebar">
    <h1>Custom Error page</h1>
    ... ...
  </ui:define>

</ui:composition>
```

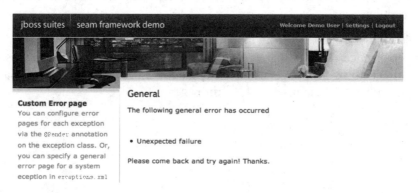

**Figure 17.3**   The `generalError.xhtml` page for `RuntimeException`

**Error Messages with @Redirect**

The @Redirect annotation can also take a message attribute to send a JSF message to the error page it redirects to.

**Using Error Pages with Seam Security**

It is easy to redirect to a custom login page when an unauthenticated user tries to access a restricted web page protected by the Seam security framework (see Chapter 18). You just need to capture and redirect the org.jboss.seam.security.NotLoggedInException.

# 17.5 The Debug Information Page

Custom error pages are nice for production systems. However, when you develop the application, you do not know when and what kinds of errors might come up. Seam and Facelets provide generic mechanisms to capture any error during development and redirect to the debug information page, so that you can accurately pinpoint the error source.

## 17.5.1 The Facelets Debug Page

To enable the Facelets debug page, you need to put Facelets in development mode in the app.war/WEB-INF/web.xml file:

```
<web-app ...>
  ... ...
  <context-param>
    <param-name>facelets.DEVELOPMENT</param-name>
    <param-value>true</param-value>
  </context-param>
</web-app>
```

If an error occurs when Facelets renders a page, it displays a professional looking error page with accurate debugging information pinpointing the line number in the Facelets XHTML file that caused the error (see Figure 17.4). The source file line number is useful because what the standard JSF stack trace gives you is useless line numbers on the servlet compiled from the view page.

The debug page also provides information about the current internal state of the JSF rendering engine. For instance, you can view the complete JSF component tree associated with the current page. You can actually launch the debug page as a pop-up from any Facelets page; you just need to put the <ui:debug hotkey="d"/> element in your Facelets page. Then, at runtime, press **Ctrl+Shift+d** to launch the debug pop-up. You can choose any hotkey other than the **d** shown here. Of course, if there is no error at this moment, the debug page shows only the component tree and scoped variables, without the stack trace.

**An Error Occurred:**

Error Parsing /hello.xhtml: Error Traced[line: 25] The element type "p" must be terminated by the matching end-tag "</p>".

```
com.sun.facelets.FaceletException: Error Parsing /hello.xhtml: Error Traced[line: 25] The element type "p" must be
    at com.sun.facelets.compiler.SAXCompiler.doCompile(SAXCompiler.java:228)
    at com.sun.facelets.compiler.Compiler.compile(Compiler.java:104)
    at com.sun.facelets.impl.DefaultFaceletFactory.createFacelet(DefaultFaceletFactory.java:192)
    at com.sun.facelets.impl.DefaultFaceletFactory.getFacelet(DefaultFaceletFactory.java:141)
    at com.sun.facelets.impl.DefaultFaceletFactory.getFacelet(DefaultFaceletFactory.java:93)
    at com.sun.facelets.FaceletViewHandler.buildView(FaceletViewHandler.java:483)
    at com.sun.facelets.FaceletViewHandler.renderView(FaceletViewHandler.java:533)
    at org.apache.myfaces.lifecycle.LifecycleImpl.render(LifecycleImpl.java:384)
    at javax.faces.webapp.FacesServlet.service(FacesServlet.java:138)
    at org.apache.catalina.core.ApplicationFilterChain.internalDoFilter(ApplicationFilterChain.java:252)
    at org.apache.catalina.core.ApplicationFilterChain.doFilter(ApplicationFilterChain.java:173)
    at org.jboss.seam.servlet.SeamExceptionFilter.doFilter(SeamExceptionFilter.java:46)
    at org.apache.catalina.core.ApplicationFilterChain.internalDoFilter(ApplicationFilterChain.java:202)
    at org.apache.catalina.core.ApplicationFilterChain.doFilter(ApplicationFilterChain.java:173)
    at org.jboss.seam.servlet.SeamRedirectFilter.doFilter(SeamRedirectFilter.java:32)
    at org.apache.catalina.core.ApplicationFilterChain.internalDoFilter(ApplicationFilterChain.java:202)
    at org.apache.catalina.core.ApplicationFilterChain.doFilter(ApplicationFilterChain.java:173)
    at org.apache.catalina.core.StandardWrapperValve.invoke(StandardWrapperValve.java:213)
    at org.apache.catalina.core.StandardContextValve.invoke(StandardContextValve.java:178)
    at org.apache.catalina.core.StandardHostValve.invoke(StandardHostValve.java:126)
    at org.apache.catalina.valves.ErrorReportValve.invoke(ErrorReportValve.java:105)
    at org.apache.catalina.core.StandardEngineValve.invoke(StandardEngineValve.java:107)
    at org.apache.catalina.connector.CoyoteAdapter.service(CoyoteAdapter.java:148)
    at org.apache.coyote.http11.Http11Processor.process(Http11Processor.java:869)
    at org.apache.coyote.http11.Http11BaseProtocol$Http11ConnectionHandler.processConnection(Http11BaseProtoco
    at org.apache.tomcat.util.net.PoolTcpEndpoint.processSocket(PoolTcpEndpoint.java:527)
    at org.apache.tomcat.util.net.LeaderFollowerWorkerThread.runIt(LeaderFollowerWorkerThread.java:80)
    at org.apache.tomcat.util.threads.ThreadPool$ControlRunnable.run(ThreadPool.java:684)
    at java.lang.Thread.run(Thread.java:613)
```

+ Component Tree

+ Scoped Variables

**Figure 17.4**    The Facelets debug page

# 17.5.2  The Seam Debug Page

If an error occurs outside the JSF Facelets page rendering operation (e.g., an error in the UI event handler method), the Facelets debug page will not catch it. We have to use the Seam debug page for this type of error.

To use the Seam debug page, you need to follow the instructions in Section 3.3 to bundle the `jboss-seam-debug.jar` and set up the Seam Exception Filter. Then, in the `app.war/WEB-INF/components.xml` file, you must enable debugging on the `core:init` component:

```
<components ...>
  <core:init jndi-pattern="booking/#{ejbName}/local" debug="true"/>
  ... ...
</components>
```

Now, any uncaught error will be redirected to the `/debug.seam` page, which displays the context information as well as the stack trace (Figure 17.5).

**- Session Context**

bookingList

bookings

facelets.ui.DebugOutput

localeSelector

loggedIn

org.jboss.seam.core.conversationEntries

resourceBundle

user

**+ Application Context**

**- Exception**

Exception during INVOKE_APPLICATION(5): java.lang.RuntimeException: Simulated DB error

```
org.jboss.ejb3.tx.Ejb3TxPolicy.handleExceptionInOurTx(Ejb3TxPolicy.java:69)
org.jboss.aspects.tx.TxPolicy.invokeInOurTx(TxPolicy.java:83)
org.jboss.aspects.tx.TxInterceptor$Required.invoke(TxInterceptor.java:197)
org.jboss.aop.joinpoint.MethodInvocation.invokeNext(MethodInvocation.java:101)
org.jboss.aspects.tx.TxPropagationInterceptor.invoke(TxPropagationInterceptor.java:7
org.jboss.aop.joinpoint.MethodInvocation.invokeNext(MethodInvocation.java:101)
org.jboss.ejb3.stateful.StatefulInstanceInterceptor.invoke(StatefulInstanceIntercept
org.jboss.aop.joinpoint.MethodInvocation.invokeNext(MethodInvocation.java:101)
org.jboss.aspects.security.AuthenticationInterceptor.invoke(AuthenticationIntercepto
org.jboss.ejb3.security.Ejb3AuthenticationInterceptor.invoke(Ejb3AuthenticationInter
org.jboss.aop.joinpoint.MethodInvocation.invokeNext(MethodInvocation.java:101)
org.jboss.ejb3.ENCPropagationInterceptor.invoke(ENCPropagationInterceptor.java:47)
org.jboss.aop.joinpoint.MethodInvocation.invokeNext(MethodInvocation.java:101)
org.jboss.ejb3.asynchronous.AsynchronousInterceptor.invoke(AsynchronousInterceptor.j
org.jboss.aop.joinpoint.MethodInvocation.invokeNext(MethodInvocation.java:101)
org.jboss.ejb3.stateful.StatefulContainer.localInvoke(StatefulContainer.java:203)
org.jboss.ejb3.stateful.StatefulLocalProxy.invoke(StatefulLocalProxy.java:98)
$Proxy111.confirm(Unknown Source)
org.jboss.seam.example.booking.HotelBooking$$FastClassByCGLIB$$c83b792d.invoke(<gene
net.sf.cglib.proxy.MethodProxy.invoke(MethodProxy.java:149)
org.jboss.seam.intercept.RootInvocationContext.proceed(RootInvocationContext.java:45
org.jboss.seam.intercept.ClientSideInterceptor$1.proceed(ClientSideInterceptor.java:
org.jboss.seam.intercept.SeamInvocationContext.proceed(SeamInvocationContext.java:55
org.jboss.seam.interceptors.RemoveInterceptor.removeIfNecessary(RemoveInterceptor.ja
sun.reflect.GeneratedMethodAccessor105.invoke(Unknown Source)
sun.reflect.DelegatingMethodAccessorImpl.invoke(DelegatingMethodAccessorImpl.java:25
java.lang.reflect.Method.invoke(Method.java:585)
org.jboss.seam.util.Reflections.invoke(Reflections.java:18)
```

**Figure 17.5** An uncaught exception without a custom error page is redirected to 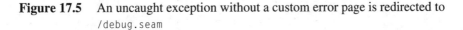`/debug.seam`

Again, the Seam `/debug.seam` page works even if there is no error. You can load that page at any time to look at the current Seam runtime context information.

Seam integrates exceptions in the business layer right into custom error pages in the presentation layer. This is yet another benefit of Seam's unified component approach. You have no more excuse for ugly error pages!

# 18

## Seam Security

**S**ecurity is, arguably, one of the most important aspects of application development. Given the cost associated with a security breach in an organization, this should be a top priority when developing an application. Unfortunately, due to its complexity, security is often an afterthought, which can lead to gaping holes in an application for malicious users to take advantage of. How can developers allocate the time necessary to completely secure an application? Imagine that your managers have already scheduled a year worth of effort to be completed in the next six months—are you doomed to be the next security breach headline on the nine o'clock news? Fortunately, when using Seam, much of this complexity is hidden, making it simple to ensure that your application is secure.

Security is a cross-cutting concern, meaning that much of the code to handle security requirements is not directly related to the business rules you are attempting to code. For example, if the method `bar()` in class `Foo` needs to be accessible only to the users who are logged in and have the role `FOO_USER`, we could easily code this into the method. If requirements change and we now want to ensure that every method in `Foo` is restricted to `FOO_USER`, we suddenly see that this code is getting constantly replicated. The same scenario applies to web pages. If we want to secure all pages in the directory `/secured`, we would like to apply this restriction only once. Seam makes it easy to handle this cross-cutting concern.

As we discuss Seam security throughout this chapter, we will walk you through the basic security features of the Rules Booking example. This example can be found in the examples distributed with the book in the `rulesbooking` folder. Rule Booking is yet another extension of the Seam Hotel Booking example utilizing basic Seam security which will be covered in the following sections as well as rules-based authorization (Chapter 22), and using a rule base (see Chapter 23). The Rules Booking example provides a rewards program to the users of the system and allows users to review the hotels they have recently booked. Obviously, these scenarios require certain role and permission checks to ensure that the system provides behavior consistent with the expectations of the business. We will demonstrate how the security features of Seam fit the requirements of this type of application.

In addition to basic security, this chapter will cover additional security features provided by Seam, such as SSL and CAPTCHA, to help you to secure your application even further. Do not wait, those hackers could be hitting your web site right now!

# 18.1  Authentication and User Roles

The most important aspect of a security framework is user authentication. Each user must log in with a username and password combo to access the restricted parts of the web application. These username and password are checked against some authentication source (e.g., LDAP, data source, etc.) to verify that the user is who he or she says. Once the user's *identity* has been verified, we can determine the role of the user within the application.

Each user may have one or several security roles, meaning he or she is authorized to access certain restricted sections or features of the application. For instance, in the Rules Booking example users are either basic users or rewards users. Rewards users have the benefit of gaining reward points each time a booking is confirmed and applying those rewards to future bookings for a saving. Basic users can simply search for and book hotels, as in our previous examples, as well as write reviews on the hotels they have recently booked. In order to differentiate between rewards users and basic users, a rewards user is associated with the `rewardsuser` role. Let's see how we can authenticate users and assign them appropriate roles.

Seam is built upon JAAS (Java Authentication and Authorization Service), a standardized solution. It also provides a simplified approach to authentication and authorization that allows you to quickly incorporate security into your application. First, you need to write a login form for the user to enter username and password. In the login form, you should bind the user credentials to the Seam built-in `#{credentials}` component. The `#{identity}` component can then be invoked to authenticate the user based on the provided credentials.

```
<div>
  Username:
  <h:inputText value="#{credentials.username}"/>
</div>
```

```
<div>
  Password:
  <h:inputSecret value="#{credentials.password}"/>
</div>

<div>
  <h:commandButton value="Account Login"
                   action="#{identity.login}"/>
</div>
```

Both the #{credentials} component and #{identity} component are scoped to the HTTP session. Once a user is logged in, he or she stays logged in until the session expires. The #{identity.login} method, in turn, invokes an "authenticator" method to perform the actual authentication work. We will discuss how to configure the authenticator method shortly. If the login succeeds, the #{identity.login} method returns the String value loggedIn, which you can use in the navigation rules to determine the next page to display. If the login fails, the #{identity.login} method returns null to redisplay the login form with an error message.

The login form home.xhtml allows the users to enter their credentials to log in to the Rewards Booking application, as shown in Figure 18.1.

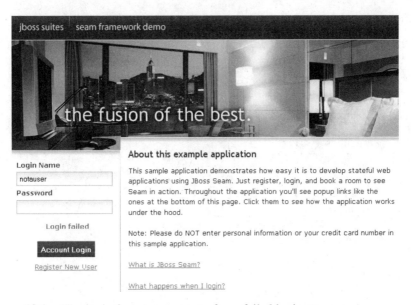

**Figure 18.1**    The login form home.xhtml after a failed login attempt

As you can see, when an attempted login fails, the user is presented with a "Login failed" message. This message can be customized by specifying the org.jboss.seam. loginFailed key in a message.properties resource file.

## Logout

The #{identity.logout} method provides a simple mechanism for logging out a user from a Seam application. It simply invalidates the current session and causes Seam to reload the current page—to be redirected to the login page if the current page is restricted.

The authentication method, invoked from #{identity.login}, must ensure that the username and password from the injected credentials instance are valid user credentials. If they are valid, the method returns true; otherwise, it returns false. After the username and password are verified, the authentication method optionally retrieves the security roles for the user and adds those roles to the Identity component via Identity.addRole(String role). The following authenticate() method is an example authentication method. It checks the User table in the database to authenticate the user and retrieves the user's roles from the same database upon successful authentication.

```
@Stateless
@Name("authenticator")
public class AuthenticatorAction implements Authenticator
{
  @In EntityManager em;

  @In Credentials credentials;
  @In Identity identity;

  @Out(required=false, scope = SESSION)
  private User user;

  public boolean authenticate()
  {
    List results = em.createQuery(
      "select u from User u where u.username=#{credentials.username}"
        + " and u.password=#{credentials.password}").getResultList();

    if ( results.size()==0 )
    {
      return false;
    }
    else
    {
      user = (User) results.get(0);

      for(Role role : user.getRoles())
      {
        identity.addRole(role.getRolename());
      }

      return true;
    }
  }
}
```

This is a very brute-force approach to authentication, but it can be useful if you must invoke existing authentication logic or perform custom authentication tasks. For Seam to know that the #{authenticator.authenticate} method is the authentication method for the application, you must declare it in the components.xml file:

```
<components xmlns="http://jboss.com/products/seam/components"
            xmlns:security="http://jboss.com/products/seam/security"
            xmlns:core="http://jboss.com/products/seam/core">

   ... ...

   <security:identity
      authenticate-method="#{authenticator.authenticate}"/>

</components>
```

As you will see in Section 18.3, Seam 2.1 includes support for many common authentication use cases through the IdentityManager component. This allows you to avoid implementing this type of custom authentication logic.

---

**Security Lifecycle Events**

Seam provides a number of lifecycle events for security actions, enabling you to hook into the framework. Examples include:

- org.jboss.seam.security.loginSuccessful is raised after a successful login attempt.

- org.jboss.seam.security.loginFailed is raised after a login attempt fails.

- org.jboss.seam.security.loggedOut is raised when the user has been logged out.

These events are enumerated in the Seam documentation and are especially useful for auditing purposes.

---

# 18.2  Declarative Access Control

Authentication by itself is not very useful; it must be combined with an authorization scheme to grant access to the application based on the user's identity. Seam makes it easy to declare access constraints on web pages, UI components, and Java methods via XML tags, annotations, and JSF EL expressions. Through this declarative approach Seam allows you to easily build a layered security architecture. Security experts often term this layered approach to security a *defense-in-depth* approach and recommend its use to deter security threats. Not only does a layered approach decrease vulnerability to external threats; it also helps to avoid security holes from simple programming error.

Seam addresses the following layers common to Seam applications:

**page access**    Restricting access to specific pages or sections of the application.

**UI components**    Restricting access to specific components on a page.

**component access**    Restricting access to Seam components at the component or method level.

**entity access**    Restricting access to specific entities.

The following sections will discuss the first three layers of security, while entity access restrictions as well as rule-based permissions will be discussed in Chapter 22.

## 18.2.1  Page Access

The first layer we will discuss is one of the most common access control scenarios which involves displaying certain web pages only when the user is logged in. That can be easily done with the `pages.xml` file. Continuing our Rules Booking example, the following listing shows that only logged-in users can access the `password.xhtml` page, as well as any pages with the `/rewards/*` URL pattern. If the user is not logged in, the `home.xhtml` page is displayed instead, as we have specified this as our `login-view-id` in the `<pages>` tag.

```
<pages ... login-view-id="/home.xhtml">
  ... ...
  <page view-id="/password.xhtml" login-required="true">
    ... ...
  <page>

  <page view-id="/rewards/*" login-required="true">
    ... ...
  <page>
</pages>
```

When using wildcards in page definitions, Seam uses the closest match to determine what attributes to apply to a page. We can use this to apply broad restrictions with exceptional cases. In our Rules Booking example, if we wanted to restrict all pages to require login except for the login page itself, we could use the following definition:

```
<pages ... login-view-id="/home.xhtml">
  ... ...
  <page view-id="*" login-required="true">
    ... ...
  <page>

  <page view-id="/home.xhtml" login-required="false">
    ... ...
  <page>
</pages>
```

Since /home.xhtml is a closer match to the login page than to the wildcard definition, login will not be required for this page. This is also useful in scenarios where restrictions are relaxed or tightened for a certain page or subset of pages.

If you want to redirect the user to the originally requested page after the login, add the following elements in your components.xml file:

```
<event type="org.jboss.seam.notLoggedIn">
  <action expression="#{redirect.captureCurrentView}"/>
</event>

<event type="org.jboss.seam.postAuthenticate">
  <action expression="#{redirect.returnToCapturedView}"/>
</event>
```

Using simple EL expressions in the <restrict> tag, we can also limit access to a page to users with a certain security role. For instance, looking again at the Rules Booking example, the following pages.xml code section indicates that the /rewards/* pages are accessible only to logged-in users with the rewardsuser role. The s:hasRole function implicitly invokes the Identity.hasRole(String role) method. This checks the roles associated with the Identity component during authentication.

```
<pages ... >
  ... ...
  <page view-id="/rewards/*">
    <description>Rewards Summary</description>
    <restrict>#{s:hasRole('rewardsuser')}</restrict>
  </page>
</pages>
```

When access is denied for the page, Seam throws a NotLoggedInException if a user is not currently logged in or an AuthorizationException if the role/permission check fails. You can use the techniques described in Chapter 17 to redirect to custom error pages when those exceptions occur.

Seam provides both s:hasRole and s:hasPermission, which we will discuss further in Chapter 22, as convenience operations. As these operations are accessible through EL expressions, they are available for pages.xml restrictions as well as within UI components and at the component level through the @Restrict annotation. All of these cases will be discussed in the following sections.

## 18.2.2  UI Components

Besides controlling access to entire web pages, our next layer of security allows you to use EL expressions to selectively display UI elements on a page to different users. This is accomplished via the rendered attribute on JSF components. The following listing shows the user information panel found in the /template.xhtml of the Rules Booking example:

```
Welcome #{user.name}
<s:link id="rewards" value="| Points: #{rewards.rewardPoints}"
        view-id="/rewards/summary.xhtml" propagation="none"
        rendered="#{s:hasRole('rewardsuser')}" />
| <s:link id="search" view="/main.xhtml" value="Search"
        propagation="none"/>
| <s:link id="settings" view="/password.xhtml" value="Settings"
        propagation="none"/>
| <s:link id="logout" action="#{identity.logout}" value="Logout"/>
```

Notice the reward points are only rendered if the user has the `rewardsuser` role. If the same template was to be used in pages that do not require a login, we could optionally display the entire user information bar based on the login status of the user. The login status of the user can be determined through the `#{identity.loggedIn}` method.

```
<s:div rendered="#{identity.loggedIn}">
  Welcome #{user.name}
  <s:link id="rewards" value="| Points: #{rewards.rewardPoints}"
          view-id="/rewards/summary.xhtml" propagation="none"
          rendered="#{s:hasRole('rewardsuser')}" />
  | <s:link id="search" view="/main.xhtml" value="Search"
          propagation="none"/>
  | <s:link id="settings" view="/password.xhtml" value="Settings"
          propagation="none"/>
  | <s:link id="logout" action="#{identity.logout}" value="Logout"/>
</s:div>
```

## 18.2.3  Component Access Control

Access control on the UI is simple to understand, but it is not sufficient. A clever cracker might be able to get past the UI layer and access methods on Seam components directly. It is important to secure components and individual Java methods in the application as well. Restricting component access is the next layer of our defense-in-depth approach. Fortunately, you can easily declare component- and method-level access constraints with Seam annotations and EL expressions. The following example shows a `changePassword()` method that is accessible only to logged-in users.

```
@Stateful
@Scope(EVENT)
@Name("changePassword")
public class ChangePasswordAction implements ChangePassword
{
  @Restrict("#{identity.loggedIn}")
  public void changePassword()
  {
    if ( user.getPassword().equals(verify) )
    {
      user = em.merge(user);
      facesMessages.add("Password updated");
      changed = true;
    }
```

```
    else
    {
      facesMessages.addToControl("verify", "Re-enter new password");
      revertUser();
      verify = null;
    }
  }
}
```

Given that all methods on the `ChangePasswordAction` are only accessible to logged-in users, we can place this restriction at the component level:

```
@Stateful
@Scope(EVENT)
@Name("changePassword")
@Restrict("#{identity.loggedIn}")
public class ChangePasswordAction implements ChangePassword
{
  // ... ...
```

Similarly, you can tag methods to be accessible only by users with a certain role. In the Rules Booking example, the `updateSettings()` method of the `RewardsManager` component is restricted to the `rewardsuser` role. This ensures that non-rewards users will not be authorized to update `Rewards` settings.

```
@Name("rewardsManager")
@Scope(ScopeType.CONVERSATION)
public class RewardsManager {
  @In User user;
  @In EntityManager em;

  @Out(required=false)
  private Rewards rewards;
  // ... ...
  @Restrict("#{s:hasRole{'rewardsuser'}}")
  public void updateSettings() {
    if(rewards.isReceiveSpecialOffers()) {
      facesMessages.add("You have successfully registered to " +
        "receive special offers!");
    } else {
      facesMessages.add("You will no longer receive our " +
        "special offers.");
    }

    rewards = em.merge(rewards);
    em.flush();
  }
  // ... ...
}
```

As before, when access is denied for the method, Seam throws the `NotLoggedIn-Exception` or the `AuthorizationException`, depending on whether the user is currently logged in. Again, you can refer to the techniques described in Chapter 17 to redirect to custom error pages when those exceptions occur.

# 18.2.4 Type-Safe Role Annotations

In addition to performing role checking through EL, annotations can be used to provide a more type-safe approach. Component methods can be annotated with these custom annotations to perform a role check based on the annotation name. The `@Admin` annotation is the only role check annotation defined by Seam security out of the box, but you are free to define as many annotations as your application requires by using the `@RoleCheck` annotation. For example, in the Rules Booking example we can define a `@RewardsUser` annotation:

```
@Target({METHOD})
@Documented
@Retention(RUNTIME)
@Inherited
@RoleCheck
public @interface RewardsUser {}
```

Simply declaring this custom annotation as a role check with the meta-annotation `@RoleCheck` activates the annotation for use in your components. The `RewardsManager` can now specify this annotation as a safeguard for updating the `rewards` instance:

```
@Name("rewardsManager")
@Scope(ScopeType.CONVERSATION)
@Transactional
public class RewardsManager {
  @In User user;
  @In EntityManager em;
  @In FacesMessages facesMessages;

  @Out(required=false)
  private Rewards rewards;

  // ... ...

  @RewardsUser
  public void updateSettings() {
    if(rewards.isReceiveSpecialOffers()) {
      facesMessages.add("You have successfully registered to " +
        "receive special offers!");
    } else {
      facesMessages.add("You will no longer receive our " +
        "special offers.");
    }

    rewards = em.merge(rewards);
    em.flush();
  }
  // ... ...
}
```

Seam security will perform a role check when the `updateSettings()` method is invoked to ensure that the currently logged-in user has the `rewardsuser` role. The role check is always performed against the lowercase representation of the annotation name.

# 18.3  Identity Management

Seam identity management provides a common API for managing users and roles. This API abstracts identity management from the underlying provider. Whether you are using a relational database, LDAP, or any other identity store, the `IdentityManager` API supports authentication as well as administrative operations. The `IdentityManager` API provides support for the following:

- Authentication against the configured identity store
- CRUD operations (create, read, update, and delete) for both users and roles
- Granting and revoking roles, changing passwords, enabling and disabling user accounts, listing users and roles

The `IdentityStore` component interacts with the underlying provider. You just need to configure the appropriate `IdentityStore` instance to be injected into the `IdentityManager` at runtime. You can create a custom provider by implementing the `IdentityStore` interface and configuring it for injection into the `IdentityManager` component.

The class diagram in Figure 18.2 represents the relationship between an application and the `IdentityManager` component. The `IdentityManager` is injected into any dependent components and abstracts the underlying provider. The `JpaIdentityStore` and the `LdapIdentityStore` are provided by Seam security out-of-the-box and will be discussed in the next few sections.

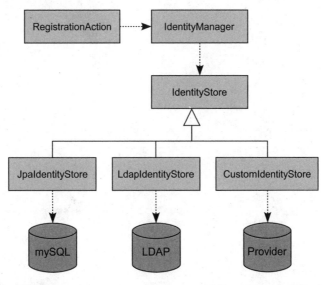

**Figure 18.2**    The `RegistrationAction` is abstracted from the underlying identity store by interacting with the `IdentityManager` API.

## 18.3.1  Using the JpaIdentityStore

The JpaIdentityStore provides identity management with a relational database. The Rules Booking example, found in the examples released with the book, demonstrates the use of the JpaIdentityStore. First, we must define the entities that will represent the users and roles. Table 18.1 lists the required annotations for these entities.

**Table 18.1** Identity Annotations

| Annotation | Use | Entity | Description |
|---|---|---|---|
| @UserPrincipal | field, method | user entity | This annotation marks the field or method containing the user's username. |
| @UserPassword | field, method | user entity | This annotation marks the field or method containing the user's password. Allows a hash algorithm to be specified. |
| @UserRoles | field, method | user entity | This annotation marks the field or method containing the roles of the user. Should be a List or Set. |
| @RoleName | field, method | role entity | This annotation marks the field or method containing the name of the role. |

The following entity definition, taken from the Rules Booking example, declares the minimal annotations required to define a user entity for use with the JpaIdentityManager:

```
@Entity
@Name("user")
@Scope(SESSION)
@Table(name="Customer")
public class User implements Serializable
{
   private String username;
   private String password;
   private List<Role> roles;

   // ... ...

   @UserPrincipal
   @Id
   @Length(min=5, max=15)
   @Pattern(regex="^\\w*$", message="not a valid username")
   public String getUsername()
   {
      return username;
   }
   public void setUsername(String username)
   {
      this.username = username;
   }
```

```
@UserPassword(hash = "md5")
@NotNull
@Length(min=5, max=15)
public String getPassword()
{
   return password;
}
public void setPassword(String password)
{
   this.password = password;
}

@UserRoles
@ManyToMany(fetch=FetchType.EAGER)
@JoinTable(joinColumns={ @JoinColumn(name="USERNAME") },
             inverseJoinColumns={ @JoinColumn(name="ID") }
)
public List<Role> getRoles()
{
   return roles;
}

public void setRoles(List<Role> roles)
{
   this.roles = roles;
}
// ... ...
}
```

Notice the mix of JPA annotations with Seam security annotations. The JPA annotations specify how the `User` should be stored, allowing you to map the entity to a custom table definition. The Seam security annotations specify how the `JpaIdentityStore` should use this entity.

The `@UserPrincipal` annotation defines the field or method containing the user's username. Note that we specify this as an `@Id`, as the username is also considered a unique identifier for the user. The `@UserPassword`-annotated field or method contains the user's password. The `hash` attribute specifies the hash algorithm to use to encrypt the user's password. By default, Seam supports the standard `MessageDigest` algorithms found in the Java Cryptography Architecture specification. Table 18.2 enumerates the possible `hash` values.

**Table 18.2** Standard `MessageDigest` Algorithms

| Algorithm | Description |
|---|---|
| md5 | The default hash algorithm used if the `hash` attribute is not specified. The MD5 message digest algorithm is defined in RFC 1321. |
| sha | Another option defined by the Secure Hash Standard (SHS). |
| none | Specifies that Seam should not hash the user's password. This is not recommended in a production environment, as this presents a security risk. |

The @UserRoles annotation applies to the collection that contains the roles the user is associated with. Now, let's take a look at the Role entity.

```
@Entity
public class Role implements Serializable {
 private Long id;
 private String rolename;

 // ... ...

 @Id @GeneratedValue
 public Long getId() {
  return id;
 }

 public void setId(Long id) {
  this.id = id;
 }

 @RoleName
 public String getRolename() {
  return rolename;
 }

 public void setRolename(String rolename) {
  this.rolename = rolename;
 }

 // ... ...
 }
```

The Role entity only requires that the @RoleName annotation be specified.

---

**@RoleName May Not Be Unique**

In the Role entity, a generated @Id is used, not relying on the @RoleName to be unique. This helps to ensure extensibility in case this schema needs to be extended for use across multiple applications with differing user bases but potentially clashing role names.

---

Now, we just need to configure the JpaIdentityStore in our components.xml file:

```
<components xmlns="http://jboss.com/products/seam/components"
            xmlns:drools="http://jboss.com/products/seam/drools"
            xmlns:security="http://jboss.com/products/seam/security"
            xmlns:xsi="http://www.w3.org/2001/XMLSchema-instance"
            xsi:schemaLocation=
              "http://jboss.com/products/seam/security
              http://jboss.com/products/seam/security-2.1.xsd
              http://jboss.com/products/seam/components
              http://jboss.com/products/seam/components-2.1.xsd">
  ... ...
  <security:jpa-identity-store entity-manager="#{em}"
    user-class="org.jboss.seam.example.booking.MemberAccount"
    role-class="org.jboss.seam.example.booking.MemberRole" />
```

```
<persistence:managed-persistence-context
  name="em"
  auto-create="true"
  persistence-unit-jndi-name=
    "java:/EntityManagerFactories/bookingEntityManagerFactory"/>
  ... ...
</components>
```

Note that the `JpaIdentityStore` definition specifies the `EntityManager`. This is only required if you specify a component name for your Seam-managed persistence context (SMPC) instance as something other than the general naming convention, `entityManager`. See Chapter 11 for details on configuring an SMPC instance.

In addition, we do not need to configure the `IdentityManager`, as the `JpaIdentityStore` is assumed as the default `IdentityStore`. In the next section, you will see how to specify an `IdentityStore`.

Once this has been configured, we can use the `IdentityManager` for both authentication and administrative functions. For example, previously we defined the following authentication view snippet:

```
<div>
  Username:
  <h:inputText value="#{credentials.username}"/>
</div>

<div>
  Password:
  <h:inputSecret value="#{credentials.password}"/>
</div>

<div>
  <h:commandButton value="Login" action="#{identity.login}"/>
</div>
```

During authentication, the `JpaIdentityStore` generates the necessary query, based on the field annotated with `@UserName` as well as the user-entered value of `#{credentials.username}`, to retrieve the user from the persistent store. Once retrieved, the `JpaIdentityStore` compares the entered `#{credentials.password}` value with the field annotated with `@UserPassword`.

What if you need to access the user entity from the context after authentication? This is easy to do by using the `JpaIdentityStore.EVENT_USER_AUTHENTICATED` event.

```
@Name("authenticationObserver")
public class AuthenticationObserver
{
  @Observer(EVENT_USER_AUTHENTICATED)
  public void userAuthenticated(User user) {
    Contexts.getSessionContext().set("user", user);
  }
}
```

In addition, administrative functions can be performed, such as adding users or roles. The `register.xhtml` form allows a new user to register with the application (Figure 18.3).

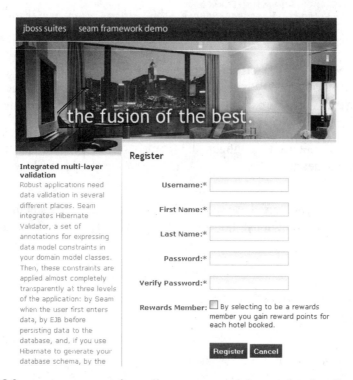

**Figure 18.3**    `register.xhtml` form allows a user to register and optionally receive reward points.

The following listing from the `RegisterAction` demonstrates how a user is added during registration.

```
@Stateful
@Scope(EVENT)
@Name("register")
public class RegisterAction implements Register
{
  @In private User user;
  @In private StatusMessages statusMessages;
  @In private IdentityManager identityManager;

  // ... ...

  private boolean rewardsUser;

  public void register()
  {
    if ( user.getPassword().equals(verify) )
    {
```

```
        try {
          new RunAsOperation(true) {
            public void execute() {
              identityManager.createUser(user.getUsername(),
                user.getPassword(), user.getFirstName(),
                user.getLastName());
              if(rewardsUser)
                identityManager.grantRole(user.getUsername(),
                  "rewardsuser");
            }
          }.run();

          statusMessages.add(
            "Successfully registered as #{user.username}");
          registered = true;
        } catch(IdentityManagementException e) {
          statusMessages.add(e.getMessage());
        }
      }
    else
    {
      statusMessages.addToControl("verify", "Re-enter your password");
      verify=null;
    }
  }
}
// ... ...

public boolean isRewardsUser()
{
  return rewardsUser;
}
public void setRewardsUser(boolean rewardsUser)
{
  this.rewardsUser = rewardsUser;
}
}
```

Here, we inject the `IdentityManager` and use it to register a new user. The `createUser()` method creates a new user based on the provided attributes. Note that the user's first name and last name have been specified. This makes use of two additional field- or method-level annotations provided by Seam security, namely `@FirstName` and `@LastName`. In addition, should the user request to be a rewards user, we grant the `rewardsuser` role. This role must exist in the table mapped to the role entity.

### Executing an Operation with Temporary Security Privileges

The `RunAsOperation` component allows you to execute an operation with a temporary set of privileges. By extending this component with an inner class definition and passing a `true` value to its constructor, we execute the `createUser()` and `createRole()` operations, allowing all security checks to pass. This is necessary, as the example allows any user to register with the application, without having an administrator create user accounts. We also could have specified a set of roles to execute the operation with by using the `addRole()` method provided by the `RunAsOperation` API.

## 18.3.2   Using the LdapldentityStore

The LdapIdentityStore provides an identity store that allows users and roles to be stored inside an LDAP directory. The LdapIdentityStore is very simple to use. The following example demonstrates the configuration of a fictional LDAP directory running on the host directory.solutionsfit.com:

```
<components xmlns="http://jboss.com/products/seam/components"
            xmlns:drools="http://jboss.com/products/seam/drools"
            xmlns:security="http://jboss.com/products/seam/security"
            xmlns:xsi="http://www.w3.org/2001/XMLSchema-instance"
            xsi:schemaLocation=
              "http://jboss.com/products/seam/security
              http://jboss.com/products/seam/security-2.1.xsd
              http://jboss.com/products/seam/components
              http://jboss.com/products/seam/components-2.1.xsd">
  ... ...

  <security:ldap-identity-store
    server-address="directory.solutionsfit.com"
    bind-DN="cn=Manager,dc=solutionsfit,dc=com"
    bind-credentials="secret"
    user-DN-prefix="uid="
    user-DN-suffix=",ou=Person,dc=solutionsfit,dc=com"
    role-DN-prefix="cn="
    role-DN-suffix=",ou=Roles,dc=solutionsfit,dc=com"
    user-context-DN="ou=Person,dc=solutionsfit,dc=com"
    role-context-DN="ou=Roles,dc=solutionsfit,dc=com"
    user-role-attribute="roles"
    role-name-attribute="cn"
    user-object-classes="person,uidObject"
    enabled-attribute="enabled"
  />

  <security:identity-manager identity-store="#{ldapIdentityStore}"/>
  ... ...
</components>
```

The users are stored within this directory under the context ou=Person, dc=solutionsfit,dc=com, and are identified via the uid attribute corresponding to their username. Roles are stored in their own context, ou=Roles, dc=solutionsfit,dc=com, and referenced from the user's entry through the roles attribute. Role entries are identified by their common name configured by the cn attribute. This corresponds to the role name. An enabled-attribute has been specified which allows users to be disabled by setting the value of this attribute to false.

Notice the configuration of the IdentityManager. When using the LdapIdentityStore, it is required that you specify the identity-store, as the IdentityManager attempts to use the JpaIdentityStore by default. In addition, should you choose to implement your own IdentityStore, the configuration would be the same. Simply reference the IdentityStore component by component name.

### Using a Different Identity Store for Users and Roles

Seam security does not restrict you to using one `IdentityStore` for both users and roles. Instead, you can use the `identity-store` attribute to configure user retrieval and the `role-identity-store` attribute to configure role retrieval:

```
<security:identity-manager
  identity-store="#{ldapIdentityStore}"
  role-identity-store="#{jpaIdentityStore}" />
```

Here, we configure an `LdapIdentityStore` for user retrieval and a `JpaIdentityStore` for role retrieval.

# 18.4  Additional Security Features

In addition to authentication and authorization, Seam offers other security features allowing you to improve the security of your application with minimal effort. Throughout this section, we will demonstrate how simple it can be to strengthen the security of your application using Seam.

## 18.4.1  Simplified SSL

Enabling SSL is highly recommended for web applications where sensitive information is passed between the client and server and is always recommended for login pages. Without SSL, malicious users can sniff the credentials of a user and use these credentials to access the application with the user's identity. SSL (Secure Sockets Layer) is a cryptographic Internet communications protocol that is considered to be secure. Essentially, SSL creates a handshake between the server and the client where a stateful connection is negotiated. Once the negotiation is complete, all server/client communication is encrypted for transport between the communication endpoints.

This means that your application is now reasonably protected from man-in-the-middle attacks and eavesdroppers. So, how do we get this level of security? This is actually quite simple when using Seam, assuming your application server has been configured to accept HTTPS requests. HTTPS is simply HTTP interaction over the SSL communication protocol. Review the documentation for enabling SSL communication for your specific application server. In general, this involves enabling communication over port 443.

Once your application server is configured, enabling this communication within your application is as simple as placing a configuration parameter in your `pages.xml` file. The following enables secure communication for a login page:

```
... ...
<page view-id="/login.xhtml" scheme="https"/>
... ...
```

If an HTTP request is received for the `login.xhtml` page, Seam will automatically redirect the request as an SSL request. So, if the user typed `http://localhost/myApp/login.seam` into his or her URL bar, the URL will be automatically redirected to `https://localhost/myApp/login.seam` by Seam. Redirecting to an HTTPS URL performs HTTP communication over a secure SSL connection. Similarly, if a successful login redirects the user to a non-SSL page, Seam will automatically redirect the request as a HTTP request. This greatly simplifies a mixed communication protocol in web applications.

In addition, you can configure your application to use a default scheme. The following listing demonstrates a mixed communication protocol where SSL is only used for the user login:

```
... ...
<page view-id="*" scheme="http" />

<page view-id="/login.xhtml" scheme="https"/>
... ...
```

Remember that the overhead of SSL communication is minimal once the initial hand-shake has occurred. So, if you are using SSL in your application, you should carefully consider where its use is appropriate.

Finally, you must configure the ports to use for communication. These can vary based on the environment; it is recommended to configure this in `components.xml` to allow using profiles (see Section 5.2.3). The following listing demonstrates this configuration:

```
<components
  xmlns="http://jboss.com/products/seam/components"
  xmlns:navigation="http://jboss.com/products/seam/navigation"
  xmlns:xsi="http://www.w3.org/2001/XMLSchema-instance"
  xsi:schemaLocation=
    "http://jboss.com/products/seam/navigation
    http://jboss.com/products/seam/navigation-2.1.xsd
    http://jboss.com/products/seam/components
    http://jboss.com/products/seam/components-2.1.xsd">

  <navigation:pages http-port="8080" https-port="8443" />
  ... ...
</components>
```

The ports have now been defined for both HTTP and HTTPS. We could also use wild-cards in the port values to allow the ports to be swapped, based on the environment, through the `components.properties` file.

## 18.4.2 Telling Humans and Computers Apart with CAPTCHA

CAPTCHA is a Completely Automated Public Turing test to tell Computers and Humans Apart. CAPTCHAs are useful to reduce spamming (e.g., automated postings to blogs and forums) and malicious resource expenditure (e.g., expensive search queries or large file download requests). CAPTCHAs vary in their complexity, depending on the level of security required, but can be quite effective.

Generally, CAPTCHAs involve presenting the user with some challenge that is simple for a human to solve but difficult for a computer. For example, by default Seam presents a simple math problem to the user in the form of an image; the user must provide a correct answer to move forward. As the match problem is presented in the form of an image, it is difficult for an automated agent to provide a correct answer—but not impossible. Seam makes it easy to use a simple CAPTCHA while providing the flexibility to increase the level of security as your application grows.

The Rules Booking example provides an example of using a CAPTCHA within a form. In order to use the Seam CAPTCHA, you must first configure the `SeamResourceServlet`, which generates the CAPTCHA image, in your `web.xml`:

```
... ...
<servlet>
  <servlet-name>Seam Resource Servlet</servlet-name>
  <servlet-class>
    org.jboss.seam.servlet.SeamResourceServlet
  </servlet-class>
</servlet>

<servlet-mapping>
  <servlet-name>Seam Resource Servlet</servlet-name>
  <url-pattern>/seam/resource/*</url-pattern>
</servlet-mapping>
... ...
```

Once the `SeamResourceServlet` has been configured, it is quite simple to add a CAPTCHA to a form. The following listing comes from the `review.xhtml` page in our Rules Booking example:

```
... ...
<h:graphicImage value="/seam/resource/captcha"/>
<h:inputText id="verifyCaptcha" value="#{captcha.response}"
             required="true">
  <s:validate />
</h:inputText>
<div class="errors">
  <h:message for="verifyCaptcha"/>
</div>
... ...
```

The challenge is automatically validated when the user provides a response, and if the provided answer is incorrect, a message will be displayed through the `<h:message for="verifyCaptcha"/>` tag. In addition, you can override the built-in Seam CAPTCHA component to provide custom CAPTCHA messages. The Rules Booking example provides an example of this in the class `org.jboss.seam.examples. booking.security.BookingCaptcha`. A simplified version of this CAPTCHA generation algorithm is shown in the following listing:

```
@Name("org.jboss.seam.captcha.captcha")
@Scope(ScopeType.SESSION)
@Install(precedence=Install.APPLICATION)
public class BookingCaptcha extends Captcha
{
  // ... ...

  public String getRandomWord() {
    String[] randomWords = { "Seam", "Framework",
      "Experience", "Evolution", "Java EE" };

    Random random = new Random();

    return randomWords[random.nextInt(4)];
  }

  @Override @Create
  public void init()
  {
    String randomWord = getRandomWord();

    setChallenge(randomWord);
    setCorrectResponse(randomWord);

    log.info(
      "Initialized custom CAPTCHA with challenge: #0", getChallenge());
  }

  // ... ...
}
```

Obviously, this is not very difficult to crack, but as shown in the Rules Booking example, we can make it much more challenging to decode the image displayed to the user by randomizing the placement of letters, adding random obscuring images, etc. Your imagination is the only limitation in a custom CAPTCHA implementation, but be aware that custom CAPTCHAs are generally easy for bots to crack.

JCaptcha (http://jcaptcha.sourceforge.net) provides an open source alternative to a custom CAPTCHA implementation. JCaptcha is an open source Java framework for Captcha definition and integration. JCaptcha provides a customizable CAPTCHA image generation engine that is very difficult to crack, but can be somewhat difficult for users to read.

reCAPTCHA (http://recaptcha.net) provides yet another free alternative to a custom Captcha implementation. reCAPTCHA is not only easier to read, it helps to digitize books that were published prior to the digital age. Words that cannot be read by computers are sent as CAPTCHAs for humans to decipher. It is a bit more difficult to set up and use due to the use of a web service, but a Java API is provided. To learn more, visit the reCAPTCHA site.

# Part IV

## AJAX Support

**L**everaging JavaServer Faces (JSF), Seam offers excellent support for cutting-edge web technologies. In this part, we discuss several ways to make your web pages more dynamic, more responsive, and more user-friendly using the AJAX (Asynchronous JavaScript and XML) technology. You can easily add AJAX features to Seam applications and access Seam backend components using a specialized asynchronous JavaScript library.

# 19

## Custom and AJAX UI Components

Asynchronous JavaScript and XML (AJAX) is a rich web UI approach pioneered by Google. The term itself was coined by Jesse James Garret of Adaptive Path in 2005. The idea is to use JavaScript to retrieve dynamic content from the server and then update the UI components on the web page without refreshing the entire page. For example, on a Google Maps (http://maps.google.com) web page, you can use the mouse to pan and zoom the map without page reload. The map page captures the user's mouse events via JavaScript and makes AJAX calls back to the server to retrieve new maps to display based on the mouse events. The user simply sees that the map gets updated as he or she moves the mouse. Another well-known AJAX example is Google Suggest (www.google.com/webhp?complete=1&hl=en). The search box in Google Suggest makes an AJAX call to the server whenever you type something in the box. The server returns a list of suggested search phrases based on the current content in the box, and the page displays the selectable list as a pop-up window underneath the box. This instant search-and-update action happens in real time as the user types, so it feels as if the smart text field is "guessing" the user's intention all the time.

AJAX allows a web page to become a rich application by itself. From the user perspective, AJAX web pages are responsive and intuitive. In fact, most Web 2.0 sites today have some AJAX elements. The AJAX UI is essentially a dynamic UI rendered by network-aware JavaScript in the browser.

So, what are the challenges to use AJAX with JSF and Seam web applications? After all, JSF and Seam enable you to use arbitrary HTML tags and JavaScript bits on the web page. You can certainly use any JavaScript library to build whatever web UI you want. The real challenge is to integrate those JavaScript-rendered UI with backend business components. For instance, you could use an off-the-shelf JavaScript library to render a rich text editor on the web page, but how do you bind the user's input text in the editor box to a backend component (e.g., a string property on a Seam EJB3 entity bean)? The JavaScript-rendered dynamic UI is not a JSF component, and it will not interpret the JSF EL (i.e., the `#{obj.property}` notation) for backing bean references.

A naive approach is to write a special HTTP servlet to handle AJAX requests from JavaScript code. This servlet can then interact with objects in the `FacesContext` or `HttpSession` to save the user input or generate AJAX response to the JavaScript. However, the problem with this approach is that it includes a lot of manual coding for both the client-side JavaScript and the server-side Java Servlet. An AJAX servlet developer must be very careful with the states of the server-side objects. This is obviously not the ideal solution. Is there an easier way to support AJAX in JSF and Seam applications?

Fortunately, as a cutting-edge web framework, JSF and Seam provide several elegant ways to integrate AJAX support in your web applications. In this book, we will primarily discuss the following three approaches:

- The first approach is to reuse AJAX-enabled JSF UI components. The benefits of this approach are simplicity and power: You do not need to write a single line of JavaScript or AJAX servlet code, yet the component itself knows how to render JavaScript and AJAX visual effects; the JavaScript code and the backend communication mechanism are encapsulated in the component itself. AJAX services are implemented in the Seam backend components bound to the UI component. We cover this approach later in this chapter.

- The second approach is to use a generic AJAX component library for JSF, such as the Ajax4jsf library. The benefit is that it enables you to add AJAX functionality to any existing JSF component. Again, it does not require writing any JavaScript or AJAX servlet code, but it cannot render visual effects beyond rerendering certain JSF components. Since all AJAX requests happen within the JSF component lifecycle, the backend value binding just works without any additional code. We will cover this approach in Chapter 20.

- The last approach is to use the Seam Remoting JavaScript library to access backend Seam components directly when a page event happens. With it, you can access the backend components via JSF EL in the JavaScript calls. This approach works with any third-party JavaScript library and provides the most flexibility. We will cover this approach in Chapter 21.

Let's begin with the first approach in this chapter. We will use the open source RichFaces JSF component library to illustrate how to use AJAX components in Seam applications. RichFaces works virtually out of the box with Seam. As you will see in examples, there is no need to change your standard configuration—just drop in the components in your view pages and you are ready to go! The example application for this chapter is the `ajax` project in the book's source code bundle. This is an AJAXified version of the Integration example we discussed earlier in the book.

---

**What Is RichFaces?**

RichFaces is an AJAX-enabled rich JSF component library. It was originally developed by Exadel, subsequently purchased and open sourced by Red Hat. RichFaces integrates well into the Red Hat Developer Studio to provide drag-and-drop UI assembly for Seam-based web applications.

In this chapter, we only show several examples of RichFaces widgets. To see a complete gallery of widgets in action, visit http://livedemo.exadel.com/richfaces-demo/index.jsp.

---

# 19.1  Autocompletion Text Input Example

The first AJAX example we showcase in the `ajax` example is an autocompletion text input field similar to the one in Google Suggest.

The text input field for the person name (on the `hello.xhtml` page) can automatically suggest a list of popular names based on your partial input. For instance, if you type in the string `"an"`, names `"Michael Yuan"` and `"Norman Richards"` are suggested because they both contain `"an"`. The JavaScript associated with the text box captures every keystroke in the box, makes AJAX calls to retrieve autocompletion suggestions, and then displays those suggestions. Figure 19.1 shows how the autocompletion text field guesses a list of names based on the user's partial input.

**Figure 19.1**    The AJAX autocompletion text field in action

The autocompletion text field requires some complex interaction between the browser and the server. But with the well-encapsulated RichFaces component, you do not need to worry about anything; you simply drop the `<rich:suggestionbox>` component into your web page wherever the suggestion drop-down box is supposed to appear (typically, below the text input field that takes the suggestion). The following listing shows how the suggestion box works:

```
<html xmlns="http://www.w3.org/1999/xhtml"
      xmlns:ui="http://java.sun.com/jsf/facelets"
      xmlns:h="http://java.sun.com/jsf/html"
      xmlns:f="http://java.sun.com/jsf/core"
      xmlns:s="http://jboss.com/products/seam/taglib"
      xmlns:rich="http://richfaces.org/rich">
... ...

<h:inputText value="#{person.name}" id="suggestion"/>
<rich:suggestionbox height="200" width="200"
                    selfRendered="true"
                    for="suggestion"
                    suggestionAction="#{manager.getNameHints}"
                    var="hint">
  <h:column>
    <h:outputText value="#{hint}"/>
  </h:column>
</rich:suggestionbox>
```

The `for` attribute points to the `id` of a text input field. Whatever the user chooses from the suggestion box will be automatically put into the target text field. The suggestion box is activated and updated with every keystroke in its target text field.

Since the suggestions are essentially a list of text items in a table, you can think of the `<rich:suggestionbox>` component as an `<h:dataTable>` component—it takes a list of suggestions from a backing bean method, iterates through the list, and displays the content in `h:column` elements. The suggestion list comes from the `suggestionAction` attribute and is iterated over the EL variable name specified in the `var` attribute.

In our example, the `#{manager.getNameHints}` method is called with every keystroke to update the suggestion list. The current value in the text field is passed to that method as an argument. The method has to return a data structure that can be used by an `h:dataTable`. That means a `List` of any type of object would be fine. This is the code for this backend method:

```
@Stateful
@Name("manager")
public class ManagerAction implements Manager {

    String [] popularNames = new String [] {
      "Gavin King", "Thomas Heute", "Michael Yuan",
      "Norman Richards", "Bill Burke", "Marc Fleury",
      "Jacob Orshalick"
    };

    public List <String> getNameHints (Object p) {
      String prefix = (String) p;
      int maxMatches = 10;

      List <String> nameHints = new ArrayList <String> ();
```

```
        int totalNum = 0;
        if (prefix.length() > 0) {
          for (int i=0; i<popularNames.length; i++) {
            if (popularNames[i].toLowerCase()
              .indexOf(prefix.toLowerCase())!=-1
              && totalNum < maxMatches) {

              nameHints.add(popularNames[i]);
              totalNum++;

              System.out.println("Add " + popularNames[i]);
            }
          }
        } else {
          for (int i=0; i<maxMatches && i<popularNames.length; i++) {
            nameHints.add(popularNames[i]);
          }
        }
        return nameHints;
    }
    ... ...
}
```

That's it! Within minutes, we have an AJAX-enabled example application, and we have not written a single line of JavaScript or DHTML code.

# 19.2 Rich Input Control Examples

The autocompletion example is a classic use case of AJAX. However, when people talk about rich web experience, they actually mean more than just AJAX. They also include rich UI controls that make use of JavaScript and DHTML effects. In this example, we show you how easy it is to use rich UI input widgets, such as a number spinner and an inline text edit widget.

A number spinner lets you choose a number to enter. Unlike a generic text input field, a number spinner gives the user a much stronger visual clue in terms of what data is expected by the server.

An inline text editor shows a piece of regular text which becomes a text editor when you click on it. It allows you to edit a document-style page without the page being cluttered by regular text input fields. Figure 19.2 shows both widgets in action.

The following code is all you need to get both widgets working on our `hello.xhtml` page:

```
<rich:inputNumberSpinner value="#{person.age}"/>
... ...
<rich:inplaceInput defaultLabel="click to enter your email"
                   value="#{person.email}"
                   showControls="true"/>
```

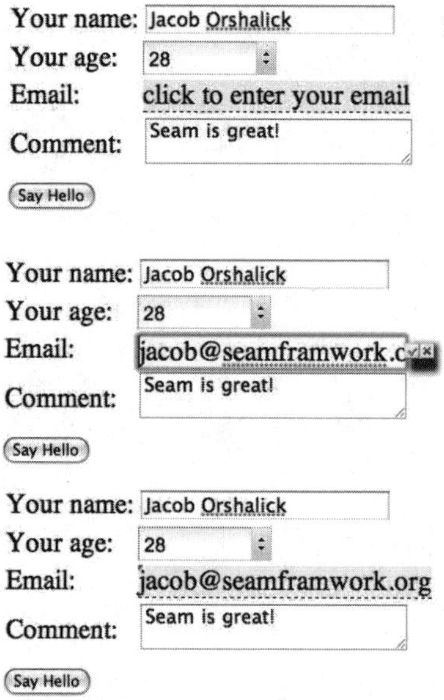

**Figure 19.2**    The input number spinner and the inline text editor

# 19.3   A Scrollable Data Table

Our last RichFaces example is a scrollable data table. Displaying large data tables has always been tricky in web development. Ideally, the table needs to provide the ability to page from one set of results to the next or previous, so that a big table does not produce a very large web page which is unreadable and takes forever to load. However, implementing paging is a tedious process, as the server must manage the paging state of the table.

RichFaces provides a drop-in solution for this problem—just replace your regular data table with a RichFaces data table. It is automatically paged with a scroller. As you move from page to page, the content is retrieved from the server on the fly via AJAX. The following listing shows the scrollable data table in `fans.xhtml`:

```
<rich:dataTable width="483" id="fansList" rows="5" columnClasses="col"
                value="#{fans}" var="fan">
  <f:facet name="header">
    <rich:columnGroup>
      <h:column>Name</h:column>
      <h:column>Age</h:column>
      <h:column>Email</h:column>
      <h:column>Comment</h:column>
      <h:column>Action</h:column>
      <h:column>Action</h:column>
    </rich:columnGroup>
  </f:facet>
```

```
<rich:column>#{fan.name}</rich:column>
<rich:column>#{fan.age}</rich:column>
<rich:column>#{fan.email}</rich:column>
<rich:column>#{fan.comment}</rich:column>
<rich:column>
  <h:commandButton value="Delete" action="#{manager.delete}"/>
</rich:column>
<rich:column>
  <a href="person.seam?pid=#{fan.id}">Edit</a>
</rich:column>
</rich:dataTable>

<rich:datascroller align="left" for="fansList" maxPages="20"/>
```

The `rich:datascroller` component under the table provides the UI for paging. Its `for` attribute points to the table it scrolls. Figure 19.3 shows the table with the scroller.

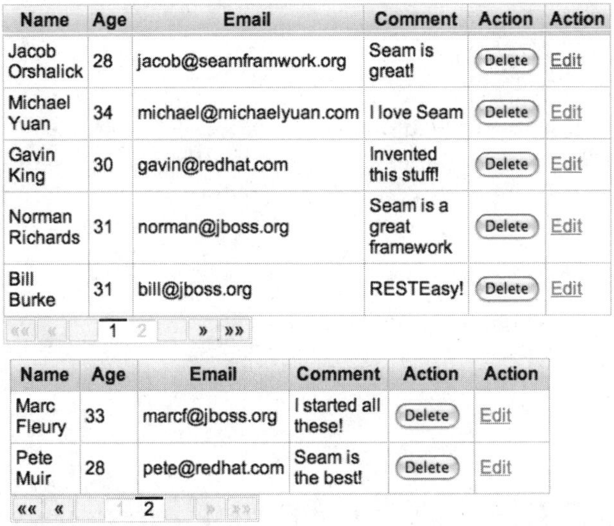

| Name | Age | Email | Comment | Action | Action |
|------|-----|-------|---------|--------|--------|
| Jacob Orshalick | 28 | jacob@seamframwork.org | Seam is great! | Delete | Edit |
| Michael Yuan | 34 | michael@michaelyuan.com | I love Seam | Delete | Edit |
| Gavin King | 30 | gavin@redhat.com | Invented this stuff! | Delete | Edit |
| Norman Richards | 31 | norman@jboss.org | Seam is a great framework | Delete | Edit |
| Bill Burke | 31 | bill@jboss.org | RESTEasy! | Delete | Edit |

«« « 1 2 » »»

| Name | Age | Email | Comment | Action | Action |
|------|-----|-------|---------|--------|--------|
| Marc Fleury | 33 | marcf@jboss.org | I started all these! | Delete | Edit |
| Pete Muir | 28 | pete@redhat.com | Seam is the best! | Delete | Edit |

«« « 1 2 » »»

**Figure 19.3** Data table with scroller

# 19.4 Using RichFaces with Seam

RichFaces works out of the box with Seam. There is very little configuration needed. You just need to include the RichFaces JARs and declare the `rich:` namespace in your XHTML files so that you can use those components.

The `richfaces-impl.jar` and `richfaces-ui.jar` files must be included in `app.war/WEB-INF/lib`, and the `richfaces-api.jar` file needs to be in EAR's `lib` path:

```
mywebapp.ear
|+ app.war
   |+ web pages
   |+ WEB-INF
       |+ web.xml
       |+ faces-config.xml
       |+ other config files
       |+ lib
           |+ jboss-seam-ui.jar
           |+ jboss-seam-debug.jar
           |+ jsf-facelets.jar
           |+ richfaces-impl.jar
           |+ richfaces-ui.jar
|+ app.jar
|+ lib
   |+ jboss-seam.jar
   |+ jboss-el.jar
   |+ richfaces-api.jar
   |+ commons...jar
|+ META-INF
   |+ application.xml
   |+ other config files
```

In the `web.xml` file, you can also configure the "skin" of the RichFaces widgets to control their look and feel. In our example, we use the `blueSky` skin:

```
<web-app ...>
  ... ...
  <context-param>
    <param-name>org.richfaces.SKIN</param-name>
    <param-value>blueSky</param-value>
  </context-param>
  ... ...
</web-app>
```

# 19.5   Other JSF Component Libraries

By standardizing the web component architecture in Java EE, JSF has fostered a marketplace for component libraries. Besides ICEfaces, more than a dozen commercial and open source vendors are competing in this marketplace, providing a decent selection of high-quality JSF components for web developers. Here is a list of some of the well-known third-party JSF component packages. JSF community web sites, such as http://jsfcentral.com and http://java.net, maintain more complete and up-to-date lists of component vendors.

- ICEfaces (www.icefaces.com) is a high-quality AJAX JSF component library that works well with Seam. Compared to RichFaces, it requires a little more configuration, but supports an alternative set of rich widgets. There is an ICEfaces example application included in the standard Seam distribution.

- The Apache MyFaces Tomahawk project (http://myfaces.apache.org/tomahawk) develops rich web UI components such as advanced data tables, tabbed panels, calendars, color pickers, etc., as well as input data validators beyond the standard ones. Tomahawk components are all released under the Apache Open Source License.

- Oracle Application Development Framework (ADF) Faces was one of the first commercial JSF component suites. It provides more than 80 UI components, including alternatives to all standard components. The ADF components have a great look-and-feel, and they can all be skinned to different themes. ADF components also boast high performance because each component is rendered via partial page updates (AJAX style, without page reload). Oracle has donated the ADF Faces source code to the open source Trinidad project (http://incubator.apache.org/adffaces) in the Apache foundation.

- The Woodstock project (https://woodstock.dev.java.net) is an open source project to develop AJAX-based enterprise-ready JSF web UI components. It already has more than a dozen components available.

- The Sun BluePrint Catalog (https://bpcatalog.dev.java.net) provides AJAX-enabled JSF components under the BSD license. Those components are primarily provided for educational purposes.

- The ILOG JView JSF components (www.ilog.com/products/jviews) render professional-looking business charts from data models. This is one of the leading business data visualization products.

- Otrix (www.otrix.com) provides commercial AJAX JSF components for trees, menus, data grids, etc.

Most JSF component libraries include both UI components and validator components. As we discussed in Chapter 12, custom JSF validators are useful when corresponding Seam validators are not available. The following example shows how to use the credit card validator component in the Apache Tomahawk library:

```
Credit Card Number:
<h:inputText id="creditCard" required="true"
             value="#{customer.creditCard}">
  <t:validateCreditCard />

</h:inputText>
* <h:message for="creditCard" styleClass="error"/>
```

Custom JSF component libraries help Seam applications stay at the cutting edge of web presentation technologies. As developers, we should leverage them to build better applications.

# 20

## Enabling AJAX for Existing Components

In the previous chapter, we showed how easy it is to use prepackaged AJAX JSF components. However, developing those components is not a trivial exercise; it requires not only JavaScript/AJAX skills, but also a deep knowledge of how JSF works. In most cases, it is not cost-effective to write your own AJAX JSF components unless you plan to reuse them extensively. Most developers limit themselves to the components third-party vendors already offer.

However, what if the existing components do not do exactly what you want? What if the available components are simply too expensive? Such situations occur often in real-world enterprise applications. We need an AJAX solution that is not only easy to use, but also flexible enough to address different customization requirements. In this chapter, we introduce Ajax4jsf, which provides flexible and customizable AJAX support for JSF components. This is the second AJAX approach, as discussed at the beginning of Chapter 19.

Ajax4jsf is an open source JSF component library developed by Exadel as the basis of Exadel's own proprietary AJAX JSF components. The unique feature that sets Ajax4jsf apart from other AJAX JSF frameworks is that Ajax4jsf can add AJAX functionality to any existing JSF component. In fact, it can turn any JSF operation already in your application into an AJAX operation and then display the result via a partial page update (i.e., without page reload). If you want to learn more about Ajax4jsf, visit its web site at https://ajax4jsf.dev.java.net.

Ajax4jsf works by submitting JSF requests via AJAX and then rerendering specific elements on the page based on the updated state of the backend components. To demonstrate how it works, let's use a revised Hello World example again. The sample code is available in the `ajax4jsf` project. The project uses the Facelets + Seam + Ajax4jsf stack of technologies.

# 20.1  AJAX Validator Example

One of the simplest and most useful examples for showcasing Ajax4jsf is AJAX validation on input fields. In Chapter 12, we saw how Hibernate validator annotations and Seam JSF tags work together to validate form inputs according to database constraints and display nice-looking error messages. However, these error messages are displayed only after you submit the form. AJAX can greatly improve the validation workflow: The JavaScript on the web page could send the user input in each field back to the server for validation immediately after the field loses focus; if the validation fails, the error message is displayed immediately without the form being submitted.

However, it is very difficult to add AJAX support into the Seam JSF validation process through "regular" AJAX techniques. The Seam JSF validation process is almost completely declarative, and no "hook" exists for the client-side JavaScript to trigger the server-side validation functions or access the validation messages. Ajax4jsf solves this problem by integrating AJAX support right into the existing JSF components and the standard JSF lifecycle.

Below is an example of an AJAX-validated input field (see Figure 20.1). The `<s:validate/>` tag indicates that this input field should be validated by the `@NotNull` `@Email` Hibernate validator on `Person.getEmail()`, and the `<s:decorate>` tag highlights the input field with images, background, and border when a validation error occurs. See Chapter 12 for more on how those tags work. What's important here is the `<a4j:support>` tag, which we will discuss shortly.

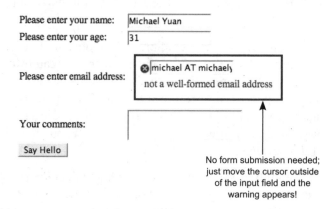

Figure 20.1 image content:

**Seam Hello World**

Please enter your name:  [ Michael Yuan ]

Please enter your age:  [ 31 ]

Please enter email address:  [ ⊗ michael AT michaely

not a well-formed email address ]

Your comments:  [ ]

[ Say Hello ]

No form submission needed; just move the cursor outside of the input field and the warning appears!

**Figure 20.1**  AJAX validation of input field

```
Please enter email address:<br/>
<a4j:outputPanel id="emailInput">
  <s:decorate>
    <h:inputText value="#{person.email}" size="15">
      <s:validate/>
      <a4j:support event="onblur" reRender="emailInput"/>
    </h:inputText>
  </s:decorate>
</a4j:outputPanel>
```

Compared to the non-AJAX version of `<h:inputText>`, the AJAX-enabled JSF component encloses an `<a4j:support>` element. That's it! The `event` attribute specifies the JavaScript event upon which the AJAX call is invoked. In this case, whenever the input text field loses focus (i.e., the `onblur` event happens), Ajax4jsf submits the text in the field to the component's backend binding property (i.e., the `#{person.email}` property) via a JSF `POST` operation. The AJAX submission goes through the regular Seam JSF validation process. After the AJAX request is processed, Ajax4jsf rerenders the component with the `emailInput` ID, which is the entire decorated input component itself. If any error occurs, it shows up in the rendering (see Figure 20.1). We need an `<a4j:outputPanel>` element here to give the entire decorated input field a JSF ID.

Of course, using the `reRender` attribute, you can rerender any component on the page upon completing the AJAX call. You can even rerender multiple components: Just assign multiple component IDs, separated by commas, to the `reRender` attribute. The rerendered components reflect the new state of the server-side components after the AJAX call.

---

**The `<a4j:outputPanel>` Component**

Why do we need the `<a4j:outputPanel>` element here? Can't we just use `<s:decorate id="emailInput">`? The problem is that the `<s:decorate>` element is not rendered when there is no error (i.e., when the form is first loaded). Therefore, no `emailInput` HTML element exists for the Ajax4jsf JavaScript to rerender without a page refresh.

The `<a4j:outputPanel id="emailInput">` element guarantees that the HTML element with the proper JSF ID will be in the page. This is very useful for wrapping page elements (e.g., a piece of XHTML text in a Facelets page) that do not have proper JSF IDs. You can enclose multiple JSF components as well as any XHTML text in the `<a4j:outputPanel>` element, and they will all be rerendered together after the AJAX call is completed. Indeed, we recommend that you use the `<a4j:outputPanel>` element to wrap all your Ajax4jsf `reRender` components.

---

In the previous example, the `a4j:support` component rerenders a JSF component after the AJAX call returns. You can also tell the browser to execute arbitrary JavaScript upon the completion of the AJAX response. Just add the JavaScript function call to the `oncomplete` attribute of the `a4j:support` tag:

```
<h:inputText value="#{person.email}" size="15">
  <s:validate/>
  <a4j:support event="onblur"
               reRender="emailInput"
               oncomplete="alertUser()"/>
</h:inputText>
```

# 20.2  Programmatic AJAX

The validator example is nice and simple, but it does not really involve any programming because everything is declarative. For most innovative AJAX applications, however, we would want to execute our own application-specific code in the AJAX interaction.

For instance, in the following example, we use an AJAX call to check whether a person's name is already in the database as soon as the user types something in the input field (see Figure 20.2). The database query here is custom logic that is not easily handled by any existing validation framework. This feature is often implemented to support an on-the-fly username availability check on site registration forms.

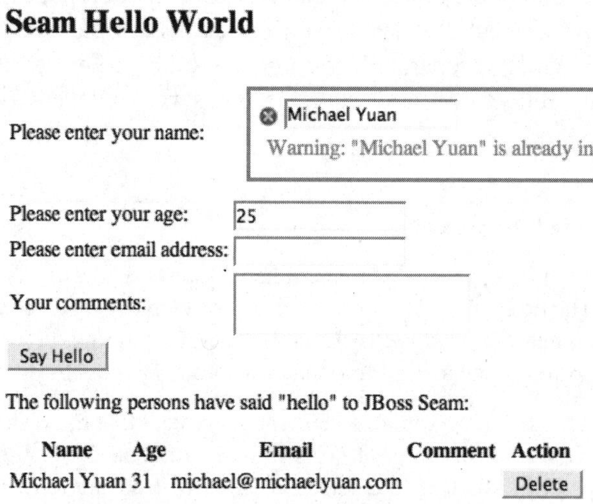

**Seam Hello World**

Please enter your name:
  ⊗ Michael Yuan
  Warning: "Michael Yuan" is already in the system.

Please enter your age:  25
Please enter email address:
Your comments:

Say Hello

The following persons have said "hello" to JBoss Seam:

| Name | Age | Email | Comment | Action |
|------|-----|-------|---------|--------|
| Michael Yuan | 31 | michael@michaelyuan.com | | Delete |

**Figure 20.2**   AJAX interaction with custom logic

In Ajax4jsf, the custom code (i.e., the code to check the database in this example) is executed in JSF backing component methods. Those methods are invoked in the standard JSF lifecycle when an Ajax4jsf request is submitted. We use them to control what is displayed in the AJAX-rerendered component after the call is completed. Now, let's check out how it works.

This is the JSF component for the name input field:

```
Please enter your name:
... ...
<h:inputText value="#{manager.name}" size="15">
  <a4j:support event="onblur" reRender="nameInput"/>
</h:inputText>
```

Again, the a4j:support element indicates that whenever the input text field loses focus (i.e., onblur), Ajax4jsf submits the value of this component to its backend binding property (i.e., the #{manager.name} property). When the AJAX request is processed, Ajax4jsf rerenders the component with the nameInput ID.

The following is the nameInput component. The #{manager.nameErrorMsg} backing bean property controls the display of the nameInput component. If the property is not an empty string, the component highlights the text field with an error icon and message. So in the AJAX interaction, we need to add code to alter the #{manager.nameErrorMsg} value at the backend before the AJAX call returns.

```
<a4j:outputPanel id="nameInput">
  <f:subview rendered="#{!empty(manager.nameErrorMsg)}">
    <f:verbatim><div class="error"></f:verbatim>
    <h:graphicImage styleClass="errorImg" value="error.png"/>
  </f:subview>

  <h:inputText value="#{manager.name}" size="15">
    <a4j:support event="onblur" reRender="nameInput"/>
  </h:inputText>

  <f:subview rendered="#{!empty(manager.nameErrorMsg)}">
    <h:outputText styleClass="errorMsg"
                  value="#{manager.nameErrorMsg}"/>
    <f:verbatim></div></f:verbatim>
  </f:subview>
</a4j:outputPanel>
```

At the onblur event, the AJAX request causes JSF to invoke the setName() method on the manager component to bind the component value. The setName() method contains the custom logic for this AJAX interaction: It checks whether the name is already available in the database. If the name already exists, the setName() method sets the nameErrorMsg property, which is then displayed when the nameErrorMsg component is rerendered after the AJAX call is returned asynchronously.

```
@Stateful
@Name("manager")
public class ManagerAction implements Manager {

  ... ...

  String name;
```

```
public void setName (String name) {

  this.name = name;

  List <Person> existing = em.createQuery(
    "select p from Person p where name=:name")
    .setParameter("name", name).getResultList();

  if (existing.size() != 0) {
    nameErrorMsg = "Warning: \"" + name +
                   "\" is already in the system.";
  } else {
    nameErrorMsg = "";
  }
  return;
}
public String getName () {
  return name;
}

String nameErrorMsg;
public void setNameErrorMsg (String nameErrorMsg) {
  this.nameErrorMsg = nameErrorMsg;
}
public String getNameErrorMsg () {
  return nameErrorMsg;
}
}
```

# 20.3  AJAX Buttons

Ajax4jsf can turn any JSF `commandButton` or `commandLink` into an AJAX operation. The AJAX buttons or links submit the form via a JavaScript call and rerender specified components on the page based on the new backend state after the server-side JSF event handler method for the button is invoked.

To demonstrate this feature, let's AJAX-enable the **Delete** buttons in the data table for `fans`. When you click on any of those buttons, the current fan is removed from the database and the `dataTable` component is rerendered to reflect the change. This page update is done in AJAX fashion—that is, no page reload occurs. That is especially useful when you have a very long data table. A whole page refresh would lose the current scrollbar position, and you would have to scroll from the top again (see Figure 20.3).

To use an AJAX submission button, you just need to replace the `h:commandButton` (or `h:commandLink`) with `a4j:commandButton` (or `a4j:commandLink`). As in the case with the `a4j:support` component, the `a4j` components take a `reRender` property to specify which components are to be updated when the AJAX call returns. Here is our new AJAX `dataTable`:

## The Seam Greeters

The following persons have said "hello" to JBoss Seam:

| Name | Age | Email | Comment | Action |
|------|-----|-------|---------|--------|
| Michael Yuan | 31 | michael@michaelyuan.com | | Delete |
| John Doe | 25 | john@redhat.com | | Delete |
| Jane Roe | 28 | jane@redhat.com | Hello Seam! | Delete |
| Bill Gates | 40 | bill@microsoft.com | I love Seam! | Delete |

Delete a row without a page refresh

## The Seam Greeters

The following persons have said "hello" to JBoss Seam:

| Name | Age | Email | Comment | Action |
|------|-----|-------|---------|--------|
| Michael Yuan | 31 | michael@michaelyuan.com | | Delete |
| John Doe | 25 | john@redhat.com | | Delete |
| Jane Roe | 28 | jane@redhat.com | Hello Seam! | Delete |

**Figure 20.3**  AJAX deletion of a table row

```
<h:form>
<h:dataTable id="fans" value="#{fans}" var="fan">
  <h:column>
    <f:facet name="header">
      <h:outputText value="Name" />
    </f:facet>
    <h:outputText value="#{fan.name}"/>
  </h:column>

  ... ...

  <h:column>
    <f:facet name="header">
      <h:outputText value="Action" />
    </f:facet>
    <a4j:commandButton type="submit"
                       value="Delete"
                       reRender="fans"
                       action="#{manager.delete}"/>
  </h:column>
</h:dataTable>
</h:form>
```

That's it; you have no more backend code to write. When a user clicks on the **Delete** button, the backend component sees a standard JSF form submission which goes through the standard JSF lifecycle. The Ajax4jsf framework takes care of the AJAX plumbing automatically.

Via the `onclick` and `oncomplete` attributes, you can specify arbitrary JavaScript functions to be executed before the AJAX call is made and after the AJAX call is completed. In the following example, we change the cursor shape to a waiting symbol when we start the AJAX call and restore it when the AJAX response is received and the components are updated.

```
<a4j:commandButton type="submit"
                    value="Delete"
                    reRender="fans"
                    onclick="showWaitCursor()"
                    oncomplete="restoreCursor()"
                    action="#{manager.delete}"/>
```

# 20.4  AJAX Containers

In standard JSF, a button click submits the entire form to the server and then triggers the event handler method. The full form submission is often not necessary with AJAX requests. We sometimes need to submit only one or two related input components to the backend for the AJAX call to function correctly. Submitting the entire form would be a waste of bandwidth in this case. Ajax4jsf provides a special tag `a4j:region` to limit the part of the form you want to submit. Only components included in the `<a4j:region>...</a4j:region>` element are submitted when a user clicks on an AJAX button inside the region. The `a4j:region` component is also known as an AJAX container because it contains the AJAX activity within parts of the page. Other AJAX container tags include `a4j:form` and `a4j:page`. Refer to the Ajax4jsf documentation for information on their use.

The AJAX container tags take an optional `ajaxListener` property, which points to a backend method that is to be invoked whenever an AJAX event happens on any component in the region. So, we can trigger backend event handler methods directly from a JSF input component, without manually clicking on a button.

# 20.5  Other Goodies

Besides AJAX input components and AJAX buttons and links, the Ajax4jsf library provides some other important components to facilitate AJAX development.

The `a4j:poll` component periodically polls the server and rerenders specified components based on the current state of the server. For instance, you might want to display a progress bar for a long-running server process. The page would periodically poll the server to partially update a progress bar based on the server process's current progress.

The `a4j:mediaOutput` component enables you to use a server-side method to paint an image and then display it in the browser. The server-side `paint()` method can use any of the Java SE 2D and Swing drawing APIs. That enables you to render dynamic custom graphics in the browser. This is great for simple visual effects associated with AJAX calls (e.g., the progress bar mentioned earlier would be a good fit).

The `a4j:include` component can include an external JSF page in the current page. The included page can update itself and navigate from one page to another without affecting its host page. Think of it as an embedded HTML frame without the hassles associated with frames. That enables you to write in-page AJAX wizards.

The `a4j:status` and `a4j:log` components display AJAX interactions between the client and server in real time. They are very useful for debugging purposes.

The Ajax4jsf library has more cool components. Refer to its documentation for more details.

# 20.6  Using Ajax4jsf with Seam

Similar to RichFaces, Ajax4jsf works out of the box with Seam. It does not require any configuration. All you need to do is to package the Ajax4jsf library JAR files with the application. The `ajax4jsf.jar` is the main Ajax4jsf component library, and the `oscache-xxx.jar` is a dependent library that Ajax4jsf requires. We put both files in the WAR file (i.e., the `app.war`). This is the packaging structure for the JAR files in `ajax4jsf.ear`:

```
ajax4jsf.ear
|+ META-INF
|+ lib
|+ app.war
|   |+ WEB-INF
|   |   |+ lib
|   |   |   |+ ajax4jsf.jar
|   |   |   |+ oscache-2.3.2.jar
|   |   |   |+ jboss-seam-ui.jar
|   |   |   |+ jboss-seam-debug.jar
|   |   |   |+ jsf-facelets.jar
|+ app.jar
```

Of course, you also need to declare the `a4j:` namespace in your XHTML pages to use those components.

# 20.7   Pros and Cons

Ajax4jsf turns regular JSF components into AJAX-enabled components. It works with existing JSF applications and requires little change to existing code. Ajax4jsf is easy to learn, easy to understand, and much more versatile than the prepackaged component approach discussed in Chapter 19.

However, Ajax4jsf also has its limitations. Since the AJAX update is based on rerendering JSF components, it is difficult to add fancy JavaScript effects; you must make extensive changes to the components themselves, which, as we discussed, is not an easy task. Sure, you can use the `a4j:mediaOutput` component to render custom graphics, but it is slow for animations and other visual effects from the server side. Also, since Ajax4jsf uses the same lifecycle as regular JSF, it has to submit all JSF state information in each AJAX call. That results in excessive bandwidth usage and slow response when you use client-side state saving in JSF.

To fully resolve those issues, we must look at solutions that provide tighter integration with JavaScript. That is the topic for the next chapter.

# 21

# Direct JavaScript Integration

**W**e have discussed two approaches for supporting AJAX in Seam applications. Both require zero JavaScript or XML communication code—but they also have some drawbacks.

The componentized AJAX UI approach (Chapter 19) is easy, but you are limited to what the vendor offers. You face a steep learning curve if you want to implement an AJAX-enabled JSF component to render your own custom visual effects or backend logic. The Ajax4jsf approach (Chapter 20) works well in the JSF context, but it is difficult to implement components with visual effects (e.g., drag-and-drops, fades, pop-ups) beyond the standard HTML widgets already supported by the existing JSF components. In addition, it is bandwidth-intensive to wrap JSF requests in AJAX calls, especially if you use client-side state saving.

With so many free high-quality JavaScript libraries available, it seems silly not to take advantage of them just because you are limited by JSF component vendors, right? Fortunately, Seam provides a JavaScript remoting framework that enables you to access any Seam backend component from the JavaScript UI. Thus, you can easily bind user input captured in a JavaScript UI widget to the backend, or use the backend component to generate AJAX data to alter the web page display dynamically.

In this chapter, we demonstrate how to use Seam Remoting JavaScript library to connect Seam server-side components with HTML/JavaScript UI elements. In the last section, we will give concrete examples of integrating the popular Dojo JavaScript toolkit into Seam applications.

# 21.1   AJAX Validator Example (Reloaded)

In Chapter 20, we showed how to use AJAX to validate a name typed in by the user in the Seam Hello World example. The user's name is sent to the server, as soon as the user fills out the web form, and is checked against the database. If the name already exists in the database, a warning message is displayed next to the text input field—all without a form submission. In the first example in this chapter, we will reimplement this feature using the Seam Remoting approach. The example code in this section is in the `remote` project in the source code bundle. When the application is running, you can access it at `http://localhost:8080/remote/`.

To use Seam Remoting, make sure that the `jboss-seam-remoting.jar` file is included in your EAR's `lib` directory, as remoting works on EJB session beans.

## 21.1.1  Server-Side Component

First, we need a method in the backend Seam component to check the input name against the database. We add a `checkName()` in the `ManagerAction` class:

```
@Stateful
@Scope(SESSION)
@Name("manager")
public class ManagerAction implements Manager {
  ... ...
  public boolean checkName (String name) {
    List <Person> existing = em.createQuery(
      "select p from Person p where name=:name")
      .setParameter("name", name).getResultList();

    if (existing.size() != 0) {
      return false;
    } else {
      return true;
    }
  }
}
```

Now comes the important part: In the session bean interface, you must tag the method with the `@WebRemote` annotation for it to be accessible through the Seam Remoting JavaScript.

```
@Local
public interface Manager {
  ... ...
  @WebRemote
  public boolean checkName (String name);
}
```

The Seam resource servlet handles all AJAX calls from the client-side JavaScript to the `@WebRemote`-annotated methods. The AJAX calls are routed via the `seam/resource/remoting/*` URL. AJAX-related resource files (e.g., dynamically generated JavaScript, see later) are also served via this special URL. In Section 3.3, we already explained how to configure the resource servlet. You just need to add the following lines in your `web.xml` file:

```
<servlet>
  <servlet-name>Seam Resource Servlet</servlet-name>
  <servlet-class>org.jboss.seam.servlet.ResourceServlet</servlet-class>
</servlet>

<servlet-mapping>
  <servlet-name>Seam Resource Servlet</servlet-name>
  <url-pattern>/seam/resource/*</url-pattern>
</servlet-mapping>
```

## 21.1.2 Triggering a JavaScript Event on a Web Page

With the backend method ready, let's check out how the AJAX call is triggered on a web page.

```
<h:inputText id="name"
             value="#{person.name}"
             onfocus="hideCheckNameError()"
             onblur="checkName()"
             size="15"/>
<span id="nameError" style="display:none">
  You have already said hello! :)
</span>
<h:message for="name" />
```

The `onblur` property on `<h:inputText>` indicates the JavaScript method to invoke when the text field loses focus—so, when the user finishes the input and clicks outside the field, the `checkName()` JavaScript method is invoked. The JavaScript method takes the input text in the field and invokes the `ManagerAction.checkName()` method on the server side via an AJAX call. The return value of the AJAX call determines whether the error message in the `<span>` element should be shown. Let's look at how the JavaScript `checkName()` method works.

---

**Hiding and Showing the `span` Element**

The `style="display:none"` property indicates that the `span` element for the error message is not displayed initially. JavaScript can display it if the `ManagerAction.checkName()` method returns `false`. The JavaScript `hideCheckNameError()` method makes sure that the error message is hidden when the text field is activated again. The following are the `hideCheckNameError()` and `showCheckNameError()` methods for manipulating the `span` element:

```
function showCheckNameError () {
  var e = document.getElementById("nameError");
  if (!(e === null)) {
    e.style.visibility = "inherit";
    e.style.display = "";
  }
}

function hideCheckNameError () {
  var e = document.getElementById("nameError");
  if (!(e === null)) {
    e.style.visibility = "hidden";
    e.style.display = "none";
  }
}
```

## 21.1.3  Making an AJAX Call

The heart of the AJAX operation involves making the AJAX call and then getting the result asynchronously. In the page where you need to make AJAX calls, load the `seam/resource/remoting/resource/remote.js` JavaScript. The Seam resource servlet assembles and serves this script on the fly. For each Seam component that contains `@WebRemote`-annotated methods, Seam generates a custom JavaScript for accessing this component as well. In our example, we load the `interface.js?manager` JavaScript for accessing the Seam backend component named `manager`.

```
<script type="text/javascript"
        src="seam/resource/remoting/resource/remote.js">
</script>

<script type="text/javascript"
        src="seam/resource/remoting/interface.js?manager">
</script>
```

Now you can get a JavaScript version of the `manager` component via a `Seam.Component.getInstance("manager")` call. The call to the JavaScript `manager.checkName()` method is then translated into an AJAX call to the server-side `manager.checkName()` method. We get the text from the text field and use the `manager.checkName()` method to check whether it already exists in the server-side database:

```
<script type="text/javascript">
  // Seam.Remoting.setDebug(true);

  // Don't display the loading indicator
  Seam.Remoting.displayLoadingMessage = function() {};
  Seam.Remoting.hideLoadingMessage = function() {};

  // Get the "manager" Seam component
  var manager = Seam.Component.getInstance("manager");
```

```
    // Make the async call with a callback handler
    function checkName () {
      var e = document.getElementById("form:name");
      var inputName = e.value;
      manager.checkName(inputName, checkNameCallback);
    }

  ... ...
</script>
```

---

### Creating a JavaScript Object for an Entity Bean or JavaBean POJO Component

The `Seam.Component.getInstance()` method obtains a singleton stub object for a Seam session bean. You can make AJAX method calls against the session bean. But for a Seam entity bean or simple JavaBean components, you need to create the corresponding JavaScript objects using the `Seam.Component.newInstance()` method. All the getter and setter methods on the entity bean (JavaBean) are available in the JavaScript object. You can edit the entity objects and then pass them as call arguments in AJAX calls against session bean components.

---

The JavaScript and server-side `manager.checkName()` methods take the same call arguments. As we mentioned in the previous sidebar, you can even construct an entity bean instance in JavaScript and then pass it to a remote AJAX method as a call argument. However, there's one more twist: The JavaScript method takes an additional asynchronous callback handler as a call argument. The `manager.checkName()` call is invoked asynchronously so that the JavaScript does not block the UI waiting for the response, which could potentially take a long time because the call goes through the network. So, instead of waiting for the return value from the remote call, we pass in a JavaScript callback handler, `checkNameCallback()`, and let the JavaScript method `manager.checkName()` return immediately. The `checkNameCallback()` method is invoked with the server-side method's return value when the server method finishes. The callback handler then decides whether to display the error message based on the return value.

```
<script type="text/javascript">
  ... ...

  function checkNameCallback (result) {
    if (result) {
      hideCheckNameError ();
    } else {
      showCheckNameError ();
    }
  }

  ... ...
</script>
```

In an earlier sidebar, we saw how the `hideCheckNameError()` and `showCheckNameError()` methods hide and display the `span` element for the error message.

That's it for the simple example. Of course, the server-side name validation is hardly exciting—we already did it with no JavaScript in Chapter 20. But it does serve as an example for more complex use cases. In the next section, we will look at a more complicated example.

---

**The Comment Field**

As you probably noticed in the `remote/hello.seam` form, the user comment field is not a regular HTML text area. You click on the text to edit it and then click on the **Save** button to persist the new comment. That is done with the Dojo inline editing widget which we discuss in Section 21.3.2.

---

# 21.2  AJAX Progress Bar

The Seam AJAX Progress Bar example is a more sophisticated AJAX example for Seam Remoting. We use it to demonstrate how to use AJAX widgets that are completely unrelated to JSF components and how to poll for AJAX content. The source code is in the `ProgressBar` directory in the source code bundle. After you build it and deploy the `progressbar.ear` into your JBoss AS, you can access the application at `http://localhost:8080/progressbar/`. On the `progressbar.seam` page, click on the **Go** button to start the progress bar (Figure 21.1). When the progress bar reaches 100 percent, the server redirects to the `complete.seam` page.

**Figure 21.1**    The AJAX Progress Bar in Seam

## 21.2.1  Seam Components

When you click on the **Go** button, the `progressBarAction.doSomething()` Seam method is invoked as the event handler.

```
<h:commandButton value="Go!"
                 action="#{progressBarAction.doSomething}"/>
```

The `progressBarAction.doSomething()` method performs whatever the task is that takes a long time to complete and, in the process, updates the `progress` component stored in the session context:

```
@Stateless
@Name("progressBarAction")
@Interceptors(SeamInterceptor.class)
public class ProgressBarAction implements ProgressBar {

  @In(create = true)
  Progress progress;

  public String doSomething() {
    Random r = new Random(System.currentTimeMillis());
    try {
      for (int i = 0; i < 100;)
      {
        Thread.sleep(r.nextInt(200));
        progress.setPercentComplete(i);
        i++;
      }
    }
    catch (InterruptedException ex) {
    }
    return "complete";
  }
  public Progress getProgress() {
    return progress;
  }
}
```

The `progress` component is just a JavaBean with properties related to the progress bar:

```
@Name("progress")
@Scope(ScopeType.SESSION)
public class Progress {
  private int percentComplete;

  public int getPercentComplete() {
    return percentComplete;
  }
  public void setPercentComplete(int percentComplete) {
    this.percentComplete = percentComplete;
  }
}
```

To provide a mechanism for the client JavaScript to access the `progress` component via AJAX calls, we tag the `getProgress()` method with the `@WebRemote` annotation:

```
@Local
public interface ProgressBar {
  String doSomething();
  @WebRemote Progress getProgress();
}
```

## 21.2.2   Accessing Seam Components from JavaScript

Now, load the necessary JavaScript for accessing the `progressBarAction` component:

```
<script type="text/javascript"
        src="seam/resource/remoting/resource/remote.js">
</script>

<script type="text/javascript"
        src="seam/resource/remoting/interface.js?progressBarAction">
</script>

<script type="text/javascript">
  //<![CDATA[
    // Seam.Remoting.setDebug(true);

    // Don't display the loading indicator
    Seam.Remoting.displayLoadingMessage = function() {};
    Seam.Remoting.hideLoadingMessage = function() {};

    // Get the progressBarAction Seam component
    var progressBarAction =
      Seam.Component.getInstance("progressBarAction");

    ... used the progressBarAction object ...
  // ]]>
</script>
```

You can now invoke the `progressBarAction.getProgress()` method with a callback. The current `progress` object is passed to the callback when the server-side AJAX method exits. The `progressCallback()` function uses the `progressBar` object defined in the `slider.js` file to actually draw the updated progress bar. Finally, since we need to obtain the progress periodically to update the progress bar, we wrap the asynchronous `progressBarAction.getProgress()` call in a `setTimeout()` JavaScript function, which calls the wrapped function every time the timeout elapses (250 milliseconds in our case).

```
<script type="text/javascript">
  //<![CDATA[
    ... ...
    // Make the async call with a callback handler
    function getProgress() {
      progressBarAction.getProgress(progressCallback);
    }
```

```
  // The callback function for receiving the AJAX response
  // and then updating the progress bar
  function progressCallback(progress) {
    progressBar.setPosition(progress.percentComplete);
    if (progress.percentComplete < 100)
      queryProgress();
  }

  // Wrap the async call in setTimeout so that it is
  // called again and again to update the progress bar
  function queryProgress() {
    setTimeout("getProgress()", 250);
  }

  // ]]>
</script>
```

This JSF snippet ties together the `commandButton` component, the server-side `progressBarAction.doSomething()` method, and the `queryProgress()` JavaScript method for AJAX interaction:

```
<h:form onsubmit="queryProgress();return true;">
  <h:commandButton value="Go!"
                   action="#{progressBarAction.doSomething}"/>
</h:form>
```

When the user clicks on the **Go** button, the browsers sends in a request to start the `progressBarAction.doSomething()` method on the backend and, at the same time, starts the `queryProgress()` JavaScript function. While the browser is waiting for the `progressBarAction.doSomething()` method to complete, the `queryProgress()` method keeps updating the progress bar via AJAX calls to the `progressBarAction.getProgress()` method.

# 21.3  Integrating the Dojo Toolkit

Now you have seen how to use Seam Remoting to develop vanilla AJAX applications. But in reality, many fancy AJAX web applications use third-party JavaScript libraries to add rich UI widgets and effects. In this section, we examine how to integrate third-party JavaScript libraries into Seam applications. We will use the popular Dojo toolkit as an example. Again, the sample application is in the `remote` source code project.

---

**What Is Dojo?**

Dojo is an open source JavaScript library for rich web applications. AJAX developers use it widely. You can learn more about Dojo from its web site, http://dojotoolkit.org.

---

Aside from communication and data modeling utilities, third-party JavaScript libraries usually provide two types of UI widgets: visual effects and enhanced user input controls.

## 21.3.1  Visual Effects

Widgets of this type are for rich UI effects. They include visual effects such as animation, fade in/out, drag-and-drops, etc., as well as navigation/layout widgets, such as tabs, accordion, trees, etc. The Dojo JavaScript functions retrieve XHTML elements by their IDs or types and then operate on those elements to create the desired visual effects. For those functions and widgets, Seam applications are no different from other HTML web applications. You just need to enclose a content segment in <div> tags with the appropriate IDs. That is especially easy with Facelets (see Section 3.1) because Facelets pages are simply XHTML pages with JSF components. To make our point, let's look at two simple Dojo examples. The following listing shows how to create a three-tab panel in Dojo. The content in the first two tabs is loaded when the page is loaded, and the third tab's content is loaded from another page when you click on it.

```
<div id="mainTabContainer" dojoType="TabContainer" selectedTab="tab1">
  <div id="tab1" dojoType="ContentPane" label="Tab 1">
    <h1>First Tab</h1>
    ... HTML and JSF component tags for tab content ...
  </div>
  <div id="tab2" dojoType="ContentPane" label="Tab 2">
    ... More HTML and JSF component tags for tab content ...
  </div>
  <a dojoType="LinkPane" href="somepage.seam"
     refreshOnShow="true">Tab 3</a>
  ... ...
</div>
```

For another example, let's use Dojo JavaScript functions to fade in and fade out a part of the web page enclosed in the <div> tags:

```
<a href="javascript:void(dojo.lfx.html.fadeOut('fade', 300).play())">
Fade out</a> |
<a href="javascript:void(dojo.lfx.html.fadeIn('fade', 300).play())">
Fade in</a> |
<a href="javascript:void(dojo.html.setOpacity(
                         document.getElementById('fade'), 0.5))">
Set opacity = 50%</a>

<div id="fade">
... XHTML and JSF components to be faded in/out by the above links ...
</div>
```

As you can see, these examples have nothing specific to Seam. You can enclose any number of Seam JSF components between those <div> tags, and the Dojo JavaScript will work just fine.

It gets more complicated when a Dojo JavaScript function needs to directly operate on a JSF component. For most cases, you can just enclose the JSF component in a pair of `<div>` tags. If that is not possible, you must manually figure out the ID of the rendered JSF component. That is typically pretty easy; you just need to look at the HTML source of the generated page. Note, however, that those generated IDs do change from one JSF implementation to the next.

## 21.3.2 Input Widgets

The second type of Dojo widgets includes the input widgets that replace the standard HTML input fields. For instance, Dojo provides a rich text editor, an inline text editor, a GUI date/time picker, and many other useful input widgets. Since those widgets are not JSF components, we cannot directly bind their values to a backing bean property. Seam Remoting can really help here. Figure 21.2 shows a Dojo rich text editor in the `hello.xhtml` form. It generates HTML-styled comments.

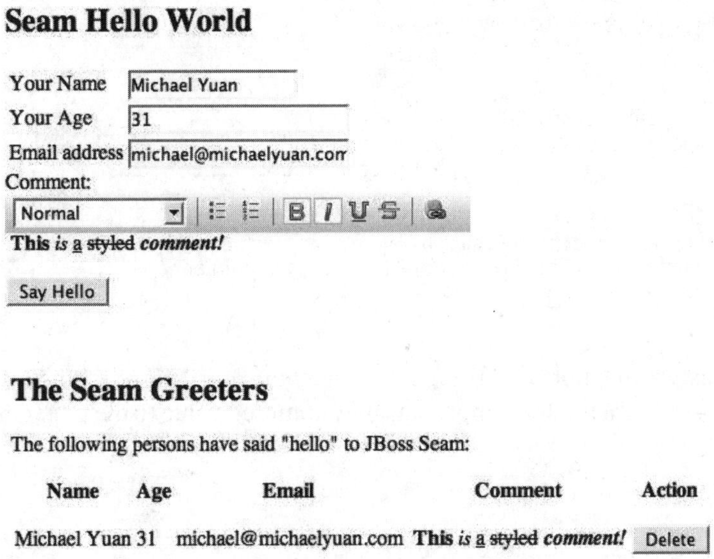

**Figure 21.2**    A Dojo rich text editor

The following is the relevant code for the web page. Most of it is just standard Dojo. When the form submits, the comment in the rich text editor is not submitted to JSF because the Dojo rich text widget does not have any JSF backend value binding. Therefore, we invoke the JavaScript function `submitComment()` to submit the comment separately when the user clicks on the **Say Hello** button.

```
<script src="dojo-0.3.1-editor/dojo.js"
        type="text/javascript">
</script>
```

```
<script type="text/javascript">
  dojo.require("dojo.widget.Editor");
</script>

... ...

Comment:<br/>
<div id="comment" dojoType="Editor"></div>

<h:commandButton type="submit" value="Say Hello"
                 onclick="submitComment()"
                 action="#{manager.sayHello}"/>
```

This is the code for the `submitComment()` JavaScript function. Notice that we do not pass in a callback function to the Seam Remoting call here because we do not need to process the return value.

```
<script language="javascript">
  ... ...

  // Get the "manager" Seam component
  var manager = Seam.Component.getInstance("manager");

  ... ...

  function submitComment () {
    var ed = dojo.widget.byId("comment");
    manager.setComment (ed.getEditorContent());

    // This works too
    // var eds = dojo.widget.byType("Editor");
    // manager.setComment (eds[0].getEditorContent());
  }
</script>
```

Of course, as we mentioned earlier, the `#{manager.setComment}` method must be a Seam `@WebRemote` method. It simply sets the submitted value to the `person` component.

```
@Local
public interface Manager {
  ... ...

  @WebRemote
  public void setComment (String comment);
}

... ...

@Name("manager")
public class ManagerAction implements Manager {
  ... ...

  public void setComment (String comment) {
    person.setComment (comment);
  }
}
```

**An Alternative**

An alternative way to use the Dojo rich text component is to render it into an HTML `textarea` instead of a `div`. The rich text in the `textarea` is submitted as an HTTP request parameter when the user submits the form. Although you still cannot directly bind a Dojo `textarea` to a Seam component, you can at least retrieve the HTTP request parameter at the backend via the `@RequestParameter` injection (see Chapter 15). In most cases, this is probably easier than the Seam Remoting approach.

The rich text editor is simple. Now let's take a look at a more complex example: a Dojo inline editor on the `hello.xhtml` form. The idea is that a comment appears to be normal text until you click on it; then it becomes an editable text field, where you can change the comment and save it to the backend (Figure 21.3).

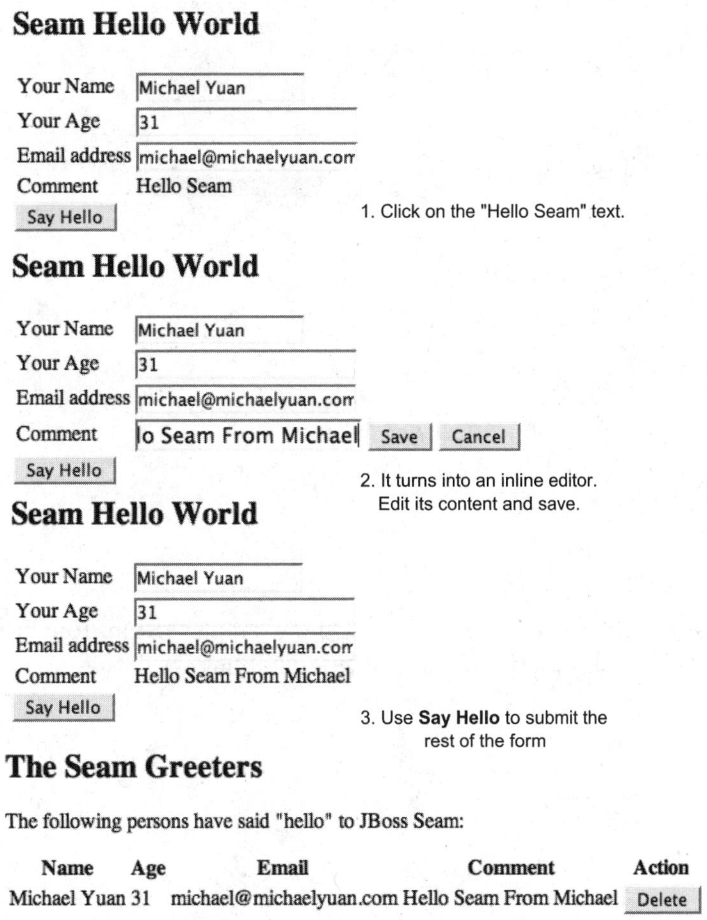

**Figure 21.3**   A Dojo inline editor

The JavaScript code is a little more involved here. We give the inline editor widget an `onSave` handler method, `submitComment()`, which saves its current content to the backend via Seam Remoting. As you can see, even with this widget, a single line of Seam Remoting code handles the backend communication.

```
<script src="dojo-0.3.1-editor/dojo.js"
        type="text/javascript">
</script>
<script type="text/javascript">
  dojo.require("dojo.widget.InlineEditBox");
  dojo.require("dojo.event.*");
</script>

<script language="javascript">
  ... ...

  // Get the "manager" Seam component
  var manager = Seam.Component.getInstance("manager");

  function submitComment (newValue, oldValue) {
    manager.setComment (newValue);
  }

  function init () {
    var commentEditor = dojo.widget.byId("comment");
    commentEditor.onSave = submitComment;
  }

  dojo.addOnLoad(init);
</script>

... ...

<tr>
  <td>Comment</td>
  <td>
    <div id="comment" dojoType="inlineEditBox">
    Hello Seam
    </div>
  </td>
</tr>
```

Although the examples we gave here are Dojo examples, Seam Remoting can work with any third-party JavaScript library. The possibilities are limitless!

# Part V

## Business Processes and Rules

Apart from data-driven web applications, Seam supports business process-driven web applications via the jBPM business process engine. It also supports business rules via the Drools engine (also known as JBoss Rules). With several simple annotations, you can attach Seam stateful components to business processes that require actions from multiple users and can survive multiple server reboots. Each user is automatically presented with the tasks the process requires. Business processes and rules are integrated into the very heart of the Seam framework: Seam leverages jBPM workflow to manage the JSF pageflow in a stateful manner, and the Seam security framework makes heavy use of the Drools engine to manage access security rules. We cover all these important use cases in this part of the book.

# 22

Rule-Based Security
Framework

**B**usiness processes are closely related to business rules. Seam integrates the Drools (also known as JBoss Rules) engine to support sophisticated rules. In fact, Seam itself uses Drools to implement an innovative security framework for web applications. In this chapter, we demonstrate how business rules are used to manage security.

Managed security is one of those "half-measure solutions" in enterprise Java. The standard Java EE security model works okay for the simplest cases (e.g., to require login to access part of the site). But more often than not, developers struggle against the standard Java EE security schemes and work around them instead of using them.

The Seam security model, on the other hand, is based on rules. You can specify who is permitted to access which page, which UI element, and which bean method. As with everything else in Seam, all Seam security rules are stateful. That means each rule's outcome depends on the current state of the application context. You can therefore give certain users access to certain application features only when some runtime conditions are met. The Seam security framework offers great power and flexibility for almost every use case a web application might encounter.

## 22.1  Rule-Based Access Control

In Chapter 18, we saw the extensive security features provided by Seam that enable you to authenticate, authorize, and manage application users through their `#{credentials}` and roles. The features we discussed are already quite impressive by themselves, but we have not touched business rules yet. Business rules take access control to a whole new level, unseen in previous generations of Java security frameworks.

- Using business rules, you can put all security configuration in one file and simplify the `Restrict` tags and annotations. That is a huge plus when you have a large web site with many user roles and many potential entry points because all access rules can be reviewed and analyzed at once. It also allows nonprogrammers to develop rules using GUI tools that the Drools project provides.

- Business rules give you per-instance access controls based on the current state of the application. We will discuss this further in Section 22.4.

Of course, the downside of using access rules is that you must bundle the Drools JAR files and configuration files with the application (see Chapter 23). But that is a small price to pay for such advanced features.

Let's begin by reimplementing the role-based access control scheme in rules.

# 22.2  Configuring Rule-Based Permissioning

Seam security provides a framework for resolving permissions. Simply by implementing the `PermissionResolver` interface, you can inject any approach for resolving user permissions. While this gives ultimate flexibility, in most cases one of the two Seam implementations will suit your permissioning needs. The following implementations are provided by Seam:

`RuleBasedPermissionResolver`   This is the permission resolver discussed throughout this chapter. It uses Drools to resolve rule-based permission checks and provides extensive flexibility in permissioning, allowing use of a terse scripting language for authoring permission checks.

`PersistentPermissionResolver`   This permission resolver stores object permissions in a persistent store, such as a relational database. If you require ACL (Access Control List) security restrictions where a list of permissions must be attached to an object, this permission resolver will suit your needs. It is discussed in depth in the Seam Reference Documentation.

To configure the `RuleBasedPermissionResolver`, you will first need to define a `security.drl` file in the classpath. This file will contain the rules fired to perform permission checks. A rule base can then be configured which is referenced by the permission resolver.

```
<components xmlns="http://jboss.com/products/seam/components"
            xmlns:drools="http://jboss.com/products/seam/drools"
            xmlns:security="http://jboss.com/products/seam/security"
            xmlns:xsi="http://www.w3.org/2001/XMLSchema-instance"
            xsi:schemaLocation="http://jboss.com/products/seam/drools
               http://jboss.com/products/seam/drools-2.1.xsd
               http://jboss.com/products/seam/security
               http://jboss.com/products/seam/security-2.1.xsd">
  <security:rule-based-permission-resolver
    security-rules="#{securityRules}"/>

  <drools:rule-base name="securityRules">
    <drools:rule-files>
      <value>/META-INF/security.drl</value>
    </drools:rule-files>
  </drools:rule-base>
  ... ...
```

We will cover the details of how to build and deploy the application with Drools in Section 23.3, but for now let's take an in-depth look at permissioning using rules.

# 22.3  Simple Access Rules

Before we discuss the access rules, let's first explain how the `Restrict` tag or annotation really works under the hood. When you have an empty `Restrict`, it is equivalent to making a call to the `#{identity.hasPermission}` method. The shorthand version of the EL is `#{s:hasPermission(...)}`. To understand how this works, let's return to the Rules Booking example discussed in Chapter 18. Previously, we used the `#{s:hasRole}` operation to determine authorization, but let's see how this can be accomplished using rules-based permissioning.

```
@Name("rewardsManager")
@Scope(ScopeType.CONVERSATION)
public class RewardsManager {
  @In EntityManager em;

  @Out(required=false)
  private Rewards rewards;
  // ... ...
  @Restrict
  public void updateSettings() {
    if(rewards.isReceiveSpecialOffers()) {
      facesMessages.add("You have successfully registered to " +
        "receive special offers!");
    } else {
      facesMessages.add("You will no longer receive our special offers.");
    }
    rewards = em.merge(rewards);
    em.flush();
  }
  // ... ...
}
```

The empty @Restrict annotation is equivalent to the following:

```
@Restrict("#{s:hasPermission('rewardsManager', 'updateSettings')}")
```

The first call parameter is the component name (the target), and the second parameter is the method name (the action). They form the basis of the security rule. To allow only the users with the rewards role to access this method, we have the following rule in the security.drl, our Drools configuration file:

```
package MyApplicationPermissions;

import org.jboss.seam.security.PermissionCheck;
import org.jboss.seam.security.Role;

rule RewardsUser
when
  c: PermissionCheck(target == "rewardsManager",
                        action == "updateSettings")
  Role(name == "rewardsuser")
then
  c.grant();
end;
```

The name of the rule can be arbitrary. The important point is that the rule is triggered when the #{rewardsManager.updateSettings} method is called, and access is granted when the current user has the rewardsuser role. Each Role that the user has is inserted as a fact into the WorkingMemory. This allows you to check any role the user may be associated with.

The PermissionCheck is a Seam component created prior to invoking the security rules. The component is inserted into the WorkingMemory and is used to identify the rule that determines the user's permissions and to grant permission if the rule is successful. There is no magic going on here. The initialized values of the PermissionCheck component ensure the uniqueness of the intended security rule.

Seam checks the status of the PermissionCheck component once rule execution is complete. If the grant() method has been invoked, the permission check will return true.

---

**Check for Logged-in Users**

If you want to grant access to all logged-in users, regardless of their roles, you can check whether the Principal object exists. The Principal object is created in the login process. To do that, use exists Principal() to replace the Role(name == "rewardsuser") line in the rule we discussed earlier.

---

The `<restrict>` tag rules for web pages are similar. Since no component names and method names exist here, the default `target` is the JSF `view-id` of the page, and the default `action` is `render`. For instance, the following page configuration results in a `#{s:hasPermission('/rewards/summary.xhtml', 'render')}` call when the `/rewards/summary.xhtml` page is accessed:

```
<pages>

    ... ...

    <page view-id="/rewards/summary.xhtml">
      <restrict/>
    </page>

</pages>
```

This is the security rule for `rewardsuser`-only access to the page:

```
rule CanUserViewRewards
when
   c: PermissionCheck(target == "/rewards/summary.xhtml",
                        action == "render")
   Role(name == "rewardsuser")
then
   c.grant()
end;
```

# 22.4  Per-Instance Access Rules

So far, we have only mentioned executing rules against security object instances (i.e., `Principals` and `Roles`). By passing an object from the Seam stateful context to the security check method, you can create rules that grant access only when certain runtime conditions are met. The `target` we discussed before in the `PermissionCheck` is not required to be a string. It can be any object from the context, even a Seam component. The `target` instance will be inserted into the `WorkingMemory` as a `Fact` from the current context.

Returning to the Rules Booking example, the user is prompted with a list of previous bookings on the `main.xhtml` view (Figure 22.1). The user can then review one of the bookings by selecting the **Write Review** link (Figure 22.2).

You are only allowed to review a `Hotel` if you are logged in and have previously booked the `Hotel`. This restriction can be placed on the `submit()` method of the `HotelReviewAction`, as shown in the following listing:

Current Hotel Bookings

| Name | Address | Check in date Check out date | Room Preference | Payment | Conf # | Action |
|------|---------|------------------------------|-----------------|---------|--------|--------|
| W Hotel | Union Square, Manhattan NY, NY | Sat Sep 27 00:00:00 CDT 2008 Fri Oct 10 00:00:00 CDT 2008 | Cozy Room | $5,850.00 | 1 | Cancel Write Review |

**Figure 22.1**    `main.xhtml`: After a hotel is booked, the user can review that hotel based on his or her stay.

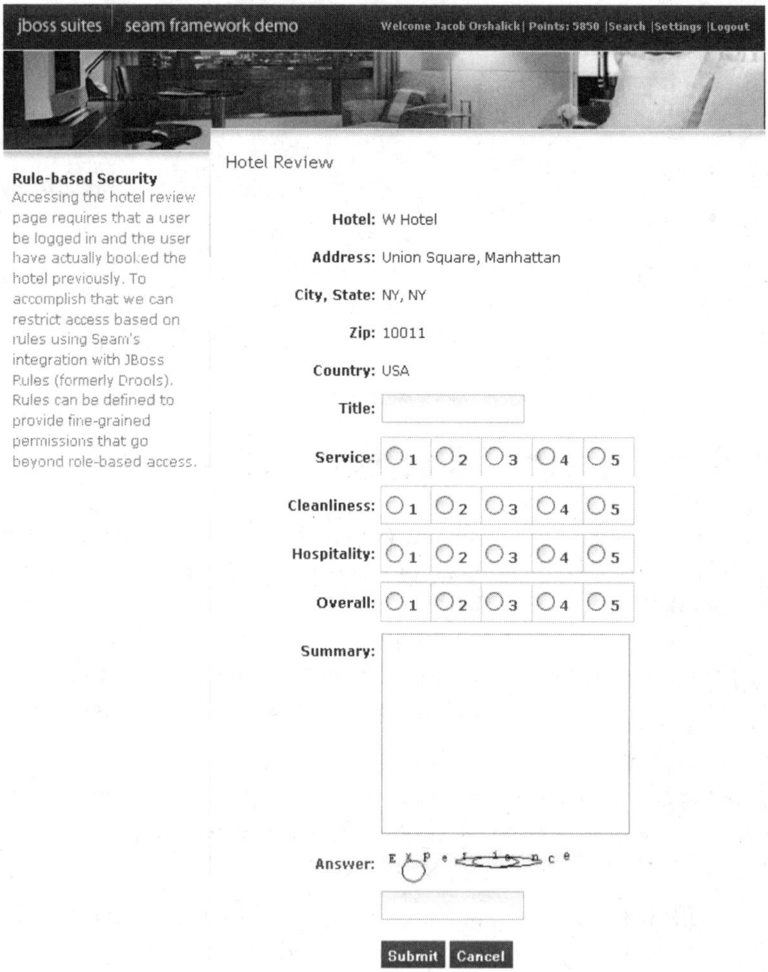

**Figure 22.2**    `review.xhtml`: Users are restricted in writing reviews based on security rules.

```
@Name("hotelReview")
@Stateful
public class HotelReviewAction implements HotelReview
{
  // ... ...
  @In private EntityManager em;

  @In(required=false)
  @Out(required=false)
  private Hotel hotel;

  @End
  @Restrict("#{s:hasPermission(hotelReview, 'review')}")
  public void submit()
  {
    log.info("Submitting review for hotel: #0", hotel.getName());

    hotel.addReview(review);
    em.flush();
   // ... ...
  }
  // ... ...
}
```

This restriction results in execution of the HotelReviewer security rule. Note that the s:hasPermission invocation passes the hotelReviewer component as the target. Components or entities can be passed as a PermissionCheck target instead of a string. This results in the component instance being added as an additional Fact available in the WorkingMemory for firing rules.

```
rule HotelReviewer
when
  exists Principal()
  $hotelReview: HotelReview($bookings: bookings, $hotel: hotel)
  exists ( Booking( hotel == $hotel ) from $bookings )
  c: PermissionCheck(target == $hotelReview, action == "review")
then
  c.grant();
end;
```

Essentially, the rule first determines whether the user is logged in, by ensuring that the Principal exists in WorkingMemory. The rule then ensures that the Hotel the user is attempting to review exists in the user's bookings. Notice the power of the rule definition—it is easy to express complex conditions through the Drools syntax. For more information on defining rules, see Chapter 23.

The state of the hotelReview component is used to determine whether the user has permission to review the Hotel. As you can imagine, the restrictions could be extended. We would likely also want to ensure that the checkoutDate of the Booking has passed and that the user has not previously written a review for this Booking. Writing additional checks becomes simple.

Checking on submit is really a last resort—but this is good practice given our defense-in-depth approach. It would also be a good idea to completely restrict access to the `review.xhtml` page if the user is not authorized.

```
<page view-id="/review.xhtml" conversation-required="true">
  <description>Hotel Review: #{hotel.name}</description>
  <restrict>#{s:hasPermission(hotelReview, 'review')}</restrict>
  <navigation from-action="#{hotelReview.submit}">
    <redirect view-id="/main.xhtml"/>
  </navigation>
  <navigation from-action="#{hotelReview.cancel}">
    <redirect view-id="/main.xhtml"/>
  </navigation>
</page>
```

As demonstrated in Section 18.2.1, it is simple to restrict access to specific web pages using the `<restrict>` tag. Here we once again specify our restriction to ensure that a user cannot access `review.xhtml` without appropriate permissions.

# 22.5  Securing Your Entities

The lowest layer of security in Seam allows you to secure entities. It is easy to apply security restrictions to read, insert, update, and delete actions for entities. Annotating an entity with `@Restrict` will ensure that a permission check is fired each time a persistence operation occurs. The default security check that is performed is a permission check of `entity:action`, where `entity` is the entity instance that the permission check is being performed against. The entity instance is inserted as a `Fact` into the `WorkingMemory`. The action is dependent on the persistence operation being performed: `read`, `insert`, `update`, or `delete`. As before, it is possible to specify an EL expression in the `@Restrict` annotation to further customize this behavior.

To secure all actions for the `Rewards` entity, simply annotate the entity with `@Restrict`:

```
@Entity
@Name("rewards")
@Restrict
@Table(name="Reward_Member")
public class Rewards {
  // ... ...
```

Now a permission check can be defined for `delete` actions:

```
when
  Role(name == "administrator")
  $rewards : Rewards(rewardPoints == 0)
  c: PermissionCheck(target == $rewards, action == "delete")
then
  c.grant();
end;
```

In this case, an administrator is given permission to delete the `Rewards` record associated with a user if it is inactive. Entity lifecycle methods can be used to further pinpoint when a security check should be invoked. In the above example, a security check would be attempted for all persistence operations, although we are only interested in `delete` actions. In this case, we could simply annotate a method with `@PreRemove` and `@Restrict` and remove the `@Restrict` annotation from the top of the entity.

```
@PreRemove @Restrict
public void preRemove() {}
```

This results in a security check being executed only when the entity is being removed. As you can see, it is not required that the method perform any operation, simply that it be annotated with the entity lifecycle annotation and `@Restrict`. The entity lifecycle annotations for executing permission checks are `@PostLoad`, `@PrePersist`, `@PreUpdate`, and `@PreRemove`. The permissions executed for each case are `read`, `insert`, `update`, and `delete` respectively.

Entity security checks must be enabled through an `EntityListener` if you are using EJB3. The `EntityListener` is configured by placing the following definition in the `META-INF/orm.xml` file of your project:

```
<?xml version="1.0" encoding="UTF-8"?>
<entity-mappings
  xmlns="http://java.sun.com/xml/ns/persistence/orm"
  xmlns:xsi="http://www.w3.org/2001/XMLSchema-instance"
  xsi:schemaLocation="http://java.sun.com/xml/ns/persistence/orm
                      http://java.sun.com/xml/ns/persistence/orm_1_0.xsd"
  version="1.0">

  <persistence-unit-metadata>
    <persistence-unit-defaults>
      <entity-listeners>
        <entity-listener
          class="org.jboss.seam.security.EntitySecurityListener"/>
      </entity-listeners>
    </persistence-unit-defaults>
  </persistence-unit-metadata>

</entity-mappings>
```

In addition, similar to the type-safe role annotations we saw in Section 18.2.4, Seam provides type-safe annotations for standard CRUD-based permissions. Table 22.1 lists the annotations provided out of the box.

These annotations can be specified on the method or parameter where a security check should be performed. If placed on a method, the target class for which the permission will be checked must be specified. The following example ensures that a user has permission to delete a `Rewards` instance:

**Table 22.1**  Type-Safe Annotations for Standard CRUD-Based Permissions

| Annotation | Use | Description |
|---|---|---|
| @Read | method, parameter | Declares a type-safe permission check to determine whether the current user has read permission for the specified class. |
| @Update | method, parameter | Declares a type-safe permission check to determine whether the current user has update permission for the specified class. |
| @Insert | method, parameter | Declares a type-safe permission check to determine whether the current user has insert permission for the specified class. |
| @Delete | method, parameter | Declares a type-safe permission check to determine whether the current user has delete permission for the specified class. |

```
public void removeRewards(@Delete Rewards rewards) {
   ...
 }
```

The same permission check we defined previously would be executed in this case. Just as with role annotations, you can define your own type-safe permission checks using the @PermissionCheck meta-annotation.

Per-instance access rules enable developers to control application behavior dynamically. This is quite useful in applications requiring more than just a simple role-based access scheme for security. Seam makes it easy to implement complex security rules in your application in a concise and expressive manner.

# 23

## Integrating Business Rules in Web Applications

**I**n Chapter 22, we saw how to use rules to describe and enforce security policies in your web application. The security rules in Seam are powered by the Drools framework. Using the same underlying Drools engine, we can easily add generic business rules in Seam applications as well.

The easiest way to use rules in Seam is probably to piggyback on top of the security rules infrastructure. We can just put business rules in `app.ear/META-INF/security.drl` and use `#{s:hasPermission(...)}` to check whether to present certain navigation or business function choices to the user.

In this chapter, we will first continue working on the Rules Booking example application, which uses business rules embedded inside security rules. After that, we will discuss generic Drools use cases and explain how to reload rules without restarting the server.

## 23.1  Embedded Rules

To illustrate how business rules work with security rules, we added a reward points system to the Rules Booking application. The business rules that control whether to let the user pay his or her current booking with points are the same rules that determine whether to show the **Apply Rewards** button to the user. This type of natural synergy allows us to build simple rule-based applications from `security.drl`.

Before we dive into the actual rules, let's check out the application first.

## 23.1.1  Rule-Based Behavior

To see the rule-based rewards system in action, first log into the Rules Booking example with username and password demo/demo. After you book a hotel room, you can see your current reward points at the top right of the page. Each reward point is worth 10c.

Now, try to book another hotel room. Figures 23.1 to 23.3 show the process. If you have enough points to cover the entire cost of the new booking, you will be presented with a new navigation option to redeem the reward points. If you do redeem, the reward points are deducted from your account, and your cost for the booking is reduced to zero. The business rule here is to determine whether the user has enough reward points to redeem, and present the option as needed.

**Nesting conversations**
Nested conversations allow the application to capture a consistent continuable state at various points in a user interaction, thus insuring truly correct behavior in the face of backbuttoning and workspace management.

**Continuing the conversation**

Try going back and selecting a different room. You will notice a new nested conversation in the list of workspace

## Payment

**Name:** W Hotel

**Address:** Lexington Ave, Manhattan

**City, State:** NY, NY

**Zip:** 10011

**Country:** USA

**Room Preference:** Fantastic Suite

**Total payment:** $9,000.00

**Discounted payment:** $9,000.00

**Check In Date:** Sun Apr 27 00:00:00 GMT 2008

**Check Out Date:** Tue May 06 00:00:00 GMT 2008

**Figure 23.1**    Payment screen when you do not have enough points

## 23.1.2  Applying Rules

The reward business rule is applied to the payment.xhtml page via the #{s:hasPermission('rewards', 'payment', rewardsManager)} security check. The page displays the **Apply Rewards** button when the check is satisfied.

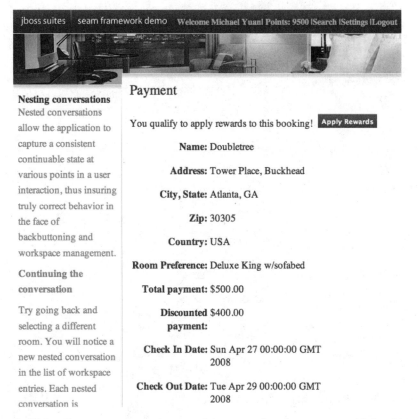

**Figure 23.2** Payment screen when you have enough points to cover this booking

```
<s:div styleClass="entry"
       rendered="#{s:hasPermission('rewards','payment',rewardsManager)}">
  <h:outputText value="You qualify to apply rewards to this booking!"/>
  <h:commandButton action="#{rewardsManager.requestConfirmation}"
                   value="Apply Rewards" immediate="true"/>
</s:div>
```

The check is mapped to the RewardsForPayment rule in security.drl. We pass in the rewardsManager object to the rule.

```
rule RewardsForPayment
when
  c: PermissionCheck(name == "rewards", action == "payment")
  Role(name == "rewards")
  RewardsManager($userRewards : rewards, $hotel : hotel,
                 $rewardPointsCost : rewardPointsCost)
  Hotel( name != "W Hotel" ) from $hotel
  Rewards( eval( rewardPoints >= $rewardPointsCost) )
          from $userRewards
then
  c.grant();
end;
```

**Figure 23.3**    Redeeming the points

The rules engine first determines that the current user has the role of `rewards` (i.e., has signed up for the rewards program during registration). It extracts the `rewards`, `hotel`, and `rewardPointsCost` properties from the `rewardsManager` object passed into the rule. The rule requires that the `rewardPointsCost` be less than `rewards.rewardPoints`, meaning that the user has enough points to cover this entire booking. The rule also requires that the hotel is not a "W Hotel," providing a mechanism for hotels to opt out of the rewards program.

Once the `RewardsForPayment` rule is satisfied, the **Apply Rewards** button is displayed and the `#{rewardsManager.requestConfirmation}` action becomes available for the user to go on with the rewards redemption workflow.

---

**Bundle Drools Library JARs**

You need to bundle Drools library JARs with your application in order to make the `security.drl` rules work. See Section 23.3 for details.

---

# 23.2  Generic Rules

As we see in this chapter, piggybacking business rules in `security.drl` is a convenient way to use rules. It makes sense for many use cases, since we typically want to do a security check with business rules in case someone directly types in a URL to access additional features (e.g., the reward points program) without going through the rule engine first.

Of course, the rules engine can also be used in contexts that are not related to security at all. For instance, we might use rules to compute the hotel room price. Every user sees a different price based on how many points he or she has accumulated. You can see the discount amount reflected in the **Discounted payment** fields in Figures 23.1 and 23.2. There is no "security" restriction in this use case.

In addition, the application might use dynamically updatable rules—to update the rules without redeploying the server. In this section, we will cover these use cases. But first, let's get ourselves familiar with a key concept in Drools: the working memory.

## 23.2.1  The Working Memory

The way a rules engine works is by creating a memory space called *working memory* to hold all objects that the rules will be applied to. When the application asks the rules engine to run, it applies the rules to all objects in the working memory and modifies the objects as needed. The application waits until the rules are completed and checks the final states of the objects in the working memory before proceeding.

So, the first step in our application is to create a working memory instance and make it accessible as a Seam component. That is done in the `app.war/WEB-INF/components.xml` file:

```
<drools:rule-base name="pricingpolicy"
                  rule-files="/META-INF/pricingpolicy.drl"/>
<drools:managed-working-memory name="pricingWM"
                               rule-base="#{pricingpolicy}"/>
```

The Seam runtime first creates a rule base from the specified rules file. It then creates a working memory component named `pricingWM` and makes it available to all Seam components. The rules are defined as follows:

```
package MyApplicationPrices;

import org.jboss.seam.example.booking.action.HotelReview;
import org.jboss.seam.example.booking.action.RewardsManager;
import org.jboss.seam.example.booking.entities.Booking;
import org.jboss.seam.example.booking.entities.Hotel;
import org.jboss.seam.example.booking.entities.Rewards;
```

```
rule HighDiscount
when
  $booking : Booking ()
  exists( Rewards( rewardPoints >= 3000 ))
then
  $booking.setDiscountRate (0.8);
end

rule MidDiscount
when
  $booking : Booking ()
  exists( Rewards( rewardPoints >= 2000 ))
then
  $booking.setDiscountRate (0.85);
end

rule LowDiscount
when
  $booking : Booking ()
  exists( Rewards( rewardPoints >= 1000 ))
then
  $booking.setDiscountRate (0.9);
end

rule NoDiscount
when
  $booking : Booking ()
  exists( Rewards( rewardPoints < 1000 ))
then
  $booking.setDiscountRate (1.0);
end
```

Each rule references a `Booking` type object and a `Rewards` type object from the working memory. The rule examines the `rewardPoints` property on the `Rewards` object, and makes changes to the `Booking` object accordingly. For instance, if the `rewardPoints` is more than 3000, the `HighDiscount` rule would set the `discountRate` on the `Booking` object to 0.8, meaning that this booking will be at 80% discount from its original price.

## 23.2.2 Using the Working Memory

Next, in order to run the rules in a Seam component, we first inject the `pricingWM` working memory instance.

```
public class HotelBookingAction implements HotelBooking {
  ... ...
  @In (create=true)
  private WorkingMemory pricingWM;
  ... ...
}
```

In our case, we run the rules when the `payment.xhtml` page is loaded to figure out the discount price for the current booking.

```
<page view-id="/payment.xhtml" conversation-required="true">
  ... ...
  <action execute="#{hotelBooking.applyPricingRules}"/>
  ... ...
</page>
```

In the page action method #{hotelBooking.applyPricingRules}, we insert the current booking object and rewards object into the working memory, and then fire the rules. The booking and rewards objects are the Booking and Rewards type objects referenced in the rule mentioned in the previous section.

```
public class HotelBookingAction implements HotelBooking {
  ... ...
  public void applyPricingRules () throws Exception {
    pricingWM.insert(rewards);
    pricingWM.insert(booking);
    pricingWM.fireAllRules();
  }
  ... ...
}
```

After all the rules are executed, the booking object should have the discountRate property set according to the rewards points.

The rest of the application just goes on to display this discounted price and charge the credit card accordingly when the user checks out.

## 23.2.3 Dynamically Updatable Rules

In this example, our business rules are fixed and bundled in the EAR file. However, in the real world, business rules are often subject to change. A business analyst draws up rules in Excel spreadsheets or GUI-based designers and exports them to .drl files. We cannot redeploy the server every time the rules change.

Instead, Drools provides a mechanism to periodically pull rules from a network location to update its existing rules. That allows a business analysts to change the behavior of the system at runtime. You can configure the online rules repository location in your app.war/WEB-INF/components.xml file:

```
<drools:rule-agent name="myRules"
                   url="http://host/rules"
                   local-cache-dir="/var/rules/cache"
                   poll="30"
                   configuration-name="appRules" />
```

In the above configuration, the rules repository is located at http://host/rules/appRules.drl. Drools polls the repository every 30 minutes and caches the downloaded rules files locally at /var/rules/cache/appRules.drl.

# 23.3   Building and Deployment

As we discussed in Chapter 22 and earlier in this chapter, you need to reference the
`*.drl` files in the `app.war/WEB-INF/components.xml` file. Obviously, for the rules to
take effect, you need to bundle the `*.drl` files as well as Drools JARs in the application.

The following snippet from `build.xml` shows the necessary JAR files you need for
deploying Drools support on JBoss AS. You may need other JAR files to deploy to non-
JBoss application servers. Please refer to Drools documentation for more details. The
`*.drl` files are bundled in `app.ear/META-INF/` so that they can be referenced from
`classpath:/META-INF/`.

```
<target name="ear">
  <mkdir dir="${build.jars}"/>

  <ear destfile="${build.jars}/${projname}.ear"
       appxml="${resources}/META-INF/application.xml">

    <fileset dir="${build.jars}"
             includes="*.jar, *.war"/>

    <metainf dir="${resources}/META-INF">
      <include name="jboss-app.xml" />
      <include name="security.drl" />
      <include name="pricingpolicy.drl" />
    </metainf>

    <fileset dir="${seam.home}">
      <include name="lib/jboss-seam.jar"/>
      <include name="lib/jboss-el.jar" />
      <include name="lib/commons-lang.jar" />
      <include name="lib/commons-beanutils.jar" />
      <include name="lib/commons-digester.jar" />
      <include name="lib/richfaces-api.jar" />

      <!-- include drools dependencies -->
      <include name="lib/antlr-runtime.jar" />
      <include name="lib/core.jar" />
      <include name="lib/janino.jar" />
      <include name="lib/mvel14.jar" />
      <include name="lib/drools-core.jar" />
      <include name="lib/drools-compiler.jar" />
    </fileset>
  </ear>
</target>
```

If you are building a WAR file for the application for Tomcat deployment, you
will need to bundle the JAR files in `app.war/WEB-INF/lib` and the `*.drl` files in
`app.war/WEB-INF/classes/META-INF` directories.

# 23.4  Conclusions

In this chapter, we discussed how to add business rules to a Seam web application. The easiest approach is to piggyback on the security rules if your business rules have implications on access control. It is also easy to integrate standalone business rules through a working memory instance injected into your Seam component.

In the next two chapters, we will discuss how to integrate business processes into Seam applications. And then, in Chapter 25, we will discuss how to integrate business processes with rules to eliminate much of the business logic coding in your application!

# 24

## Managing Business Processes

Business process management is a crucial aspect in today's enterprise applications. Instead of hardcoding the business flow in the application, business process engines allow the application to change its operation on the fly via configuration changes. Such flexibility allows the application to quickly adapt to changing business requirements.

Although many enterprise applications can benefit from configurable business processes, in reality, relatively few of them actually use business process engines. The reason is that the integration between web applications and business process engines is hard. Most developers would rather hardcode the business flow than deal with the integration problems. Seam changes that by enabling very easy integration with the popular jBPM (Business Process Manager) framework.

Seam's jBPM integration has deep roots in the framework's stateful design. A remarkable thing about Seam is that it provides a consistent state management framework for everything from conversation states to jBPM business process states. Seam makes it easy to attach jBPM processes to Seam stateful components (e.g., EJB3 stateful session beans).

In previous chapters, we showed that Seam is a great framework for developing stateful web applications. However, all our stateful application examples so far have only dealt with application states associated with a single web user, and that stateful data have lasted only minutes to hours. In business process-driven applications, the application state is often long-running, involving multiple tasks and multiple actors. For instance, let's examine a simple use case scenario: An author edits a document that a manager must approve before sending it to the publisher. This very simple example involves several tasks (writing, approving, sending the manuscript, publishing) and several actors (author, manager, publisher). Seam, together with jBPM, captures all the process information in a single document and then integrates the process into the application code.

This chapter doesn't cover the details of the jBPM framework. Instead, we will focus on showing you how to integrate business processes into Seam applications. The sample application for this chapter is the `ticketing` project in the source code bundle. If you don't know anything about jBPM, fear not: The first part of this chapter gives you the jBPM basics so you can start writing your business processes. If you are familiar with jBPM concepts and vocabulary, you can skip the first section.

# 24.1   jBPM Concepts and Vocabulary

The key concepts in a business process are states and tasks. Generally, the system spends most of its time waiting for user actions. Each user action (e.g., loading a web page or triggering an event handler by clicking a button) would force the system to perform some task and switch itself into a new waiting state. The system goes through a series of those waiting states to accomplish a business task that requires multiperson collaboration. Figure 24.1 shows a very simple business process.

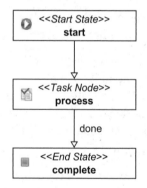

**Figure 24.1**    A simple business process

In jBPM, a process is defined in a process definition XML file. Whenever you want to use a process definition, you must create a process instance to hold and save the data related to that particular instance. In a sense, the process definition is analogous to a Java class, and the process instance is like a Java object.

You can create a process definition XML file by hand, or you can create it visually using the JBoss Eclipse IDE. Figure 24.2 shows an example order-fulfillment process in the JBoss Eclipse IDE's visual process designer. The process describes how to approve (or reject) an order based on certain conditions. To create a process, you first define each potential application state as a node (either a graphical node element in the designer or an XML element in the actual process definition file). Then, for each node, you define

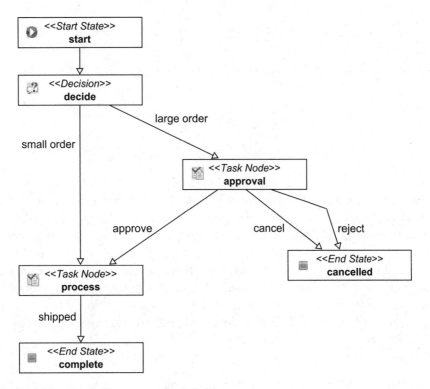

**Figure 24.2**    Designing a process definition

transition rules to move the system from the current state to a state represented by another node.

The JBoss Eclipse IDE generates the following XML file for the process definition shown in Figure 24.2. As you can see, the XML file is intuitive and highly readable; it is not difficult to create by hand.

```
<process-definition name="OrderManagement">
  <start-state name="start">
    <transition to="decide"/>
  </start-state>

  <decision name="decide" expression="#{orderApproval.howLargeIsOrder}">
    <transition name="large order" to="approval"/>
    <transition name="small order" to="process"/>
  </decision>

  <task-node name="approval" end-tasks="true">
    <task name="approve" description="Review order">
      <assignment pooled-actors="reviewers"/>
    </task>
    <transition name="cancel"  to="cancelled"/>
    <transition name="approve" to="process"/>
    <transition name="reject"  to="cancelled"/>
  </task-node>
```

```
    <task-node name="process">
      <task name="ship" description="Ship order">
        <assignment pooled-actors="#{shipperAssignment.pooledActors}"/>
      </task>
      <transition name="shipped" to="complete">
        <action expression="#{afterShipping.log}"/>
      </transition>
    </task-node>

    <end-state name="complete"/>
    <end-state name="cancelled"/>

  </process-definition>
```

You can probably guess what this process does. Basically, we defined an initial state and a final state; in the middle, we added a decision node to let the system pick the right way to take in our graph, depending on a Seam expression. We also defined two task nodes and transitions between those nodes and other nodes. If the system is in a task node, it must complete the task first and then transit to another state node, depending on the task outcome. The `assignment` tag lets us pass the process to other actors. Finally, we used `action` to call a method whenever the `shipped` transition is triggered. If you want to learn more about jBPM and its process definition language, refer to the official jBPM documentation at www.jboss.org/products/jbpm/docs.

---

**Referencing Seam Components in a Process Definition**

You can bind Seam components directly to jBPM process definition documents using the #{} notation, much like what we use in JSF pages. The process can reference values from Seam data components to automatically invoke Seam session bean methods as transition actions.

---

In the next section, for the sake of clarity and simplicity, we will provide a new example of a ticketing process commonly found on customer service web sites. The example project is in the `ticketing` directory in the book's source code bundle. It integrates a business process for employees to assign open support tickets to themselves and then answer and close the assigned tickets.

# 24.2  Application Users and jBPM Actors

As we mentioned, a business process typically involves multiple collaborators. The process definition spells out which tasks can be assigned to whom. The jBPM runtime maintains a list of actors that can be assigned to tasks. For instance, in the Ticketing example, the `answer` task, which requires the user to reply to a ticket, should be visible (and accessible) only to the `admin` actor:

```
<task-node name="process">
  <task name="answer" description="#{ticket.title}">
    <assignment pooled-actors="admin" />
  </task>
  ... ...
</task-node>
```

To integrate a business process into your web application, the first challenge is to map your web users to jBPM actors. Multiple web users can have the same jBPM actor role. For instance, multiple web users (e.g., every employee in the company) can be the `admin` actor in the Ticketing example. The jBPM actor role is thus similar to a permission group in traditional role-based authorization systems.

The Seam jBPM API makes it easy to assign jBPM actor roles to web users. The `login.xhtml` page in the Ticketing example enables the user to log in either as a `user` (to raise tickets) or as an `admin` (to answer tickets). We need to assign different jBPM actor roles depending on whether the user clicked on the **As user** or **As admin** buttons when logging in. Here is the relevant code snippet on the `login.xhtml` page:

```
<h:inputText value="#{user.username}" />

... ...

<h:commandButton type="submit" value="As user"
                 action="#{login.loginUser}"/>
<h:commandButton type="submit" value="As admin"
                 action="#{login.loginAdmin}"/>
```

Seam maintains the jBPM actor role for the current user in a built-in component called `#{actor}`. The application can choose its desired user authentication mechanism. After the user is authenticated, the application updates the `actor` component for the actor role of the user who just logged in. Since the `actor` component is session-scoped, the actor role is maintained as long as the user is logged in. The following is the Seam event handler method for the **As user** button in the Ticketing example application. When we call `#{login.loginUser}`, we tell the jBPM `actor` component that the current user has the `user` role. The jBPM engine then figures out which tasks or processes should be available for this user.

```
@Stateful
@Name("login")
@Scope(ScopeType.SESSION)
public class LoginAction implements Login {

  @In(create = true)
  private Actor actor;

  @In
  private User user;
```

```
public String loginUser() {
  // Check user credentials etc.
  actor.setId(user.getUsername());
  actor.getGroupActorIds().add("user");
  return "home";
}
// ... ...
}
```

We can also assign multiple actor roles to the user currently logged in. For instance, when the user logs in as admin in the Ticketing example, we tell jBPM that the current user has both the user and admin roles so that process tasks for both actors become available to the user.

```
public String loginAdmin() {
  // Check user credentials etc.
  actor.setId(user.getUsername());
  actor.getGroupActorIds().add("user");
  actor.getGroupActorIds().add("admin");
  return "home";
}
```

In Section 24.4.3.2, we will discuss how to assign tasks to users with jBPM actor roles.

# 24.3  Creating a Business Process

Earlier in Chapters 7 and 8, you saw that Seam defines several scopes for its components. One of the key Seam scopes is the process scope. The process instance itself clearly defines the lifecycle of this scope. Any state information attached to this process instance survives after the machine reboots. The process instance can be shared among user sessions because you can assign tasks to different users.

In this section, we will discuss how to create a business process definition, start it in your application, and create data components associated with the process.

## 24.3.1  Defining the Process

As an example, let's try to define the business process in the Ticketing example. The system works like this: A user enters a question into a system and waits for the administrators to respond (Figure 24.3); when an administrator logs in, he can assign the task to himself and reply to the question (Figure 24.4).

The following is the business process definition in the ticketProcess.jpdl.xml file. Immediately after the process starts, it transitions to the process node and waits in that state. When an admin user logs in, that user must complete the answer task to move forward. When the answer task is completed, the system transitions to the complete

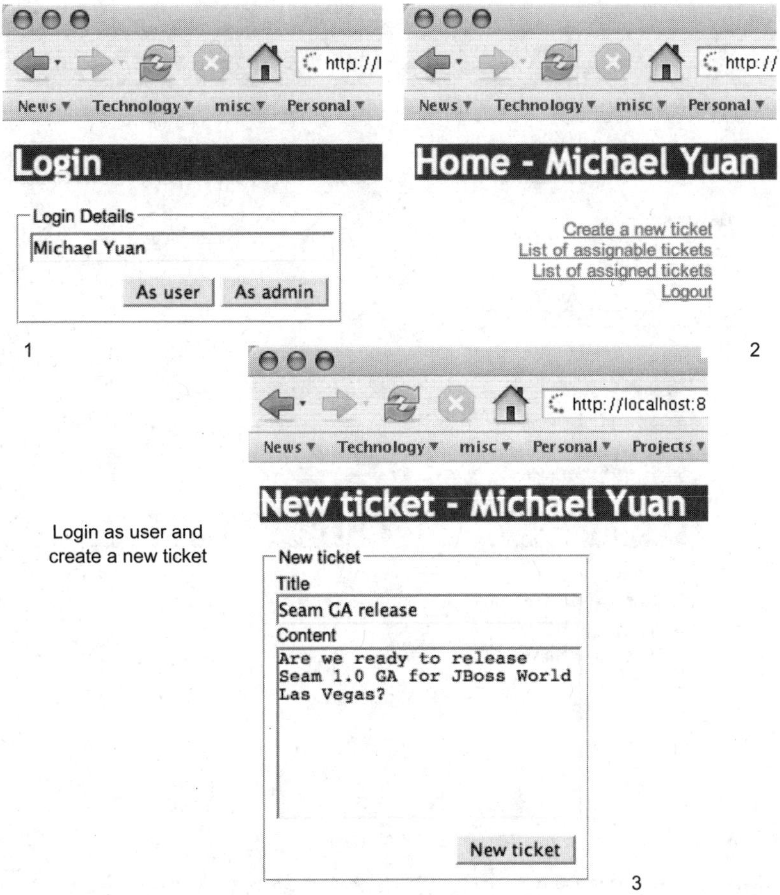

**Figure 24.3**    The process for the user: logging in and creating a ticket

node while executing the action method `myLogger.myLog()`. The process ends, and the
process instance is destroyed at the `complete` state.

```
<process-definition name="TicketProcess">
  <start-state name="start">
    <transition to="process"/>
  </start-state>

  <task-node name="process">
    <task name="answer" description="#{ticket.title}">
      <assignment pooled-actors="admin" />
    </task>
    <transition name="done" to="complete">
      <action expression="#{myLogger.myLog}" />
    </transition>
  </task-node>

  <end-state name="complete"/>
</process-definition>
```

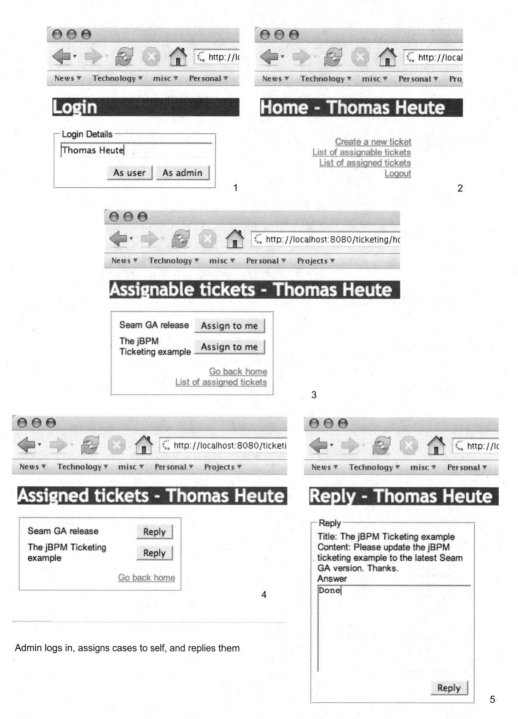

**Figure 24.4**    The process for the administrator: logging in, assigning tickets to self, and replying to the tickets

## 24.3.2  Creating a Business Process Instance

A business process must be triggered by a user action. In our example, when the user clicks on the **New ticket** button on the web page, the system creates a new business process for that ticket, with the `ticket` object attached in the process scope. The process ends when the administrator replies to the ticket and the system logs the reply. To implement this, we annotated the **New ticket** button event handler method with a `@CreateProcess` annotation. Each process definition has a name that is the unique parameter to pass to the `@CreateProcess` annotation.

```
@Stateless
@Name("ticketSystem")
public class TicketSystemAction implements TicketSystem {
  @CreateProcess(definition="TicketProcess")
  public String newTicket() {
    return "home";
  }
  ... ...
}
```

Now, whenever a user invokes the `newTicket()` method, a process instance based on the `TicketProcess` process definition is created. One business process instance exists for each new ticket created. The web user can select which business process he or she wants to work on by passing the `taskId` HTTP request parameter to the web pages (see Section 24.4.2 for more).

---

**What about Stateful Session Beans?**

In this example, we put the business logic in the stateless session bean `TicketSystemAction` and used POJO components for the stateful data associated with the process (see Section 24.3.3). We do this for clarity: It enables us to first discuss how to implement the business logic in the business process and then to cover how the state is maintained in the process.

When you understand how the system works, you can easily mesh the two and use business process-scoped stateful session beans to implement both business logic and application state. We leave this as an exercise for the reader.

---

## 24.3.3  Binding Data Objects in Process Scope

A business process always has data associated with it. In the Ticketing example, a `Ticket` object is associated with each process instance. Using `#{ticket}`, you can refer to the `Ticket` object associated with the current process both in the process definition document and on the JSF page. In Section 24.4.3, we discuss how to select a business process as "current." In this section, we focus on how to bind a data object with a business process instance.

To bind a value to the business process scope, you can directly use @Out(scope=BUSINESS_PROCESS) for all primitives and Strings. If you want to store more complex objects, you must make sure they are serializable. Having a POJO stored as a serialized object in your database is probably not the best way; instead, you can store such an object as an entity bean and just store the ID of the bean to the process instance. This example merely shows you that storing serializable objects in a process instance is possible. Another linked problem is that, since the object is serialized, you can't retrieve a variable if you have to change the class definition. In a real-world scenario, only the entity bean identifier is linked to the business process, and modifying the entity bean definition usually affects only the database table definition.

---

### Do Not Intercept

The example uses the Ticket class as a Seam component annotated with @Intercept(InterceptionType.NEVER). This means that Seam will not intercept this Java bean. As of this writing, interceptable Java beans cannot be bound to a business process because they cannot be unserialized after a server shutdown.

---

```java
import java.io.Serializable;
import org.jboss.seam.*;

@Name("ticket")
@Intercept(InterceptionType.NEVER)
@Scope(ScopeType.BUSINESS_PROCESS)
public class Ticket implements Serializable {

  private String title;
  private String content;
  private String answer;

  public String getContent() {
    return content;
  }
  public void setContent(String content) {
    this.content = content;
  }
  public String getTitle() {
    return title;
  }
  public void setTitle(String title) {
    this.title = title;
  }
  public String getAnswer() {
    return answer;
  }
  public void setAnswer(String answer) {
    this.answer = answer;
  }
}
```

This object can be attached to a business process instance and "lives" with it.

# 24.4 Managing Tasks

Tasks are central elements in a business process. After a business process is created, it waits for the user to complete the tasks defined in the process. Whenever the user completes a task, the process moves forward and decides which task the user needs to do next. To support business processes in web applications, Seam provides a mechanism for associating web actions (e.g., button clicks) with tasks. In this section, we explain how this works.

## 24.4.1 Implementing Business Logic for Tasks

Tasks in a jBPM business process definition are just nodes in the XML file. The process itself does not specify the business logic—that is, what actions are needed for each task and how the task is completed. It just needs to know when the user starts and completes a task so that the process can move on to the next task node.

In a Seam jBPM application, the business logic for each task is implemented in Java and JSF code. The user starts and completes a task by going through web pages. Therefore, we need to tell the application which web UI event starts a task and which event ends the task. For instance, in the Ticketing example application, the **Reply** button should start the `answer` task. To do that, we annotate the UI event handler method of the **Reply** button (i.e., the `TicketSystemAction.reply()` method) with the `@BeginTask` annotation. In this example, the `reply()` method simply redirects to the reply page. The ticket information on that page is available in the Seam `#{ticket}` component associated with this business process instance (see Section 24.3.3). In a stateful session bean, the `@BeginTask`-annotated method usually fetches and initiates data for the task.

```
@Stateless
@Name("ticketSystem")
public class TicketSystemAction implements TicketSystem {

  ... ...

  @BeginTask
  public String reply() {
    return "reply";
  }
  ... ...
}
```

The `#{ticketSystem.reply}` method returns `reply`, which directs JSF to display the `reply.xhtml` page. A task can take several web pages to complete, spanning multiple Seam session bean methods. The `@BeginTask` annotation declares the first method to invoke to start a task. From there, the user can go over multiple pages and session bean methods to complete the task. At the end of the task, the `@EndTask` annotation declares the last method in the task. In our example, the **Answer** button's event handler sends out the reply, completes the task, and causes the process to move to the next state. If more than one transition from the current task node exists, you must specify which transition to pass by giving the transition name to the @EndTask annotation (@EndTask("approve"), for example).

```
@Stateless
@Name("ticketSystem")
public class TicketSystemAction implements TicketSystem {
  ... ...

  @EndTask
  public String sendAnswer() {
    // send the answer to user
    return "home";
  }
  ... ...
}
```

When the task is completed, the process moves on to the next task. The web user can then assign the task and work on it until the process completes.

---

### Tasks with Multiple Transitions

The following example, taken from the DVD demo store that comes with the Seam distribution, shows how to handle multiple transitions in a task node. During the task, the Seam stateful session bean component determines which transition to invoke and then guides the user to invoke the appropriate @EndTask method to finish the task.

```
@BeginTask
public String viewTask() {
  order = (Order) em.createQuery("from Order o " +
    "join fetch o.orderLines " +
    "where o.orderId = :orderId")
      .setParameter("orderId", orderId)
      .getSingleResult();
  return "accept";
}

@EndTask(transition="approve")
public String accept() {
  order.process();
  return "admin";
}

@EndTask(transition="reject")
public String reject() {
  order.cancel();
  return "admin";
}
```

The transition to trigger is defined in the @EndTask annotation, and the returned string is the JSF outcome to display the next view page.

---

## 24.4.2  Specifying a Task to Work On

The @BeginTask and @EndTask annotations do not take task name parameters. So, how does the application know that the #{ticketSystem.reply()} method is supposed to start an answer task, not some other task defined in the process? Furthermore, if the application has multiple business processes running at the same time, multiple answer tasks may be waiting in different processes (i.e., different tickets) at any given time. How does the system know which of those answer tasks it is supposed to begin in response to a particular **Reply** button?

The answer here is to use the taskId HTTP request parameter. In jBPM, each task in the "waiting" state has a unique ID. If multiple tasks exist in a process, only the one that is currently waiting for user action has a valid ID. You can apply @BeginTask, @EndTask, or other methods to a task with a specific ID. For instance, the following **Reply** button applies to the waiting task with ID 123. The taskId is conceptually similar to the conversationId we discussed in Chapter 9.

```
<h:commandLink action="#{ticketSystem.reply}">
  <h:commandButton value="Reply"/>
  <f:param name="taskId" value="123"/>
</h:commandLink>
```

Using this technique, we can associate any button or link with the task it intends to operate on. Furthermore, we can associate a web page with a specific task or business process. For instance, when you load the reply.seam?taskId=123 URL, the #{ticket} component on the reply.xhtml page is already loaded with the business process-scoped #{ticket} component associated with taskId 123. The reply.xhtml page is therefore really simple:

```
Title: #{ticket.title}
...
Content: #{ticket.content}
...
Answer: <h:inputTextarea value="#{ticket.answer}"/>
...
<h:commandLink action="#{ticketSystem.sendAnswer}">
  <h:commandButton value="Reply"/>
  <f:param name="taskId" value="#{param.taskId}"/>
</h:commandLink>
```

When the user clicks on the **Reply** button, the current taskId for the page is passed on to the #{ticketSystem.sendAnswer} method. The sendAnswer() method also knows which task it is operating on. As we discussed before, it ends the task and causes the business process to move on.

Of course, in the real world, we do not hardcode the taskId (e.g., 123) into the web pages. Instead, we ask the system to dynamically generate taskIds for the tasks available to the currently logged-in user. That is the topic of Section 24.4.3.

# 24.4.3   Selecting a Task in the UI

We just saw that web actions are associated with jBPM tasks via the `taskId` parameter. Each available task in the waiting state has a `taskId`. But how do users determine the available `taskId`s, and how can they assign tasks to themselves or other users? This is possible via built-in Seam jBPM components.

---

**Business Processes and Conversations**

We can draw an analogy here between business processes and long-running conversations. When a user has multiple long-running conversations, he or she can choose one to join by switching the browser window or selecting from the `#{conversationList}`. Business processes are not tied to browser windows; the Seam components in this section are the business process equivalents to `#{conversationList}`.

---

## 24.4.3.1   The pooledTaskInstanceList Component

The `pooledTaskInstanceList` component finds all the task instances that can be assigned to the logged-in user. This can be used, for example, in a ticketing system where an admin gets the list of unassigned tasks he or she can work on. This example code could be used (e.g., on the `assignableTickets.xhtml` page):

```
<h:dataTable value="#{pooledTaskInstanceList}" var="task">
  <h:column>
    <f:facet name="header">Id</f:facet>
    #{task.id}
  </h:column>
  <h:column>
    <f:facet name="header">
      Description
    </f:facet>
    #{task.description}
  </h:column>
</h:dataTable>
```

As we specified in the process definition file (see Section 24.3), the `#{task.description}` is the `#{ticket.title}` in the task's process scope.

## 24.4.3.2   The pooledTask Component

This component is typically used inside a `#{pooledTaskInstanceList}` data table. It provides a unique method of assigning a task to the current logged-in actor. The `id` of the task to assign must be passed as a request parameter so that the action method (i.e., the `@BeginTask` method) can determine which task it starts for. To use this component, you can write the following code; the #{task.id} comes from the #{pooledTaskInstanceList} iterator (see the previous section):

```
<h:commandLink action="#{pooledTask.assignToCurrentActor}">
  <h:commandButton value="Assign"/>
  <f:param name="taskId" value="#{task.id}"/>
</h:commandLink>
```

### 24.4.3.3 The taskInstanceList Component

This component's goal is to get all the task instances that have been assigned to the logged-in user. In the Ticketing example, this component is used in the assignedTickets.xhtml page to show a list of processes (i.e., tickets) already assigned to the user.

```
<h:dataTable value="#{taskInstanceList}" var="task">
  <h:column>
    <f:facet name="header">Id</f:facet>
    #{task.id}
  </h:column>
  <h:column>
    <f:facet name="header">
      Description
    </f:facet>
    #{task.description}
  </h:column>
</h:dataTable>
```

### 24.4.3.4 The taskInstanceListByType Component

This component can be seen as a filtered version of the previous component. Instead of returning the whole list of task instances, this component returns only the task instances of a certain type.

```
<h:dataTable value="#{taskInstanceListByType['todo']}" var="task">
  <h:column>
    <f:facet name="header">Id</f:facet>
    #{task.id}
  </h:column>
  <h:column>
    <f:facet name="header">
      Description
    </f:facet>
    #{task.description}
  </h:column>
</h:dataTable>
```

In a nutshell, you can use jBPM to define the process, use Seam stateful session beans to handle the tasks and transitions in the process, and then use Seam's built-in components to tie the process actions to UI elements on the JSF page.

# 24.5 Business Process-Based Page Navigation Flow

As we saw in Chapter 3, Seam improves JSF's pageflow management by introducing `pages.xml`. In `pages.xml`, we can define page parameters, actions, as well as stateful navigation rules based on the internal state of the application.

With jBPM support, Seam further expands the stateful pageflow management facility to support actual business processes as pageflows. This is another important aspect of jBPM integration in Seam. To best illustrate how a business process-based pageflow works, check out the `numberguess` example in the book's source code bundle. The application has two processes attached to the `numberGuess.xhtml` and `confirm.xhtml` pages, respectively.

```
<pages>
  <page view-id="/numberGuess.xhtml">
    <begin-conversation join="true" pageflow="numberGuess"/>
  </page>
  <page view-id="/confirm.xhtml">
    <begin-conversation nested="true" pageflow="cheat"/>
  </page>
</pages>
```

The `numberGuess.xhtml` page displays a form for you to guess a random number generated by the application. After you enter a guess, the application tells you whether it is too high or too low and asks you to guess again until you reach the right number. This is the `numberGuess.xhtml` page:

```
<h:outputText value="Higher!"
  rendered="#{numberGuess.randomNumber gt numberGuess.currentGuess}"/>
<h:outputText value="Lower!"
  rendered="#{numberGuess.randomNumber lt numberGuess.currentGuess}"/>
<br/>
I'm thinking of a number between
#{numberGuess.smallest} and
#{numberGuess.biggest}. You have
#{numberGuess.remainingGuesses} guesses.
<br/>
Your guess:
<h:inputText value="#{numberGuess.currentGuess}"
             id="guess" required="true">
  <f:validateLongRange maximum="#{numberGuess.biggest}"
                       minimum="#{numberGuess.smallest}"/>
</h:inputText>

<h:commandButton value="Guess" action="guess"/>
<s:button value="Cheat" view="/confirm.xhtml"/>
<s:button value="Give up" action="giveup"/>
```

The **Guess** and **Give up** buttons map to `guess` and `giveup` transitions in the business process associated with the page. The `giveup` transition is simple: It just redirects to the `giveup.xhtml` page, where you can click on buttons mapped to `yes` and `no` actions. The `guess` transition is slightly more complex: Seam first executes the `#{numberGuess.guess}` method, which compares the user's guess to the random number and saves the current guess. Then the process goes on to the `evaluateGuess` decision node. The `#{numberGuess.correctGuess}` method compares the current guess with the random number. If the outcome is `true`, the process moves to the `win` node and displays the `win.xhtml` page.

```
<pageflow-definition name="numberGuess">

  <start-page name="displayGuess" view-id="/numberGuess.xhtml">
    <redirect/>
    <transition name="guess" to="evaluateGuess">
      <action expression="#{numberGuess.guess}"/>
    </transition>
    <transition name="giveup" to="giveup"/>
  </start-page>

  <decision name="evaluateGuess"
            expression="#{numberGuess.correctGuess}">
    <transition name="true" to="win"/>
    <transition name="false" to="evaluateRemainingGuesses"/>
  </decision>

  <decision name="evaluateRemainingGuesses"
            expression="#{numberGuess.lastGuess}">
    <transition name="true" to="lose"/>
    <transition name="false" to="displayGuess"/>
  </decision>

  <page name="giveup" view-id="/giveup.xhtml">
    <redirect/>
    <transition name="yes" to="lose"/>
    <transition name="no" to="displayGuess"/>
  </page>

  <page name="win" view-id="/win.xhtml">
    <redirect/>
    <end-conversation/>
  </page>

  <page name="lose" view-id="/lose.xhtml">
    <redirect/>
    <end-conversation/>
  </page>

</pageflow-definition>
```

The following are the `#{numberGuess.guess}` and `#{numberGuess.correctGuess}` methods. With the support of business process, these methods need to contain only business logic code—they do not need to couple it with the navigation logic.

```java
@Name("numberGuess")
@Scope(ScopeType.CONVERSATION)
public class NumberGuess {
  ... ...
  public void guess() {
    if (currentGuess > randomNumber) {
      biggest = currentGuess - 1;
    }
    if (currentGuess < randomNumber) {
      smallest = currentGuess + 1;
    }
    guessCount ++;
  }

  public boolean isCorrectGuess() {
    return currentGuess == randomNumber;
  }
}
```

If the user loads the `confirm.xhtml` page, the `cheat` process starts. If you click on the button mapped to the `yes` action, the `#{numberGuess.cheated}` is invoked to mark you as a cheater, and the process moves on to the `cheat` node to display the `cheat.xhtml` page:

```xml
<pageflow-definition name="cheat">

  <start-page name="confirm" view-id="/confirm.xhtml">
    <transition name="yes" to="cheat">
      <action expression="#{numberGuess.cheated}"/>
    </transition>
    <transition name="no" to="end"/>
  </start-page>

  <page name="cheat" view-id="/cheat.xhtml">
    <redirect/>
    <transition to="end"/>
  </page>

  <page name="end" view-id="/numberGuess.xhtml">
    <redirect/>
    <end-conversation/>
  </page>

</pageflow-definition>
```

### The Back Button

When navigating using a stateful pageflow model, you have to make sure that the application decides what is possible. Think about the transitions: If you passed a transition, you cannot go back unless you make it possible in your pageflow definition. If a user decides to press the **Back** button in the browser, that could lead to an inconsistent state. Fortunately, Seam automatically brings the user back to the page that she should be seeing. This enables you to make sure that a user will not twice place her $1 million order just because she accidentally pressed the **Back** button and submitted it again.

# 24.6  jBPM Libraries and Configuration

To use jBPM components, you must bundle the `jbpm-x.y.z.jar` file in your application's JAR file (i.e., the `app.jar` inside the EAR file). We recommend JBPM 3.1.2
or above.

You also must add the following configuration files to the root of your EAR file:
`*.jpdl.xml` defines the business processes, `jbpm.cfg.xml` configures the jBPM engine,
and `hibernate.cfg.xml` configures the database that stores the process states.

```
ticketing.ear
|+ ticketProcess.jpdl.xml
|+ hibernate.cfg.xml
|+ jbpm.cfg.xml
|+ app.war
|+ app.jar
|   |+ class files
|   |+ jbpm-3.1.2.jar
|   |+ seam.properties
|   |+ META-INF
|+ jboss-seam.jar
|+ el.api.jar
|+ el-ri.jar
|+ META-INF
```

The `jbpm.cfg.xml` file overrides the default attributes in the jBPM engine. Most importantly, you must disable the jBPM transaction manager for persistent data because Seam
now manages database access.

```
<jbpm-configuration>
  <jbpm-context>
    <service name="persistence">
      <factory>
        <bean
            class="org.jbpm.persistence.db.DbPersistenceServiceFactory">
          <field name="isTransactionEnabled">
            <false/>
          </field>
        </bean>
      </factory>
    </service>
  </jbpm-context>
</jbpm-configuration>
```

The jBPM engine stores the process state in a database to make the process long-
lived—even after the server reboots. The `hibernate.cfg.xml` file configures which
database to store the jBPM state data in and loads jBPM data mapping files to set up
database tables. In this example, we just save the jBPM state data in the embedded
HSQL database at `java:/DefaultDS`. Many jBPM mapping files exist; we will not list
all of them here. You can refer to the `hibernate.cfg.xml` file in the `ticketing` project
to find out more.

```
<hibernate-configuration>
  <session-factory>
    <property name="dialect">
      org.hibernate.dialect.HSQLDialect
    </property>
    <property name="connection.datasource">
      java:/DefaultDS
    </property>
    <property name="transaction.factory_class">
      org.hibernate.transaction.JTATransactionFactory
    </property>
    <property name="transaction.manager_lookup_class">
      org.hibernate.transaction.JBossTransactionManagerLookup
    </property>
    <property name="transaction.flush_before_completion">
      true
    </property>
    <property name="cache.provider_class">
      org.hibernate.cache.HashtableCacheProvider
    </property>
    <property name="hbm2ddl.auto">update</property>

    <mapping resource="org/jbpm/db/hibernate.queries.hbm.xml"/>

    <mapping .../>
  </session-factory>
</hibernate-configuration>
```

In addition, you must tell the Seam runtime where to find the `*.jpdl.xml` files. You do this by adding a `core:Jbpm` component in the `components.xml` file:

```
<components>
  ... ...
  <core:Jbpm processDefinitions="ticketProcess.jpdl.xml"/>
</components>
```

Overall, Seam greatly simplifies the development of business process-driven web applications. Traditional web developers might find the business process concepts a little confusing initially. But when you get past the basic syntax, you will find this approach extremely easy to use and very powerful. Seam lowers the bar for applying business processes in web applications.

# 25

Integrating Business
Processes and Rules

So far, we have discussed how to integrate the Drools rules engine (Chapters 22 and 23) and the jBPM business process engine (Chapter 24) as separate services into Seam applications. Business processes and rules are naturally complementary to each other. At each node of the process, we can fire a set of rules to decide what to do next, based on the current state of the application. This way, we can express a large chunk of our business logic in a declarative manner and avoid much of the business logic coding in Java.

In this chapter, we will reimplement the number guess game from Section 24.5, but using declarative rules, instead of hardcoded business logic in Java, to manage the flow of the application. This example is adapted from the Seam official examples.

The game asks you to guess the random number it chooses. Every time you make a guess, the system tells you whether the guess is too high or too low, and adjusts the permitted number range for the next guess. You are allowed to make 10 guesses in each game. If you make a correct guess, the game displays the "you won" page. If you make 10 wrong guesses, the game displays the "you lost" page.

## 25.1  The Process

From the game description above, the game really only has three states: waiting for the player to enter a guess; declaring a win; and declaring a loss. After the player inputs a guess, the application figures out which of the three states it needs to enter next, and the process repeats itself. Based on that, we have the following business process defined:

```
<pageflow-definition ... name="numberGuess">

  <start-page name="displayGuess"
              view-id="/numberGuess.xhtml">
    <redirect/>
    <transition name="guess" to="drools"/>
  </start-page>

  <decision name="drools">

    <handler class="org.jboss.seam.drools.DroolsDecisionHandler">
      <workingMemoryName>workingMemory</workingMemoryName>
      <assertObjects>
        <element>#{game}</element>
        <element>#{guess}</element>
      </assertObjects>
    </handler>

    <transition to="displayGuess"/>
    <transition name="lose" to="lose"/>
    <transition name="win" to="win"/>

  </decision>

  <page name="win" view-id="/win.xhtml">
    <end-conversation />
    <redirect/>
  </page>

  <page name="lose" view-id="/lose.xhtml">
    <end-conversation />
    <redirect/>
  </page>

</pageflow-definition>
```

The business process is started when the user loads the `numberGuess.xhtml` page and Seam creates the `game` component.

```
@Name("game")
@Scope(ScopeType.CONVERSATION)
public class Game {

  private int biggest;
  private int smallest;
  private int guessCount;

  @Create
  @Begin(pageflow="numberGuess")
  public void begin() {
    guessCount = 0;
    biggest = 100;
    smallest = 1;
  }

  ... ...
}
```

The process starts in the `displayGuess` state. When the user enters a guess and clicks on the **Guess** button, the state transits to `drools`. In the `drools` node, the rules are applied to determine if the user entered the correct guess. If the guess is incorrect and the maximum number of tries has not been reached, the application transits back to the `displayGuess` state with the `numberGuess.xhtml` page showing the current range of allowable guesses. Otherwise, the system transits to the `win` or `lose` state based on the rules and displays the appropriate web page.

The `workingMemory` component used in the `drools` node is created in `components.xml`, as we discussed in the previous chapter.

```
<components ...>
  <drools:rule-base name="ruleBase"
                    rule-files="numberguess.drl"/>
  <drools:managed-working-memory name="workingMemory"
                                 rule-base="#{ruleBase}"/>

  <bpm:jbpm>
    <bpm:pageflow-definitions>
      <value>pageflow.jpdl.xml</value>
    </bpm:pageflow-definitions>
  </bpm:jbpm>

</components>
```

# 25.2  The Rules

The following rules are applied in the `drools` node to determine which page to navigate to next and what information to display on the page:

```
package org.jboss.seam.example.numberguess

import org.jboss.seam.drools.Decision

global Decision decision
global int randomNumber
global Game game

rule High
  when
    Guess(guess: value > randomNumber)
  then
    game.setBiggest(guess-1);
end

rule Low
  when
    Guess(guess: value < randomNumber)
  then
    game.setSmallest(guess+1);
end
```

```
rule Win
  when
    Guess(value==randomNumber)
  then
    decision.setOutcome("win");
end

rule Lose
  when
    Game(guessCount==9)
  then
    if ( decision.getOutcome()==null )
    {
      decision.setOutcome("lose");
    }
end

rule Increment
  salience -10
  when
    Guess()
  then
    game.incrementGuessCount();
end
```

When the rule High is satisfied, the guess is too high. In this case, the rule engine decreases the upper limit of the next guess, increases the guess count, and sets the no decision outcome. The numberGuess.xhtml page will be displayed next with the new upper limit and guess count.

When the rule Win is satisfied, the rule engine sets the decision outcome to win. The win outcome is automatically set to the transition name of the business process node. The pageflow then brings the user to the win.xhtml page.

The key integration points between Drools and the pageflow engine are as follows:

- The drools node shows that a business process can automatically invoke the rules engine against a working memory.

- The rule's outcome is automatically set to the name of the business process transition to the next state.

# 25.3 Conclusions

The example application in this chapter shows how to use a business process with the rules engine in a Seam web application. The Java classes in this example are mostly simple Java beans which supply data binding for the web forms. All the application flow and business logic is declaratively expressed in configuration files and handled by a business process engine and rules engine. This type of declarative programming can be very powerful when you have fast-changing business logic in your system.

# Part VI

---

# Testing Seam Applications

Testing has become a crucial component in modern software development processes. As a POJO framework, Seam was designed from the ground up for easy testability. Seam goes beyond and above what other POJO frameworks do when it comes to testing. Seam actually provides its own testing framework based on TestNG, which makes it easy to write automated, out-of-the-container unit and integration tests for Seam applications. In the next two chapters, you learn how easy it is to write test cases for Seam applications. We also explain how to set up a proper testing environment for out-of-the-container testing.

# 26

Unit Testing

The wide adoption of agile software development methods, such as Test-Driven Development (TDD), has made unit testing a central task for software developers. An average-sized web project can have hundreds, if not thousands, of unit test cases. Hence, testability has become a core feature for software frameworks.

Plain Old Java Objects (POJOs) are easy to unit-test. You just instantiate a POJO, using the standard Java `new` keyword, and run its methods in any unit-testing framework. It is no coincidence that the spread of agile methodologies and POJO-based frameworks happened at the same time in the last couple years. Seam is a POJO-based framework designed for easy unit testing.

Enterprise POJOs do not live in isolation. They must interact with other POJOs and infrastructure services (e.g., a database) to perform their tasks. The standard TDD and agile practice is to "mock" the service environment in the testing environment—that is, to duplicate the server APIs without actually running the server. However, the mock services are often difficult to set up and depend on the testing framework you choose. To address this challenge, Seam comes with a `SeamTest` class that greatly simplifies the mocking tasks. The `SeamTest` facility is based on the popular TestNG framework, and it mocks all Seam services in your development environment.

In this chapter, we will discuss how to use the `SeamTest` class to write TestNG unit tests. Our test cases are written against the `stateful` example application discussed in Chapter 7. To run the tests, enter the `stateful` project folder and run the command `ant test`. The build script runs all tests we have in the `test` directory and reports the results in the command console as follows:

```
$ant test

... ...

[testng] PASSED: simulateBijection
[testng] PASSED: unitTestSayHello2
[testng] PASSED: unitTestSayHello
[testng] PASSED: unitTestStartOver

[testng] ===============================================
[testng]    HelloWorld
[testng]    Tests run: 4, Failures: 0, Skips: 0
[testng] ===============================================
```

The test results are also available in HTML format in the `build/testout` directory (Figure 26.1).

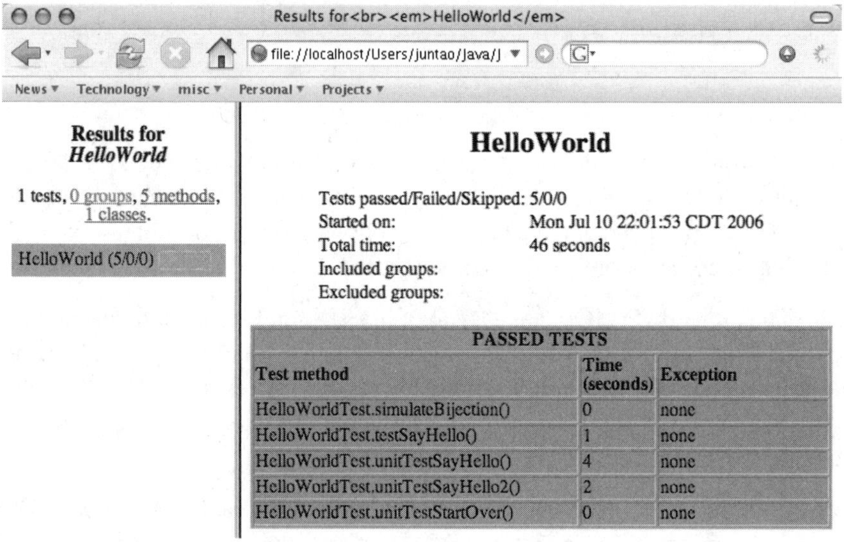

**Figure 26.1**    The test results for the `stateful` project

As we discuss in Appendix B, you can use the `stateful` project as a template and place your own test cases in the `test` directory. This way, you can reuse all configuration files, library JARs, and the build script. But for the curious, we explain exactly how the build script sets up the classpath and configuration files to run the tests in Appendix B.

---

**What Is TestNG?**

TestNG is a "next generation" testing framework intended to replace JUnit. It supports many categories of developer tests, including unit tests, integration tests, end-to-end tests, etc. Compared with JUnit, TestNG tests are more flexible and easier to write.

Like Seam, TestNG makes extensive use of Java annotations to simplify the code. That makes it a natural choice for Seam application developers. More importantly, TestNG provides superior built-in support for mock objects, which are crucial for a testing framework. Seam takes advantage of this capability and comes with a custom mock framework in the `SeamTest` class. We cover the use of the `SeamTest` class in this and the next chapters.

In this chapter, we provide a basic introduction to TestNG, to get you started with the framework. All the examples should be fairly self-explanatory. If you are interested in learning more about TestNG, visit the TestNG web site, http://testng.org.

# 26.1  A Simple TestNG Test Case

Let's start with a simple method in the `ManagerAction` class to illustrate the key elements of a TestNG unit test case.

```
public class ManagerAction implements Manager {

  public void startOver () {
    person = new Person ();
    confirmed = false;
    valid = false;
  }
  ... ...
}
```

The following method tests the `ManagerAction.startOver()` method. It instantiates a `ManagerAction` **POJO**, runs the `startOver()` method, and checks that the value `manager.confirmed` is indeed set to `false`. It is extremely simple, but it has all the basic elements of a unit test.

```
public class HelloWorldTest extends SeamTest {

  @Test
  public void unitTestStartOver() throws Exception {
    Manager manager = new ManagerAction ();
    manager.startOver();
    assert !manager.getConfirmed ();
  }
  ... ...
}
```

Notice the `@Test` annotation on the `unitTestStartOver()` method. It tells TestNG that this method is a test case and should be executed by the test runner. The `HelloWorldTest` class inherits from `SeamTest`, which gives test methods access to mock facilities built into `SeamTest`. We do not use any mock services in this simple test case, but you will see their usefulness in the next section.

TestNG enables you to have multiple test classes and multiple test run configurations. In each test run configuration, you can choose to run one or several test classes. A test configuration is defined in an XML file in the classpath. In the `testing.xml` test configuration file, we tell TestNG that it should run the test cases in the `HelloWorldTest` class:

```
<suite name="HelloWorld" verbose="2" parallel="false">

  <test name="HelloWorld">
    <classes>
      <class name="HelloWorldTest"/>
    </classes>
  </test>

</suite>
```

Now we use TestNG's built-in Ant task to run the test configuration. With the correct classpath set up, we just need to pass in the test configuration file. Here is a snippet from the `stateful` project's `build.xml` file:

```
<target name="test" depends="compile">

  <taskdef resource="testngtasks" classpathref="lib.classpath"/>
  ... ...
  <testng outputdir="${build.testout}">
    <jvmarg value="-Xmx800M" />
    <jvmarg value="-Djava.awt.headless=true" />
    <classpath refid="test.classpath"/>
    <xmlfileset dir="${test}" includes="testng.xml"/>
  </testng>

</target>
```

The test results appear on the console, as well as in HTML format in the `build/testout` directory, as described above.

# 26.2  Simulating Dependency Bijection

Dependency bijection (see Chapter 1) is extensively used in Seam applications. Although bijection is easy for developers, it poses challenges for unit tests. Seam dependency bijection annotations can work directly on private data fields. Without getter/setter methods (or constructor methods), the test framework does not have access to those private fields, and therefore cannot wire together POJOs and services for testing. An example is the `person` field in the `ManagerAction` class; it is annotated with both `@In` and `@Out`, but it does not have getter/setter methods. How can the unit test case in TestNG manipulate the `ManagerAction.person` field?

```
@Stateful
@Name("manager")
@Scope (SESSION)
public class ManagerAction implements Manager {
  @In @Out
  private Person person;
  ... ...
}
```

This is where the mock facilities in the `SeamTest` class become useful. The `SeamTest` class provides the `getField()` and `setField()` methods to simulate bijection and operate directly on Seam component's private fields. The following example shows how to use the `getField()` and `setField()` methods. We first inject a `Person` object and test whether the injection succeeds. Then we run the `ManagerAction.startOver()` method, which refreshes the `person` field, and test the result to be outjected. It is important to cast the `getField()` result to the proper object type.

```
public class HelloWorldTest extends SeamTest {
  @Test
  public void simulateBijection() throws Exception {
    Manager manager = new ManagerAction ();
    Person in = new Person ();
    in.setName ("Michael Yuan");

    // Inject the person component
    setField (manager, "person", in);
    Person out = (Person) getField(manager, "person");
    assert out != null;
    assert out.getName().equals("Michael Yuan");

    manager.startOver();

    out = (Person) getField(manager, "person");
    assert out != null;
    assert out.getName() == null;
  }
  ... ...
}
```

---

**Accessing Private Fields?**

The Java specification does not allow access to private fields from outside the class. How does `SeamTest` do it, then? The `SeamTest` class runs its own embedded Seam runtime, which instruments the class bytecode to get around the restriction of the regular JVM.

---

# 26.3 Mocking the Database and Transaction

Almost all Seam applications store their data in relational databases. Developers must unit-test database-related functionality. However, database testing outside the server container is difficult. You must mock all the persistence-related container services, including creating a fully functional EJB3 `EntityManager`, connecting to an embedded database, and managing database transactions. The `SeamTest` class makes it easy to mock the database services.

The first thing you need to do is create an `EntityManager`. The `persistence.xml` file contains information on how to connect to the embedded database. In order to bootstrap the entity manager in a Java SE test environment, we need to specify a non-JTA data source for testing (similar to the setup discussed in Chapter 4). So, we have the following `test/persistence.xml` file; it is loaded in the classpath when we run the tests but not packaged in the EAR:

```
<persistence>
  <persistence-unit name="helloworld"
                    transaction-type="RESOURCE_LOCAL">
    <provider>
      org.hibernate.ejb.HibernatePersistence
    </provider>
    <non-jta-data-source>java:/DefaultDS</non-jta-data-source>
    <properties>
    ... ...
    </properties>
  </persistence-unit>
</persistence>
```

You should first create an `EntityManagerFactory` by passing the persistence unit name in the `persistence.xml` file to a static factory method. From the `EntityManagerFactory`, you can create an `EntityManager` and then inject it into your Seam component using the `SeamTest.setField()` method discussed in the previous section.

```
EntityManagerFactory emf =
  Persistence.createEntityManagerFactory("helloworld");
EntityManager em = emf.createEntityManager();

Manager manager = new ManagerAction ();
setField(manager, "em", em);
```

---

**Persistence Context Name**

In a seam-gen project, the persistence unit name defaults to the project name. So, if you are porting the book's example applications to a seam-gen project, don't forget to change the persistence unit name for the `createEntityManagerFactory()` method before you run the tests.

---

Now you can test any database methods in your Seam POJO. All database operations are performed against an embedded HSQL database bundled in the test environment. You do not need to set up this database yourself if you use the project template in the book's source code bundle (see Appendix B). If you write any data into the database, you must enclose the `EntityManager` operations in a transaction, for example:

```
em.getTransaction().begin();
String outcome = manager.sayHello ();
em.getTransaction().commit();
```

The following is a complete listing of the `unitTestSayHello()` test case, which tests the `ManagerAction.sayHello()` method in `stateful`. It ties together everything we've discussed.

```
public class HelloWorldTest extends SeamTest {

  @Test
  public void unitTestSayHello() throws Exception {

    Manager manager = new ManagerAction ();

    EntityManagerFactory emf =
      Persistence.createEntityManagerFactory("helloworld");
    EntityManager em = emf.createEntityManager();
    setField(manager, "em", em);

    Person person = new Person ();
    person.setName ("Jacob Orshalick");
    setField(manager, "person", person);
    setField(manager, "confirmed", false);

    em.getTransaction().begin();
    manager.sayHello ();
    em.getTransaction().commit();

    List <Person> fans = manager.getFans();
    assert fans!=null;
    assert fans.get(fans.size()-1).getName().equals("Jacob Orshalick");

    person = (Person) getField (manager, "person");
    assert person != null;
    assert person.getName() == null;

    em.close();
  }
  ... ...
}
```

# 26.4  Loading the Test Infrastructure

As we discussed in Section 26.1, we define the tests in the `test/testng.xml` file and run them in the `testng` Ant task. The Java source code for all the test cases is located in the `test` directory.

To run the tests, especially the mock database tests (see Section 26.3) and integration tests (see Chapter 27), the test runner must first load the JBoss Embeddable EJB3 container and the Seam runtime. All the Seam configuration files for the application must be on the classpath (or in `META-INF` and `WEB-INF` directories on the classpath), just as they would be in a real application server.

---

**Using Seam-gen**

Projects that seam-gen generates already have the test infrastructure properly set up. You just need to put the `*Test.xml` (i.e., the `testng.xml` equivalent) files and the test case source files in the `test` directory and run `ant test`. You can use the `EntityManager` and other EJB3 services in the test cases.

---

You can use the same configuration files for testing as for deployment, except for the `WEB-INF/components.xml` and `META-INF/persistence.xml` files. The `test/components.xml` and `test/persistence.xml` files are copied to the test classpath when we run the tests. We have covered the `test/persistence.xml` file before. The change we need to make to `components.xml` is the JNDI name pattern. We do not need the EAR name prefix in the EJB3 bean JNDI name pattern because no EAR file exists in the tests. This change is not needed if you are testing a Seam POJO application (see example application `jpa`).

```
<components ...>
   ... same as deployment ...
   <core:init jndi-pattern="#{ejbName}/local" debug="false"/>
</components>
```

To load the testing infrastructure, you also need to put the support library JARs and configuration files on the test classpath. Those files are located in the `$SEAM_HOME/lib`, `$SEAM_HOME/lib/test`, and `$SEAM_HOME/bootstrap` directories in the sample code bundle. You must be careful to exclude JARs and directories that might have duplicate configuration files in them, such as `components.xml`. The following are the relevant parts of the `build.xml` file for running the tests:

```
<property name="lib" location="${seam.home}/lib" />
<property name="applib" location="lib" />
<path id="lib.classpath">
  <fileset dir="${lib}" includes="*.jar"/>
  <fileset dir="${applib}" includes="*.jar"/>
</path>
<property name="testlib" location="${seam.home}/lib/test" />
<property name="eejb.conf.dir" value="${seam.home}/bootstrap" />
<property name="resources" location="resources" />

<property name="build.test" location="build/test" />
<property name="build.testout" location="build/testout" />

... ...
```

```xml
<target name="test" depends="compile">

  <taskdef resource="testngtasks" classpathref="lib.classpath"/>

  <mkdir dir="${build.test}"/>

  <javac destdir="${build.test}" debug="true">
    <classpath>
      <path refid="lib.classpath"/>
      <pathelement location="${build.classes}"/>
    </classpath>
    <src path="${test}"/>
  </javac>

  <copy todir="${build.test}">
    <fileset dir="${build.classes}" includes="**/*.*"/>
    <fileset dir="${resources}" includes="**/*.*"/>
  </copy>

  <!-- Overwrite the WEB-INF/components.xml -->
  <copy todir="${build.test}/WEB-INF" overwrite="true">
    <fileset dir="${test}" includes="components.xml"/>
  </copy>
  <!-- Overwrite the META-INF/persistence.xml -->
  <copy todir="${build.test}/META-INF" overwrite="true">
    <fileset dir="${test}" includes="persistence.xml"/>
  </copy>

  <path id="test.classpath">
    <path path="${build.test}" />

    <fileset dir="${testlib}">
      <include name="*.jar" />
    </fileset>

    <fileset dir="${lib}">
      <exclude name="jboss-seam-ui.jar" />
      <exclude name="jboss-seam-wicket.jar" />
      <exclude name="interop/**/*" />
      <exclude name="gen/**/*" />
      <exclude name="src/**/*" />
    </fileset>

    <path path="${eejb.conf.dir}" />
  </path>
  <testng outputdir="${build.testout}">
    <jvmarg value="-Xmx800M" />
    <jvmarg value="-Djava.awt.headless=true" />
    <classpath refid="test.classpath"/>
    <xmlfileset dir="${test}" includes="testng.xml"/>
  </testng>

</target>
```

The beauty of this test setup is that the test runner bootstraps the entire runtime environment for Seam. Thus, you can run not only unit tests, but also integration tests that fully utilize the JSF EL to simulate real-world web interactions.

# 27

---

# Integration Testing

Unit tests are useful, but they have limitations. By definition, unit tests focus on POJOs and their methods. All the mock infrastructure was there to make it possible to test those POJOs in relative isolation. That means we do not get to test whether the POJO correctly interacts with the framework itself. For instance, how do you test whether an outjected component has the correct value in Seam runtime context? How do you know that the JSF interactions and EL expressions have the desired effects? This is where we need integration testing to test live POJOs inside the Seam and JSF runtime. Unlike the white box unit tests, the integration tests treat the application from the user's point of view.

Integration tests can also be much simpler than unit tests, especially when they involve database operations and other container services. In integration tests, we test live Seam components instead of the test-instantiated POJOs in unit test cases. An embedded Seam runtime started by `SeamTest` manages those live Seam components. That embedded Seam runtime provides the exact same services as the Seam runtime in JBoss AS servers. You do not need to mock the bijection or manually set up the `EntityManager` and transactions for database access.

If you use the book's example projects as a template (e.g., the `stateful` example) or use seam-gen to generate your projects, you are ready to go with the integration tests. Just add your own test cases, as described shortly, to the `test` directory and run `ant test`. No extra configuration or setup is needed.

---

**Ins and Outs of Server Container Testing**

A simple form of integration testing is to deploy the application in JBoss AS and run the tests manually through a web browser. But for developers, the key requirement for easy testability is automation. Developers should be able to run integration tests unattended and view the results in a nicely formatted report. Ideally, the tests should run directly inside the development environment (i.e., JDK 5.0 or directly inside an IDE) without starting any server or browser.

---

The biggest challenge in testing live Seam components is to simulate the JSF UI interactions. How do you simulate a web request, bind values to Seam components, and then invoke event handler methods from the test case? Fortunately, the Seam testing framework has made all this easy. In the next section, we will start from a concrete test example in `integration`.

In a Seam web application, we access Seam components through `#{}` EL expressions in JSF pages. To access those components from TestNG test cases, the Seam test framework does two things. First, it provides a mechanism to simulate (or "drive") the entire JSF interaction lifecycle from the test code. Second, it binds test data to Seam components via JSF EL expressions or reflective method calls. Let's check out those two aspects in our test code.

# 27.1  Simulating JSF Interactions

In each web request/response cycle, JSF goes through several steps (phases) to process the request and render the response. Using the `FacesRequest` inner classes inside `SeamTest`, you can simulate test actions in each JSF phase by overriding the appropriate methods. The `FacesRequest` constructor can take a string argument for the target `view-id` of this script, followed by any number of page parameters you define in the `pages.xml`. The test runner then just calls those lifecycle methods in the order of JSF lifecycle phases. The following snippet shows the basic structure of a typical script to test the submission of a web form.

```
public class HelloWorldTest extends SeamTest {

  @Test
  public void testSayHello() throws Exception {

    new FacesRequest("/mypage.xhtml") {

      @Override
      protected void updateModelValues() throws Exception {
        // Bind simulated user input data objects to Seam components
      }
```

```
      @Override
      protected void invokeApplication() {
        // Invoke the UI event handler method for
        // the HTTP POST button or link
      }

      @Override
      protected void renderResponse() {
        // Retrieve and test the response data objects
      }

    }.run();

  }

  ... ...
}
```

The `updateModelValues()` method updates Seam data components based on the values in the user input fields. The `invokeApplication()` method invokes the event handler method for the form submission button. It makes use of the data component constructed in the `updateModelValues()` stage. The `renderResponse()` method checks the outcome of the event handler method, including any components that are to be outjected. In the next several sections, we will look at those methods in more detail.

---

**JSF Lifecycle Phases**

JSF has five phases in a request/response cycle; refer to a JSF book to understand what exactly the server does in each phase. In this chapter, we will demonstrate the three most commonly used JSF phases. Each JSF lifecycle phase has a corresponding method in the `SeamTest.Script` class. You need to override a lifecycle method only if you need to perform tasks in its corresponding lifecycle phase.

---

# 27.2 Using JSF EL Expressions

So, how exactly do you "bind the test data to Seam components" and "invoke Seam event handler methods"? In regular JSF, we use EL expressions to bind data and actions, which JSF resolves when the form is submitted. In the test script, we can also use JSF EL expressions. The Seam testing framework resolves these.

You can use the `getValue()` and `setValue()` methods in `SeamTest` to bind value objects to Seam components via EL expressions. The `SeamTest.invokeMethod()` method invokes a Seam component method specified in an EL expression. The following example shows the complete test script. In `updateModelValues()`, we bound the string `"Michael Yuan"` to the `#{person.name}` component. In `invokeApplication()`, we invoke the

#{manager.sayHello} event handler method. Then, in the renderResponse() method, we retrieve the #{manager.fans} component and verify its content.

```
public class HelloWorldTest extends SeamTest {

  @Test
  public void testSayHello() throws Exception {

    new FacesRequest("/hello.xhtml") {

      @Override
      protected void updateModelValues() throws Exception {
        setValue("#{person.name}", "Michael Yuan");
        setValue("#{person.age}", 30);
        setValue("#{person.email}", "michael@mail.com");
        setValue("#{person.comment}", "test");
      }

      @Override
      protected void invokeApplication() {
        assert getValue ("#{person.name}").equals("Michael Yuan");
        invokeMethod("#{manager.sayHello(person)}");
      }

      @Override
      @SuppressWarnings("unchecked")
      protected void renderResponse() {
        ListDataModel fans = (ListDataModel) getValue("#{fans}");

        assert fans != null;
        fans.setRowIndex(0);
        Person fan = (Person) fans.getRowData();
        assert fan.getName().equals("Michael Yuan");
      }

    }.run();

  }

  ... ...
}
```

Notice that bijection happens automatically here. The test runner knows how to inject the EntityManager and other components. When we get the #{fans} component, it is already wrapped in the ListDataModel type since it is annotated with @DataModel in the code. Everything behaves exactly as if it were running in an application server container.

That's it for the test script. The EL expressions enable us to write test cases that closely resemble the JSF page. We can test Seam components and EL expressions at the same time.

# 27.3   Transactional Data Source

When you use the `FacesRequest` facility and invoke methods via EL expressions, Seam automatically wraps those method calls in transactions. So, there is no need to start and commit the transactions by hand, as we did in unit tests. That also allows us to use JTA data sources unchanged from the EAR in the testing environment.

Below is the `persistence.xml` we used for integrated testing. Notice that you need to specify a transaction manager lookup class so that the test application can locate the JBoss transaction manager in the testing environment outside of the JBoss AS container.

```
<persistence>
  <persistence-unit name="helloworld">
  <provider>org.hibernate.ejb.HibernatePersistence</provider>
  <jta-data-source>java:/DefaultDS</jta-data-source>
    <properties>
      <property name="hibernate.dialect"
                value="org.hibernate.dialect.HSQLDialect"/>
      <property name="hibernate.transaction.flush_before_completion"
                value="true"/>
      <property name="hibernate.hbm2ddl.auto" value="create-drop"/>
      <property name="hibernate.show_sql" value="true"/>
      <property name="hibernate.transaction.manager_lookup_class"
         value="org.hibernate.transaction.JBossTransactionManagerLookup"/>
    </properties>
  </persistence-unit>
</persistence>
```

The ability to use transactional data source allows integration tests to closely mimic the execution environment inside the application server and thereby improves testing accuracy.

Aside from the `persistence.xml`, you can set up integration tests exactly the same way as you set up unit tests, as shown in Section 26.4.

# Part VII

## Production Deployment

Seam applications can deploy on all Java EE 5.0- and J2EE 1.4-compliant application servers, as well as the Tomcat Servlet/JSP server. In this part, we cover important deployment issues, such as using a production database, tuning for performance and scalability, and setting up a server cluster.

# 28

## Using a Production Database

Seam is an ideal solution for developing database-driven web applications. However, so far in this book, for the sake of simplicity, we did not use a production-quality relational database in our example applications. Instead, all our examples used the HSQL database engine embedded into the JBoss. AS to store data. The advantage of using HSQL is that we do not need any extra configuration in the application; it is the default `java:/DefaultDS` data source in the server environment.

However, in real-world web applications, we almost always need to use a production database, such as MySQL, Oracle, Sybase, or MS SQL, to store application data. Fortunately, it is actually very easy to configure alternative database backends for a Seam application. In this chapter, we will show how to set up a MySQL database backend for the Seam Hotel Booking example. We will also cover how to setup JNDI data sources in Tomcat for Seam POJO applications.

## 28.1 Installing and Setting Up the Database

Obviously, you have to install your favorite production database server first. The database server can reside on its own computer or share the same computer as the JBoss AS instance. Most database servers also support multiple databases and multiple users. Each database is a collection of relational tables for a user or an application. Each user, identified by a username and password, has the privilege to read or write in a set of databases. For this exercise, you should install the latest MySQL server and then create a database named `seamdemo` for the Seam Hotel Booking example application. You should grant read/write privilege for the `seamdemo` database to the user `myuser` with the password `mypass`.

Next, you should initialize the database. You need to create the table structures and populate the tables with initial data (i.e., the hotel names and locations in this example). To do that for the Seam Hotel Booking example, run the `productiondb/seamdemo.sql` script on the MySQL command line against the `seamdemo` database. The following is a snippet of the `seamdemo.sql` script file:

```
DROP TABLE IF EXISTS `Booking`;
CREATE TABLE `Booking` (
  `id` bigint(20) NOT NULL auto_increment,
  `creditCard` varchar(16) NOT NULL default '',
  `checkinDate` date NOT NULL default '0000-00-00',
  `checkoutDate` date NOT NULL default '0000-00-00',
  `user_username` varchar(255) default NULL,
  `hotel_id` bigint(20) default NULL,
  PRIMARY KEY  (`id`),
  KEY `FK6713A0396E4A3BD` (`user_username`),
  KEY `FK6713A03951897512` (`hotel_id`)
);

DROP TABLE IF EXISTS `Hotel`;
CREATE TABLE `Hotel` (
  `id` bigint(20) NOT NULL auto_increment,
  `address` varchar(100) NOT NULL default '',
  `name` varchar(50) NOT NULL default '',
  `state` char(2) NOT NULL default '',
  `city` varchar(20) NOT NULL default '',
  `zip` varchar(5) NOT NULL default '',
  PRIMARY KEY  (`id`)
);
INSERT INTO `Hotel` VALUES (...),(...)...

DROP TABLE IF EXISTS `User`;
CREATE TABLE `User` (
  `username` varchar(255) NOT NULL default '',
  `name` varchar(100) NOT NULL default '',
  `password` varchar(15) NOT NULL default '',
  PRIMARY KEY  (`username`)
);
INSERT INTO `User` VALUES (...),(...)...
```

**Automatic Initialization**

The database initialization step is not absolutely necessary. For instance, in the HSQL-based examples early in the book, we configured Seam to automatically create the table schema based on the entity bean annotations (see the last section in this chapter). We then placed an `import.sql` file in the EJB3 JAR file. The SQL `INSERT` statements in the `import.sql` file are automatically executed when the application is deployed.

See the MySQL administration documentation for details on how to install the server, create databases, manage users, and run SQL scripts from the command line.

In the following sections, we show how to set up the JBoss AS to use the production database. The process can be easily automated by seam-gen (see Chapter 5). Still, we recommend you read the rest of this chapter to understand exactly what goes on inside the seam-gen automated project generator.

# 28.2  Installing the Database Driver

Next, you need to install a JDBC driver for the database. The driver allows Seam applications to interact with the database using standard JDBC API, which is required for the EJB3 persistence engine in Seam to function.

You can find JDBC drivers for your database on the database vendor's web site. For MySQL, you can download the driver for free from www.mysql.com/products/connector-j. This is just a JAR file, which you need to copy into the `server/default/lib` directory of the JBoss AS installation (replace `default` with any alternative server configuration you are using).

# 28.3  Defining a Data Source

For the application to reference the database as a data source, you must create a data source configuration file. Different application servers have different ways of doing it. In the Seam Hotel Booking example, the `productiondb/booking-ds.xml` file configures the MySQL data source for JBoss AS. It contains the URL to access the database server, the database name, and the username and password of the user who would access the database on behalf of the Java application. You must copy this file to the `server/default/deploy` directory of your JBoss AS. Then all your applications can access the `seamdemo` database on this MySQL server via a data source object obtained from the `java:/bookingDatasource` JNDI name.

```
<datasources>
  <local-tx-datasource>
    <jndi-name>bookingDatasource</jndi-name>
    <connection-url>
      jdbc:mysql://localhost:3306/seamdemo
    </connection-url>
    <driver-class>com.mysql.jdbc.Driver</driver-class>
    <user-name>myuser</user-name>
    <password>mypass</password>
  </local-tx-datasource>
</datasources>
```

# 28.4   Configuring the Persistence Engine

The `persistence.xml` file in the EJB3 JAR file's `META-INF` directory configures the underlying persistence engine for Seam. In the source code, you can find this file under the `resources/META-INF` directory.

The `persistence.xml` file specifies that the `EntityManager` object in this Seam application persists all entity beans to the `java:/bookingDatasource` database. Recall that this data source points to the `seamdemo` database on the production MySQL server. The `persistence.xml` file also configures the `EntityManager` to use the MySQL dialect of the SQL language when updating the database. The `hibernate.hbm2dll.auto=none` property specifies that the table schema is not automatically created when the application is deployed. If the property has the value `create-drop`, the database tables are created at application deployment and deleted at undeployment (or server shutdown). Finally, if the value is `update`, the database schema is updated or created, but the content is not deleted. On a production system, a database user often does not have the privileges to create or drop tables.

```
<persistence>
  <persistence-unit name="bookingDatabase">
    <provider>org.hibernate.ejb.HibernatePersistence</provider>
    <jta-data-source>java:/bookingDatasource</jta-data-source>
    <properties>
      <property name="hibernate.dialect"
                value="org.hibernate.dialect.MySQLDialect"/>
      <property name="hibernate.hbm2ddl.auto"
                value="none"/>
    </properties>
  </persistence-unit>
</persistence>
```

That's it! That's all you need to set up a MySQL backend database for the Seam Hotel Booking example application. Setting up other production databases, such as Oracle and MS SQL, is similarly easy.

# 28.5   How about Tomcat?

As we discussed early on in the book, Seam POJO applications can be deployed to plain Tomcat servers (see Chapter 4). Tomcat does not come with an embedded database or a default data source. So, we have to set up the data source in JNDI even if we just want to use an embedded database like HSQL. In the example `tomcatjpa`, we have the following lines in `tomcatjpa.war/META-INF/context.xml` to set up the data source for an HSQL server. The JNDI name is under namespace `java:comp/env/`. The `hsql.jar` is included in `tomcatjpa.war/WEB-INF/lib` to provide the JDBC driver as well as the database itself.

```
<Context path="/tomcatjpa" docBase="tomcatjpa"
         debug="5" reloadable="true" crossContext="true">

   <Resource name="jdbc/TestDB" auth="Container"
             type="javax.sql.DataSource"
             maxActive="100" maxIdle="30" maxWait="10000"
             username="sa"
             driverClassName="org.hsqldb.jdbcDriver"
             url="jdbc:hsqldb:."/>

</Context>
```

Obviously, a MySQL data source can be set up in a similar fashion using the techniques we described earlier in this chapter. However, since Tomcat does not have a JTA transaction manager, the `persistence.xml` file needs to specify explicitly that the transaction is non-JTA:

```
<persistence>
  <persistence-unit name="helloworld"
                    transaction-type="RESOURCE_LOCAL">
    <provider>org.hibernate.ejb.HibernatePersistence</provider>
    <non-jta-data-source>java:comp/env/jdbc/TestDB</non-jta-data-source>
    <properties>
      <property name="hibernate.dialect"
                value="org.hibernate.dialect.HSQLDialect"/>
       <property name="hibernate.hbm2ddl.auto"
                value="create-drop"/>
      <property name="hibernate.show_sql" value="true"/>
      <property name="hibernate.cache.provider_class"
                value="org.hibernate.cache.HashtableCacheProvider"/>
    </properties>
  </persistence-unit>
</persistence>
```

### Tomcat Redeployment Issues

Tomcat extracts and caches the `META-INF/context.xml` file from the WAR to `$TOMCAT/conf/Catalina`. The cached file does not appear to be updated when you redeploy the WAR. So, if you make changes to your data source in `META-INF/context.xml`, make sure to delete the `$TOMCAT/conf/Catalina` cache before redeploying.

If you do need to use a JTA transaction manager in your Tomcat application, you can do so via a number of third-party tools, including the JBoss Microcontainer. However, by doing so, you are essentially building a JEE application server on Tomcat, and you will probably be better off using a proper JEE application server directly. Building transaction managers in Tomcat is beyond the scope of this book.

# 29

Java EE 5.0 Deployment

As a developer, you have a variety of choices when it comes to the deployment environment for Seam applications.

If you can deploy on a Java EE 5.0-compliant application server, you have no problem. Seam is designed to work in that environment. The book examples are fully tested on the default profile of JBoss AS 4.0.5+. With minimal modifications to configuration files and JAR files, your Seam application could easily run in JBoss AS 5.0 and Sun's GlassFish Application Server.

If you do not have a Java EE 5.0 application server but have access to a J2EE 1.4 server, you can write your applications in Seam POJOs instead of EJB3 beans. This approach is discussed in Chapter 4. As we mentioned, however, Seam POJOs are not as feature-rich as EJB3 components.

Finally, Tomcat fans can deploy both EJB3-based and POJO-based Seam applications on plain Tomcat servers. The Tomcat deployment uses the JBoss Microcontainer to load the necessary services.

In this chapter, we will focus on Java EE 5.0 deployment of Seam applications.

## 29.1  JBoss AS 4.0.5

Strictly speaking, JBoss AS 4.0.5 is not a Java EE 5.0-compliant application server—but it provides the two most important pieces: EJB3 and JSF support. To deploy Seam applications in JBoss AS 4.0.5, you must install the server from the GUI installer and choose the EJB3 profile. See Appendix A for more details. All the examples in this book are configured to run in the JBoss AS 4.0.5 EJB3 profile.

# 29.2   JBoss AS 4.2.x and 5.x

JBoss AS 4.2.x and 5.x embed the JSF Reference Implementation (RI) instead of the Apache MyFaces implementation embedded in JBoss AS 4.0.5. The JSF RI implements JSF 1.2 specification. To deploy Seam applications in JBoss AS 4.2.x and 5.x, you need to configure the `web.xml` file in `app.war/WEB-INF/` and comment out the MyFaces listener:

```
<!-- MyFaces -->
<!--
<listener>
  <listener-class>
org.apache.myfaces.webapp.StartupServletContextListener
  </listener-class>
</listener>
-->
```

Next, you need to enable the `SeamELResolver` in order for Seam to resolve component names correctly in web pages. To do that, add the following element to your `faces-config.xml` file in `app.war/WEB-INF/`. Also, you need to update the XML namespaces in `faces-config.xml` to JSF 1.2. Below is an example:

```
<faces-config version="1.2"
              xmlns="http://java.sun.com/xml/ns/javaee"
              xmlns:xsi="http://www.w3.org/2001/XMLSchema-instance"
              xsi:schemaLocation="http://java.sun.com/xml/ns/javaee
              http://java.sun.com/xml/ns/javaee/web-facesconfig_1_2.xsd">

  <application>
    <el-resolver>
      org.jboss.seam.jsf.SeamELResolver
    </el-resolver>
  </application>

  <lifecycle>
    <phase-listener>
      org.jboss.seam.jsf.SeamPhaseListener
    </phase-listener>
  </lifecycle>

  ... more config ...

</faces-config>
```

Finally, since the JSF 1.2 RI libraries already bundle the `el-ri.jar` and `el-api.jar` files, you can remove those JARs from your EAR archive and remove references to them from the `mywebapp.ear/META-INF/application.xml` file.

# 29.3  GlassFish

GlassFish is Sun's open source Java EE 5.0 application server. Every Seam release since the 1.0 GA has been tested on GlassFish. In this section, we will look at what configuration files you must change to make the book's examples (as well as seam-gen projects) run on GlassFish. This is more involved than running Seam applications on JBoss AS.

First, we highly recommend that you use Hibernate as the Java Persistence API (JPA) provider in GlassFish. By default, GlassFish uses TopLink Essentials (a.k.a. the watered-down "lesser TopLink") for JPA implementation. It might be fine for basic JPA needs, but Seam makes good use of Hibernate-specific features, such as Hibernate validators and filters. In fact, it would be foolish not to use the Hibernate JPA with Seam, considering how easy it is to install Hibernate JPA in GlassFish: By including Hibernate JARs in your EAR, you can enable Hibernate JPA for a single application. Or, you can simply copy Hibernate JARs to GlassFish's `lib` directory and enable Hibernate JPA for all applications. To use the Hibernate JPA, just choose the proper persistence provider in your `persistence.xml` file, as we will do below.

If you have to use the "lesser TopLink" JPA, we also have a TopLink build target in the `examples/glassfish` project. Be aware that you need to load the database manually for the hotel data, because TopLink does not read the `import.sql` file.

All the changes from a JBoss deployment to a GlassFish deployment concern the configuration files and library JARs only.

Since GlassFish uses the JSF 1.2 RI and not MyFaces, you should make the same changes we discussed in Section 29.2. They include: commenting out the context listener for MyFaces in `web.xml`, adding a `SeamELResolver` in `faces-config.xml`, and removing the `el-ri.jar` and `el-api.jar` files from the EAR and `application.xml`.

GlassFish requires you to declare all EJB3 session bean reference names in the `web.xml` file for the web application to access the beans. This is a rather tedious process. You must add the following lines in `web.xml` for each session bean in your application:

```
<ejb-local-ref>
  <ejb-ref-name>
    projectname/ManagerAction/local
  </ejb-ref-name>
  <ejb-ref-type>Session</ejb-ref-type>
  <local>Manager</local>
  <ejb-link>ManagerAction</ejb-link>
</ejb-local-ref>
```

Then, if you need to inject an EJB3 session bean (A) into another session bean (B) using the `@In` annotation, you also need to declare bean A in the JAR file containing bean B. That must be done if bean A and bean B are in the same JAR file. You must add the ejb-local-ref element to the META-INF/ejb-jar.xml file bundled in the JAR file containing bean B. That is tedious, and is a serious inconvenience of GlassFish.

```
<ejb-jar ...>
  <enterprise-beans>
    <session>
      <ejb-name>BeanA</ejb-name>
      <ejb-local-ref>
        <ejb-ref-name>
          projname/BeanB/local
        </ejb-ref-name>
        <ejb-ref-type>Session</ejb-ref-type>
        <local>BeanBInterface</local>
        <ejb-link>BeanB</ejb-link>
      </ejb-local-ref>
    </session>

    ... more injections ...

  </enterprise-beans>

  ... ...

</ejb-jar>
```

You also need to tell Seam the session bean naming pattern you just used in web.xml so that Seam can locate those beans. Make sure you have the following in the components.xml file:

```
<core:init jndi-pattern="java:comp/env/projectname/#{ejbName}/local"
           debug="true"/>
```

To use the Hibernate JPA with GlassFish's built-in JavaDB (Derby database), you need a persistence.xml file similar to the following. To use other databases, refer to the GlassFish manual.

```
<persistence ...>
  <persistence-unit name="bookingDatabase">
    <provider>
      org.hibernate.ejb.HibernatePersistence
    </provider>
    <jta-data-source>jdbc/__default</jta-data-source>
    <properties>
      <property name="hibernate.dialect"
                value="org.hibernate.dialect.DerbyDialect"/>
      <property name="hibernate.hbm2ddl.auto"
                value="create-drop"/>
      <property name="hibernate.show_sql"
                value="true"/>
      <property name="hibernate.cache.provider_class"
      value="org.hibernate.cache.HashtableCacheProvider"/>
    </properties>
  </persistence-unit>
</persistence>
```

Finally, you need to bundle the following JAR files in your EAR in addition to any library files you already need for JBoss AS deployment:

`hibernate*.jar`   Hibernate3, Annotation, EntityManager JARs

`thirdparty-all.jar`   Combined third-party JARs for Hibernate JPA support outside of JBoss AS

`jboss-archive-browsing.jar`   Required for Hibernate EntityManager

`commons-beanutils-1.7.0.jar`   Required by Seam outside of JBoss AS

`commons-digester-1.6.jar`   Required by Seam outside of JBoss AS

Now the application should deploy in GlassFish.

# 30

## Performance Tuning and Clustering

**S**eam drastically improves application developer productivity via extensive use of annotated POJOs, dependency bijection, and runtime service interceptors. Developers
write less code because Seam generates and executes much of the boilerplate code behind
the scenes. However, the developer convenience comes with a price: The more work
Seam needs to do, especially at runtime, the slower the system performs. Today, as
computer hardware performance continues to improve and prices continue to drop,
improving developer productivity is a higher priority than raw performance.

However, for high-volume web applications, we must carefully evaluate, and try to
compensate for, the performance impacts from the Seam runtime. For starters, we
should tune our Seam applications to make the most of the existing hardware. If a single
server is insufficient, we should also understand how to scale a Seam application by
leveraging a server cluster. In this chapter, we discuss how to tune and scale Seam
applications.

### Annotations and Performance

Different Seam annotations are processed at different stages of the application lifecycle,
and they may have big implications on performance. Basic configuration annotations such
as `@Stateful` and `@Name` are processed at application deployment. They increase only the
application startup time and do not impact runtime performance. In fact, in other enterprise
Java frameworks, this type of deployment information is specified in XML files. XML
parsing is often slower than annotation processing, which means Seam does not have any
additional performance overhead.

However, some annotations, such as the dependency bijection annotations (e.g., @In and @Out), trigger Seam runtime interceptors before and after each method call or property access. They do have a performance impact.

# 30.1   Tuning Performance on a Single Server

The following common JBoss best practices apply to tuning a Seam application on a single server.

## 30.1.1   Avoid Calling by Value

In an EAR deployment in JBoss AS, you have the options to enable calling by value and deployment isolation. The options are defined in your $JBOSS/server/default/deploy/ear-deployer.xml file:

```
<mbean code="org.jboss.deployment.EARDeployer"
       name="jboss.j2ee:service=EARDeployer">
  <!-- Isolate all ears in their own class loader space -->
  <attribute name="Isolated">true</attribute>
  <!-- Enforce call by value to all remote interfaces -->
  <attribute name="CallByValue">true</attribute>
</mbean>
```

Seam automatically generates dynamic proxy objects to make calls from JSF components to EJB3 session beans. If you enable calling by value, the call parameters and return values are serialized in the process. The benefit is that the JSF and EJB3 tiers of the application are properly separated. This is useful when you have multiple versions of the same Java classes deployed on the same server or when you need to port applications from other application servers to JBoss AS.

However, calling by value is also slow because object serialization and deserialization are very CPU-intensive. Calling a method by value could be 10 times slower than a regular call by reference. Most Seam applications are designed to run inside the same JVM on JBoss AS, so we recommend that you do not enable calling by value if you can.

## 30.1.2   JVM Options

First, always start the JVM using the -server option. It does a number of optimizations up front, trading faster runtime performance for longer startup time.

Next, it is important to give the JVM as many resources as possible. The most important resource for the JVM is the amount of RAM. Since all server-side state data (e.g., HTTP sessions and stateful session beans) are stored in the RAM, it is crucial for high-load servers (i.e., whose with lots of concurrent users) to have a large amount of RAM. On a typical server box, you should allocate at least 75 percent of the physical RAM to the JVM. You can do that via the JVM startup options in the `JAVA_OPTS` property in the `bin/run.conf` file (use the `bin\run.bat` file on Windows). We use the same value for the `-Xmx` (maximum RAM) and `-Xms` (minimum RAM) options to force the JVM to use the specified amount of RAM. For instance, the `-Xmx6g` `-Xms6g` options start the JVM with 6GB of RAM.

---

**64-bit Systems**

On a 32-bit system, the JVM has access to a maximum of only 2GB of RAM. On a 64-bit system, including AMD64 and Intel EMT64, you can allocate far more RAM to the JVM—but you must use a 64-bit JVM to take advantage of the additional RAM.

However, a too large memory heap could also hurt performance because it takes too long for the garbage collector to sweep through it. We have observed the JVM behaving erratically under stress when the heap is several gigabytes big. In this case, especially when the system has multiple CPUs, we recommend that you run multiple JBoss AS instances or simply multiple virtual machines (e.g., VMWare) on the same server. You can use a load balancer to distribute the load to those virtual machines, as described later in this chapter.

---

Modern JVMs use very sophisticated algorithms to run garbage collection. Garbage collection should run in parallel to other tasks so that the heap is being continuously cleaned up. That avoids the long server pause when the garbage collector stops other processes to clean up a large heap. To run the parallel garbage collector, you can specify the `-XX:+UseParallelGC` `-XX:+UseParallelOldGC` option for the JVM.

Finally, performance tuning is often application-specific and requires empirical observations. You can tweak many other JVM options for improving performance and debugging. For instance, you can fine-tune the garbage collection algorithm in the JVM to minimize the GC pauses in your specific use case. Different JVMs (e.g., the Sun JVM, BEA JRockit JVM, and IBM JVM) also have different options for performance tuning. We recommend that you read a JVM tuning guide for more information.

## 30.1.3 Reducing Logging

By default, both Seam and MyFaces log a lot of information. Much of that information is for application developers and has little use in a production environment. Excessive logging I/O operations could really be the bottleneck on a high-load server. To reduce logging on a production server, you can increase the logging level for the `org.jboss` classes to the `INFO`. Just uncomment the following lines in the `server/default/conf/log4j.xml` file; that gets rid of much of the logging from Seam:

```
<log4j:configuration>

... ...

<category name="org.jboss">
  <priority value="INFO"/>
</category>

<category name="javax.faces">
  <priority value="INFO"/>
</category>

</log4j:configuration>
```

## 30.1.4  Tuning the HTTP Thread Pool

In JBoss AS, a separate thread answers each HTTP request. When the application has many concurrent users, much of the CPU time is spent managing those threads. Optimizing thread management is a key to improving the application performance under high load.

To avoid excessive thread creation and termination, JBoss AS maintains a pool of threads. When a new HTTP request comes in, the server retrieves a worker thread from the pool to process the request. After the response is rendered, the worker thread is returned to the pool and made available to process another HTTP request. You can specify a maximum size for the thread pool. If all the threads in the pool are currently being used, new requests must wait until a thread finishes its work and becomes available. To fully utilize CPU resources, the size of the thread pool should be at least five times the number of available CPUs on the server. However, too many threads can impede performance: The CPU then has to spend more time switching contexts between threads than processing requests.

Another constraint on thread pool size is the number of HTTP keepalive connections (see the associated sidebar). You can configure the maximum number of keepalive connections on the server; each connection corresponds to an active user. If all connections are keepalive, the number of connections is essentially the number of concurrent users the server can handle. Additional users will then receive the connection timeout error. However, each keepalive connection also ties up a worker thread, so your thread pool size must be at least as big as the number of keepalive connections. For a high-load server, you might have a large number of keepalive connections, which would require too many threads to be effective.

An obvious fix is to have a modest number of keepalive connections and a modestly larger thread pool. The spare threads, which are not tied to the keepalive connections, are used to service the users overflowing the keepalive limit. This way, some users get the keepalive connection and enjoy better performance, while others have slower regular connections but still get service. You can optimize the right mix of threads and keepalive connections only through trial and error for your specific server needs.

**Keepalive Connections**

A keepalive connection allows a web browser to reuse the same network connection for multiple HTTP requests. It eliminates the overhead of creating and destroying multiple connections. All modern web browsers use HTTP keepalive connections by default. However, for a connection be keepalive, the server also must support it. As you can see here, the server has the flexibility to decide which users get keepalive connections, depending on its own load.

The two thread-related settings just discussed are in the HTTP `Connector` element in the `server/default/deploy/jbossweb-tomcat55.sar/server.xml` file. The `maxThreads` attribute determines the size of the thread pool, and the `maxKeepAliveRequests` attribute determines the maximum number of keepalive connections. If the `maxKeepAliveRequests` attribute is `-1`, the server will allow an unlimited number of keepalive requests until the thread pool is exhausted.

```
<Server>

  <Service name="jboss.web"
           className="org.jboss.web.tomcat.tc5.StandardService">

    <Connector port="8080"
               address="${jboss.bind.address}"
               maxThreads="250"
               maxKeepAliveRequests="100"
               strategy="ms"
               maxHttpHeaderSize="8192"
               emptySessionPath="true"
               enableLookups="false"
               redirectPort="8443" acceptCount="100"
               connectionTimeout="20000"
               disableUploadTimeout="true"/>

  </Service>

</Server>
```

# 30.1.5 Choosing Between Client- and Server-Side State Saving

JSF can save its internal component state in the user's HTTP session (server-side state saving) or in the browser as hidden form fields (client-side state saving). Server-side state saving consumes the server's memory and is generally harder to scale because of the need to replicate the session data in a cluster (see later in this chapter). Client-side state saving, on the other hand, distributes the state management load to the users' browsers.

However, when it comes to CPU performance, client-side state saving is much slower because of the need to serialize objects. Thus, you must decide whether memory or CPU is the more likely bottleneck of your application and choose the appropriate state-saving method. You can select the state-saving method in the application's WEB-INF/web.xml file:

```
<webapp>

... ...

<context-param>
  <param-name>
    javax.faces.STATE_SAVING_METHOD
  </param-name>
  <param-value>server</param-value>
</context-param>

</webapp>
```

## 30.1.6   Using a Production Data Source

JBoss AS's default data source, java:/DefaultDS, points to the embedded HSQL database shipped with the server. Although the HSQL database is fine for application development, it is not suitable for production environments. It is a major performance bottleneck and becomes unstable under high load. Be sure to set up a data source with a production database for your applications. Refer to Chapter 28 for more on how to set up the production data source.

---

**Data Access Is the Bottleneck**

In most real-world applications, the database access layer is the most likely performance bottleneck. Therefore, you must optimize the database access as much as possible.

---

## 30.1.7   Using a Second-Level Database Cache

Seam applications use EJB3 entity beans to model relational database tables. In most applications, only a small subset of the database records is frequently used. To improve performance, we should cache the entity beans representing those frequently accessed records in the application memory, instead of making repeated database roundtrips for the same bean objects. In this section, we give a quick explanation of how object caching works; for more details on this subject, refer to Chapter 32.

To use the entity bean cache, you must annotate the bean class. All bean instances from the class are automatically cached after the first access until the EntityManager updates the underlying database table.

```
@Entity
@Name("person")
@Cache(usage=CacheConcurrencyStrategy.READ_ONLY)
public class Person implements Serializable {

  private long id;
  private String name;

  @Id @GeneratedValue
  public long getId() { return id;}
  public void setId(long id) { this.id = id; }

  public String getName() { return name; }
  public void setName(String name) {
    this.name = name;
  }
}
```

In the `persistence.xml` file for those entity beans, specify the distributed JBoss TreeCache as the cache implementation:

```
<entity-manager>
  <name>myapp</name>
  <jta-data-source>java:/DvdStoreDS</jta-data-source>
  <properties>

    ... ...

    <property name="hibernate.cache.provider_class"
              value="org.jboss.ejb3.entity.TreeCacheProviderHook"/>
    <property name="hibernate.treecache.mbean.object_name"
              value="jboss.cache:service=EJB3EntityTreeCache"/>

  </properties>
</entity-manager>
```

The cached objects are stored in "regions." Each region has its own size and cache expiration settings. Instances of the `Person` entity bean are stored in a cache region named `/Person` (the cache region name matches the fully qualified Java class name for the entity bean). The regions are configured in the JBoss AS's `server/default/deploy/ejb3-entity-cache-service.xml` file:

```
<server>
  <mbean code="org.jboss.cache.TreeCache"
         name="jboss.cache:service=EJB3EntityTreeCache">
    <depends>jboss:service=Naming</depends>
    <depends>jboss:service=TransactionManager</depends>

    ... ...

    <attribute name="EvictionPolicyConfig">
      <config>
        <attribute name="wakeUpIntervalSeconds">
          5
        </attribute>
```

```
<region name="/_default_">
  <attribute name="maxNodes">
    5000
  </attribute>
  <attribute name="timeToLiveSeconds">
    1000
  </attribute>
</region>

<region name="/Person">
  <attribute name="maxNodes">
    10
  </attribute>
  <attribute name="timeToLiveSeconds">
    5000
  </attribute>
</region>

<region name="/FindQuery">
  <attribute name="maxNodes">
    100
  </attribute>
  <attribute name="timeToLiveSeconds">
    5000
  </attribute>
</region>

    ... ...

    </config>
  </attribute>
</mbean>
</server>
```

In addition to caching entity bean instances, we can use the regions to cache the EJB3 query results. For instance, the following code caches the query result in the /FindQuery cache region. For the query cache to be effective, you must cache the entity bean of the query result as well. In this case, we must cache the Person entity bean:

```
List <Person> fans =
  em.createQuery("select p from Person p")
    .setHint("org.hibernate.cacheRegion", "/FindQuery")
    .getResultList();
```

For more information on using second-level database cache in JBoss EJB3, refer to the JBoss documentation.

## 30.1.8  Using Database Transactions Carefully

In Chapter 11, we discussed both database transactions and a nontransactional extended persistence context. Without a transaction manager, we typically flush the persistence context at the end of the conversation and send all database updates in a batch. That offers two performance advantages to the transactional approach:

- The database updates are flushed in a batch at the end of the conversation instead of being flushed at the end of each request/response cycle (i.e., at the end of a thread). That reduces unnecessary database roundtrips during the conversation.

- The nontransactional database update is significantly faster than a transactional one.

Of course, the drawback of this approach is that if the database (or connection to the database) fails in the middle of the update batch, the database is only partially updated.

A good compromise is to build up the database changes in stateful Seam components throughout the conversation and then use a single transactional method at the end of the conversation to update the `EntityManager`. This way, we avoid the roundtrips in the conversation and still take advantage of the transactional support when we actually access the database. For more details on this technique, refer to Section 11.2.

# 30.2  Clustering for Scalability and Failover

With proper optimization, a Seam application can handle most low- to medium-load scenarios on a single commodity server. However, true enterprise applications must also be scalable and fail-tolerant.

- Scalability means that we can handle more load by adding more servers. It "future-proofs" our applications. A cluster of X86 servers is probably much cheaper than a single mainframe computer that handles a comparable load.

- Fail tolerance means that when a server fails (e.g., because of hardware problems), its load is automatically transferred to a failover node. The failover node should already have the user's state data, such as the conversational contexts; thus, the user will not experience any disruption. Fail tolerance and high reliability are crucial requirements in many enterprise environments.

As an enterprise framework, Seam was designed from the ground up to support clustering. In the rest of this section, we will discuss how to optimize your clustering settings. Detailed instructions on JBoss AS clustering setup are beyond the scope of this book; you can find more details in JBoss Application Server Clustering Guide (www.jboss.org/jbossas/docs).

---

**Installing the Clustered Profile**

Make sure that you selected the `ejb3-clustered` profile in the JBoss AS installer (or JEMS installer). This profile contains the necessary library JARs and configuration files to run clustered EJB3 (and, hence, Seam) applications.

---

## 30.2.1   Sticky Session Load Balancing

All HTTP load balancers support *sticky sessions*, which means that requests in the same session must be forwarded to the same JBoss node unless there is a failover. You must turn on sticky sessions in your setup. In the ideal world, all nodes in a replicated cluster have the same state, and the load balancer can forward any request to any node. However, in a real cluster, the network and CPU resources are limited, so it takes time to actually replicate the state from node to node. Without sticky sessions, the user will get random HTTP 500 errors when the request hits a node that does not yet have the latest replicated state.

---

**Apache Tomcat Connector**

Apache Tomcat Connector (a.k.a. mod_jk 1.2, see http://tomcat.apache.org/connectors-doc) is a popular software-based load balancer for Tomcat (and, hence, JBoss AS). It uses an Apache web server to receive user requests and then forwards them on to the JBoss AS nodes via the AJP v1.3 protocol. It is important that the maximum number of concurrent users in the load-balancer Apache server must match the sum of concurrent users in the JBoss AS nodes.

We recommend that you use the worker or winnt MPM (Multi-Processing Module) in Apache together with mod_jk. The older pre-fork MPM is not thread-based and performs poorly when there are many concurrent users.

---

## 30.2.2   State Replication

In a failover cluster, state replication between nodes is one of the biggest performance bottlenecks. A JBoss AS cluster has three separate replication processes going on. The following configuration files are relative to the `server/default/deploy` directory:

- The HTTP session data replication is configured via the `tc5-cluster.sar/META-INF/jboss-service.xml` file.

- The EJB3 stateful session bean (i.e., Seam stateful component) replication is configured via the `ejb3-clustered-sfsbcache-service.xml` file.

- The EJB3 entity bean cache (i.e., distributed second-level cache for the database) replication is configured via the `ejb3-entity-cache-service.xml` file.

All three configuration files are similar: They all use the JBoss TreeCache service to cache and replicate objects. We recommend that you set the `CacheMode` attribute to `REPL_ASYNC` for asynchronous replication. In the asynchronous replication mode, the server node does not wait for replication to finish before it serves the next request. This is much faster than synchronous replication, which blocks the system at several wait points.

The `ClusterConfig` element in each configuration file specifies the underlying communication protocol stack for the replication traffic. Through the JGroups library, JBoss AS supports many network protocol stacks for `ClusterConfig`. It is important to optimize the stack to achieve the best performance. From our experiments, we believe that the TCP/IP NIO stack is the best choice for most small clusters. Refer to the JBoss AS documentation for more on the clustering protocol stack.

## 30.2.3 Failover Architectures

The simplest cluster architecture combines all server nodes in a single cluster and gives all nodes an identical state through replication. Although the single-cluster architecture is simple, it is generally a bad idea in real-world applications. As each node replicates its state to all other nodes in the cluster, the replication workload increases geometrically with the number of nodes in the cluster. This is clearly not a scalable architecture when the cluster grows beyond four or eight nodes. For good performance, we recommend partitioning the cluster into node pairs.

Using the buddy replication feature in JBoss Cache 1.4.0, you can group the nodes into pairs. You can also set up the load balancer to retry the correct failover node when a node in a pair fails.

If the load balancer hits both nodes in the buddy pair (using sticky sessions, of course), the failover node receives twice the traffic if the other node fails. That is not an elegant failover mechanism because the user would experience congestion. An alternative architecture is asymmetric failover: The load balancer hits only one node in each buddy pair, and the other node is reserved as a replicated failover node. You need more redundant hardware in this setup, but the cluster has the same computational capabilities during the failover.

Performance tuning is a complex subject, especially in a cluster. You must carefully evaluate your application's needs and devise the best strategy. The information in this chapter is intended merely to provide some simple guidelines.

# Part VIII

## Emerging Technologies

Seam has driven the development of the Web Beans specification (JSR-299) and continues to incorporate emerging technologies to simplify web development. In this part, we will demonstrate how Seam allows you to execute timer jobs in your application using Quartz, how you can develop highly scalable applications with multilayer caching, and how to simplify your development using the Groovy scripting language. In addition, we will provide an introduction to Web Beans which will eventually serve as the core of Seam and is poised to change the face of web development with Java EE.

# 31

Scheduling Recurring Jobs from a Web Application

**M**anaging recurring tasks is a key requirement for enterprise applications. For instance, you might need to collect payments from your customers every week, generate a report for payroll on the first day of every month, etc. How do you do it? Well, you can require your users to click on the **Collect payment** manually every week. But good enterprise software is all about automatizing away those tedious, error-prone, manual tasks. We must allow a user say **Collect payment every week** once, and the server should take it over from now on.

However, an issue with web applications is that their interaction model is too much request/response focused. Every action the server takes is the result of a user request. Web actions do not normally happen automatically without user intervention. It requires special setup to have a long-running automatic timer in a web application.

Seam provides a simple mechanism to schedule recurring tasks right from web actions. In this chapter, we will first show you how to schedule simple recurring jobs via Seam annotations. Then, we will discuss how to configure the backend job store to manage persistent jobs that are automatically restarted when the server reboots. We will also explain how to schedule complex, Unix cron job-like recurring tasks in Seam. Finally, we will show how to start recurring tasks at server startup without explicit user intervention.

The sample application in this chapter is the `quartz` example the book's source code bundle.

# 31.1   Simple Recurring Events

To schedule a simple recurring task from the web, you first put the task itself in a method. Then, you annotate the method with the @Asynchronous annotation. The scheduling configuration—such as when to begin, the recurring frequency, and when to stop—is passed as annotated method's call parameters. In the following example, we have a task that simply withdraws some amount of money from the customer's account at a fixed time interval. The account to process and the payment amount to deduct are specified in the payment object.

```
@Asynchronous
@Transactional
public QuartzTriggerHandle schedulePayment (
                          @Expiration Date when,
                          @IntervalDuration Long interval,
                          @FinalExpiration Date stoptime,
                          Payment payment) {

  payment = entityManager.merge(payment);

  if (payment.getActive()) {
    BigDecimal balance = payment.getAccount().adjustBalance(
                         payment.getAmount().negate());
    payment.setLastPaid(new Date());
  }
  return null;
}
```

The @Expiration, @IntervalDuration, and @FinalExpiration annotations mark the parameters that provide the task's start time, frequency (in milliseconds), and end time. Notice that the method declares that it returns a QuartzTriggerHandle object, but we do not construct that object in the method. We merely return a null value. Seam intercepts the method and returns an appropriate QuartzTriggerHandle automatically to its caller. We will touch on this point later.

Now, to schedule this task, you invoke the schedulePayment() method from a web action method. It could be an event handler of a web button or link, or a page action method if you want to schedule the event when a page is loaded. Every time a user invokes the saveAndSchedule() method from the web, a new timer for the task is created.

```
@In PaymentProcessor processor;

// This method is invoked from a web action
public void saveAndSchedule() {

  // The payment, paymentDate, paymentInterval, and
  // paymentEndDate objects are constructed from the
  // web UI based on the user input.

  // This is the @Asynchronous method.
```

```
QuartzTriggerHandle handle =
  processor.schedulePayment(paymentDate, paymentInterval,
                            paymentEndDate, payment);
payment.setQuartzTriggerHandle( handle );
savePaymentToDB (payment);
}
```

The `QuartzTriggerHandle` object returned from the `schedulePayment()` method is serializable. You can save this object in the database if you want to access the timer later. For instance, the following web action method, `cancel()`, shows how you can get hold of a running timer from the database and stop it before its end date expires.

```
public void cancel() {
  Payment payment = loadPaymentFromDB (paymentId);
  QuartzTriggerHandle handle = payment.getQuartzTriggerHandle();
  payment.setQuartzTriggerHandle(null);
  removePaymentFromDB (payment);

  try {
      handle.cancel();
  } catch (Exception e) {
      FacesMessages.instance().add("Payment already processed");
  }
}
```

Similarly, you can pause and resume any timer in the system as needed.

---

**One-off Long-Running Tasks**

The `schedulePayment()` method returns immediately after it is invoked, and the timer task automatically runs as scheduled in the background. The web user does not have to wait for the task to complete. That makes it easy to invoke long-running background tasks from the web without blocking the user. For instance, you can make the task start immediately and run only once. The event handler method returns immediately after the user presses the button, and you can display a nice message asking the user to check back for the results later.

---

# 31.2 Configuring the Quartz Scheduler Service

As many other features in Seam, you can choose to use alternative implementations of the timer behind the asynchronous methods. While you can use the standard EJB3 timer service to manage asynchronous methods, we recommend that you use the Quartz scheduler service. Quartz provides richer features than the EJB3 timer, and it does not require the application to run inside a JEE 5 application server.

Quartz is a widely used open source scheduler. It supports several different job scheduling mechanisms, including using the Unix cron expressions to schedule jobs (see below in this chapter). It supports job persistence in databases, as well as in memory. To read more about Quartz, visit its official web site at www.opensymphony.com/quartz.

To set up Quartz, you need to bundle the `quartz.jar` file in your application (look for it in the official Seam distribution, or your can download Quartz directly from its project web site). Quartz versions 1.5 and 1.6 are supported. You should place the `quartz.jar` file either in `app.war/WEB-INF/lib` for WAR deployment or in `app.ear/lib` for EAR deployment.

Next, add the following lines in `components.xml` to tell Seam to start the Quartz scheduler service:

```
<components ... ...
  xmlns:async="http://jboss.com/products/seam/async"
  xmlns:xsi="http://www.w3.org/2001/XMLSchema-instance"
  xsi:schemaLocation="... ...
                      http://jboss.com/products/seam/async
                      http://jboss.com/products/seam/async-2.0.xsd">

  ... ...

  <!-- Install the QuartzDispatcher -->
  <async:quartz-dispatcher/>

</components>
```

Finally, you probably also want to store Quartz jobs in a database so that the scheduler can survive server restarts. To do that, first run the required SQL setup script in Quartz distribution against your database server to create the job stores in your favorite relational database. You can typically find the SQL scripts in the `/docs/dbTables` directory of the Quartz distribution. Most popular relational databases are supported. Then, add a `seam.quartz.properties` file in your classpath (i.e., the `app.war/WEB-INF/classes` directory) to configure Quartz to use this particular data source. Below is the content of a typical `seam.quartz.properties` file. Just replace the `dbname`, `username`, and `password` with the credentials of the Quartz database tables you just set up.

```
org.quartz.scheduler.instanceName = Sched1
org.quartz.scheduler.instanceId = 1
org.quartz.scheduler.rmi.export = false
org.quartz.scheduler.rmi.proxy = false

org.quartz.threadPool.class = org.quartz.simpl.SimpleThreadPool
org.quartz.threadPool.threadCount = 5

org.quartz.jobStore.class = org.quartz.impl.jdbcjobstore.JobStoreTX
org.quartz.jobStore.driverDelegateClass =
  org.quartz.impl.jdbcjobstore.StdJDBCDelegate
org.quartz.jobStore.dataSource = myDS
org.quartz.jobStore.tablePrefix = QRTZ_
```

```
org.quartz.dataSource.myDS.driver = com.mysql.jdbc.Driver
org.quartz.dataSource.myDS.URL = jdbc:mysql://localhost:3306/dbname
org.quartz.dataSource.myDS.user = username
org.quartz.dataSource.myDS.password = password
org.quartz.dataSource.myDS.maxConnections = 30
```

As you can see, this is really just a standard `quartz.properties` file. We append `seam.` before it to signify that it is used to configure Quartz services inside Seam.

# 31.3 Scheduling Cron Jobs

With the Quartz scheduler configured, let's try to schedule a timer task with Unix cron expressions. Unix cron expressions are widely used to schedule recurring events on enterprise systems. They are much richer and much more powerful than the fixed interval timers. To read more about the cron syntax for scheduling, check out http://en.wikipedia.org/wiki/Cron.

To use a cron expression, just replace the `@IntervalDuration`-annotated method argument with an `@IntervalCron`-annotated cron expression. You can still use the `@Expiration` and `@FinalExpiration` parameters to specify the start and end dates for the job.

```
@Asynchronous
@Transactional
public QuartzTriggerHandle schedulePayment (
                        @Expiration Date when,
                        @IntervalCron String cron,
                        @FinalExpiration Date stoptime,
                        Payment payment) {

   ... ...

   return null;
}
```

The following web action method schedules the automatic payment task to run at 12:05 AM and 12:10 AM every Monday and on 10th of every month.

```
QuartzTriggerHandle handle =
   processor.schedulePayment(payment.getPaymentDate(),
                        "5,10 0 10 * 1",
                        payment.getPaymentEndDate(),
                        payment);

payment.setQuartzTriggerHandle( handle );
```

That's it. Integrating Unix cron jobs has never been easier!

# 31.4   Scheduling Jobs When Starting Up

So far, we have seen how to schedule recurring tasks via web actions. We can do it by pressing a button, clicking on a link, or simply loading a web page (by making the asynchronous method a page action method). But sometimes, we want to start a scheduled task as soon as the Seam application starts up, with no user input at all.

The obvious way to do it is to call the asynchronous method in the @Create method of an APPLICATION-scoped Seam component, and start that component from components.xml. The component could be something like this:

```
@Name("paymentStarter")
@Scope(ScopeType.APPLICATION)
public class PaymentStarter {

  @Create
  public void startup() {
    // Check if the recurring payment's
    // QuartzTriggerHandle already exists
    // in the database.

    if (!paymentExists) {
      startPayment ((new Date()), 3600 * 24 * 7);
    }
  }

  @Asynchronous
  @Transactional
  public QuartzTriggerHandle startPayment (
                        @Expiration Date when,
                        @IntervalDuration long interval) {

    ... ...

    return null;
  }
}
```

In components.xml, make sure to start the component after the scheduler component and any other dependencies.

```
<components ... ...>

  ... ...

  <!-- Install the QuartzDispatcher -->
  <async:quartz-dispatcher/>

  ... ...

  <component name="paymentStarter"/>

</components>
```

Of course, you can also start the component by annotating it with the @Startup annotation. Just make sure to specify dependencies in @Startup so that the component is started after the Quartz scheduler starts.

```
@Name("paymentStarter")
@Scope(ScopeType.APPLICATION)
@Startup(depends={"quartzDispatcher"})
public class PaymentStarter {

    ... ...

}
```

# 31.5  Conclusion

With Quartz and EJB3 timer integration, Seam makes it easy to schedule recurring tasks from web applications. It also makes it easy to execute long-running tasks asynchronously on a separate thread to avoid blocking the UI. This is a very useful feature that can come handy in many application scenarios.

# 32

Improving Scalability with
Multilayered Caching

In most enterprise applications, the database must be shared across application instances in a clustered environment and even across completely different applications. This often leads to the database being the primary performance bottleneck. Performance can also be hindered by expensive calculations that are often repeated. We can help to relieve both of these constraints through caching. Caching is simply storing some temporary data in a way that is inexpensive to access. This temporary data may duplicate data elsewhere, in the case of data access caching, or store the result of some expensive calculation.

As you will note in our definition, applications can benefit from caching whether they are I/O bound or CPU bound. I/O bound means that the time taken to complete the computation is directly dependent on how long it takes to get the data. To retrieve data from a database incurs the overhead of marshalling and unmarshalling data, setting up and tearing down connections, and network latency. CPU bound means that the time it takes for the application to complete a computation is dependent on the speed of the CPU and main memory. Let's take a look at some real-world examples.

- While performance profiling a recent non-user-facing application, it was noted that 90% of processing time was spent in data access, while CPU usage was very low. This was a good indication that the application was I/O bound. By enabling the second-level cache of the ORM provider and caching some strategic entities, a 60% performance gain was achieved.

- While performance profiling a recent user-facing application, it was noted that on certain pages, 80% of processing time was spent rendering very large data tables, while I/O access was very low. The ORM provider was caching the rendered data through its second-level cache, but the calculations for rendering were very expensive. These data tables changed infrequently and were heavily used, leading to repetitive, CPU-intensive rendering. Caching the page fragments that contained the data tables led to a 70% performance gain—and very happy users.

As you can see, applications can greatly benefit from caching to improve performance. In addition, caching helps to reduce load on resources. Obviously, if we reduce our data access by half, that time becomes available to others using those shared resources; the same applies to CPU time as well. As you will see throughout this chapter, it is easy to improve scalability and reduce load with caching when using Seam.

# 32.1  Multilayered Caching

Caching in a Seam application is performed at multiple layers of the application. Each layer plays a role in helping your application to scale. Figure 32.1 breaks down caching by the traditional application tiers.

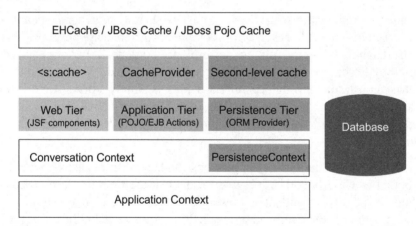

**Figure 32.1**    The multiple layers of caching in a Seam application, broken down by tier

The first level of caching is the database. This level is certainly useful and important, but can only go so far. At some point, the application must pick and choose when a trip to the database is actually needed. Figure 32.1 shows where caching is available throughout the application layers to avoid a database roundtrip.

The persistence tier has two levels of caching. In Chapter 11, we talked about the `PersistenceContext` which maintains a cache of what has been retrieved from the database throughout a conversation with a user. The `PersistenceContext` maintains the first-level cache. ORM solutions also provide a second-level cache for data which is shared among users and updated rarely. Hibernate provides direct integration with each of the cache providers supported by Seam, as we will discuss later.

We discussed the use of conversations in Chapter 8. Conversations allow you to maintain a cache of state related to the current user interaction across requests. In addition to the conversation context, the application context can be used to cache nontransactional state. Be aware that the application context is not replicated across nodes in a cluster. A good example of nontransactional state is configuration data.

In addition, Seam provides direct integration with cache providers (e.g., EHCache or JBoss Cache) to enable caching in the web tier of an application. As you will see in Section 32.3, the `CacheProvider` component is made directly available to your POJO or EJB actions through injection. In addition, we will demonstrate the use of the `<s:cache/>` JSF component which allows fragments of your web pages to be cached.

The Rules Booking example enables users to write reviews about their stay at a hotel. These reviews are then displayed with the hotel when users view the details of that hotel (Figure 32.2).

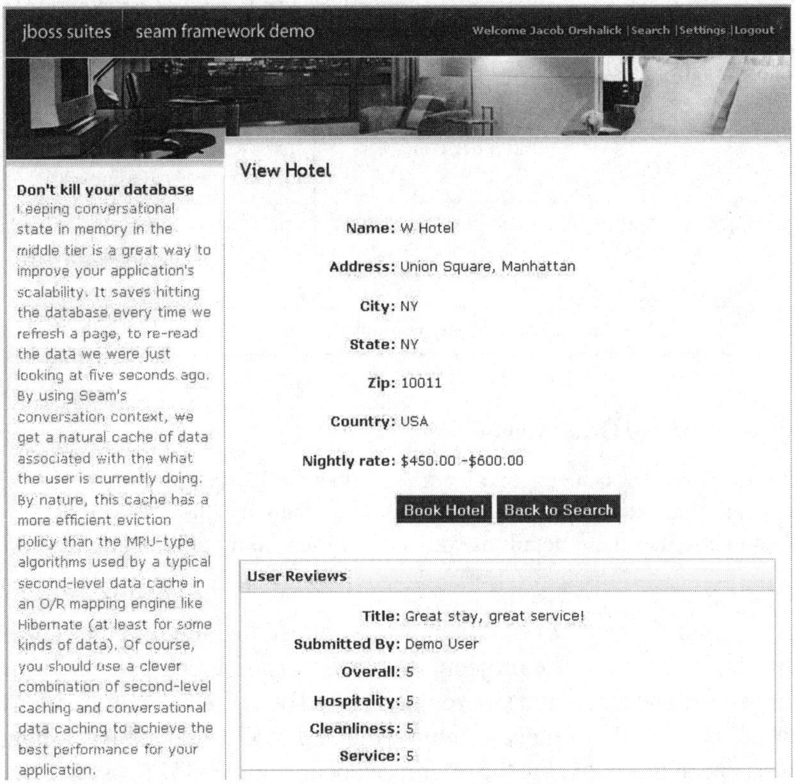

**Figure 32.2** `hotel.xhtml` displays the details of the hotel along with any user reviews.

While additional reviews can be added, this data is unlikely to change often. With that in mind, performance could be improved through caching. Instead of making a roundtrip to the database to retrieve this data on each hotel view, we can simply access an in-memory cache. This saves the latency of network communication as well as CPU cycles in the database, freeing up processing time for other tasks.

# 32.2   Integrating a Cache Provider through Seam

Seam makes it simple to achieve this performance gain through integration with a cache provider. There are three cache providers supported by Seam out of the box: JBoss Cache, JBoss POJO Cache, and EHCache. Table 32.1 describes the JARs that must be included in the `lib` directory of your EAR archive for each cache provider.

**Table 32.1**  Cache Provider Compatibility and Required JARs

| Cache Provider | Compatibility | Required Jars |
|---|---|---|
| JBoss Cache 1.x | JBoss 4.2.x and other containers | `jboss-cache.jar`—JBoss Cache 1.4.1, `jgroups.jar`—JGroups 2.4.1 |
| JBoss Cache 2.x | JBoss 5.x and other containers | `jboss-cache.jar`—JBoss Cache 2.2.0, `jgroups.jar`—JGroups 2.6.2 |
| JBoss POJO Cache 1.x | JBoss 4.2.x and other containers | `jboss-cache.jar`—JBoss Cache 1.4.1, `jgroups.jar`—JGroups 2.4.1, `jboss-aop.jar`—JBoss AOP 1.5.0 |
| EHCache | suitable for use in any container | `ehcache.jar`—EHCache 1.2.3 |

**Using JBoss Cache in Other Containers**

If you are using JBoss Cache in containers other than the JBoss Application Server, additional dependencies must be satisfied. The JBoss Cache wiki (http://wiki.jboss.org/wiki/JBossCache) provides these details as well as additional configuration options.

For JBoss Cache, a `treecache.xml` file must be defined to configure the cache for your application. The `rulesbooking` project provides an example `treecache.xml` configuration intended for a nonclustered environment. The JBoss Cache configuration contains quite a bit of configuration related to clustering and replication. This configuration is beyond the scope of this book, but the reference documentation for JBoss Cache provides in-depth documentation of these settings. The following listing from the Rules Booking example demonstrates how to configure the location of your `treecache.xml` file in `components.xml` for a JBoss Cache 1.x provider:

```
<?xml version="1.0" encoding="UTF-8"?>
<components xmlns="http://jboss.com/products/seam/components"
  xmlns:cache="http://jboss.com/products/seam/cache"
  xmlns:xsi="http://www.w3.org/2001/XMLSchema-instance"
  xsi:schemaLocation=
    "http://jboss.com/products/seam/cache
     http://jboss.com/products/seam/cache-2.1.xsd
     http://jboss.com/products/seam/components
     http://jboss.com/products/seam/components-2.1.xsd">

  <cache:jboss-cache-provider configuration="treecache.xml" />
  ... ...
```

EHCache uses its default configuration if none is provided, but it is quite simple to specify a custom configuration. As with JBoss Cache, the cache namespace allows you to configure an EHCache provider, as shown in the following listing:

```
<?xml version="1.0" encoding="UTF-8"?>
<components xmlns="http://jboss.com/products/seam/components"
  xmlns:cache="http://jboss.com/products/seam/cache"
  xmlns:xsi="http://www.w3.org/2001/XMLSchema-instance"
  xsi:schemaLocation=
    "http://jboss.com/products/seam/cache
     http://jboss.com/products/seam/cache-2.1.xsd
     http://jboss.com/products/seam/components
     http://jboss.com/products/seam/components-2.1.xsd">

  <cache:eh-cache-provider configuration="ehcache.xml" />
  ... ...
```

Each supported cache provider has an associated element in the `http://jboss.com/products/seam/cache` namespace for configuration.

Once the necessary JARs and configuration files have been included in the application archive, it is easy to make use of the Seam `CacheProvider` component. An instance can be directly injected by name into a component in your application with the `@In` annotation. The `HotelReviewAction` demonstrates this injection:

```
import org.jboss.seam.cache.CacheProvider;

// ... ...

@Name("hotelReview")
@Stateful
public class HotelReviewAction implements HotelReview
{
  @In private CacheProvider<PojoCache> cacheProvider;

  // ... ...
```

Once injected, it is easy to add and remove elements from the cache through the `CacheProvider` API. Table 32.2 lists some of the key methods of the `CacheProvider` API.

**Table 32.2** The `CacheProvider` API

| Method | Description |
|---|---|
| `put(String region, String key, Object object)` | Places an object in the cache, given a region and a key. |
| `get(String region, String key)` | Retrieves an object from the cache, given a region and a key. |
| `remove(String region, String key)` | Removes the object from the cache, based on the provided region and key. |

Note that you can work directly with the underlying cache provider simply by invoking `cacheProvider.getDelegate()`. This can be useful for performing implementation-specific operations, such as managing the cache tree with JBoss Cache. The drawback of accessing the delegate is that it directly couples your component to the underlying cache implementation, making it more difficult to change later.

---

**Using the Tree Cache with JBoss Cache**

JBoss Cache maintains objects in the cache in a tree form. This means that objects are cached under specific nodes in the tree, making it easy to organize cached object instances. This organization allows you to strategically clear objects from the cache when necessary. Nodes are identified in the tree by their fully qualified names (FQNs). In general, providing a node name is as simple as providing a `String`, but it is possible to create a complex tree form in the cache. See the JBoss Cache reference guide at http://www.jboss.org/jbosscache/docs for further information.

---

# 32.3  Simplified Caching with Seam

Now that we have seen a bit of the API, let's take a look at how it can be used. As mentioned previously, the Rules Booking example makes use of the `CacheProvider` to reduce database roundtrips on hotel reviews. In order to cache these reviews, the example demonstrates using the `<s:cache>` UI component provided by Seam. The `<s:cache>` component allows page fragments to be cached simply by surrounding the section of the page you want to cache with this tag. Inside the tag, specify the region where the object should be stored and the key that uniquely identifies the object instance. In general, the key will be the database ID of the entity or some other unique identifier.

```
<s:cache key="#{hotel.id}" region="hotelReviews">
  <h:dataTable value="#{hotel.reviews}" var="review">
    <h:column>
      <f:facet name="header">
        User Reviews
      </f:facet>

      <div class="label">Title:</div>

      <div class="output">
        <h:outputText value="#{review.title}" />
      </div>

      ... ...

    </h:column>
  </h:dataTable>
</s:cache>
```

Notice the use of #{hotel.id} as the cache key. This key is guaranteed to be unique for the hotel instance being viewed, ensuring that the appropriate reviews will be loaded from the cache. Seam automatically takes care of the caching for us. On first access, Seam checks the cache and realizes that an entry is not available for the defined region and key. The h:dataTable is then rendered by lazily loading the reviews from the database. Upon rendering, Seam captures the result and places it in the cache at the defined region and key. On subsequent accesses, Seam retrieves these results from the cache instead of making the roundtrip to load the reviews.

So, what if we need to refresh this data? If a user adds a new review for a hotel, it is important to ensure that the review is included the next time someone views the hotel. This can be achieved through several means. The first is a custom expiration policy. Expiration policies allow you to define exactly when an object should be evicted from the cache. There are several policies available through the JBoss Cache implementations as well as EHCache. This first approach places control of the eviction in the hands of the cache provider. It is always recommended that a reasonable expiration policy be specified. These expiration policies are beyond the scope of this book, but are well documented in the providers' reference guides.

The second approach places this control in the hands of the application. It is often useful to combine these approaches. This second approach is demonstrated by the Rules Booking example. When a review is added, the HotelReviewAction removes the hotel reviews for the hotel being reviewed from the cache:

```
@Name("hotelReview")
@Stateful
public class HotelReviewAction implements HotelReview
{
  @In private CacheProvider<PojoCache> cacheProvider;

  // ... ...
```

```
@End
@Restrict("#{s:hasPermission('hotel', 'review', hotelReview)}")
public void submit()
{
    log.info("Submitting review for hotel: #0", hotel.getName());

    hotel.addReview(review);
    em.flush();

    cacheProvider.remove("hotelReviews", hotel.getId());

    facesMessages.add("Submitted review for hotel: #0", hotel.getName());
}
}
```

The reviews are easy to remove using the `CacheProvider` API. The `HotelReviewAction` simply invokes the `remove` operation with the `region` and `key` combination identifying the page fragment that should be removed from the cache.

---

### Configuring Your Cache Provider for Second-Level Caching with Hibernate

If you are using Seam with Hibernate and have configured your cache provider, setting up Hibernate's second-level caching becomes a snap. To use the JBoss Cache you must first ensure that `jgroups.jar` is included in the `lib` of your application server instance. Then, simply add the following settings in your `persistence.xml`:

```
<properties>
    <property name="hibernate.cache.use_second_level_cache"
            value="true"/>
    <property name="hibernate.cache.provider_class"
            value="org.hibernate.cache.TreeCacheProvider"/>
    ... ...
</properties>
```

JBoss Cache is currently the only transactional cache supported by Hibernate out of the box. Using JBoss Cache, you have the choice of `read-only` and `transactional` concurrency strategies. EHCache is even easier to configure and provides a simple read-write cache. EHCache only requires the following settings in your `persistence.xml`:

```
<properties>
    <property name="hibernate.cache.use_second_level_cache"
            value="true"/>
    <property name="hibernate.cache.provider_class"
            value="org.hibernate.cache.EhCacheProvider"/>
    ... ...
</properties>
```

---

Applications can greatly benefit from caching, improving their performance and reducing load on resources. The multilayered caching provided by Seam makes it easy to achieve these goals and develop highly scalable web applications.

# 33

## Making Seam Groovy

$\textbf{A}$re you a Groovy developer? No, this is not a question of style, this is a question of languageuse choice. The Java platform is currently under a welcome invasion of dynamic languages, with polyglot programming piquing the Java community's interest. Polyglot programming—described by Neal Ford in http://memeago-ra.blogspot.com/2006/12/ polyglot-programming.html—encourages us to use the right tool for the job. Each language has its strengths and weaknesses, so polyglot programming allows us to strategically choose a language to fit a specific system requirement.

Groovy is unique in that it is a dynamic language that runs on the JVM and does not require you to put away any of the Java frameworks you are accustomed to, or relearn a new language from scratch. Instead, Groovy aims to provide the features of a dynamic language by building on top of Java rather than throwing it away. This is very attractive for organizations that want to take advantage of the benefits of dynamic languages while maintaining their existing Java investment.

We discussed RAD (Rapid Application Development) with Seam in Chapter 5, but Groovy helps to take RAD to the next level. Using Seam with Groovy has many advantages:

- Rapid development with dynamic language features, but with the choice to use Java when well-suited to a particular problem

- Maintaining and improving on the solid foundation that Java EE provides

- Continued use of existing Java investments as Groovy classes can directly use Java classes

- When used with seam-gen (see Chapter 5), immediate updates of changes to Groovy files without redeployment

Seam makes it easy to use Groovy in your application. As you will see in Section 33.3, there are no special interfaces or hooks to implement.

The power of Groovy is best explained through demonstration of its dynamic features, so this chapter will guide you through the Groovy Time-Tracking application. Groovy Time-Tracking is an open source project that can be found at http://code.google.com/p/groovy-seam. This application demonstrates the power of Groovy while making use of both Seam and JPA without a single Java class.

The first two sections of the chapter serve as an introduction to Groovy and show some examples of the syntactic sugar that Groovy provides in a Seam application. If you are already familiar with Groovy, skip to Section 33.3 to find out how to use Groovy in your Seam applications.

# 33.1  Groovy Entities

Groovy simplifies the implementation of your domain model. We are firm believers in *domain-driven design*; see Eric Evans' classic book (*Domain-Driven Design*, 2004) for a great read that teaches us that the domain model is where the business logic belongs. Implementing business logic is where Groovy really shines. Let's start off by looking at the Groovy way to initialize a timesheet.

```
@Entity
class GroovyTimesheet
{
  @Id @GeneratedValue
  Long id

  @OneToMany
  @JoinColumn(name="TIMESHEET_ID")
  List<GroovyTimeEntry> entries = new ArrayList<GroovyTimeEntry>()

  GroovyTimesheet(PayPeriod payPeriod, int month, int year)
  {
    (payPeriod.getStartDate(month, year)..
      payPeriod.getEndDate(month, year)).each
    {
      entries << new GroovyTimeEntry(hours:0, date:it)
    }
  }

  // ... ...
}
```

What is going on here? Essentially, we define a range of dates that are iterated over. The `PayPeriod` is a simple enum that determines the start and end dates of a pay period. By specifying (`payPeriod.getStartDate(month, year)..payPeriod.getEndDate(month, year)`), we define a range of dates. Groovy understands the meaning of a range of dates, allowing us to express this in a very concise manner (try expressing this in Java and you'll get the picture). In addition, we use the `each` operation on this range. This operation allows us to define a closure that executes as Groovy loops through our range of dates, a day at a time. This way, we initialize each `GroovyTimeEntry` instance for the pay period.

Also, notice the use of the `<<` operator (or the `leftShift` operator). This operator, defined for a `List`, allows us to add elements to the list. The `GroovyTimeEntry` instance is initialized using the default constructor. By default, named constructor parameters can be specified in any order to initialize an object instance. If you define a constructor, this is no longer provided by default. Finally, notice the use of the keyword `it` in the closure we defined for the `each` operation. The keyword `it` provides the value of the current element in the iteration. In our instance, as we loop through the date range, each date will be fed to the `GroovyTimeEntry` constructor.

---

**That Code Won't Compile, You Missed the Semicolons!**

Groovy supports a very relaxed syntax making it optional to add semicolons. This is of course up to personal preference, but after some debate with colleagues, the semicolons were deemed unnecessary noise. When using Groovy, the decision is up to you!

---

Of course we must also define the `GroovyTimeEntry`. The following listing demonstrates the simplicity of this definition:

```
@Entity
class GroovyTimeEntry {
  @Id @GeneratedValue
  Long id

  BigDecimal hours
  Date date
}
```

Is that all the code? Looks pretty nice, doesn't it? As mentioned above, the default constructor allows us to specify named parameters. In addition, getters and setters are automatically provided for each of our attributes.

You've probably noticed the use of JPA annotations here. This is perfectly legal, and your Groovy class will be a JPA entity. The same is true for Seam components annotated with `@Name`. How does this work? Groovy classes are compiled to Java bytecode under the covers, so all JEE and Seam features are available to your Groovy classes at runtime. Just use the `groovyc` compiler, or include the `groovyc` Ant task into your build.

Now, what if we want to add `GroovyTimeEntry` instances to the `GroovyTimesheet` instance programmatically? The following code implements this:

```
@Entity
class GroovyTimesheet {
  // ... ...

  void leftShift(GroovyTimeEntry entry) {
    entries << entry
  }
  // ... ...
}
```

As mentioned above, the `leftShift` operator is provided by Groovy and can be overloaded by your custom implementations. By defining a custom `leftShift` implementation, we are now able to add a `GroovyTimeEntry` instance through the following:

```
// ... ...
timesheet << new GroovyTimeEntry(new Date())
// ... ...
```

Operator overloading isn't limited to `leftShift`. We can also overload other operators, such as +:

```
// ... ...
BigDecimal plus(GroovyTimeEntry entry) {
  this.hours + entry.hours
}
// ... ...
```

This allows us to add the hours of two `GroovyTimeEntry` instances using the simple + operator. Notice that a return is not specified. This is optional, as the last line is assumed to be a return statement.

---

### Unit Testing with Groovy

Groovy offers simplified JUnit testing by extending the `GroovyTestCase` class. This allows you to use Groovy syntax with additional JUnit assertion statements. The following test demonstrates the readability Groovy can lend to your test cases:

```
void testOverloadedPlusOperation() {
  int expectedHours = 9

  assertEquals("Should result in ${expectedHours} hours", expectedHours,
    new GroovyTimeEntry(hours : 5) + new GroovyTimeEntry(hours : 4))
}
```

It is easy to see that, by using a named argument constructor, we are initializing the hours for each `GroovyTimeEntry` instance. The `GString` allows us to easily specify the expected result in the assertion failure message. This is a very basic test, and as you can imagine, using the Groovy constructs we've discussed, you can easily create very complex unit tests.

---

# 33.2 Groovy Actions

Now that we have seen the benefits of using Groovy to define our entities, what about our Seam actions? They can also benefit from the dynamic features that Groovy provides. Let us again look at the Groovy Time-Tracking application.

Groovy Time-Tracking allows users to enter timesheets on a project-by-project basis. An administrator can update the details of each `Project` instance as well as associate users with projects (Figure 33.1).

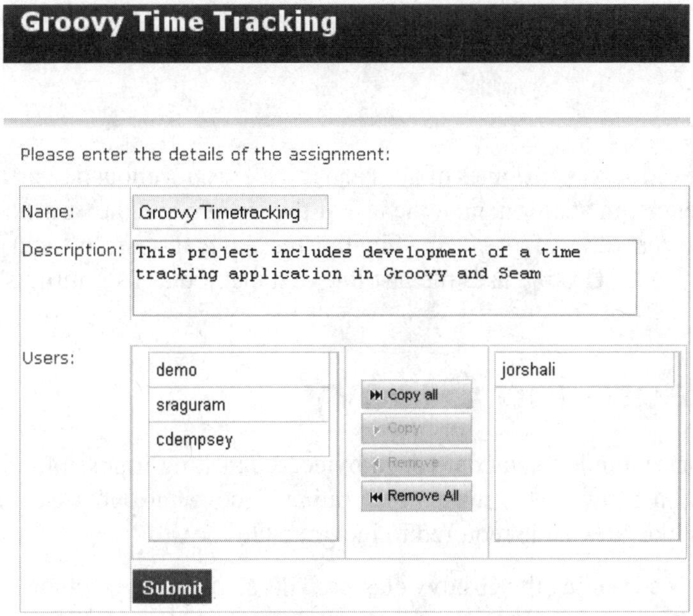

**Figure 33.1** `projectEdit.xhtml`: The user can update the project name, description, and the developers assigned to the project.

The assigned users are displayed with the RichFaces `pickList` component:

```
<td>Users:</td>
<td>
  <rich:pickList value="#{editProject.userIds}">
    <f:converter converterId="javax.faces.Long" />
    <s:selectItems value="#{users}" itemValue="#{user.id}"
                   var="user" label="#{user.username}" />
  </rich:pickList>
</td>
```

When a `Project` is selected, the users assigned to the `Project` must be displayed in the selected list. Groovy provides some syntactic sugar that makes the `EditProjectAction.select()` method very attractive:

```
@Name("editProject")
@Scope(CONVERSATION)
class EditProjectAction {
  // ... ...

  List<Long> userIds

  String select() {
    project = projectSelection
    userIds = new ArrayList<Long>()

    project.users.each {
      userIds << it.id
    }

    "/projectEdit.xhtml"
  }
  // ... ...
}
```

As before, we can access attributes of `EditProjectAction` without having to implement getters and setters. In addition, note the use of the closure and the `leftShift` operator (`<<`) to create the `List` of `userIds`. Finally, the navigation result can be specified without a `return` as Groovy uses the last line of a method as its return value.

# 33.3   Integrating Groovy

Groovy classes compile to standard Java bytecode, making it possible to use Groovy anywhere you use Java. This makes integrating Groovy into your Seam application simple. Let's look at what is required to integrate Groovy.

The first step is compiling the Groovy classes. This step must be included in your build for production release, but it is not necessary during development if your application uses seam-gen (see the sidebar below). Not to worry, this only requires a simple addition to the build:

```
<path id="lib.classpath">
  <pathelement path="/path/to/groovy-all.jar" />
  ... ...
</path>

... ...

<target name="compile">
  <taskdef name="groovyc"
           classname="org.codehaus.groovy.ant.Groovyc"
           classpathref="lib.classpath" />
  <mkdir dir="${build.classes}"/>
  <groovyc destdir="${build.classes}" classpathref="lib.classpath">
    <src path="${src}"/>
  </groovyc>
</target>
```

The code snippet above comes from the Groovy Time-Tracking example and demonstrates how Groovy compilation can be added to your Ant build. Ensure that the `groovy-all.jar` archive is included in the classpath and define the `org.codehaus.groovy.ant.Groovyc` task definition. Once the task is defined, the `groovyc` task is executed against the directory where Groovy classes have been defined (the `src` directory).

---

**Joint Compilation**

Note that the task definition shown here only provides compilation of Groovy classes. This requires that all Java classes that a Groovy class depends on be precompiled when Groovy compilation occurs, and vice versa. The `groovyc` task provides the capability to intermix Groovy and Java classes without constraint through joint compilation. See the documentation of the `groovyc` task for configuration details.

---

**Using Groovy with Seam-gen**

When using a seam-gen application with Groovy, place your `.groovy` files in the `src/hot` folder to gain hot-deployment support. This provides a truly RAD approach to using Groovy (no pun intended), as Groovy classes are interpreted at runtime. Note that Groovy classes should always be compiled for production use or performance testing, as interpretation is quite expensive. For more information on seam-gen refer to Chapter 5.

---

Whether you are using seam-gen or including compiled Groovy bytecode, the Groovy runtime must be made available in the classpath during execution. This simply requires including a `groovy-all.jar` archive into the WAR or EAR you deploy:

```
<target name="ear">
  <mkdir dir="${build.jars}"/>

  <ear destfile="${build.jars}/${projname}.ear"
      appxml="${resources}/META-INF/application.xml">
    <fileset dir="${build.jars}" includes="*.jar, *.war"/>
    <metainf dir="${resources}/META-INF">
      <include name="jboss-app.xml" />
    </metainf>
    <fileset dir="${lib}">
      <include name="jboss-seam.jar"/>
      ... ...
    <include name="groovy-all.jar" />
    </fileset>
  </ear>
</target>
```

The above task generates an EAR archive and includes the `groovy-all.jar`. Now the Groovy runtime environment will be available to the Groovy classes during execution.

# 34

## Introduction to Web Beans

Seam has evolved web development in the Java EE environment, and now Web Beans is poised to revolutionize it. The Web Beans specification (JSR-299) is a collaborative community effort heavily influenced by Seam and Guice (http://code.google.com/p/google-guice). Web Beans not only intends to standardize many of the concepts introduced by these frameworks, but improves on them to define the next-generation web development model. In "The Web Beans Manifesto" (http://relation.to/Bloggers/TheWebBeansManifesto) the specification lead, Gavin King, described the theme of Web Beans as "loose coupling with strong typing."

Loose coupling provides the dynamic behavior that makes a system flexible. Unfortunately, loose coupling is often achieved by sacrificing type safety. XML configuration is by far the worst culprit in most frameworks, but even Seam sacrifices type safety with its injection constructs by relying on component names. So, how can we achieve loose coupling while maintaining type safety? This is a core objective of the Web Beans component model.

Web Beans will standardize a type-safe component model that applies across application tiers. This finally unifies the web tier and the EJB tier which greatly simplifies Java web development. Much of the component model will feel very familiar now that you have learned the component model of Seam, but you will notice that the Web Beans model introduces additional type safety as well as powerful new constructs. Throughout the chapter, we will take a look at what Web Beans provides by revisiting the Hotel Booking example.

# 34.1   Defining a Web Beans Component

Web Beans provides a container that injects any necessary dependencies at runtime, based on the current context (Figure 34.1). Notice that we mention the context here—as with Seam, when injecting components or values, context counts!

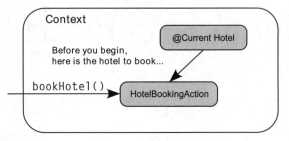

**Figure 34.1**     The current `Hotel` is provided by Web Beans from the context for booking.

Without any further delay, let's take a look at our first Web Beans component. The listing below declares the `HotelSearchingAction` from the Hotel Booking example we saw previously as a Web Beans component:

```
@Production            // Deployment Type
@Named("hotelSearching")  // Component Name
@ConversationScoped       // Context Scope
@Stateful
public class HotelSearchingAction implements HotelSearching {
  // ... ...
```

The first annotation looks a bit foreign to a Seam user, but its behavior is quite familiar. The `@Production` annotation is a *deployment type*. Deployment types, first and foremost, identify classes as Web Beans components. By annotating `HotelSearchingAction` with `@Production`, we are identifying it as a component. In addition, deployment types specify install precedence and environment availability similar to the `@Install` annotation provided by Seam, which we discussed in Section 7.2.1.

As with Seam, this allows you to override components provided by the Web Beans implementation, by a framework, or even application components for the purpose of testing. The `@Production` annotation is the annotation provided for use with your components, but it is quite simple to specify your own deployment types with the `@DeploymentType` annotation. Note that any custom deployment types must also be enabled in the `web-beans.xml` file which we will discuss shortly.

The `@Named` annotation gives this component a name. As with Seam, this component can now be referenced by name through EL. For example, should we want to reference the search string for querying hotels, we can now use `#{hotelSearching.searchString}`. The `@ConversationScoped` annotation specifies that this component should be scoped to the conversation. We will discuss the conversation scope as defined by Web Beans shortly.

Note that the `@Stateful` annotation defines this component as a stateful session bean. EJBs can be defined as Web Beans components, but as with Seam, Web Beans components are not required to be EJBs. In fact, an EJB doesn't even have to be a Web Beans component to define Web Beans-injected fields! As long as the EJB runs within a Web Beans container, the fields will be injected by the container.

---

**How Does Web Beans Find My Components?**

Similar to the `seam.properties` marker file in Seam, when the Web Beans container finds a `web-beans.xml` file in the classpath or in an archive, it will scan for Web Beans components. In addition, the `web-beans.xml` file allows you to configure components, define custom deployment types, configure interceptors, and much more. Of course, given the goal of type safety, configuration in this file should be limited and in most cases not necessary.

---

# 34.2  Component Injection

In the tradition of dependency injection, Web Beans aims to separate API from implementation. As a quick refresher, dependency injection is an inversion of the control technique that forms the core of modern-day frameworks. Traditionally, objects have held the responsibility for obtaining references to the objects they collaborate with. These objects are extroverted as they reach out to get their dependencies. This leads to tight coupling and hard-to-test code. Instead, we can allow the Web Beans container to provide the dependencies for us based on the current context.

Once a component has been defined by specifying a deployment type, it will be instantiated by the container when injected by another component or an EJB, or when referenced through EL. Web Beans has no concept of outjection, but all components and context values are contextual. This means we can achieve the same level of decoupling you are used to with Seam. Let's take a look at the `HotelBookingAction` defined as a Web Beans component:

```
@Named("hotelBookingAction")
@ConversationScoped
@Production
@Stateful
public class HotelBookingAction implements HotelBooking {
  @Current User user;
```

```
    Booking booking;
    // ... ...

    @PersistenceContext
    EntityManager entityManager;

    public void bookHotel(long hotelId) {
      // ... ...

      Hotel hotel = entityManager.find(Hotel.class, hotelId);

      booking = new Booking(hotel, user);
    }

    // ... ...

    public Booking getBooking() {
      return booking;
    }
  }
```

Notice that we are interested in the @Current User instance. Web Beans injects the User from the context. Just like Seam, the User will be looked up from the context, but unlike Seam, this lookup is based on the attribute type and any *binding types*. @Current is considered a binding type and is the default binding type, if none are provided. Thus, our HotelBookingAction has a binding type of @Current.

A binding type simply qualifies the specific component instance we are interested in for a particular type. This ensures that if multiple implementations of the requested type are available, the correct instance is chosen. For example, let's say we need to authorize payments for bookings. First, we define a simple interface that allows payment processing:

```
public interface PaymentService {
  public boolean authorizePayment(Payment payment);
}
```

Initially, the Booking application may only support credit card payments. In this case, it is easy to define a component that supports the PaymentService API:

```
@Production
@Named
@Stateless
public class CreditCardPaymentService implements PaymentService {
  public boolean authorizePayment(Payment payment) {
    // ... ...
  }
}
```

Note that we used the @Named annotation but did not specify a name. The CreditCardPaymentService is given the default name in this case, creditCardPaymentService, which is simply the class name with the first letter converted to lowercase.

This component can now be injected into the HotelBookingAction to authorize payments simply by specifying the default @Current binding type.

```
@Named("hotelBookingAction")
@ConversationScoped
@Production
@Stateful
public class HotelBookingAction implements HotelBooking {
  @Current PaymentProcessor paymentProcessor;

  // ... ...

  public void confirm() {
    boolean isAuthorized =
      paymentProcessor.authorize(booking.getPayment());

    if(isAuthorized) {
      entityManager.persist(this.booking);
      // ... ...
    }
  }
  // ... ...
}
```

So, what if we now need to support rewards payments? This requires the use of a binding type to qualify the implementation that should be injected by the container:

```
@Production
@Named
@Stateless
@CreditCard
public class CreditCardPaymentService implements PaymentService {
  // ... ...
```

This binding type can now be specified at the injection point to ensure that we receive the CreditCardPaymentService without creating a direct dependency on this type:

```
@Named("hotelBookingAction")
@ConversationScoped
@Production
@Stateful
public class HotelBookingAction implements HotelBooking {
  @CreditCard PaymentProcessor paymentProcessor;

  // ... ...
}
```

Binding types are defined with the @BindingType meta-annotation. The following definition specifies the @CreditCard binding type:

```
@BindingType
@Target({FIELD, PARAMETER, TYPE})
@Retention(RUNTIME)
public @interface CreditCard {}
```

Here, we have declared that this annotation can be specified at the FIELD, PARAMETER, and TYPE level. In our examples above, we have used the FIELD and TYPE definition, but what about PARAMETER? As you will see in Section 34.3, arguments can be injected into methods as parameters.

---

**Creation of Simple Web Beans Components versus EJBs**

Construction of POJO Web Beans components invokes the constructor of that Web Beans component. This makes it possible to use constructor injection through constructor parameters and perform any required setup. EJBs, on the other hand, are retrieved from JNDI, meaning that their creation is controlled by the EJB container but their lifecycle methods are available for any post-construction setup.

---

# 34.3  Producer Methods

Producer methods are similar to @Factory methods in Seam in that they declare a method that creates some context object(s)—but the similarities end there. Producer methods are much more flexible than @Factory methods and provide the same type safety as the new component model. Let's take a look at an example producer method:

```
@Named
@ConversationScoped
@Production
@Stateful
public class HotelSearchingAction implements HotelSearching {
  private String search;

  // ... ...

  @Produces @ConversationScoped @Named("hotels")
  public List<Hotel> queryHotels()
  {
    // query for hotels and return result
  }

  // ... ...
}
```

The @Produces annotation identifies this method as a producer method. You'll also notice familiar annotations described in the previous sections. If #{hotels} is accessed in the view or a list of hotels is injected through @Current List<Hotel>, our producer method will be invoked to provide the injected objects. The `hotels` are also scoped to the lifecycle of the current conversation context, which will be discussed in Section 34.4.

This producer method could also be rewritten as follows; here, the name of the hotel list is again `hotels`, but this time it is assumed by the JavaBean naming convention:

```
@Named
@ConversationScoped
@Production
@Stateful
public class HotelSearchingAction implements HotelSearching {
  private String search;

  // ... ...

  @Produces @ConversationScoped
  public List<Hotel> getHotels()
  {
    // query for hotels and return result
  }
}
```

The binding types we discussed previously can also be used to differentiate between producer methods defined for the same type. For instance, we may want to define multiple methods that retrieve lists of hotels:

```
@Named
@ConversationScoped
@Production
@Stateful
public class HotelSearchingAction implements HotelSearching {
  // ... ...

  @Produces @ConversationScoped @All
  public List<Hotel> getAllHotels()
  {
    // query for all hotels and return result
  }

  @Produces @ConversationScoped @MostPopular
  public List<Hotel> getMostPopularHotels()
  {
    // query for most popular hotels and return result
  }
}
```

We can also inject objects into producer methods. This is useful in the scenarios where decision making is required for component injection. For instance, when we discussed the `PaymentService`, we saw that multiple implementations could potentially be injected. We could differentiate them by a binding type, but what if the `PaymentService` needed depends on the current context? The following example demonstrates how this could be achieved with a producer method:

```
@Production
public class PaymentServiceResolver {
  @Produces
  public PaymentService getPaymentService(
      @CreditCard PaymentService creditCardPaymentService,
      @Rewards PaymentService rewardsPaymentService,
      @Current Booking booking) {
    PaymentService paymentService;
    PaymentType paymentType = booking.getPayment().getPaymentType();

    switch(paymentType) {
      case CREDIT_CARD : paymentService = creditCardPaymentService;
        break;
      case REWARDS : paymentService = rewardsPaymentService;
        break;
      default:  throw new IllegalStateException("A PaymentType has "
        + "been defined without an associated PaymentService");
    }

    return paymentService;
  }
}
```

The `@Current PaymentService` in this case is determined based on the state of the `@Current Booking` instance. As you can see, this allows us to achieve fine-grained control over component or object injection.

Now, let's take a look at the contexts we've alluded to throughout the chapter so far.

# 34.4  The Context Model

The context model provided by Web Beans will feel very familiar to a Seam or JSF developer. The context model includes the standard JSF scopes with the addition of the conversation scope, introduced by Seam, and the dependent scope, exclusive to the Web Beans specification. All scopes outside of the dependent scope are considered normal scopes, while the dependent scope is termed a pseudoscope. Don't get too hung up on the terminology; in a nutshell, a pseudoscope is just a scope that does not behave like the normal scopes. The exact definition can be found in the specification. Before we get too far, let's first review the standard JSF contexts in relation to Web Beans.

**request context**   The life of the context spans a single web request. To scope a component to the request context, it should be annotated with `@RequestScoped`.

**session context**   The context is propagated between requests that occur in the same HTTP servlet session, and destroyed when the session is invalidated or times out. To scope a component to the session context, it should be annotated with `@SessionScoped`.

**application context** This context is shared among all servlet requests to the same web application context. To scope a component to the application context, it should be annotated with `@ApplicationScoped`.

As with Seam, Web Beans defines a conversation context and a conversation is associated with every JSF request. To define a component as conversation-scoped, it should be annotated with `@ConversationScoped`. The Web Beans conversation model is very similar to the Seam model we discussed in Section 8.2.2 with a few subtle differences. Figure 34.2 represents the potential states of a conversation in the Web Beans model.

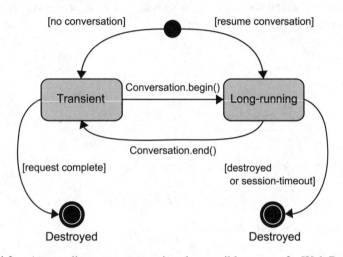

**Figure 34.2** A state diagram representing the possible states of a Web Beans conversation

A conversation is either *transient* or *long-running*. A transient conversation is essentially synonymous with a temporary conversation in Seam. A transient conversation is associated with every request unless a long-running conversation is being resumed. The transient conversation, along with its context, is destroyed once the request completes. A long-running conversation is maintained in the `HttpSession` between requests, allowing the conversation to be resumed on a subsequent request. As with Seam, a conversation is automatically propagated across a redirect.

Note the use of the `Conversation` API in Figure 34.2 to transform a conversation from transient to long-running and vice versa. As all requests are associated with a transient conversation by default, invoking the `Conversation.begin()` method informs the Web Beans container that the conversation context should be stored in the `HttpSession` to be resumed on a later request. In contrast, invoking the `Conversation.end()` method informs the container that the conversation should be marked as transient, meaning it will be destroyed at the end of the request.

How do we resume long-running conversations? As mentioned previously, the current conversation is propagated across a redirect automatically. In addition, if the user submits a form that was rendered in the context of a long-running conversation, that conversation will be resumed for the request. Note that this provides the same multiwindow and multitab operation as that enjoyed by Seam applications. As with Seam, a simple GET request results in a new transient conversation, allowing multiple concurrent long-running conversations within the same user session. For an example of multiwindow operation, refer back to Chapter 8.

Now that we've discussed the semantics, let's take a look at the syntax of beginning and ending a long-running conversation:

```
@Named
@ConversationScoped
@Production
@Stateful
public class HotelBookingAction implements HotelBooking {
  @Current Conversation conversation;

  // ... ...

  public void bookHotel(long hotelId) {
    conversation.begin();

    Hotel hotel = entityManager.find(Hotel.class, hotelId);

    this.booking = new Booking(hotel, user);
  }
  // ... ...

  public void confirm() {
    entityManager.persist(this.booking);

    conversation.end();
  }
  // ... ...
}
```

As you can see, we can inject the @Current Conversation instance. Once injected, it is quite simple to begin and end the long-running conversation through the Conversation API. When the user decides to book a hotel, we begin a long-running conversation to maintain the booking context between requests. On confirmation, we can safely end the long-running conversation and allow it to be destroyed at the end of the request.

Note that each time a user attempts to book a hotel, a new conversation is started. This means the same user can be booking multiple alternative hotels between multiple windows or tabs without a problem, as these conversations each have a distinct conversation context.

The new scope introduced by Web Beans is the @Dependent pseudoscope. This scope simply means that the component is bound to the lifecycle of the component it is injected into and no two components can share the same instance. If you are familiar with the Unified Modeling Language (UML), this is similar to a composite relationship, as shown in Figure 34.3.

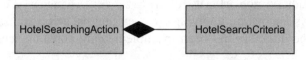

**Figure 34.3**    A composite relationship between the HotelSearchingAction and the HotelSearchCriteria

In Figure 34.3, the HotelSearchingAction composes a HotelSearchCriteria instance. This means that if the HotelSearchingAction is destroyed, the HotelSearchCriteria is destroyed as well. In this case, the HotelSearchingCriteria component would be annotated with @Dependent.

# 34.5  Component Stereotyping

Stereotypes are not a new concept. In fact, the Unified Modeling Language (UML) used them as extensibility mechanisms for defining new model elements that have specific properties suitable to your problem domain. Sounds familiar?

Figure 34.4 demonstrates some of the stereotypes we have come across so far.

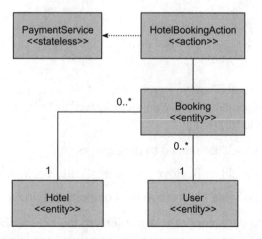

**Figure 34.4**    Class diagram representing stereotypes, as defined by the Unified Modeling Language (UML)

Obviously, this indicates certain semantics specific to each class we see in Figure 34.4. Generally, the semantics of a stereotype are described in some appended documentation and have to be incorporated into the code through patterns.

In Figure 34.4, you see an example of an existing Java stereotype, `<<entity>>`. Classes can simply be annotated with `@Entity` to gain the cross-cutting behavior associated with entities. In addition, notice the use of `<<stateless>>` which would simply translate to the `@Stateless` annotation implying cross-cutting behavior (transactional, object-pooling, etc.). The difficulty has been in implementing domain-specific stereotypes, such as `Action`.

Up to this point, there has been no simple approach to implementing this concept in a domain-specific setting with Java. Sure, you could use inheritance along with the template method pattern or other patterns to capture commonalities in components, but there was no simple way to inject the cross-cutting behavior that a stereotype implies. Through the Web Beans stereotype approach, this behavior can be specified declaratively, just as it is within the model, and the properties can be applied through interception.

If you recall, both the `HotelBookingAction` and the `HotelSearchingAction` share common annotations. These repetitive annotations can become needless noise in common component definitions such as actions. In addition, should actions require some change to cross-cutting behavior, we would have to seek out each implementation to make the necessary annotation changes—a clear violation of the DRY (Don't Repeat Yourself) rule. To define the `<<action>>` shown in Figure 34.4, we could create the following stereotype:

```
@ConversationScoped
@Production
@Named
@Stereotype
@Target(TYPE)
@Retention(RUNTIME)
public @interface Action {}
```

Notice the use of the `@Stereotype` annotation. This meta-annotation states that the `@Action` is a stereotype and that any annotations are to be applied to the component. Our `@Action` states the following:

- The component should be scoped to the conversation.

- The component should be deployed as an application component.

- The default name should be given to the component if no name is declared.

We can now clean up the component definitions of the `HotelBookingAction` and the `HotelSearchingAction`, as demonstrated in the following listing:

```
@Stateful
@Action
public class HotelSearchingAction implements HotelSearching {
    ... ...
}

@Stateful
@Action
public class HotelBookingAction implements HotelBooking {
    ... ...
}
```

Let's say we now need all `@Action` components to be `@Transactional` and `@Secure`. This is obviously quite simple with our new definition:

```
@Transactional
@Secure
@ConversationScoped
@Production
@Named
@Stereotype
@Target(TYPE)
@Retention(RUNTIME)
public @interface Action {}
```

No additional configuration is necessary, as the `@Transactional` and `@Secure` interceptor bindings (see Section 34.6) ensure that the appropriate interceptors are enabled for our component to take care of transaction management and ensure that the instance is secure. Implementation of patterns suddenly becomes simple, even for junior developers.

So what does all this buy us? For one, the implementation speaks to you in the same way the UML diagram does. If we look at the `HotelBookingAction` class, we know that it is an `@Action` which indicates certain intrinsic behavior associated with the class. This intrinsic behavior is passed in a completely type-safe manner through annotations. In addition, we gain the ability to easily test our components as the cross-cutting behavior will be introduced in a container environment. We can only test our logic and not worry about the cross-cutting aspects knowing they will be introduced at runtime.

Let's now take a look at the interceptor binding types which provide the constructs for the implicit cross-cutting behavior that we want to achieve with stereotypes.

# 34.6 Implementing Cross-Cutting Behavior

What if you need to implement your own cross-cutting behavior? For instance, you may need to audit all user actions initiated on a particular component. This is possible by implementing your own interceptors and *interceptor binding types*. An interceptor binding type is simply an annotation that is annotated with `@InterceptorBindingType`. Let's take a look at our auditing example:

```
@InterceptorBindingType
@Target({TYPE, METHOD})
@Retention(RUNTIME)
public @interface Audited {}
```

Once an interceptor binding type has been defined, we can define a Web Beans interceptor that is annotated with our @Audited annotation as well as the @Interceptor annotation:

```
@Audited @Interceptor
public class AuditInterceptor {
  @AroundInvoke
  public Object aroundInvoke(InvocationContext invocationContext) {
    // do auditing logic ...
  }
}
```

Note that this interceptor is compliant with the EJB specification of an interceptor. In fact, all Web Beans interceptors are completely EJB-compliant with the addition of the @Interceptor annotation and an interceptor binding type. Now that we have defined both the interceptor binding type and the interceptor, we can incorporate our cross-cutting behavior into the HotelBookingAction:

```
@Action
@Stateful
public class HotelBookingAction implements HotelBooking {
  // ... ...

  private Booking booking;

  @PersistenceContext
  private EntityManager entityManager;
  // ... ...

  @Audited
  public void confirm() {
    entityManager.persist(this.booking);
    // ... ...
  }
}
```

Here, we annotated the confirm() method with @Audited. As this binds the interceptor to the confirm() method, our interceptor logic will take care of the auditing for us. Applying cross-cutting behavior becomes simple and keeps the implementation decoupled from our component. In addition, custom interceptors can be applied to the stereotypes we saw in Section 34.5, allowing you to create components with intrinsic domain-specific behavior.

# 34.7  Conclusion

Web Beans is poised to revolutionize web development as it becomes the new Java web development standard. Web Beans will standardize a type-safe component model that applies across application tiers, finally unifying the web tier and the EJB tier. This will simplify Java web development while making systems more flexible. You can find out more about the Web Beans specification at http://jcp.org/en/jsr/detail?id=299. To keep up with announcements, visit http://seamframework.org/WebBeans.

# Installing and Deploying JBoss AS

**J**Boss Seam is developed and tested on the latest JBoss Application Server (AS). It is built on top of many JBoss services, such as JBoss AOP (Aspect Oriented Programming), Hibernate, EJB3, JSF, JBoss Cache, and JBoss Transaction Manager. Seam provides a simple, unified programming model for accessing all those heavy-duty enterprise services.

The build scripts for all example applications in this book build EAR files that can be deployed in the JBoss AS (see Appendix B on how to build the example applications).

---

**Running Seam Applications Outside the JBoss AS**

Although the JBoss AS is the best server for Seam, you can also run Seam applications outside the JBoss AS if you have to do so. See Chapter 4 for more.

---

## A.1 JDK 5.0 Is Required

You can run the `java -version` command from your operating system's command line to check the version of your current JDK installation. If you are running a JDK earlier than 5.0, you need to upgrade. Linux/UNIX and Windows users can download the latest JDK from Sun's web site at http://java.sun.com/j2se/1.5.0/download.jsp. Mac OS X users should download the beta version of Apple JDK 5.0 from www.apple.com/java.

To run JBoss AS successfully, you also need to set the `JAVA_HOME` environment variable and point it to your JDK 5.0 installation directory. On a Windows system, you can do that via the system **Control Panel** tool; click on the following items from the desktop: **Start**, **Control Panel**, **System**, **Advanced**, **Environment Variables**. On a UNIX/Linux/Mac OS X system, you can do it via shell scripts.

# A.2  Installing JBoss AS

Installing the JBoss AS is as easy as downloading the ZIP file of the distribution and unzipping its content into any local directory of your choosing. The latest stable JBoss AS distributions can be found at www.jboss.org/jbossas/downloads. The examples in this book are tested in JBoss AS 4.2.3 GA.

If you are using JDK 6.x, please make sure that you download the JBoss AS distribution built for JDK 6. You can tell those distribution files by their filenames (e.g., `jboss-4.2.3.GA-jdk6.zip`).

---

**What about the Seam Library?**

An independent Seam container needs to be loaded for each Seam application, so be sure to include the `jboss-seam.jar` file in the application EAR file. The same goes for the `jboss-seam-ui.jar` file and the `jsf-facelets.jar` file—you must include them in your EAR file (in fact, in the WAR file) to support Seam-specific UI tags and Facelets. See Appendix B for more details.

---

# A.3  Deploying and Running Applications

To deploy a Seam application, you only need to copy the EAR application file (i.e., the build target from the source code) into the JBoss AS's `server/default/deploy` directory.

In our examples, you need to first set up the `build.properties` file in the root directory of the examples to point to the JBoss AS installation directory. Then, just run `ant` and `ant deploy` to deploy the application.

To start the server, run `bin/run.sh` (or `bin\run.bat` on Windows). You can now access the Seam web application URL, `http://localhost:8080/myapp/` (replace *myapp* with the application URL configured in your EAR or WAR file).

---

**JBoss AS 4.0.5**

If you are using JBoss AS 4.0.5, you will need to use the `all` configuration in order to use EJB3 session beans.

---

# Using Example Applications as Templates

In Chapter 5, we saw how to use seam-gen to generate an application template for your Seam project. The seam-gen template contains common configuration files, a build script, all support libraries, and even a sample application. It supports Eclipse/NetBeans IDE integration, out-of-the-container testing, and fast edit/save/reload development cycles. It is the best place to start building your Seam applications.

However, the seam-gen template project has a rather large footprint because it needs to include all support library JARs inside the project. It also lacks flexibility to support non-JBoss deployments. For the readers of this book, an alternative is to use the book's example projects as templates for your own projects. This is more involved than seam-gen, but it gives you more flexibility—and perhaps helps you learn more about Seam in the process. In this appendix, we will discuss how to customize the book's sample applications.

The projects in the book's source code bundle rely on library JARs in the Seam 2.1 distribution, which can be retrieved from http://seamframework.org/Download. Each example project uses the `build.properties` file found at the base of the distribution. Simply open this file and edit the properties as follows:

- `jboss.home` is the location of your local JBoss instance (the examples have been tested against JBoss AS 4.2.3.GA).

- `seam.home` is the location of the latest Seam distribution (the examples have been tested against JBoss Seam 2.1.0.GA).

Once you have made these changes, simply execute `ant main deploy`. This will build the example and deploy it to the configured JBoss instance.

# B.1   Simple EJB3-Based Web Applications

The `integration` example is the best starting place for an EJB3-based Seam web application. This is the directory structure of the source project:

```
mywebapp
|+ src
   |+ Java Source files
|+ view
   |+ web pages (.xhtml), CSS, and images
|+ resources
   |+ WEB-INF
      |+ web.xml
      |+ components.xml
      |+ faces-config.xml
      |+ pages.xml
   |+ META-INF
      |+ persistence.xml
      |+ application.xml
      |+ jboss-app.xml
      |+ ejb-jar.xml
   |+ seam.properties
|+ lib
   |+ App specific lib JARs
|+ test
   |+ components.xml
   |+ persistence.xml
   |+ testng.xml
   |+ Java source for test cases
|+ nbproject
   |+ NetBeans integration and support
|+ build.xml
```

To customize the project for your application, follow these steps:

- Add Seam components and other classes in the `src` directory.

- Add web pages, images, and other web resources in the `view` directory.

- Edit the `build.xml` to include any third-party library files required for your application through either the `war` or `ear` task. For instance, you can include the Ajax4jsf JARs, as we did in Chapter 20.

- Change the `resources/WEB-INF/navigation.xml` file to define the navigation rules (i.e., the pageflow) in the new application.

- Edit the `resources/WEB-INF/pages.xml` file to include page parameters for RESTful pages (see Chapter 15), page actions, and stateful navigation rules (see Section 24.5).

- Change the `resources/META-INF/persistence.xml` file to specify custom persistence options for the new application, if any (see Chapter 28 for some examples).

- Change the application name as follows:

- Change the project name "integration" in the build.xml file to your own project name (e.g., "mywebapp").

- Change the resources/META-INF/application.xml file to reflect your application's context root URL.

- Change the class loader name in resources/META-INF/jboss-app.xml to a unique name that fits your application.

- Change the JNDI name pattern in the resources/WEB-INF/components.xml file to match your application name (i.e., "mywebapp").

---

**JSP versus Facelets XHTML**

The integration project template uses Facelets as the presentation technology. We highly recommend using Facelets in your Seam applications (see Section 3.1). Still, if you really want to use JSP for web pages, you can use the helloworld example as the template. The setup is similar to the integration project setup we discuss here.

---

Then run ant in the project directory to build the application. The build result is in the build/jars/mywebapp.ear file. This is the structure of the EAR archive:

```
mywebapp.ear
|+ app.war
    |+ web pages (.xhtml), CSS, images
    |+ WEB-INF
        |+ web.xml
        |+ components.xml
        |+ faces-config.xml
        |+ pages.xml
        |+ lib
            |+ jsf-facelets.jar
            |+ jboss-seam-ui.jar
            |+ jboss-seam-debug.jar
|+ app.jar
    |+ Java classes
    |+ seam.properties
    |+ META-INF
        |+ persistence.xml
        |+ ejb-jar.xml
|+ jboss-seam.jar
|+ lib
    |+ jboss-seam-el.jar
|+ META-INF
    |+ application.xml
    |+ jboss-app.xml
```

If you have unit tests or integration tests for the application, you can put the test cases (the .java files) and the testng.xml file in the test directory in the project. An alternative components.xml file is already in the test directory. The difference between test/components.xml and resources/WEB-INF/components.xml is that the test version does not have the application name in its JNDI pattern (see Section 26.4)—because the tests are run outside the application server container. So if you customize the `resources/WEB-INF/components.xml` file in your application, you must make the same changes to the `test/components.xml` file. This is an example `test/components.xml` file:

```
<components ...>
  // same as resources/WEB-INF/components.xml

  <core:init jndi-pattern="#{ejbName}/local" debug="false"/>

  <core:ejb installed="true"/>
</components>
```

Likewise, there is a test version of the `persistence.xml` file, which explicitly specifies the JBoss Transaction Manager lookup in the testing environment. You probably also want to have Hibernate create and drop the database tables on the fly when you start and finish your tests.

```
<persistence>
  <persistence-unit name="helloworld">
    <provider>org.hibernate.ejb.HibernatePersistence</provider>
    <jta-data-source>java:/DefaultDS</jta-data-source>
    <properties>
      ... ...
      <property name="hibernate.hbm2ddl.auto" value="create-drop"/>
      <property name="hibernate.transaction.manager_lookup_class"
        value="org.hibernate.transaction.JBossTransactionManagerLookup"/>
    </properties>
  </persistence-unit>
</persistence>
```

When you run `ant test` in the project directory, the build script runs all the tests defined in the `test/testng.xml` file and outputs the test results both to the console and to the `build/testout` directory.

For your reference, we list the complete `build.xml` script here:

```
<project name="HelloWorld" default="main" basedir=".">

  <description>Hello World</description>
  <property name="projname" value="myapp" />

  <property file="../build.properties"/>
  <property name="jboss.deploy"
            location="${jboss.home}/server/default/deploy"/>

  <property name="lib" location="${seam.home}/lib" />
  <property name="applib" location="lib" />
```

```xml
<path id="lib.classpath">
  <fileset dir="${lib}" includes="*.jar"/>
  <fileset dir="${applib}" includes="*.jar"/>
</path>

<property name="testlib" location="${seam.home}/lib/test" />
<property name="eejb.conf.dir" value="${seam.home}/bootstrap" />

<property name="resources" location="resources" />

<property name="src" location="src" />
<property name="test" location="test" />
<property name="view" location="view" />

<property name="build.classes" location="build/classes" />
<property name="build.jars" location="build/jars" />
<property name="build.test" location="build/test" />
<property name="build.testout" location="build/testout" />

<target name="clean">
  <delete dir="build"/>
</target>

<target name="main" depends="compile,war,ejb3jar,ear"/>

<target name="compile">
  <mkdir dir="${build.classes}"/>
  <javac destdir="${build.classes}"
         classpathref="lib.classpath"
         debug="true">
    <src path="${src}"/>
  </javac>
</target>

<target name="test" depends="compile">

  <taskdef resource="testngtasks" classpathref="lib.classpath"/>

  <mkdir dir="${build.test}"/>

  <javac destdir="${build.test}" debug="true">
    <classpath>
      <path refid="lib.classpath"/>
      <pathelement location="${build.classes}"/>
    </classpath>
    <src path="${test}"/>
  </javac>

  <copy todir="${build.test}">
    <fileset dir="${build.classes}" includes="**/*.*"/>
    <fileset dir="${resources}" includes="**/*.*"/>
  </copy>

  <!-- Overwrite the WEB-INF/components.xml -->

  <copy todir="${build.test}/WEB-INF" overwrite="true">
    <fileset dir="${test}" includes="components.xml"/>
  </copy>
```

```xml
<!-- Overwrite the META-INF/persistence.xml -->

<copy todir="${build.test}/META-INF" overwrite="true">
  <fileset dir="${test}" includes="persistence.xml"/>
</copy>

<path id="test.classpath">

  <path path="${build.test}" />

  <fileset dir="${testlib}">
    <include name="*.jar" />
  </fileset>

  <fileset dir="${lib}">
    <!-- Don't include seam-ui -->
    <exclude name="jboss-seam-ui.jar" />
    <exclude name="jboss-seam-wicket.jar" />
    <exclude name="interop/**/*" />
    <exclude name="gen/**/*" />
    <exclude name="src/**/*" />
  </fileset>

  <path path="${eejb.conf.dir}" />

</path>

<testng outputdir="${build.testout}">
  <jvmarg value="-Xmx800M" />
  <jvmarg value="-Djava.awt.headless=true" />
  <classpath refid="test.classpath"/>
  <xmlfileset dir="${test}" includes="testng.xml"/>
</testng>

</target>

<target name="war" depends="compile">
  <mkdir dir="${build.jars}"/>

  <war destfile="${build.jars}/app.war"
       webxml="${resources}/WEB-INF/web.xml">
    <webinf dir="${resources}/WEB-INF">
      <include name="faces-config.xml" />
      <include name="components.xml" />
      <include name="navigation.xml" />
      <include name="pages.xml" />
    </webinf>
    <lib dir="${lib}">
      <include name="jboss-seam-ui.jar" />
      <include name="jboss-seam-debug.jar" />
      <include name="jsf-facelets.jar" />
    </lib>
    <fileset dir="${view}"/>
  </war>
</target>
```

```xml
<target name="ejb3jar" depends="compile">
  <mkdir dir="${build.jars}"/>

  <jar destfile="${build.jars}/app.jar">
    <fileset dir="${build.classes}">
      <include name="**/*.class"/>
    </fileset>
    <fileset dir="${resources}">
      <include name="seam.properties" />
    </fileset>
    <fileset dir="${applib}">
      <include name="*.jar" />
    </fileset>
    <metainf dir="${resources}/META-INF">
      <include name="persistence.xml" />
      <include name="ejb-jar.xml" />
    </metainf>
  </jar>
</target>

<target name="ear">
  <mkdir dir="${build.jars}"/>

  <ear destfile="${build.jars}/${projname}.ear"
      appxml="${resources}/META-INF/application.xml">
    <fileset dir="${build.jars}" includes="*.jar, *.war"/>
    <metainf dir="${resources}/META-INF">
      <include name="jboss-app.xml" />
    </metainf>
    <fileset dir="${seam.home}">
      <include name="lib/jboss-seam.jar"/>
      <include name="lib/jboss-el.jar"/>
    </fileset>
  </ear>
</target>

<target name="deploy">
  <copy file="${build.jars}/${projname}.ear" todir="${jboss.deploy}"/>
</target>

<target name="undeploy">
  <delete file="${jboss.deploy}/${projname}.ear"/>
</target>
</project>
```

# B.2  POJO-Based Web Applications

If you want to use Seam POJOs and forgo the EJB3 session beans, you can choose the `jpa` project as the template (see Chapter 4). This project builds the application into a WAR file deployable in the J2EE 1.4-compliant profile of the JBoss AS 4.0.5+. With a little tuning, you can build WAR files deployable on any J2EE 1.4 application server (e.g., WebLogic or Sun Application Server).

The following listing shows the structure of the `jpa` project:

```
mywebapp
|+ src
   |+ Java Source files
|+ view
   |+ web pages (.xhtml), CSS, and images
|+ resources
   |+ WEB-INF
      |+ web.xml
      |+ components.xml
      |+ faces-config.xml
      |+ pages.xml
      |+ jboss-web.xml
   |+ META-INF
      |+ persistence.xml
   |+ seam.properties
|+ lib
   |+ App specific lib JARs
|+ test
   |+ persistence.xml
   |+ testng.xml
   |+ Java source for test cases
|+ nbproject
   |+ NetBeans integration and support
|+ build.xml
```

To customize the project for your application, follow these steps:

- Add Seam components and other classes in the `src` directory.

- Add web pages, images, and other web resources in the `view` directory.

- Edit the `build.xml` file to include any third-party library files required for your application through either the `war` or `ear` task. For instance, you can include the Ajax4jsf JARs, as we did in Chapter 20.

- Change the `resources/WEB-INF/navigation.xml` file to define the navigation rules (i.e., the pageflow) in the new application.

- Edit the `resources/WEB-INF/pages.xml` file to include page parameters for RESTful pages (see Chapter 15), page actions, and stateful navigation rules (see Section 24.5).

- Change the `resources/META-INF/persistence.xml` file to specify custom persistence options for the new application, if any (see Chapter 28 for some examples). For Hibernate applications, modify the `resources/hibernate.cfg.xml` file as needed.

- Change the application name as follows:

  - Change the project name `"jpa"` in the `build.xml` file to your own project name (e.g., `"mywebapp"`).

  - Change the `resources/WEB-INF/jboss-web.xml` file to reflect your application's context root URL as needed.

Run `ant` in the project directory to build the `build/jars/mywebapp.war` application archive. Required application library JARs are included in the `WEB-INF/lib` directory. This is the content of the WAR file:

```
mywebapp.war
|+ web pages (.xhtml), CSS, and images
|+ WEB-INF
   |+ lib
      |+ jboss-seam.jar
      |+ jboss-seam-ui.jar
      |+ jboss-seam-el.jar
      |+ jboss-seam-debug.jar
      |+ jsf-facelets.jar
      |+ hibernate3.jar
      |+ hibernate-annotations.jar
      |+ hibernate-entitymanager.jar
      |+ ejb3-persistence.jar
      |+ app.jar
         |+ META-INF
            |+ persistence.xml
         |+ Java classes
         |+ seam.properties
   |+ web.xml
   |+ faces-config.xml
   |+ components.xml
   |+ jboss-web.xml
   |+ pages.xml
```

Running tests in a POJO project is the same as in an EJB3 project. The unit tests and integration tests are located in the `test` directory. Since we have no EJBs here, there is no need to have a test-specific version of `components.xml` for the POJO application. This is the `build.xml` script to build the WAR application from the Seam POJO project:

```
<project name="HelloWorld" default="main" basedir=".">
  <description>Hello World</description>
  <property name="projname" value="jpa" />

  <property file="../build.properties"/>
  <property name="jboss.deploy"
            location="${jboss.home}/server/default/deploy"/>

  <property name="lib" location="${seam.home}/lib" />
  <property name="applib" location="lib" />
  <path id="lib.classpath">
    <fileset dir="${lib}" includes="*.jar"/>
    <fileset dir="${applib}" includes="*.jar"/>
  </path>

  <property name="testlib" location="${seam.home}/lib/test" />
  <property name="eejb.conf.dir" value="${seam.home}/bootstrap" />
  <property name="resources" location="resources" />
  <property name="src" location="src" />
  <property name="test" location="test" />
  <property name="view" location="view" />
  <property name="build.classes" location="build/classes" />
  <property name="build.jars" location="build/jars" />
```

```xml
<property name="build.test" location="build/test" />
<property name="build.testout" location="build/testout" />

<target name="clean">
  <delete dir="build"/>
</target>

<target name="main" depends="compile,pojojar,war"/>

<target name="compile">
  <mkdir dir="${build.classes}"/>
  <javac destdir="${build.classes}"
         classpathref="lib.classpath"
         debug="true">
    <src path="${src}"/>
  </javac>
</target>

<target name="test" depends="compile">
  <taskdef resource="testngtasks" classpathref="lib.classpath"/>

  <mkdir dir="${build.test}"/>

  <javac destdir="${build.test}" debug="true">
    <classpath>
      <path refid="lib.classpath"/>
      <pathelement location="${build.classes}"/>
    </classpath>
    <src path="${test}"/>
  </javac>

  <copy todir="${build.test}">
    <fileset dir="${build.classes}" includes="**/*.*"/>
    <fileset dir="${resources}" includes="**/*.*"/>
  </copy>
  <!-- Overwrite the META-INF/persistence.xml -->
  <copy todir="${build.test}/META-INF" overwrite="true">
    <fileset dir="${test}" includes="persistence.xml"/>
  </copy>

  <path id="test.classpath">
    <path path="${build.test}" />

    <fileset dir="${testlib}">
      <include name="*.jar" />
    </fileset>

    <fileset dir="${lib}">
      <!-- Don't include seam-ui -->
      <exclude name="jboss-seam-ui.jar" />
      <exclude name="jboss-seam-wicket.jar" />
      <exclude name="interop/**/*" />
      <exclude name="gen/**/*" />
      <exclude name="src/**/*" />
    </fileset>

    <path path="${eejb.conf.dir}" />
  </path>
```

```xml
    <testng outputdir="${build.testout}">
      <jvmarg value="-Xmx800M" />
      <jvmarg value="-Djava.awt.headless=true" />
      <classpath refid="test.classpath"/>
      <xmlfileset dir="${test}" includes="testng.xml"/>
    </testng>
</target>

<target name="pojojar" depends="compile">
  <mkdir dir="${build.jars}"/>

  <jar destfile="${build.jars}/app.jar">
    <fileset dir="${build.classes}">
      <include name="**/*.class"/>
    </fileset>
    <fileset dir="${resources}">
      <include name="seam.properties" />
    </fileset>
    <fileset dir="${applib}">
      <include name="*.jar" />
    </fileset>
    <metainf dir="${resources}/META-INF">
      <include name="persistence.xml" />
    </metainf>
  </jar>
</target>

<target name="war" depends="pojojar">
  <mkdir dir="${build.jars}"/>

  <war destfile="${build.jars}/${projname}.war"
       webxml="${resources}/WEB-INF/web.xml">
    <webinf dir="${resources}/WEB-INF">
      <include name="faces-config.xml" />
      <include name="components.xml" />
      <include name="navigation.xml" />
      <include name="pages.xml" />
      <include name="jboss-web.xml" />
    </webinf>
    <lib dir="${lib}">
      <include name="jboss-seam.jar" />
      <include name="jboss-el.jar" />
      <include name="jboss-seam-ui.jar" />
      <include name="jboss-seam-debug.jar" />
      <include name="jsf-facelets.jar" />
      <!--
      <include name="hibernate3.jar" />
      <include name="hibernate-entitymanager.jar" />
      <include name="hibernate-annotations.jar" />
      <include name="hibernate-commons-annotations.jar" />
      <include name="ejb3-persistence.jar" />
      -->
    </lib>
    <lib dir="${build.jars}" includes="app.jar"/>
    <fileset dir="${view}"/>
  </war>
</target>
```

```
<target name="war405" depends="pojojar">
  <mkdir dir="${build.jars}"/>

  <war destfile="${build.jars}/${projname}.war"
       webxml="${resources}/WEB-INF/web.xml">
    <webinf dir="${resources}/WEB-INF">
      <include name="faces-config.xml" />
      <include name="components.xml" />
      <include name="navigation.xml" />
      <include name="pages.xml" />
      <include name="jboss-web.xml" />
    </webinf>
    <lib dir="${lib}">
      <include name="jboss-seam.jar" />
      <include name="jboss-el.jar" />
      <include name="jboss-seam-ui.jar" />
      <include name="jboss-seam-debug.jar" />
      <include name="jsf-facelets.jar" />
      <include name="jsf-api.jar" />
      <include name="jsf-impl.jar" />
      <include name="hibernate3.jar" />
      <include name="hibernate-entitymanager.jar" />
      <include name="hibernate-annotations.jar" />
      <include name="hibernate-commons-annotations.jar" />
      <include name="ejb3-persistence.jar" />
    </lib>
    <lib dir="${build.jars}" includes="app.jar"/>
    <fileset dir="${view}"/>
  </war>
</target>

<target name="deploy">
  <copy file="${build.jars}/${projname}.war" todir="${jboss.deploy}"/>
</target>

<target name="undeploy">
  <delete file="${jboss.deploy}/${projname}.war"/>
</target>
</project>
```

For plain Tomcat deployment of Seam POJO applications, refer to the `tomcatjpa`
example for more details.

# B.3  More Complex Applications

The two applications we have discussed in this appendix are simple web applications.
If your application uses advanced Seam features, you must package additional JAR
files and configuration files in the EAR or WAR archives.

- The Drools JARs and configuration files are needed to support the rule-based web
  security framework in Seam. Refer to Chapter 22 for more details.

- The jBPM JAR and configuration files are needed to support business processes and stateful pageflows in Seam applications. Refer to Chapter 24 for more details.

- PDF support requires the `jboss-seam-pdf.jar` file and the `itext-*.jar` file in the `WEB-INF/lib` directory of the WAR archive. Refer to Section 3.4.1 for more details.

- Facelets-based email template support requires the `jboss-seam-mail.jar` file in the `WEB-INF/lib` directory of the WAR archive. Refer to Section 3.4.2 for more details.

- Wiki text support requires the `antlr-*.jar` file in the `WEB-INF/lib` directory of the WAR archive. Refer to Section 3.4.3 for more details.

# Using Maven

Most example applications in this book use Ant as the build system. Ant is simple and straightforward. However, since the first edition of this book, we have seen an increasing adaption of Maven to manage builds. Maven provides declarative dependency management, which fits well with Seam applications since Seam integrates many third-party libraries and frameworks. In this appendix, we "mavenize" the Integration example application to show you how to use Maven to build Seam applications. The result application is in the `maven-ear` example.

First, let's look at the structure of the source code. In order to build an EAR application in Maven, you need to put each component of the EAR in a separate Maven module. The `ejb` module builds the EJB JAR; the `war` builds the WAR; and the `ear` module assembles them together into an EAR.

```
maven-ear
|+ pom.xml
|+ ejb
   |+ pom.xml
   |+ src
      |+ main
         |+ java
            |+ EJB beans, Seam POJOs etc.
         |+ resources
            |+ seam.properties
            |+ META-INF
               |+ ejb-jar.xml
               |+ persistence.xml
```

```
|+ war
   |+ pom.xml
   |+ src
      |+ main
         |+ java
            |+ Java classes specific to the WAR
         |+ resources
            |+ seam.properties
         |+ webapp
            |+ XHTML files
            |+ WEB-INF
               |+ components.xml
               |+ web.xml
               |+ faces-config.xml
               |+ pages.xml
|+ ear
   |+ pom.xml
```

The directory structure here follows Maven's standard convention. For instance, Maven knows to look for Java sources in src/main/java, classpath resources (e.g., configuration files) in src/main/resources, and web content in src/main/webapp. That saves us a lot of time trying to specify and figure out the source structure.

As you can see, there are no JARs in this structure. All the JARs needed for building and packaging are downloaded from central Maven repositories off the Internet.

The four pom.xml files are the core of the build system. Let's look at them one by one.

The pom.xml file in the project root directory defines the defaults for this project. It specifies things like the group ID of the entire project, which Maven repositories to use, and the default version number and scope for each dependency. It gives us a central place to view and update the version numbers for each dependency—much better than the old way of examining each dependency JAR individually. If a dependency has the provided scope, it means that the dependency is provided by the runtime environment (i.e., the application server) on the classpath. Hence, Maven will only include the provided dependencies in the compiling classpath, but will not include those JARs in the final EAR, WAR, or JAR builds.

```xml
<project ...>
  <modelVersion>4.0.0</modelVersion>
  <groupId>seambook</groupId>
  <artifactId>maven-ear-example</artifactId>
  <packaging>pom</packaging>
  <version>1.0</version>
  <name>maven-ear-example</name>
  <url>http://maven.apache.org</url>

  <repositories>
    <repository>
      <id>official-repo</id>
      <name>The official maven repo</name>
      <url>http://repo1.maven.org/maven2/</url>
    </repository>
```

```xml
    <repository>
      <id>jboss-repo</id>
      <name>The JBoss maven repo</name>
      <url>http://repository.jboss.org/maven2/</url>
    </repository>
</repositories>

<dependencyManagement>
  <dependencies>
    <dependency>
      <groupId>javax.servlet</groupId>
      <artifactId>servlet-api</artifactId>
      <version>2.5</version>
      <scope>provided</scope>
    </dependency>

    <dependency>
      <groupId>javax.ejb</groupId>
      <artifactId>ejb-api</artifactId>
      <version>3.0</version>
      <scope>provided</scope>
    </dependency>

    <dependency>
      <groupId>org.hibernate</groupId>
      <artifactId>hibernate</artifactId>
      <version>3.2.5.ga</version>
      <scope>provided</scope>
    </dependency>
    <dependency>
      <groupId>org.hibernate</groupId>
      <artifactId>hibernate-entitymanager</artifactId>
      <version>3.3.1.ga</version>
      <scope>provided</scope>
    </dependency>
    <dependency>
      <groupId>org.hibernate</groupId>
      <artifactId>hibernate-annotations</artifactId>
      <version>3.3.0.ga</version>
      <scope>provided</scope>
    </dependency>
    <dependency>
      <groupId>org.hibernate</groupId>
      <artifactId>hibernate-validator</artifactId>
      <version>3.0.0.ga</version>
      <scope>provided</scope>
    </dependency>

    <dependency>
      <groupId>org.jboss.seam</groupId>
      <artifactId>jboss-seam</artifactId>
      <version>2.0.0.GA</version>
      <exclusions>
        <exclusion>
          <groupId>javax.el</groupId>
          <artifactId>el-api</artifactId>
        </exclusion>
      </exclusions>
    </dependency>
```

```xml
    <dependency>
      <groupId>org.jboss.seam</groupId>
      <artifactId>jboss-seam-ui</artifactId>
      <version>2.0.0.GA</version>
      <exclusions>
        <exclusion>
          <groupId>javax.el</groupId>
          <artifactId>el-api</artifactId>
        </exclusion>
      </exclusions>
    </dependency>

    <dependency>
      <groupId>org.jboss.seam</groupId>
      <artifactId>jboss-seam-debug</artifactId>
      <version>2.0.0.GA</version>
      <exclusions>
        <exclusion>
          <groupId>javax.el</groupId>
          <artifactId>el-api</artifactId>
        </exclusion>
      </exclusions>
    </dependency>

    <dependency>
      <groupId>org.jboss.seam</groupId>
      <artifactId>jboss-el</artifactId>
      <version>2.0.0.GA</version>
      <exclusions>
        <exclusion>
          <groupId>javax.el</groupId>
          <artifactId>el-api</artifactId>
        </exclusion>
      </exclusions>
      <type>jar</type>
    </dependency>

    <dependency>
      <groupId>com.sun.facelets</groupId>
      <artifactId>jsf-facelets</artifactId>
      <version>1.1.14</version>
    </dependency>

    <dependency>
      <groupId>javax.faces</groupId>
      <artifactId>jsf-api</artifactId>
      <version>1.2_04-p02</version>
      <scope>provided</scope>
    </dependency>

    <dependency>
      <groupId>javax.faces</groupId>
      <artifactId>jsf-impl</artifactId>
      <version>1.2_04-p02</version>
      <scope>provided</scope>
    </dependency>
  </dependencies>
</dependencyManagement>
```

```
<modules>
  <module>ejb</module>
  <module>war</module>
  <module>ear</module>
</modules>

<build>
  <plugins>
    <plugin>
      <artifactId>maven-antrun-plugin</artifactId>
      <executions>
        <execution>
          <id>echohome</id>
          <phase>validate</phase>
          <goals>
            <goal>run</goal>
          </goals>
          <configuration>
            <tasks>
              <echo>JAVA_HOME=${java.home}</echo>
            </tasks>
          </configuration>
        </execution>
      </executions>
    </plugin>
    <plugin>
      <groupId>org.apache.maven.plugins</groupId>
      <artifactId>maven-compiler-plugin</artifactId>
      <configuration>
        <source>1.5</source>
        <target>1.5</target>
      </configuration>
    </plugin>
  </plugins>
</build>

</project>
```

The `ejb/pom.xml` declares the compile-time dependency of the classes in the EJB module. It should declare all its dependencies as `provided` since those dependencies will be provided by the application server or included in the EAR. Notice that the dependencies here have no version number since they are inherited from the parent `pom.xml` in the project root directory.

```
<project>

<parent>
  <groupId>seambook</groupId>
  <artifactId>maven-ear-example</artifactId>
  <version>1.0</version>
</parent>

<modelVersion>4.0.0</modelVersion>
<groupId>seambook</groupId>
<artifactId>maven-ear-example-ejb</artifactId>
<name>maven-ear-example - ejb</name>
<version>1.0</version>
```

```
<url>http://maven.apache.org</url>

<build>
  <finalName>ejb</finalName>
</build>

<dependencies>

  <dependency>
    <groupId>org.jboss.seam</groupId>
    <artifactId>jboss-seam</artifactId>
    <scope>provided</scope>
  </dependency>

  <dependency>
    <groupId>javax.ejb</groupId>
    <artifactId>ejb-api</artifactId>
    <scope>provided</scope>
  </dependency>

  <dependency>
    <groupId>org.hibernate</groupId>
    <artifactId>hibernate</artifactId>
  </dependency>
  <dependency>
    <groupId>org.hibernate</groupId>
    <artifactId>hibernate-entitymanager</artifactId>
  </dependency>
  <dependency>
    <groupId>org.hibernate</groupId>
    <artifactId>hibernate-annotations</artifactId>
  </dependency>
  <dependency>
    <groupId>org.hibernate</groupId>
    <artifactId>hibernate-validator</artifactId>
  </dependency>

</dependencies>

</project>
```

The war/pom.xml declares the dependencies for the WAR module. Every dependency that does not have a provided scope will be included in the WAR's WEB-INF/lib directory. All the compiled Java classes will be included in WEB-INF/classes.

```
<project>
  <parent>
    <groupId>seambook</groupId>
    <artifactId>maven-ear-example</artifactId>
    <version>1.0</version>
  </parent>
  <modelVersion>4.0.0</modelVersion>

  <artifactId>maven-ear-example-war</artifactId>
  <name>maven-ear-example - web</name>
  <packaging>war</packaging>
  <url>http://maven.apache.org</url>
```

```
    <build>
      <finalName>maven-ear-example-war</finalName>
    </build>

  <dependencies>

    <dependency>
       <groupId>seambook</groupId>
       <artifactId>maven-ear-example-ejb</artifactId>
       <version>1.0</version>
       <scope>provided</scope>
    </dependency>

    <dependency>
       <groupId>org.jboss.seam</groupId>
       <artifactId>jboss-seam-ui</artifactId>
    </dependency>

    <dependency>
       <groupId>org.jboss.seam</groupId>
       <artifactId>jboss-seam-debug</artifactId>
    </dependency>

    <dependency>
       <groupId>com.sun.facelets</groupId>
       <artifactId>jsf-facelets</artifactId>
    </dependency>

    <!-- The "provided" dependencies are
         only need for compilation -->

    <dependency>
       <groupId>javax.servlet</groupId>
       <artifactId>servlet-api</artifactId>
    </dependency>

    <dependency>
       <groupId>org.jboss.seam</groupId>
       <artifactId>jboss-seam</artifactId>
       <scope>provided</scope>
    </dependency>

    <dependency>
       <groupId>javax.faces</groupId>
       <artifactId>jsf-api</artifactId>
    </dependency>

    <dependency>
       <groupId>javax.faces</groupId>
       <artifactId>jsf-impl</artifactId>
    </dependency>

    <dependency>
       <groupId>org.hibernate</groupId>
       <artifactId>hibernate-validator</artifactId>
    </dependency>

  </dependencies>
</project>
```

The `ear/pom.xml` is executed last in the build process. It assembles the JARs together into an EAR file. All modules and library JARs in the EAR need to be declared as dependencies. Then, in the `maven-ear-plugin` part of the script, we specify the type of each module and where it should be placed in the EAR archive. Maven will build the `application.xml` accordingly on the fly. Similarly, we can also specify the JBoss loader in the build so that it will generate a `jboss-app.xml` for us.

```xml
<project>

  <parent>
    <groupId>seambook</groupId>
    <artifactId>maven-ear-example</artifactId>
    <version>1.0</version>
  </parent>

  <modelVersion>4.0.0</modelVersion>
  <artifactId>maven-ear-example-ear</artifactId>
  <name>maven-ear-example - ear</name>
  <packaging>ear</packaging>
  <url>http://maven.apache.org</url>

  <dependencies>

    <dependency>
      <groupId>seambook</groupId>
      <artifactId>maven-ear-example-ejb</artifactId>
      <type>ejb</type>
      <version>1.0</version>
    </dependency>

    <dependency>
      <groupId>seambook</groupId>
      <artifactId>maven-ear-example-war</artifactId>
      <type>war</type>
      <version>1.0</version>
    </dependency>

    <dependency>
      <groupId>org.jboss.seam</groupId>
      <artifactId>jboss-seam</artifactId>
      <type>ejb</type>
      <version>2.0.0.GA</version>
      <exclusions>
        <exclusion>
          <groupId>javax.el</groupId>
          <artifactId>el-api</artifactId>
        </exclusion>
      </exclusions>
    </dependency>

    <dependency>
      <groupId>org.jboss.seam</groupId>
      <artifactId>jboss-el</artifactId>
    </dependency>

  </dependencies>
```

```
<build>
  <plugins>
    <plugin>
      <groupId>org.apache.maven.plugins</groupId>
      <artifactId>maven-ear-plugin</artifactId>
      <configuration>
        <jboss>
          <version>4</version>
          <loader-repository>exp:loader=exp.ear</loader-repository>
        </jboss>

        <modules>
          <webModule>
            <groupId>seambook</groupId>
            <artifactId>maven-ear-example-war</artifactId>
            <contextRoot>maven-ear-example</contextRoot>
          </webModule>

          <ejbModule>
            <groupId>seambook</groupId>
            <artifactId>maven-ear-example-ejb</artifactId>
          </ejbModule>

          <ejbModule>
            <groupId>org.jboss.seam</groupId>
            <artifactId>jboss-seam</artifactId>
          </ejbModule>

          <!-- The stuff that needs to go in the lib directory.
               They will not be included in application.xml -->

          <jarModule>
            <groupId>org.jboss.seam</groupId>
            <artifactId>jboss-el</artifactId>
            <bundleDir>lib</bundleDir>
          </jarModule>

        </modules>
      </configuration>
    </plugin>
  </plugins>
</build>

</project>
```

Maven's pom.xml files can be much longer than Ant scripts, but their declarative nature makes them a lot easier to follow and understand.

Now you have the EAR structure of a Maven project. It is easy to convert it into a WAR project for Seam POJO applications or add testing support. Check out Maven documentation for more details.

APPENDIX **D**

# Direct Access to the
# Hibernate API

**I**n most examples throughout the book, we use JPA (Java Persistence API) for the persistence logic. We use Hibernate as our JPA implementation. However, as it is an open source framework at the forefront of ORM innovation, some of Hibernate's features are not yet standardized. In particular, JPA does not yet support these features:

- The JPA query language is not as rich as that in Hibernate. For instance, JPA does not support Hibernate's query-by-criteria or query-by-example.

- Hibernate offers more methods to manage objects with detached state; JPA supports only one `merge()` operation in the `EntityManager`.

- The object type system in Hibernate is much richer than that in JPA.

- Hibernate gives you more control over the size of the extended persistence context.

If you need to use those features, you must use the Hibernate API directly. You also need to use the Hibernate API directly if you are working with legacy Hibernate code (a large number of XML mapping files and queries in existing applications belong to this category). That would mean to use Hibernate `Session` instead of the JPA `EntityManager` in your Seam components. The example used in this appendix can be found in the `hibernate` example. It is a port of the `integration` example.

## D.1 Using the Hibernate API

To use the Hibernate API to manage database objects, we inject a Hibernate `Session` instead of an `EntityManager` into the `ManagerPojo` class. The API methods in the

Hibernate `Session` are roughly equivalent to those in the `EntityManager`; they have only slightly different method names. This is the Hibernate version of the `ManagerPojo` class:

```
@Name("manager")
public class ManagerPojo {

    @In (required=false) @Out (required=false)
    private Person person;

    @In (create=true)
    private Session helloSession;

    Long pid;

    @DataModel
    private List <Person> fans;

    @DataModelSelection
    private Person selectedFan;

    public String sayHello () {
        helloSession.save (person);
        return "fans";
    }

    @Factory("fans")
    public void findFans () {
        fans = helloSession.createQuery("select p from Person p").list();
    }

    public void setPid (Long pid) {
        this.pid = pid;

        if (pid != null) {
            person = (Person) helloSession.get(Person.class, pid);
        } else {
            person = new Person ();
        }
    }

    public Long getPid () {
        return pid;
    }

    public String delete () {
        Person toDelete = (Person) helloSession.merge (selectedFan);
        helloSession.delete( toDelete );
        findFans ();
        return null;
    }

    public String update () {
        return "fans";
    }

}
```

# D.2  Configuration

When the Hibernate session component, `helloSession`, is bootstrapped (and injected), Seam looks for the `hibernate.cfg.xml` file, instead of `persistence.xml`, in the JAR files in its classpath. This is the structure for the `app.jar` file in the Hibernate application:

```
app.jar
|+ ManagerPojo.class
|+ Person.class
|+ seam.properties
|+ hibernate.cfg.xml
```

The `hibernate.cfg.xml` file has pretty much the same options as the `persistence.xml` file. It builds a Hibernate session factory and registers it under the JNDI name `java:/helloSession`. Note that you must put the database entity POJO class name in a `mapping` element. If you have multiple entity POJO classes in your application, use multiple `mapping` elements. The `mapping` elements tell Hibernate to read the ORM annotations on those classes and map them to database tables.

```
<hibernate-configuration>
  <session-factory name="java:/helloSession">
    <property name="show_sql">false</property>
    <property name="connection.datasource">
      java:/DefaultDS
    </property>
    <property name="hbm2ddl.auto">
      create-drop
    </property>
    <property name="cache.provider_class">
      org.hibernate.cache.HashtableCacheProvider
    </property>
    <property name="transaction.flush_before_completion">
      true
    </property>
    <property name="connection.release_mode">
      after_statement
    </property>
    <property name="transaction.manager_lookup_class">
      org.hibernate.transaction.JBossTransactionManagerLookup
    </property>
    <property name="transaction.factory_class">
      org.hibernate.transaction.JTATransactionFactory
    </property>

    <mapping class="Person"/>
  </session-factory>
</hibernate-configuration>
```

Finally, you must bootstrap the `helloSession` component in the `components.xml` file. The `core:hibernate-session-factory` component sets up the session factory, and the `core:managed-hibernate-session` component creates a Hibernate session named `helloSession` that can be injected into `ManagerPojo`. Note that the Hibernate session component name must match the JNDI name in `hibernate.cfg.xml` so that Hibernate knows which session factory it is supposed to use to create the session.

```
<components ...>

  <core:init debug="true"/>

  <core:manager conversation-timeout="120000"/>

  <!-- Bootstrap Hibernate -->
  <core:hibernate-session-factory/>
  <core:managed-hibernate-session name="helloSession"
                                  auto-create="true"/>

</components>
```

That's all you need to use the Hibernate API in your persistence layer.

# Index

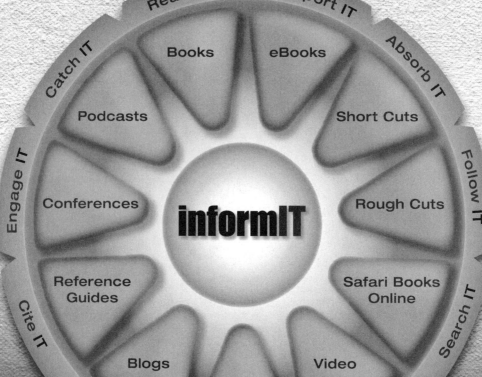